# SOCIAL
## PROBLEMS

# SOCIAL PROBLEMS

## An Advocate Group Approach

### SARA TOWE HORSFALL

**Texas Wesleyan University**

**WESTVIEW PRESS**

A Member of the Perseus Books Group

Westview Press was founded in 1975 in Boulder, Colorado, by notable publisher and intellectual Fred Praeger. Westview Press continues to publish scholarly titles and high-quality undergraduate- and graduate-level textbooks in core social science disciplines. With books developed, written, and edited with the needs of serious nonfiction readers, professors, and students in mind, Westview Press honors its long history of publishing books that matter.

Published by Westview Press,
A Member of the Perseus Books Group

Find us on the World Wide Web at www.westviewpress.com.

Every effort has been made to secure required permissions for all text, images, maps, and other art reprinted in this volume.

Westview Press books are available at special discounts for bulk purchases in the United States by corporations, institutions, and other organizations. For more information, please contact the Special Markets Department at the Perseus Books Group, 2300 Chestnut Street, Suite 200, Philadelphia, PA 19103, or call (800) 810-4145, ext. 5000, or e-mail special.markets@perseusbooks.com.

Designed by Trish Wilkinson
Set in 11 point Adobe Garamond Pro

Library of Congress Cataloging-in-Publiction Data

Horsfall, Sara.
    Social problems : an advocate group approach / Sara Towe Horsfall.
        p.   cm.
    ISBN 978-0-8133-4507-9 (pbk. : alk. paper) — ISBN 978-0-8133-4508-6 (e-book)
    1. Social problems. 2. Social change. 3. Social problems—United States.
4. Social change—United States. I. Title.
HN18.3.H67 2012
303.4—dc23                                                          2011045235

10  9  8  7  6  5  4  3  2  1

# ∷ CONTENTS

# ■ INTRODUCTION: RECREATING THE WORLD IN OUR IMAGE
## *The Need for a New Approach to Social Problems*

Over the years, whenever I taught the social problems course, I faced the dilemma of what text to use. Despite the fact that it is a common university course, most textbooks have serious flaws. First is the lack of a consistent definition. A social problem is commonly defined as a situation recognized by a group, by *someone*. That means, whoever identifies the problem is part of the discussion of the social problem. However, most texts do not examine the opinions and actions of the social actors who lobbied to bring an issue into the public eye. Even worse, the author takes the place of those social actions and advocates for the aggrieved persons. The loss of theoretical perspective turns the subject into personal opinion—albeit with a lot of supporting data.

Another serious flaw is that after the first couple of chapters, the material is nearly the same as standard introductory texts with slight adjustment of the titles: family-related problems, problems in education, population, environment, urban problems, problems in aging, crime, and so on. The social problems get lost in the discussion of sociology. This was brought home to me in one course when my students began asking, "Where are the social problems?" The class had become more about "What is sociology?" than "What are social problems?" Further, most social problems books include a discussion of the three sociological perspectives (conflict, interaction, and structure/function) and sometimes additional analysis using the three perspectives. While important to sociology, analysis of the sociological areas using the three perspectives does not always add to the understanding of social problems.

A peculiarity of social problems texts is the lack of a discussion of solutions other than government action. Government action seems to be the sociologists' "law of the hammer," leaving a whole range of actions by individuals and other organizations unexamined.

Strangely, there is no standard content to introduce social problems. Some authors talk about political conservatives and liberals, others talk about claims making, still others talk about research methods, or the basic theoretical perspectives of sociology, or values and morality. Teachers are likely to select a book that agrees with their own approach, ignoring the other approaches. Some ignore claims making entirely; others omit any talk about conservatives and liberals and so on. There is a consensus among sociologists about the groundwork in other areas. Why not in social problems?

Another neglected area in most social problems textbooks is lessons from the past. Learning from earlier successes or failures is an important part of addressing any social problem. Which solutions succeeded in bringing a positive change and which failed to do so? Prohibition springs to mind as a policy that failed; it offers great insight into social responses to governmental policies with moral components. One objective of this book is to identify relevant past solutions and bring them into the discussion.

Most textbooks do not include literature on social movements. This is an oversight, because understanding social movements can reveal how social problems are addressed in society. Social problems and social movements are two sides of the same coin. Were there no social problems, there would be no social movements or other advocate groups. Similarly, literature on social change is rarely included. But the goal of social movements and advocate groups is social change. It is helpful to understand the social change processes. In short, these two areas of sociology have much to contribute to the study of social problems.

## ⠿ TO THE INSTRUCTOR

Some social problems textbooks have started to address one or another of these issues. Some authors have modified the definition of a social problem to improve consistency. Others have focused almost entirely on solutions. Still others have pursued the logic of claims making rather than the more traditional approach. Clearly the subject area is changing. It is within that arena that this textbook is offered.[1]

Much of the material in this book is similar to other social problems texts. The important social problems are covered: health care, welfare, discrimination, illegal immigration, substance abuse, homelessness, abuse, gangs, abortion, environment, AIDS, rape, prostitution, and others. This is likely to be more than enough material for a one-semester course. While the length of discussion on each problem varies, it is as detailed or more detailed than other texts.

An obvious difference is that the material is not organized by sociological area. Instead, each problem is presented as a discrete unit. This allows for more focus on the specific problem. The goal is to present the key points with enough historical and factual data that the reader can assess the veracity of the various claims makers. It also provides an opportunity to explore particular solutions. In reality, problems are more likely to be addressed individually than as one of a group of problems.

A major addition to this book is the theoretical material presented in the first four chapters and used consistently throughout. It is intended to help conceptualize social problems and the dynamics of those involved and the process of change that is occurring. Readers are encouraged to use the definition (a social problem is defined as having six components) and other aspects of the theory throughout. As always, the role of theory is to bring to light aspects that might otherwise not be noticed.

Another major addition to the social problems topic is the inclusion of advocate groups. These are the people who identified the problem and, more importantly, have a possible solution. Rather than presenting what I think the solution might be, a solution by one advocate group is described for each social problem. This is not necessarily the best solution, but one that raises important issues. The reader is encouraged to explore other solutions (other advocate groups). Evaluating and comparing the solutions is left to the reader. A list of some advocate groups is given after the discussion of each social problem. For the most part they are representative of the different views on the topic currently.

---

1. See Appendix Three for detailed similarities and contrasts.

A brief description and current URL for each group is given in the Appendix Two. (URLs change without warning, so some links may not be functional.)

Key to this approach is presenting students with the tools they need to evaluate the claims of the various advocate groups. This is found mainly in the first chapter. Is the data accurate? Is there an obvious argument bias? Is what is suggested as a solution workable? Is it likely to be enacted? In truth, I have found that this assessment process is very difficult for students. As I tell my students, they are wonderfully naive and take anyone who uses a lot of data and sophisticated language to be an authority. Figuring out what kind of an advocate group it is, evaluating reliability, spotting ideological and/or other bias is not easy to learn. The instructor is encouraged to have assignments, class discussion, and personal advising devoted to recognizing both data and argument bias. It may seem time-consuming, but the payoff is great in terms of the students' ability to assess and digest material. Some exercises addressing this learning process are included in the online instructional material. There are also questions for thought at the end of each section.

A strength of this approach is that it allows students to develop and refine their thinking. It is expected that they will examine and/or present different solutions to a social problem. Some of the advocate group solutions will be a model for students to express their own views. Others will present them with the opportunity to "walk in the shoes" of those with whom they disagree and broaden their ability to understand others. "Trying out" different views in this way gives students a comfortable distance and reduces the risk of personal attack. It provides a "safe" environment for the discussion of liberal/conservative differences.

Finally, investigating various advocate groups gives students both an appreciation of their social environment and the information they need to be active and informed citizens of their society.

## ■■ TO THE STUDENT

This book does not give definitive answers. Rather, it will help you understand the basics of the issues and the vocabulary used to discuss them. It will also help you learn where to look for answers and how to evaluate the information you find.

The first four chapters are theory. The purpose of theory is to provide a framework for your understanding. When you see how something fits in the overall picture, it becomes easier to understand. When you systematically examine things using theory, you will discover gaps and missing parts that would otherwise be overlooked. The Analysis Worksheet in the Appendix One summarizes the main points of the theory. Although at first it may seem tedious and difficult to answer these items, by the end of the course, they should be things that you automatically seek to answer when looking at an advocate group.

Part II looks at specific problems in our society. A social problem is something recognized as a problem by someone or some group—the litmus test for including a problem in this book. Each problem has many advocate groups, sometimes well known. We look at the issues that are important to the different advocate groups in order to better understand the problem. And we need to decide if their presentation of the problem is a good one, or if they have exaggerated to make a good argument. If they do exaggerate, does it make a difference?

Some of you will go on to study social movements in greater depth in other sociology classes. It is an exciting area of inquiry. Many years ago in India I had a small office in a busy part of Bombay. The other offices up and down the hallway were occupied by entrepreneurs of all sorts, including production of clothing for export. Each office was a mini business and sometimes a mini factory. What I came to realize is that the whole building was teeming with life, each enterprise cleverly using the resources they had to develop their business and earn a living. Advocate groups in the United States are similar. Each community is teeming with them, for every cause you can imagine, and a few more. Understanding who they are, how they organize, what characteristics they have helps you to understand our society in general.

A list of advocate groups briefly described is given in Appendix Two, along with a current URL. Of course, this is not the complete list of advocate groups, just some of the prominent ones. You may wish to look for other groups that have pursued other solutions to particular problems. Whenever you visit an advocate group site, be sure to look at the "About Us" page to know the identity of the group.

One aim of this text and the class you are taking is that you become a more active participant in the society in which you live. Understanding and recognizing the issues and the arguments is an important part of being a responsible citizen. It is not expected that you will know the details of all the conflicts in and around the world. But you should be familiar with the fact that there are conflicts, and with some of the reasons why. From time to time, people will want to know what you think, and sometimes your views on an issue will matter.

An important part of being informed is vocabulary. You are likely to encounter terms that are unfamiliar to you during the course of your reading. The sociological terms or terms specific to particular problems are defined in the text as they are introduced, and given in the glossary in the back for you to refer to as needed.

An important part of being informed is also insightful understanding. The Analysis Worksheet in the Appendix will assist your analytical thinking. It doubles as an outline of the first four chapters. Refer to the Analysis section after the first advocate group solution in each chapter for my observations.

## ■■ A NOTE OF THANKS

Thanks go to many. First of all to my friends and colleagues who heard me say for years that I am writing a book on social problems. It must have seemed like a myth at times. It takes time for a theory to develop from a kernel of an idea into something that is coherent and can be used in social analysis. This has not been a solitary project. I have discussed the contents with numerous others—sociologists, nonsociologists, and of course with my students. Each provided helpful insights, critiques, and encouragement.

Students in my social problems classes gave me important feedback. They were particularly helpful in highlighting what worked and what didn't work. Three students need particular mention, Teressa Norris and Mark Elizondo, who assisted in early research, and James A. Jones, who assisted at a later stage.

Several of my friends and family members helped at different points along the way. Deanna Palla and Karla James read through early drafts and gave important comments. Susan Herrman very carefully edited much of the final draft. Candace Halliburton helped with advocate group descriptions and assisted writing the environment sections.

Thanks also go to the university for giving me the freedom to teach the class using my own theories and writing. And thanks to family members who patiently waited as I wrote.

*Sara Towe Horsfall, Ph.D.*

# Section I

## THE THEORETICAL BASIS OF THE STUDY OF SOCIAL PROBLEMS

# CHAPTER ONE

# WHAT IS A SOCIAL PROBLEM?

## ▪▪ SIX INGREDIENTS OF SOCIAL PROBLEMS

Everyone notices things in the world that need to be improved. But a social problem is more than a personal opinion about something. It has social components. For instance, those affected by a social problem will be a group (collectivity or category), not just one or two people. Also, a social problem is recognized as a problem by a group of people who feel strongly enough to take steps toward change.

Put another way, if people are suffering but no one recognizes it, there is no social problem. It becomes a social problem only when people agree that something is wrong and organize themselves to resolve it. That doesn't mean that people aren't suffering if no one recognizes it. But it does mean that their suffering hasn't filtered into social consciousness, so no one is willing to stop it.

Even those who are suffering may not consider their situation to be a social problem. They may conclude that it is due to their own failing—sin, lack of ability, bad luck, and so on. They may not be aware anyone else is suffering as they are. Or they may be resigned to their fate, believing that the effort to change things is too great and that no one cares about them. But what is defined as a social problem changes over time. Things that are not recognized as social problems today may be considered problems in the future. Recognizing something as a problem is the first step in the social change process.

How can it be that something is not a social problem if no one recognizes it? Consider child abuse. There is evidence that large numbers of children were battered in the eighteenth century and earlier. Yet it was not until the twentieth

3

century that child abuse became a public issue. In 1962 a medical journal published a report by a pediatric radiologist stating that multiple injuries at different stages of healing indicate abuse. Almost immediately professional organizations began to campaign, and twelve years later legislation outlawing child abuse was passed (Kadushin and Martin 1980; Pfohl 1977). Today child abuse is a public issue addressed by social agencies and law enforcement.

Sociologists believe that we create society. We organize ourselves, establish the rules and regulations necessary to make things work, and collectively identify goals. An early sociologist, Emile Durkheim, said that these social norms are as important as, or more important than, instinct. These consensual beliefs tell us what to do and guide our daily lives. Collective recognition and resolution of social problems is part of that creative social process.

To understand the process of defining and resolving issues, we need to know the six ingredients of social problems. First, there are those who are suffering. This is the *target group*: a collection of individuals who are treated unfairly, don't get their fair share of social and/or material resources, or face serious threats to their well-being. In short, their personal well-being (life chances, e.g., satisfaction or emotional happiness) or their social well-being (equality, representation, and other social situations) is threatened. People in the target group may not know each other, so it is more correct to call them a target category or collectivity. For simplicity's sake, I use the term *target group* to mean collectivity, category, or group.

The second ingredient is the *adverse social situation* that affects the target group. It can be changed by human effort and probably has a human or social cause. A physical disaster—a tornado or a tsunami—is not in itself a social problem but can quickly develop into one. The tsunami in Southeast Asia in 2004 created many social problems. In the immediate aftermath, large numbers of people needed food, shelter, and medical assistance. Others suffered long-term needs, such as children without parents, unemployed persons, and persons unable to locate their relatives. These and other problems were addressed by local and international governments (Korf 2007; Tang 2007). Similarly, the 9.0 earthquake that hit Japan in 2011 affected a nuclear power plant. Residents in a nearby farming community were evacuated and, because of high levels of radioactivity, will not be able to return to live there for many years, if ever.

In contrast, several tornados blew through the Fort Worth, Texas, area in 2000 and 2001. There was substantial damage but surprisingly little loss of life (Letchford, Norville, and Bilello 2000). The only real social problem that developed was concern to create a better warning system in the future.

A preventable disaster is almost always a social problem. In 1984 in Bhopal, India, a Union Carbide pesticide factory leaked forty tons of methyl isocyanate gas into the air, killing an estimated 4,000 people, many of whom lived in makeshift houses next to the power plant.[1] There had been little public recognition of the danger to these people before the disaster. Afterward, individuals, groups, and governments debated the risks of dangerous engineering defects and human error in such factories (Perrow 1984; Jasanoff 1994; Hatvalne 2010). The original event was only one part of the problem. There was also concern about the potential for future leaks and the suffering they would cause.

The third ingredient is the group of people who recognize a social problem: the *advocate group.* These individuals are motivated for different reasons, including self-interest, altruism, and idealism. If their own social or physical well-being is threatened, they are heavily invested in the solution. Or they may be moved by the suffering of others. Or they may believe that something about the situation is wrong or sinful and needs to be changed because it offends their belief system. Whatever the reason, they decide that the target group's situation should be changed. They organize themselves to bring the issue into the public arena for discussion and action. They become claims makers (more about that later).

The fourth ingredient of a social problem is the *ameliorating action*—the proposed change—and the fifth ingredient is the *action group*—the group that puts the proposed change into effect.[2] After the Fort Worth tornado in 2000, neighborhood groups (advocate groups) complained that the warning sirens were not sufficient. The complaints were persistent enough and numerous enough that the city governments (action groups) in the surrounding communities took

---

1. Subsequently 11,000 more died from aftereffects of the substance. According to the Indian government some 500,000 people were affected, including thousands of babies born with defects. In June 2010, seven former employees were convicted by an Indian court for their role in the incident.
2. Again, the terminology of "group" is not strictly correct here. The action group is usually an organization or an institution. But for simplicity's sake, when the term *action group* is used, it will mean group, organization, institution, or collectivity—whichever is appropriate.

action. The sirens were tested and upgraded, and in some cases new ones were installed (ameliorating action).

A sixth ingredient is a *will to act* to solve the social problem. Social problems often arise because people find it easier not to act. There is usually a cost attached to the action—if not a monetary cost, then a cost in personal effort or sacrifice of personal interest. To bring change, people must be willing to bear the cost. Replacing the warning sirens was relatively inexpensive, and the will to act was sufficient. Within a few weeks they were replaced or repaired. But in the case of the fertilizer factory in Bhopal, India, there was less will to act. One question that arose was, Who is responsible? When no group or agency is willing to take responsibility or has the necessary resources, the will to act falls to the government.

In sum, then, the six ingredients of a social problem are (1) an advocate group that identifies the problem, (2) an adverse social situation, (3) a victim or target group or target category, (4) an ameliorating action, (5) an action group (organization or institution), and (6) the will to act. Subsequently we can define a social problem as *a situation judged by an advocate group to be adversely affecting the personal or social well-being of a target group (or collectivity) to the extent that it needs to be redressed by means of an ameliorating action to be taken by an action group/organization or institution.* An action group will take such action once there is sufficient will to act.

## ■ HOW DO SOCIAL PROBLEMS OCCUR?

Looking to the cause, it is easy to blame social problems on people who are irresponsible, selfish, immoral, or deviant in some way—the "nuts, sluts, and perverts" (Liazos 1972). This is the tendency to blame the powerless. Legal offenders are often held to blame. Although innocent people are sometimes convicted, offenders in the criminal justice system are generally assumed to be guilty. And crime is one of the most prominent and important social problems.[3]

---

3. The Innocence Project is an organization of lawyers, students, and others who work to assist prisoners who can be proven innocent by means not available at the time of sentencing—DNA testing. Since 1992, a total of 242 people, who served an average of twelve years in prison, have been exonerated and released. For more information, go to www.innocenceproject.org.

But criminal activity is only one of many causes. Social problems arise because a society is developing or there is general ignorance of a particular situation. Some social problems arise because people pursue their own self-interest at the expense of others. Or there are competing interests. Serious social problems are associated with racism and group discrimination. There are unresolved problems whenever there is a long history of enmity and conflict between groups. This list of causes is not exhaustive, but it is diverse enough to be representative. We will examine each of these possible causes separately.

### Development

Chudacoff and Smith's (2000) fascinating account of U.S. urban growth at the turn of the last century highlights problems caused by *development.* Fear of disease (unprotected water supplies were becoming contaminated by seepage from privies and graves) and fear of fire spurred city officials to protect public water supplies. Congestion and dangerous transportation issues in nineteenth-century cities led to complaints that drivers were intentionally reckless; thus traffic regulations and fines were devised for everyone's safety and comfort. Creative solutions to these and other social problems led to the development of the modern urban infrastructure, and the early twentieth century saw "the highest standards of mass urban living in the world" (Chudacoff and Smith 2000, 136, 87, 50). Sometimes developmental problems persist, indicating the existence of factors that erode the social will, such as lack of resources, an inadequate infrastructure, or an insufficient political structure.

Technological advances also bring problems. They create new conditions and issues not addressed by existing regulations or conventions. The rapid and amorphous growth of computers and the Internet during the late twentieth century illustrates this point. Issues of censorship and control are still being discussed—nationally and worldwide.

### Aftermath of a Natural Event

A very different kind of social problem comes after a *natural event.* Hurricane Katrina in 2005 was one of the worst natural disasters to hit the United States during the twentieth century. Half a million people were evacuated, 1,600 people lost their lives, and more than 1,000 went missing (Kessler et al. 2006). From a social problems perspective, what is of interest is the way people organize themselves to respond to the possibility of disaster and the human needs arising from it. In the case of Katrina, the most publicized situation involved the low-income, primarily black residents who survived the hurricane but lacked food and shelter (Brodie et al. 2006). Many groups responded with assistance, including the local police, firemen, and Coast Guard, as well as federal agencies—FEMA (Federal Emergency Management Agency) and the Department of Homeland Security. A host of church groups, nonprofits such as the Red Cross, local organizations, and individuals in other cities also helped with shelter, basic necessities, and financial assistance during the subsequent evacuation.

The immediate outpouring of assistance was followed by several years of effort to rebuild the neighborhoods, the city, and the lives of those affected: home owners (Elliott and Pais 2006), those with increased mental health issues (Kessler et al. 2006), those who lost confidence in government officials, especially regarding issues surrounding waste disposal (Allen 2007). Other concerns focused on how the public was informed about environmental and public health threats, as well as preparedness at the local, state, and federal levels (Frickel and Vincent 2007).

### Inequality

The most prominent *inequality* is poverty, which affects close to 13 percent of the U.S. population. People who are poor suffer from a lack of basic necessities and from their relationships within the social structure (Myers-Lipton 2006). Minorities are disproportionately affected by poverty and often have reduced access to social resources because of discrimination.[4] Personal, societal, and structural factors are compounded by the underlying ideological beliefs that perpetuate the inequality. A minority child from a low-income family is less likely to attend college or university than a nonminority child from a wealthy family—even if he or she has the intelligence to succeed academically.

---

4. According to the U.S. Census Bureau, 8.3 percent of non-Hispanic whites lived in poverty, as compared with 24.9 percent of African Americans, 24.7 percent of American Indians, and 21.8 percent of Hispanics.

Sociologists call this *stratification*—organization of people according to differential access to resources and the consequent social positions in society. Problems associated with stratification have to do with health care, high rates of drug abuse, high crime areas, educational issues, political representation, and many others (Myers-Lipton 2006).

### Self-interest

*Self-interest* is a major reason that stratification develops in the first place, and an important source of other social problems. The problem is that economic theories today stress self-interest and commonly assume that "individuals in a society always act according to their self-interest or private economic incentive" (Sen 1977). Rational choice theories used by social scientists and economists also assume self-interest. This view of human nature became acceptable around the time of the Industrial Revolution, when rational self-interest for men in the business world was legitimized. The eighteenth-century doctrine of "separate spheres" had women as keepers of religion and morality, whereas men managed the political, legal, and economic affairs outside the home (Coontz 2005). These two sets of values—the moral, "feminine" values inside the home and the rational, self-oriented "masculine" values outside the home—are in conflict. The popular character Tom Sawyer highlights this discrepancy.

> The late 19th century cliché of the mischievous boy was, like the sentimentalization of women and children, an attempt to deal with one aspect of the era's central discomfiture. The very attributes that would make a man occupationally successful were unwelcome in the domestic environment of his own creation. In a situation of conflict, especially when resolution is not forthcoming, a common human response is to try to laugh; hence the mischievous boy and his exasperated female "superior." The image allowed just enough caricature of the rule-breaker and the rule maker to afford the populace a laugh, but few, it appears, truly understood the joke. The final effect of this phenomenon was perhaps its most subversive: the perception of boys' mischievous antics as masculine behavior invited reversal, so that immature or illicit activities of men could, in time, be construed as mischief that is natural and harmless. (Heininger 1984, 27–28)

Self-interest is widespread. It is the norm in a for-profit business world. There is nothing natural or harmless about the activities of senior officials at the Enron Corporation, who created a network of offshore companies to make the company look more profitable than it actually was. After the company collapsed, it became apparent who benefited at the expense of shareholders, employees, pensioners, customers, and suppliers. Even though it is generally accepted that top executives work to perpetuate their own interests (Egeberg 1995), there was an outcry about the actions of Enron officials who became a "visible symbol of the dangers of excessive self-interest" (Finkelstein et al. 2008). Dangerous self-interest, *greed* to Marxists, is a major reason for Marxist opposition to the capitalist system (Walker 2008).

### Racism and Discrimination

Racism is the belief that people with different biological traits (e.g., skin color) have different social value. Discrimination is the differential treatment of categories of people. *Racism and discrimination* involve both personal and group self-interest in noncommercial areas. After the U.S. Civil War, the South was associated with white supremacy—local residents believed that theirs was and should be a "white man's country." Fears that the newly freed slaves would upset the balance of political power were supported by theories of scientific racism and "survival of the fittest" Social Darwinism—ideas popular in the late nineteenth century.[5] When Northerners did not react to court decisions that denied protection to blacks (between 1873 and 1898), disaffected Southerners pursued their own ends (McMillen 1990). The so-called Jim Crow laws created a segregated society, depriving African Americans of the right to vote (unless they owned property), the right to be educated in the same schools as whites, and free access to public facilities. Enforcement of the Jim Crow laws was supported by an atmosphere of fear created by lynching.

---

5. Ideology contributes to racism and discrimination. Nineteenth-century eugenicists concluded that Caucasians (in particular Caucasian males, since females weren't included in the top rank) were the most developed of all the races. In *Mismeasure of Man* Stephen J. Gould documents the bias in their "scientific" studies of intelligence used to support their theories. A less obvious ideology of racism today is the common impression that Hispanic children are less likely to do well at school than white children.

Let's analyze this situation using the social problems theory presented here. Disaffected whites in the South after the Civil War considered themselves victims. In their eyes, they were the *target group*. The *adverse situation* they faced was the loss of their way of life, as well as social and political power, to people who had once been their social inferiors. During Reconstruction, in addition to having the right to vote, 2,000 blacks served in federal, state, and local offices (Foner 1993). A racist *advocate group*, the Ku Klux Klan, was formed in Pulaski, Tennessee, in 1866 to oppose the social and political changes (Martinez 2007). It soon spread to other states.

> Fear convinces Klansmen that others, somehow different from them, have negatively affected their lives. They yearn for halcyon days when no one questioned their unbridled authority. Anything or anybody challenging the status quo threatens the established order, and threats must be handled through extra legal means, if necessary. (Martinez 2007, x)

As Martinez noted, the *ameliorating action* of the KKK was to handle the threat by any means that worked. The Jim Crow laws were intended to restrict the social and political power of southern blacks and keep them disadvantaged. Fear was a means of preventing blacks from reasserting themselves. The white supremacists' *will to act* came from the political threat and economic competition they felt from African Americans and fueled their desire to maintain caste boundaries (Beck and Tolnay 1990).

The KKK is uniquely a *target group* (according to its own assessment), an *advocate group,* and an *action group*—all at the same time. They saw themselves as the victim. They worked to draw attention to their situation among others in the South and worked out a solution themselves, rather than turn to the government to resolve the issue. From their point of view, they were successful—at least for a while.

From an African American point of view—and from the view of most people today—the actions of those associated with the KKK created a segregated society that was not legally redressed until the 1960s. It took that length of time for another *advocate group* (or movement, as it turned out) to form and to develop the *will to act* on a national scale. We will revisit this problem later in the section on opposition groups.

Stratification problems (stemming from inequality or discrimination) created by self-interest usually require government intervention, since those in power do not easily give up their position of advantage. Whether they are forced to reevaluate the situation by law or they choose to do so of their own free will, the concerned parties in power often lack a global perspective of the issue. Putting their own well-being on the same level as the other parties involved is one part of a solution. This usually requires relinquishing resources, potential resources, position, or prestige.

### Competing Interests

Competing interests may technically be self-interest on a group level but can have other dimensions as well. Territorial claims are an important aspect of political interests, especially when natural resources such as water, energy, and minerals, geostrategic claims, and/or control of a population within territorial boundaries are at stake (Diehl 1999).

Competing territorial claims lie at the core of the Arab-Israeli conflict. In the late nineteenth century, Jews from Russia and eastern Europe began to conceive of the idea of a Jewish homeland to resolve their centuries-long existence as an oppressed minority scattered through many different countries (the diaspora). They began purchasing land in the Middle East—land that they thought, perhaps erroneously, was more or less unoccupied. Their secret intention was to become so numerous in the area that they could eventually claim the country as theirs. The conflict, then, came not from misunderstanding, but from the "conflicting interests and goals of the two populations. The Arabs sought instinctively to retain the Arab and Muslim character of the region and to maintain their position as the rightful inhabitants; the Zionists sought radically to change the status quo, buy as much land as possible, settle on it, and eventually turn an Arab populated country into a Jewish homeland" (Morris 2001, 49). The Jewish people received support from western forces in the region, and ultimately the modern state of Israel was born.

From a social problems perspective, Jewish and Arab *advocate groups* differ in terms of who is the victim. They propose different solutions that involve different organizations or countries to be part of the solution. In short, there are two different social problems here rather than one. Of course, most of us see it as one issue—not two. Part of the difficulty in resolving the conflict is agreeing on who is the victim, and why, and subsequently what kind of action should be taken, by whom.

Northern Ireland is another example of competing claims. Historically the roots of the problem go back to the sixteenth and seventeenth centuries, when Britain sought to reassert its control over Ireland by sending officers, soldiers, administrators, and clergy to settle and establish the country as a self-supporting contributor. The native Catholic population resisted this intrusion. The resulting conflict between the Protestant Unionists and the Catholic Nationalists has continued until today (Ruane and Todd 2000).

Yet another example of competing claims is Cyprus, where Turkish Cypriots and Greek Cypriots claim dominance of the island. The result is that the 3,571-square-mile island (approximately 40 miles across) has been divided since 1974. In 1983 the northern 1,300 square miles became the Turkish Republic of Northern Cyprus, whereas the southern part of the island is the Greek Cypriot Republic of Cyprus. A thin green line crosses the island and divides the capitol of Nicosia and has been patrolled by UN forces since 1964.

### History of Enmity and Conflict

Sometimes problems between two peoples continue long after the specific issues have been resolved. Once people have been killed, the grief of the families and friends deepens hostility to the point where even the mention of the other side stirs up animosity and suspicion. After years of conflict in the Middle East, this is true for many Jews and Arabs. It has also been true in Northern Ireland, where there has been enmity between the two sides for hundreds of years—although currently there have been several years of relative peace. It was true in Cyprus, although happily here too the situation has vastly improved.

But there are other places where a history of enmity and conflict has not been resolved. As the former Yugoslavia was breaking apart in the 1990s, Serbs, Kosovar Albanians, Croats, and Bosnian Muslims "each claimed to be defending themselves against annihilation" (MacDonald 2002, 2). Yet a century earlier, they had worked together to form the Kingdom of Serbs, Croats, and Slovenes. They were rebelling against the centuries of domination by the Byzantines, the Ottomans, and the Hapsburg Empire. And in modern times the domination continued. The Germans occupied the area during World War II, and then the communist state of Yugoslavia was formed. The Balkan saying that behind every hero stands a traitor is understandable considering the area's history. Today there are separate countries of Croatia, Slovenia, Republic of Macedonia, Bosnia and Herzegovina, Serbia, Montenegro, and Kosovo. Some conclude that the enmity between the different peoples during the 1990s was a strategy to establish independence (MacDonald 2002). Such claims only highlight the complexities involved in resolving this kind of problem.

Yet another area of historic conflict is in Rwanda, where the Tutsi and Hutu have fought each other for many years. In 1994 an estimated 800,000 Tutsis and moderate Hutus were killed by the Hutus in power, in what is now called *genocide* (BBC 2008). One version of this story was told in the movie *Hotel Rwanda*.


### Ignorance

Sometimes problems develop because of *ignorance*. When severe acute respiratory syndrome (SARS) developed in Hong Kong at the end of 2003, it was a new disease. The means of transmission was unknown, and there was no known cure; the reported death rate was 10 percent (Ap 2003; Tam et al. 2004). The epidemic highlighted the importance of understanding health factors among the population (Loh et al. 2004).

Similarly, few people realized the cause of AIDS when it appeared, or its serious consequences. In the early 1980s, when the public and medical professionals were largely silent about the disease, an estimated 100,000 to 300,000 persons on five continents became infected (Mann 1990). The disease continues to spread in countries such as India, where up to 30 percent of those exposed have never heard of it (Chatterjee 1999). As U.S. medical professionals learned more about the disease, the information was disseminated throughout the population, giving individuals an opportunity to take precautions and reduce its spread.

In sum, common causes of social problems include development, natural disasters, inequality, self-interest, racism and discrimination, competing interests, history of enmity and conflict, and ignorance. Social problems are difficulties that need to be "taken care of," or irritations that need our attention, to be fixed as quickly as possible. Social problems also offer an opportunity to improve our collective social life. They highlight areas that need to be addressed, expanded, and developed. They point to areas that require new and imaginative thinking to create adequate structures, regulations, and governance for the well-being of everyone. They are frequently a sign of healthy growth rather than something to hide and be embarrassed about. They always lead to change, and because people frequently resist change, solutions are not always welcomed or sought out. But in the end, addressing social problems today can help shape the world that we live in tomorrow. The better the solutions, the better tomorrow's world.

## ▪▪ LEVELS OF SOCIAL PROBLEMS

When analyzing social problems, we need to identify the level of the problem. This is determined primarily by the target group and the action group. Are the people in the target group from one place, or are they scattered across the country or the world? Is the action group (institution or government) local, state, national, or international? In general, widespread problems require more coordination among institutions, agencies, and governments.

A *local level* social problem will fall primarily to local authorities. Several communities may have similar problems, but each resolves its own situation. For instance, consider the problem that developed after the Fort Worth tornado in 2000. The Bank One building, a popular landmark, was effectively destroyed. This was a social problem because it occupied a complete city block in the middle of the downtown area and sat virtually empty for close to five years, raising concerns of safety, crime, and ambiance. Asbestos was discovered, which made rebuilding expensive. For two years, owners, developers, city and state officials argued. The only business that reoccupied the building was a popular restaurant on the top floor, which was forced to relocate when the building was to be imploded. Implosion was finally abandoned due to safety fears and associated costs. Three years after the tornado, concerned parties finally agreed to redevelop the building into residences, retail spaces, and public parking. Two years later the first residents moved in (Whiteley 2002; Metrocode 2009).

Other cities have faced similar problems after natural disasters. Local authorities assess the issues and resolve them—and perhaps consult others with similar issues.

*State level* problems fall under the jurisdiction of state authorities. States that have similar problems do not necessarily address them in the same way.

For example, the Amish live in religious communities separated from others. Because of their preference for horse-drawn buggies instead of cars, they present a special challenge. Their simple lifestyle puts them at risk of fatal accidents on the highways (NBC4i 2009). Since close to 80 percent of the Amish live in Ohio, Pennsylvania, and Indiana, this problem is addressed by those states but is not of concern elsewhere.

Sometimes it is not clear which authority should address a problem. Illegal immigration, for instance, is a federal issue (although a 1996 bill allowed Immigration and Customs Enforcement, or ICE, to certify state and local law enforcement officers; Carafano and Keith 2006). But people in border communities or states, or in the smaller communities where illegal immigrants settle, feel that the federal government isn't doing a good job.

For instance, in Farmers Branch, a small community in Texas, the Hispanic population has increased to 37 percent in recent years, with illegal immigrants making up a large portion of the increase. This has put a severe strain on public services in the city of only 30,000 residents. City officials passed an ordinance making it an offense to rent to undocumented persons. This was seen as a controversial action in the state and elsewhere in the country.

In 2010, after a local resident was murdered, Arizona farmers living along the Mexican border complained that the flow of illegal immigrants defaces their property and puts them at risk. Claiming that the federal government had neglected "its constitutional duty to secure the border" (CNN 2011), Governor Jan Brewer introduced a bill requiring Arizona police to verify the legal status of anyone they apprehend. The U.S. Justice Department sued, claiming that only it had that authority. The dispute has gained national attention.

At a *national level*, social problems concern all citizens in some way. Federal authorities are involved in attempts at resolution. National level issues include immigration, certain crimes, drugs, moral issues, cultural violence, and wars, such as the war in Iraq.

Sometimes actions taken by state or local level authorities are seen as part of a national identity. This is the case with the death penalty for non–U.S. citizens. Although people in the United States realize that the penalty varies from state to state, others do not. On the other hand, legalizing marijuana and euthanasia has given the Netherlands an interesting international reputation.

Last, there are problems that affect everyone on our planet. Many governments cooperate to resolve these kinds of *international level* problems. Pollution, protection of national resources, trade agreements, terrorism, extradition, and crime are some examples.

## ∷ INFORMATION AND CLAIMS MAKING

Informed citizens, advocate groups, action groups, and social researchers are all interested in information about social problems. Some professional groups, such as doctors, lawyers, teachers, social workers, and police, address social problems as part of their job, so they regularly collect information about those they serve. Action groups look to these sources and collect their own information in order to carry out the mandate they are given. The data of the federal government, one of the largest action groups (or organization), is a major resource for everyone.

Collecting and analyzing data is a topic in and of itself. There are established procedures to ensure accuracy and reliability.[6] Since most advocate groups use data that has already been collected and analyzed, it is important for us to understand how to evaluate presentations of data by claims makers.

Claims making is the process by which a person (or persons) tries to convince others of the truth and importance of an issue. In terms of social problems, it is an advocate group's efforts to convince the public and government officials (or other action groups, organizations or institutions) that there is a problem and that it needs attention. Advocate groups are the main claims makers, but action groups, social researchers, and, in fact, everyone engages in claims making at some time or another.[7] The researcher needs to know what goes into a claim.

---

6. The main ways that sociologists and other social researchers collect data are surveys, interviews and field research, case studies, and experimentation. Sociologists also use secondary data sources, including government or other known organizations such as GSS, or others, and of course the U.S. Census.

7. Because of the focus of this book, most of the discussion centers on the claims making of advocate groups. Everything that is said about claims making and claims makers can apply to all other claims-making groups or individuals.

### Social Construction and Bracketing

The first step in evaluating a claim is to understand the advocate group's reality or worldview. Everyone sees things differently, and consequently one group's solution can be another group's problem (the KKK example above). Different worldviews are possible because we, together with our friends, determine what is important and real. This is what sociologists call *social construction*—arranging the factors of one's experience into a coherent worldview. If we can understand what members of an advocate group have experienced, we will better understand their worldview. But to truly understand another worldview, researchers must set aside their own beliefs and political views and examine values, beliefs, and threats without judgment.

Setting aside one's own ideas does not mean embracing another view. Nor does it imply carelessness with details. But it does allow enough space to look carefully at the implicit and underlying motivations without dismissing them as silly, irrelevant, or wrong. Judgment is reserved for a later time. This method of setting aside one's own ideas of reality to study another reality is called "bracketing."

Once the researcher understands the group's worldview, he or she will be able to appreciate its proposed action. In some ways, the W. I. Thomas theorem is relevant here: if you think that something is real, it will be real in its consequences. The social researcher does not have to believe in the same reality as the advocate group in order to study and understand it.

A UFO study illustrates the usefulness of this approach. The researcher was not interested in whether UFOs are real or not. But he was very interested in how a belief in UFOs affects someone's actions and attitudes. The social researcher "bracketed" his own beliefs so that he could understand, without judgment, the worldview of someone who does believe in UFOs.

Approaching scientific studies in this way has become more common in recent years. Even the most objective scientists have come to accept that it is not possible to be completely objective, since everyone is influenced by his or her own worldview.

If the issue is one that the social researchers feel strongly about, it may be appropriate at a certain point for them to inform others that they are switching from the role of a social researcher to that of a claims maker. Researchers should realize that by taking on the role of a claims maker, they forfeit some authority and their claims will be evaluated along with all the others.

## Author Bias

The second step in evaluating a claim is to look for *author bias*—a distorted or misleading interpretation of the information of which the author may or may not be aware. Many advocate groups have well-known positions or political affiliations, which are reflected in the language and arguments of their claims. But knowing they have a position doesn't necessarily mean that their claim is distorted or misleading.

If the position of an advocate group is not known, the researcher should ask a series of questions about the presentation of information. Has the situation been overstated? Can known positions be recognized in the argument? What experiences in the author's background led to this view? What does the author hope to achieve from presenting this information? How does this view compare to what others think on this subject? Sometimes the author wants nothing more than to inform the reader. But at other times the author clearly wants to motivate the reader to act in a particular way. Perhaps the author wants to persuade the reader to his own worldview. Or perhaps the author wants the reader to be more sympathetic to an unpopular cause.

There is nothing wrong with listening to all sides of an issue. The conscientious researcher should understand the reasons why people have different worldviews and their interpretation of the facts. In some respects, no truly "objective" viewpoint exists. Each person looks at the world from his or her own perspective and will present facts and arguments accordingly or risk being viewed as insincere or incoherent. The researcher might even find it valuable to "walk in the shoes" of the other person—look at the situation from that perspective, in order to better understand the viewpoint being presented. ("Walking in the shoes of the other" is an opportunity to understand what the social construction process is about.)

The researcher needs to be wary of the author who, in an attempt to win over the reader, is guilty of distorting the facts or presenting the arguments in a misleading way.

If the information appears evenhanded, the researcher might want to look for other signs of a claims maker's intentions. Are there any indications of affiliation to a group or category that has a known position? Certain organizations that are referred to repeatedly may offer a clue. An article on evolution that refers to a fundamentalist Christian organization would be suspect, since most fundamentalist Christians oppose Darwinian evolution.

Identifying who published the article might give another clue. An article on science in the public school system published by the American Association for the Advancement of Science (AAAS) is likely to promote a different view than one published by the American Baptist Association (ABA). Ideally, the two sources would agree on essential points. Failing that, the researcher should weigh the data and arguments of the respective organizations while being alert to potential bias.

The social researcher should not be fooled by reputation. Just because a group has a well-known position doesn't mean it is always unreliable. For instance, one might expect a certain bias when a religious organization reports the news. But despite its religious affiliation, the *Christian Science Monitor* has been highly respected for a hundred years.

On the other hand, advocate group members who are well respected may be biased. Persons with a reputation for accuracy may nonetheless mistake their point of view for objectivity. This is apparently the case with the respected scientists Isaac Asimov, Carl Sagan, and Paul Kurtz, who cofounded the Committee for the Scientific Investigation of Claims of the Paranormal.[8] The group claims to "promote scientific inquiry" when "examining controversial and extraordinary claims." But an examination of these men's views reveals they discount the reality of spiritual phenomena.[9] Hence anyone reading articles in their publication, the *Skeptical Inquirer*, should beware of an antispiritual bias.

---

8. Changed to Committee for Skeptical Inquiry, or CSI in 2006. www.csicop.org.
9. Paul Kurtz is professor emeritus of both the CSI organization and the Council for Secular Humanism. A statement from the latter organization reads: "We are generally skeptical about supernatural claims. We recognize the importance of religious experience; we deny, however, that such experiences have anything to do with the supernatural. We have found no convincing evidence that there is a separable 'soul' or that it exists before birth or survives death. We must therefore conclude that the ethical life can be lived without the illusions of immortality or reincarnation."

It is not uncommon for scientists to have a bias against religion or spiritual affairs. After all, there has been a "war" between science and religion for approximately five hundred years (Turrell 2004).

Another example of scientists who are biased against spiritual phenomena occurred more than a century ago. In the mid-1800s, the British Association for the Advancement of Science refused to hear papers on hypnotism or mesmerism, on the basis they were insignificant to scientific research. A few years later the British Royal Society of Science refused to hear a paper on spiritualism by physicist Sir William Crookes on similar grounds (Palfreman 1979; Doyle 1975). These incidents do not reflect the image that most people have of scientists objectively examining the data. Thus we can say that even scientists claiming objectivity are subject to bias. But again, the researcher must be careful not to assume that all scientists have a similar bias.

Last, the researcher should ask if the author has something to gain from the action he or she proposes. If a ketchup manufacturer advertised that its product helped prevent cancer, it obviously stands to benefit from all the people who believe the claim and rush out to buy ketchup to prevent cancer. The claim may be completely false or only partially true (more likely in a sophisticated world). The ketchup company may be using a study that found cooked tomatoes had a particularly healthful effect on participants. But it would be difficult to consume enough ketchup to approximate the required results. Thus the statement that ketchup can help reduce cancer is not technically false, but it is misleading.

### Argument Bias

The third step in evaluating a claim is to look for *argument bias*—an attempt to convince by means other than use of data or information. Any argument made by an advocate group publication needs to be examined carefully. The researcher should be on the lookout for arguments that are intended to convince by means other than a careful weighing of the data. How specific is the argument? Does the author give details of the incidents, actions, or persons? Are the details left for the reader to figure out? Look for coherence and appropriateness. Are the claims that the author is making relevant to the question? Does the author stick to the point, going from one aspect to the next? Or does the author throw in a lot of unrelated points to stir the reader's emotions or give the impression of being knowledgeable?

An argument that uses glittering generalities will sound convincing until it is applied to a specific situation. Then the components of the argument break down. Other known tactics that are commonly used to sway someone include name-calling, plain Jane ("I'm just a simple boy"), testimonial, card stacking, bandwagon ("everyone knows"), and lies about the dead ("Before he died . . .").

### Data Bias

Evaluating *data bias* in a claim can be difficult, and the researcher should ask the following questions: What data is used to substantiate the claim? Is it verifiable? Do the facts that are presented agree with reports from other reputable sources? Are the statistics exaggerated to make the claim more dramatic? Is there too much data included? Is it up-to-date?

The researcher is like a detective, sorting through all the available evidence, deciding which is credible and which is not, who to believe, and what arguments to take with a grain of salt. The social problems expert should never dismiss a source of information as invalid because the source does not seem reliable. On the other hand, giving an unreliable source undue weight could cause the conclusions to be biased.

It is impossible for sociologists and researchers to personally verify all the data and other information presented by advocate groups, action groups, or anyone making a claim. Most of the time a quick look at the way in which data is presented will reveal a lot about any misuse of data. Beyond that, to check specific claims, the social researcher can compare the advocate group claims with other claims about the same topic. If there is general agreement among the different claims, the data is probably correct.

Think tanks are advocate groups that study social situations and provide the public with reliable information.[10] Some of these groups have a better rep-

10. To name just a few: the Brookings Institution, American Enterprise Institute, Urban Institute, Cato Institute, Tellus Institute, Heritage Foundation, American Civil Liberties Union, and Pew Research Center.

utation for accuracy than others and most have a political leaning. It is important to know which sources are reliable. A researcher needs to know where to go for data, and how to verify its accuracy. There are large areas of agreement about data among the best think tanks, regardless of their worldview. If there is a discrepancy that the researcher feels needs to be checked, the most authoritative sources of information are the Census Bureau, or known national survey organizations such as General Social Survey, the Gallup Organization, and the Inter-university Consortium for Political and Social Research (ICPSR). Other government agencies sometimes provide reliable data.

Government agencies are generally careful to collect accurate data, but occasionally there are errors. Other organizations vary in the accuracy of their data and its availability to public inquiry. Sociological studies published in peer-reviewed journals can be taken as authoritative, unless there is a particular reason for questioning the way that the study was done.

Delineating all the ways to check for data bias is beyond the scope of this chapter. But we will consider, briefly, some things to watch for. In general, bias in the data means that a conclusion is not supported as claimed.

### Wording

Look for exact meanings of the words and their implications. Scientific presentation of data is as precise as possible. A common mistake, for instance, is mixing up percentages. For instance, "The majority of the students taking the exam scored 80 percent or better" is easily misconstrued as "The majority scored above 80 percent." The word "majority," in this case, refers to the students taking the exam, not the majority of the whole class (or "population"). It is possible that only a small percentage took the exam. In that case, those who scored above 80 percent would be less than half.

### Numbers Versus Percentages

Another way statistics are used inappropriately (some say, to "lie" with statistics) is to confuse numbers and percentages. For instance, the percentage of African Americans who live in poverty is higher than the percentage of white Americans who live in poverty, yet by far the majority (in terms of numbers) of those living in poverty are white.

### Graphs

Exaggeration in graphic representation is not uncommon. A line going from 15 to 20 will appear more dramatic on a graph with a range of 10 to 25 than on a graph with a range of 0 to 50, particularly if the $x$ axis markers are compressed. Someone reporting on the number of rapes in the United States could claim a dramatic increase using the first graph, while opponents could claim a slight increase using the second graph.

### Errors in Conducting Studies

Usually evaluation of data bias will not include examining how a study was done. But occasionally nonscientific studies are given as evidence to support an advocate group claim. It is helpful to be able to recognize this when it happens.

Advocate group reports that cite data from specific studies should include enough information for the reader to find the study or the data. Census data should include the appropriate year and other pertinent information. Journal articles should include the author's name, the publication, and a date. If this information is missing, the data becomes suspect, and the researcher should not rely on it too heavily without verification.

Data that is public knowledge needs no reference. Election of U.S. presidents is a matter of public record, as are notable events such as that of September 11, 2001. At other times the datum is not public record but agrees with known facts; hence, it is believable. If it seems correct, and there is no reason not to trust the data, the researcher may decide to do so until it is discredited.

### Additional Things to Watch For

*Conceptualization:* Did the authors of the study conceptualize the study correctly? Is the concept they claim to have studied really captured in their data? For many years church attendance was used as a measure of religiosity, whereas a person could be very religious and not go to church.

*Sample and Generalization:* To make generalizations about a larger population, the sample studied must be drawn statistically (randomly). If a researcher uses a convenience sample—stopping the first ten people he sees, for instance—the results tell you nothing beyond those ten people.

*Significance*: When statistics are used, significance tells the researcher if the results are by chance. The smaller the number, the less likely the results are by chance. However, results can be statistically significant but not substantively significant, meaning the difference is not important. A study comparing grades may find that a difference between 3.15 and 3.14 is highly significant. But how much difference does .01 make? Not much.

*Cause Versus Correlation:* Most social research only points to correlation. However, correlation is often interpreted as cause. If being hungry and eating is correlated, one is tempted to say feeling hungry causes eating. But what about the times when you visit someone's home and you eat the piece of cake your host offers? In other words, the cause and correlation are not so straightforward as they seemed at first.

## ■ CONCLUSION

The concepts in this chapter help clarify what is meant by social problems. Six ingredients help us know what to look for. By identifying the *advocate group* as a minimal public to recognize a social problem, we can track the ebb and flow of particular social problems. Identifying the *action group* and the *will to act* gives us insight into the inner dynamics of the situation. Examining the way in which the advocate group makes its claims and its proposed *ameliorating action* helps us spot other aspects of the problem that are not being addressed.

In the next chapter we will examine patterns of growth and development of advocate groups. Why do people organize themselves? How do they organize? What stages of development lead to successful advocating? What kind of action will a group think is appropriate? What kind of change is the advocate group seeking? To whom will it turn to take action? What motivates the group, and what will motivate others to go along with its proposed action? What are the likely consequences of the proposed action? There are no ready-made answers to these questions. Instead, conclusions will be drawn about each advocate group based on the information presented.

In the following chapters, we will consider specific solutions to particular social problems. Some problems are very complex, with many diverse advocate groups. In each case a summary is included to help sort these out.

Government action is not the only solution, although it is important. Some problems can be addressed with government programs or legislation. Other problems are addressed successfully by nongovernmental programs and actions. There are also educational campaigns and apologies—on the part of government officials or others. And of course there are actions of individuals. It is also important to look at how people react to advocate groups, and the consequences of actions that are taken. Not all consequences are positive or intended.

Later chapters discuss several models of change, drawn from the different assumptions that people have of human nature. In addition to the well-known models of human interaction, there are models having to do with structure, and models that emphasize resources.

It is always good to take a step back and look at the situation from a broader perspective. The social researcher who examines a social problem using these analytical concepts will surely have something worthwhile to contribute to any discussion.

■ QUESTIONS FOR REVIEW

1. What are the six ingredients of a social problem?
2. What are eight common reasons social problems develop?
3. Explain author bias, argument bias, and data bias.

■ QUESTIONS FOR FURTHER THOUGHT

1. How do social problems make society better?
2. How would you evaluate the claims of Arizona governor Jan Brewer regarding illegal immigration?
3. Is the news objective? Examine the news you listen to or read on a regular basis. Is there an argument bias?
4. In what situations might government data be biased?

# CHAPTER TWO

# UNDERSTANDING ADVOCATE GROUPS

## ■■ WHO ARE THE ADVOCATE GROUPS?

I have defined an advocate group as an identifiable collection of persons who agree that something is a problem and are working to change it.[1] It is an umbrella term that includes interest groups, social movements, and sometimes a crowd or even a riot. Sociologists usually examine these collectivities separately, but to the extent that they all are identified as working for change, they are included here as advocate groups.

There are differences between interest groups and social movements. One important difference is organization. Interest groups are more formally organized. They are generally legal entities, with a formal membership, constitution, and officers. The members likely know each other, or at least know about each other. All members know the officers. They identify with the cause and with each other and by virtue of their membership, and are obligated to contribute financially or in other ways.

Social movements, on the other hand, may have little or no organizational structure. Many, if not most, have no legal standing. Aside from leaders, members or adherents have no formal obligation to contribute financially or in any other way to the movement, but supporters are likely to identify more strongly

---

1. This section relies heavily on the social movement literature, although there are significant differences. For instance, despite their considerable differences, social movements and interest groups are both included as advocate groups because they advocate for change. There is no effort to note current controversies or identify theoretical trends. Rather, theory and research are incorporated as they contribute to the understanding of advocate groups.

with the movement than members of interest groups. One characteristic of a social movement is that supporters identify on a personal level. Even so, if the movement is widespread, it is impossible for them to know each other or know much about each other.

Aside from organizational structure, the two differ in the type of action they seek. Interest groups pursue change through institutional means, such as lobbying. Social movements, in contrast, tend to favor noninstitutional means, such as protests, marches, boycotts, and the like.

A crowd, the third type of collectivity that can function as an advocate group, is a temporary gathering of persons with a similar focus who subsequently influence each other. A riot is a crowd that has become expressive and active. It is always localized (located in one geographical area, as opposed to being spread out over a wide area). Like a social movement, a crowd or a riot has no formal organization, and pursues change through noninstitutional means.

Although we can usually distinguish the type of advocate group by identifying the organizational structure and the type of action pursued, there are other characteristics of each type. We will examine them in more detail.

### Interest Groups

*Political parties* and associated political groups are the best-known interest groups. They are highly organized and structured, have a paid staff, and maintain offices in the national capital, close to the action. The active, organizing group is often small, but these groups claim to represent a large constituency on whose behalf they act. By lobbying for more than one cause, they maximize their resources. Parties have platforms that formalize the organization's positions on many current topics. Members are assumed to support the party platform. The most important strategy of political parties is to get their candidates elected to positions of power, so they can implement their reforms.

*Think tanks* also maintain close ties to politics and politicians. Most have a presence in Washington, D.C., and are frequently identified with a political party, albeit loosely. They focus on collecting and disseminating information, which they make available to politicians and government officials they want to influence. As part of their advocacy work, they make information available to others, as well. Like political interest groups, they tend to be large (although not as large as political parties) and maximize their resources by working on several issues simultaneously. There are many think tanks. Some of the better known are ACLU (American Civil Liberties Union), SPL (Southern Poverty Law Center), Pew Research Center, Urban Institute, AEI (American Enterprise Institute), Heritage Foundation, Brookings Institution, EPI (Economic Policy Institute), and Cato Institute.

*Special interest groups* focus on a single issue or related group of issues. They are usually smaller and localized. They may advocate for a concern of particular interest to their members, or they may advocate for a single social issue of concern to many people. Their usual form of social action is institutional, often government legislation—laws to protect their interests. One example of a special interest group is the NRA (National Rifle Association), which advocates less regulation of firearms. Another example of a small special interest group is MADD, or Mothers Against Drunk Driving. The focus for the NRA is of concern to its members, whereas the focus of MADD extends beyond its own membership.

### Social Movements

Social movements are likely to advocate for broader social change than special interest groups. Unlike political parties, think tanks, or special interest groups, they often form outside the sphere of political influence and thus work outside institutional or organizational channels.[2] People in social movements often believe that change within the system is not possible. Strategies and tactics are likely to include marches, boycotts, sit-ins, and other forms of protest rather than traditional lobbying and campaigning.

Social movements often have a broader appeal with large numbers of supporters or adherents. Not uncommonly, social movements develop an ideology that identifies adherents, unites them, and focuses the group's goals. Adherents

---

2. A common definition of a social movement is given by Snow et al. (2004, 11) as "collectivities acting with some degree of organization and continuity outside institutional or organizational channels for the purpose of challenging or defending extant authority or world order of which they are a part."

often adopt the movement's ideology as their own identity, which makes group members similar in their likes, dislikes, and lifestyles (McAdam and Paulsen 1997; Larana et al. 1994). Opponents or antagonists are easily recognized by their differing tastes or lifestyles. Several well-known movements are the labor unions that were very active in the early part of the twentieth century, the civil rights movement of the 1960s, the women's movement, the pro-life/pro-choice movements, and the environmentalist movement.

Researchers contend that social movements have been an important part of significant changes throughout history. They have been a major way for individuals to voice grievances and become agents of change (McAdam and Snow 1997, xviii). Participation in social movements is increasing today. "It might be argued that we live in a movement society and perhaps even a movement world" (Snow, Soule, and Kriesi 2004, 4). Examples of issues addressed by social movements today are abortion, animal rights, civil rights, human rights, democratization, environmental protection, family values, gay/lesbian rights, gender equality, governmental intrusion, gun control, immigration, labor and management conflict, nuclear weapons, religious freedom, terrorism, war, and world poverty.

### Crowds and Riots

The last two collectivities are unorganized and unstable, as well as brief in duration, but they can still be important agents of change. Local individuals who gather together influence each other in their pursuit of a common end. In the absence of formal organization, the collective action doesn't extend beyond one particular time period. Social movements "occur when they are perceived to be occurring," as do crowds and riots (Gusfield 1994, 70). When a collection of individuals with similar notions of social well-being (or lack of it) are in the right place at the right time, demonstrations, riots, and other spontaneous social eruptions can be instrumental to social change. Participants have a common purpose and become—for a short time—an advocate group.

Two examples come to mind. The first is the series of approximately twenty inner-city race riots in the 1960s. In 1964 riots erupted in Rochester, New York City, Philadelphia, Jersey City, and Chicago. In 1965 one of the worst riots developed in Watts (Los Angeles), and the following year in Cleveland, San Francisco, and Chicago. The 1967 riots in Newark and Detroit were the worst, but that same year there were also riots in Milwaukee and Minneapolis. In 1968 there were riots in Baltimore, Washington, D.C., New York City, Louisville, Kentucky, and Pittsburgh. The nation was stunned by the violence, as well as the hatred and frustration expressed by the rioters. No one formally organized the riots. The rioters spontaneously took advantage of an existing opportunity to express their dissatisfaction with inner-city life. In 1967 President Johnson appointed the National Advisory Commission on Civil Disorders. Policy makers and government officials around the country responded to improve the situation (Metzger 2000; Myers 1997).

The second example is the demonstration mounted by Chinese students and others in Tiananmen Square in China in June 1989. Initially the young people may have had some organization, but the event soon captured the world's attention and for several days seemed to grow spontaneously far beyond its original moorings. The courage displayed by the demonstrators as they challenged a harsh regime inspired awe. In the United States, Saturday cartoons were ignored as adults sat transfixed by developments half a world away. The disappointing response by the Chinese government at first made it seem that those who lost their lives did so for naught. But subsequent reforms by the Chinese government reveal that the youthful demonstrators influenced their policies (Ralston et al. 1995).

### In Sum

This discussion of special interest groups, think tanks, social movements, and crowds does not exhaust the kinds of advocate groups that exist, but it is a good start. Remember that generally, a group refers to people who identify with and interact with each other. They have a shared loyalty, experience, and interests. The term applies in a more conventional way to think tanks, special interest groups, and political parties. To call a social movement a group is a stretch, since members may not interact with each other. But as already noted, adherents of social movements often have a shared identity and even lifestyle. So it may be possible to extend the term "group" to social movements in a limited sense.

To characterize a crowd or riot as an advocate group is problematic. But if we focus on the qualities of interacting with each other (influences passing from one to another in the crowd) and having a shared experience and interests, it does fit the definition. We just have to be sure not to extend the term beyond the short period of time of collective action.

## ▞ WHY DO ADVOCATE GROUPS FORM?

Sociologists have studied social movement formation extensively and have developed theories to explain why they arise and describe their role in social change. The theories fall into three broad categories: (1) desire for structural reform, (2) reformation capacity, and (3) social reformer motivations.

Those theories will help us analyze advocate groups. Because of the differences between advocate groups and social movements, we won't use all aspects of particular theories and in most cases will use them in combination. Since this discussion is not intended to be an academic analysis of the theories, they will not be presented separately. Those who want greater detail can refer to the notes.

### Desire for Structural Reform

The first reason advocate groups form is that people are dissatisfied with the way things are and want change.[3] There is a gap between what the people want and what is available to them.

The Solidarity movement in Poland in the 1980s is a good example. The Polish people compared their living standard with that of people in western Europe, and were dissatisfied with conditions under the socialist government. Perestroika[4] encouraged intellectuals to be more open in their criticism of the socialist system. Using the intellectuals' arguments, Lech Walesa led the workers in a courageous resistance of government policies. The Catholic

---

3. This is the premise of Smelser's structural strain theory, developed in 1962. He identified six stages in the movement's development process. (1) Structural conduciveness: peculiarities of the structure create a problem. (2) Structural strain: what people perceive as ambiguities, deprivation, inconsistencies or tensions leave them dissatisfied with the situation. (3) A popular explanation of the causes and the solutions develops. (4) A precipitating incident: something happens that brings the issue to a head. (5) Mobilization for action: people spontaneously decide to join together to do something about it. (6) Inadequate response by authorities: the government tries to control the situation, but is unable to.
4. Soviet policy of restructuring intended to bring more openness.

Church supported its Polish constituents, and then further international support came from Western governments. The Polish government lacked the power to prevent a democratic government from forming. It received no assistance from the Soviet Union due to its policy of nonintervention in eastern Europe. The Solidarity movement's success was repeated in other eastern European countries, and ultimately spread to the former Soviet Union itself. Before long, seventy years of socialist rule had ended (Cirtautas 1997; Touraine et al. 1983; Harper 1993).[5]

Some researchers talk about deprivation instead of dissatisfaction.[6] People who feel deprived of something, whether money, political freedom, basic rights, or respect, will agitate to get it (Rose 1982). This is like Marx's theory that the workers (have-nots) will rebel once they realize they are being taken advantage of (class consciousness). The labor unions in this country during the first part of the twentieth century formed for this reason: workers felt underpaid, and so they joined together to negotiate higher salaries.

But not everyone is able to protest. People who are starving are too busy finding something to eat. Researchers speculate they will act only when their situation improves (McCarthy and Zald 1973, 1977). On the other hand, people who *feel* deprived, even if they are not destitute, may be quick to protest.

This distinction between *actual* and *perceived* deprivation helps explain why the 1960s race riots didn't occur in the South. African Americans in the rural South were worse off—had a lower standard of living—than those in the North, and they had more reason to protest. But in the North, because equality seemed more attainable, they felt more deprived.

This also explains why employees are more dissatisfied with their pay when they know what others are paid. With no means of comparison, no matter how low their pay, people are less likely to complain (Sweeney et al. 1990).

Another situation can be explained by this theory. Dudley Street is an economically depressed suburb of Boston. A few years back, a developer planned

---

5. This was a momentous change in political power. People living during the Soviet era had come to accept the Soviets as a fact of life. The jubilation at the fall of the Berlin Wall expressed international surprise at the end of their power.

6. This is the deprivation theory. According to relative deprivation theory, protest among the deprived will occur only when things begin to improve (Sweeney et. al. 1990; Merton 1968).

to buy up the abandoned buildings and build upscale housing. The residents organized themselves to prevent being displaced. The Dudley Street Neighborhood Initiative (DSNI) became a success after it acquired enough financial support to hire a professional organizer. Planning, persistent effort, and help from city officials led to a dramatic improvement in their neighborhood, without new development. The DSNI is now a model for other depressed neighborhoods (Medhoff and Sklar 1994).

When the target group is socially disadvantaged, others will usually advocate on its behalf. The DSNI, uniquely, was an organization with a membership of lower socioeconomic status; many members did not speak English. It was both a target group and an advocate group.

While relative deprivation explains why a disadvantaged group doesn't advocate for itself, it *does not* explain why others would advocate on its behalf. To understand the motivations of persons who advocate for others, we need other theories.

### Reformation Capacity

Another reason advocate groups form is because they can.[7] This category of theories looks at the resources needed for success. Capacity[8] is the availability of human, social, and organizational resources to be used in solving a social problem. If a group doesn't have resources, nothing will happen. Resources consist of moral, cultural, social-organizational, and human resources in addition to physical and material resources.

The people with these resources are primarily in the middle and upper classes. People in this sector of society have the time, money, influence, and inclination to work for reform. People from the middle and upper classes are well educated and financially secure, so they are free to concern themselves with current issues, as well as issues of culture and identity that focus on per-

---

7. The theories covered here are resource mobilization theory (developed in the 1970s to examine the impact of resources on a social movement, Edwards and McCarthy 2004), new social movement theory, and cultural theory.

8. In community studies, the term *capacity* refers to the human, social, and organizational resources that can be leveraged to solve collective problems (Chaskin et al. 2001, 7). The term also applies to social problems.

sonal and intimate aspects of life. This explains the increasing popularity of gay rights, abortion, New Age transformation, and so on.[9] Members of these and other advocate groups are most likely to come from the middle and upper classes.

One resource that is sometimes overlooked is cultural symbols. Appealing symbols determine who will join an advocate group. "Culture gives people the vocabulary of meanings, the expressive symbols, and the emotional repertoire" they need (Swindler 2003, 27). And if an advocate group doesn't have the political power it needs, members may use the public arena and the media to redefine the issues and situations in their favor. Their opponents also use the "giant machinery of publicity" to subvert the worldview of the other—a battle of symbolic encoding.

This approach sheds some light on the popularity of charity work among upper-class women in Victorian England. At a time when women did not work after marriage and did not hold public office, working as volunteers in humanitarian organizations to improve society gave them a place in public life. Their efforts were effective because of their access to needed resources—time, money, political influence—which they acquired primarily through their husbands and their fathers.[10]

The prison reform of the 1800s is a good example. This was an effort started by Elizabeth Fry, a Quaker who came from an educated, respected family. She first noted the treatment of female prisoners in Newgate Prison in the United Kingdom. They were housed, together with their children, in overcrowded rooms with inadequate facilities, and without legal representation. These women did not have the resources they needed to organize themselves. But even if they had, their social standing would have prevented them from being heard. Elizabeth Fry supplied them with food and clothes, organized a school for their children, and founded the Association for the Reformation of the Female Prisoners

---

9. The new social movement theory notes that such movements tend to be segmented, diffuse, and decentralized in their organizational structure, and adherents favor the use of new mobilization tactics such as nonviolence (Larana et al. 1994). New social movement theory also implies that movement members or participants are socially deficient or marginal.

10. Coincidentally, this approach provides insight into the women's movement as well. Women who worked as volunteers had the additional capacity needed to establish themselves as effective in working for women's rights and suffrage.

in Newgate (which eventually became the British Ladies' Society for Promoting the Reformation of Female Prisoners). Because of her access to social and physical resources, Fry was able to change the prison in ways that the prisoners could not (Cooper 1981; Fry and Ryder 1883).

Involvement of people from the middle and/or upper classes is also seen in the Polish Solidarity movement (discussed above) and in the American civil rights movement of the 1960s. In both cases, the majority of supporters were from the working class or were minorities. But nonminority supporters who were not from the lower class had access to the social and cultural resources the movements needed to be successful. In Poland, intellectuals clarified the issues and justified the protests. In the civil rights movement, educated northerners had financial resources, access to the government, and social status.

Timing was important in both cases. Issues do not become popular until there is a supporting vocabulary. Prior to the civil rights movement, many people objected to racial inequality, including African Americans and women. But it was not until the 1960s that integration and equal rights became popular slogans. Perhaps the rebellious atmosphere of that decade provided the civil rights movement with a needed cultural readiness.

### Reformer Motivation

The third reason advocate groups form comes from member motivation.[11] Simply put, members want or need something from the group. Early theories about social movements speculated that people who joined social movements had few friends and needed the social connections it provided. While this may still be true of some people, it doesn't describe everyone.[12]

---

11. This section draws from mass society theory, oppositional consciousness, and value-belief-norm theory.

12. The mass society theory holds that isolated people with weak social ties join social movements to acquire a sense of belonging and community. Although not very flattering, this theory does explain membership in extreme movements that are contrary to a democratic tradition. People who are alienated from traditional institutions interact with each other, form a homogeneous identity, and are susceptible to irrational behavior (Gusfield 1994; Kornhauser 1959). This theory *may* explain participation in the Branch Davidian movement in Waco, Texas, that inspired irrational and life-threatening loyalty.

Recent theories emphasize identity and ideology.[13] People join a group because they identify with others in the group, or because the group's goals inspire them or coincide with their own views and feelings. Participation in a social movement is a search for meaning and an expression of one's views. The more a social movement fulfills these demands, the more satisfying it will be to participants.

People from a disadvantaged group may join for reasons of identity and ideology, particularly if the advocate group has a cause similar to their own.[14] Some people develop a kind of "righteous anger over injustices" that they suffered or witnessed (Mansbridge and Morris 2001, 5), and are eager to work to change things. However, these same people may feel intimidated because of their lower social status, and need to address those feelings first (Morris and Braine 2001, 23).

Some people join an advocate group because of their social conscience (ideology). If something important to them is threatened and they believe they *can* help, they feel obliged to help.[15] There are at least three avenues of participation. (1) Engage in advocate group activities (demonstrate, write letters, donate money, read the literature, etc.). (2) Accept material sacrifices needed to meet the goal (pay higher prices, accept taxes, submit to regulated behavior like recycling or water bans). (3) Change personal or private behavior (reduce energy, water, or other consumption, purchase environmentally benign products, etc.) (Dietz et al. 1999).[16]

Another motivation for advocate group formation is altruism or compassion. This addresses the question of why people are willing to work for the well-being

---

13. Klandermans (2004) gave three reasons: instrumentality, identity, and ideology. Instrumentality has already been covered—people join because they want to change things (socially or politically).

14. This is the recent social movement theory of oppositional consciousness.

15. This is the newest theory of social movement formation: value-belief-norm theory.

16. These theories roughly coincide with social psychology literature. We feel obliged to do something if someone has done something good for us (norms of reciprocity). If something is unfair, according to our view of justice, we are likely to become involved. We are more likely to help if we feel guilt for something, or are in a good mood. On the other hand, we are less likely to help if we conclude it's not our concern or our turn, or if our self-esteem is threatened by helping, or if there are many others around, or if we don't have enough resources.

of others, or why they are willing to sacrifice their well-being for the sake of another.

Early sociologists talked about compassion and selfless acts of concern for the well-being of others. Comte (1973) used the term *altruism* to refer to the basic human virtue of living for others. Spencer contrasted it with egoism, the motivation for self-interest. Despite early acknowledgment of compassion and altruism, the assumption that human nature is motivated by self-interest prevailed in sociology for most of the twentieth century, perhaps because it coincided with the biological view of self-survival.

Recent research supports the idea that people are more innately social than innately selfish. Biologists have concluded that cooperation is an important part of evolution. The capacity for empathy apparently runs very deep. Studies indicate that watching someone in pain triggers a pain response (Hutchinson et al. 1999). The mirror neurons in the human brain respond to another's pain as if it were one's own; when we see someone suffering, our brain automatically responds. Indications are that the impulse to help others is more primal than to ignore someone in distress (Goleman 2006). Further, helping others is pleasurable. Brain activity associated with helping others stimulates neurons associated with the experience of pleasure and reward (Emory University Health Sciences Center 2002). That is, we derive the same pleasure from helping others as from satisfying our own desires.

Despite the skepticism and the mitigating factors, it seems obvious that this view of human nature is an important one. Advocate group members motivated by altruism or compassion do not expect anything in return but feel compelled to continue working. Of course, some may present themselves as altruistic while harboring an interest in monetary and other rewards. Determining if a person's actions are truly altruistic is difficult; sometimes only the person knows for sure. Still it is important not to discount this reason altogether.

### In Sum

Advocate groups form because some people are dissatisfied with the social structure or feel deprived in some way, although those who are absolutely deprived may not participate.

Those who found, join, and support advocate groups are likely to be from the upper and middle classes, since these are the people with the capacity to be successful. Whatever class they come from, they are motivated to participate for a variety of reasons, including: friendship with others, righteous anger, social conscience, a meaning quest, and compassion or altruism.

Once an advocate group is formed, others may join to fulfill their basic social needs, because the cultural symbols resonate with them, or—if they are from a marginal or minority group—to gain the social support of others like them.[17]

Most advocate group activity takes place in a mass arena, using cultural symbols, vocabulary, and an emotional repertoire to redefine the situation in a way that convinces others to take the action that they advocate.

## ■ THREE VIEWS OF HUMAN NATURE

As noted in Chapter 1, the worldview a group has will impact the type of solution that members seek. And a view of human nature is an important component in a worldview. If you believe that people are basically good, you will go about things in a very different way than if you believe that people are basically out to serve themselves. Three very different views of human nature have developed in the Western world. Each of them is found in advocate groups, so it is helpful to be clear concerning them.

### The Rational Human Being

This view of human nature coincides with a biological-behaviorist understanding of individuals—the "survival of the fittest" motif and the image of selfish genes. As early as the seventeenth century, philosophers such as Thomas Hobbes concluded that humans are basically selfish and competitive, and will act to benefit others only when it serves their own interests.

The economic version of this understanding of human nature came from John Stuart Mill, Adam Smith, and others who assumed that people are rational

---

17. These are called *expressive needs* by group researchers—emotional support, security, encouragement, acceptance, recognition.

and, when given the choice, will go for the biggest reward for the least cost. There are many different kinds of rewards and costs aside from financial ones.

The problem with this view of human nature is that there are times when people don't choose the biggest and the best for themselves, when they help others without expecting a reward (saving someone from a burning building). So, although this view is certainly true at times, it does not apply to all humans at all times.

Those who argue for the rational view say that sharing is simply a momentary sacrifice for a bigger reward to come. For instance, saving a person from a burning building earns the reward of public recognition. While this line of thinking has some merit, those who argue against it are usually not satisfied that it truly captures human nature. But neither can it be discounted.

People who have this view of human nature seek more restrictions to prevent selfish behavior and encourage behavior that benefits others.

### The Greater Good Human Being

The second view of human nature comes from social philosophers such as John Locke, who concluded that people will contribute to the betterment of society even if they receive no personal monetary or social reward. This is primarily because they also benefit from the establishment of a better society. Living in the seventeenth century, John Locke theorized that because people are essentially social, they will give up their individual rights to create a greater social whole. Even if people are inherently selfish, they are also social and consequently are willing to sacrifice individual rewards for a better society, because they also benefit. We do not have to debate whether that is ultimately a kind of selfishness (a person is giving up a smaller personal reward for a greater social reward). That may or may not be the case. But even without assuming either ultimate altruism or selfishness, the principle is the same: what may be called the "greater good" assumption.

In terms of solutions, people with this view of human nature will emphasize the need for information to convince people of the greater social good, assuming once that is understood, they will want to do the right thing (whatever it is).

### The Compassionate Sacrificing Human Being

The third view is that people are at heart basically good, sympathetic, and generous. (Altruism for personal gain is excluded.) This view of human nature is common in religion but not in social science. Still, an explanation of various human motivations is not complete without it. Some doubt that it is true and are entitled to their opinion. Others believe it is the highest example of human behavior. They are entitled to their opinion as well.

A notable example of this view in action is nonviolence, or Mahatma Gandhi's Satyagraha movement. By putting himself in harm's way, he was clearly appealing to the higher motivations in his opponents, the British. And he almost always received a positive response.

History is replete with examples of persons who are thought to have exemplified this ideal, from religious leaders to political figures to ordinary individuals who display occasional acts of heroism. Even popular ideas of love have an aspect of forgetting oneself in the interest of serving the other. A true, unselfish desire for the well-being of others implies a kind of sacrifice at some point. This is commonly seen in parents who are willing to give up their own lives for the sake of their child.

In terms of solutions to social problems, people who have this view of human nature will support the greatest freedom of movement and decision making for the individual, in the belief that once this motivation is stimulated, people will do the right thing.

### Discussion

In addition to understanding people's motivations for joining or participating in advocate groups, it is also important to understand the basic assumption of human nature that forms a group's worldview. The underlying assumption will determine how the problem is interpreted, and the type of solution the group will seek.

Although there are many variations, the three basic assumptions of human nature are that people (1) are rational and selfish—they will always seek the biggest and best for themselves, (2) are social and will seek the betterment of the whole above their own selfish desire, especially since they also benefit from society's improvement, and (3) are innately good and, all other things being equal, will respond to the needs of others as to their own needs.

## ▦ DYNAMICS WITHIN ADVOCATE GROUPS

What are the dynamics that work in an advocate group? It is sometimes helpful to know how people organize themselves and interact with others on a continual basis. This section uses literature on groups.

### Status

All groups have a status system that reflects the power of individual group members. High status persons normally speak more frequently, are more critical, and tend to give orders and take leadership.

### Group Norms

Groups form norms, or unspoken rules about behavior, both within the group and outside of it. Even groups that resist other societal traditions form their own traditions. For instance, if members of an unconventional group dress in more conventional business attire to improve their chances of a job, they may be criticized for giving in to the system. Members in a highly cohesive group identify with each other, sit or stand close to each other, pay attention to each other, and show affection or respect.

### Structure

Groups vary in the degree of structure they develop. A structured group has a predictable pattern of interaction and authority. The most common kind of structure is a hierarchy, a pyramid in which one or a few persons at the top have the decision-making power, and usually the highest status. But some groups have different levels of authority and status rather than a single leader and followers.

### Leaders

There are group norms and expectations about the rights and responsibilities of group members, especially the leaders. The one who influences others to pursue a specific goal is the group leader. He or she is expected to formulate goals, develop a plan, assign jobs, and recruit new members. He or she is also expected to persuade, reward, and punish members for their actions on behalf of the group, as well as monitor progress toward the goal, resolve conflicts, represent the group to others, and inspire new action.

In exchange for the leader's efforts, the followers give their loyalty, especially if the leader is generous and personable, treats people well, and distributes rewards fairly. The leader receives more endorsement when results are delivered, especially in a formal organization.

### Leadership Styles

There are three basic leadership styles: authoritarian, democratic laissez-faire, or some combination. In addition, leaders are either relationship oriented or task oriented (focused on personal relationships versus focused on the job at hand). The effectiveness of a leader varies according to the situation. During a crisis, a task oriented leader is more effective, whereas in normal times a relationship oriented leader is preferred.

Leadership styles are also influenced by the relationships leaders have with followers, the degree of structure in the group, and the leader's position of power in the group (Bass 1990; Conger, Kanungo, and Mennon 2000; Gilbert 1978; Judge and Bono 2000; Pritchard and Watson 1992; Waldman et al. 2001).

### Productivity

Whether a group is successful is sometimes difficult to determine. One measure is whether it achieves its goal. Another measure is how many resources it uses. If the output of a group is high relative to its input, it is considered efficient. It is also considered efficient if it meets its objective. Groups vary widely in their levels of productivity.

A group that doesn't achieve its goal on the first try will inspire greater effort and loyalty—to the group, to the goal, and to the leaders. But if a group fails repeatedly, members will become dissatisfied, the leadership will change; in extreme cases, the group may dissolve.

Group size and the task at hand affect productivity. If the group has a *disjunctive task*—the group relies on the strongest or best member for a good outcome—size is not important. If it has a *conjunctive task*, group productivity rests on the weakest member; the larger the group, the lower the productivity.

Interdependent tasks require high levels of communication, coordination, and member performance monitoring. In general, if group members are committed and the group goal is explicit about member participation, the group will have a high level of performance. (Wit et al. 1989; Wit and Wilke 1988).

### Impact on Participants

The effect of the group on individuals is called *social facilitation*, for example, making a speaker feel nervous during a speech. In general, people who are accomplished and confident do better when others are present or when competing. People who are not accomplished or lack confidence don't do as well when others are present.

Even when the goals are clear and members are committed, some members may do less. An increase in group size leads to less individual effort, even though the overall output of the group doesn't change. Some members may become social loafers or *free riders*, using group resources but not contributing. The free rider problem affects some groups more severely. Persons who don't believe their contribution makes a difference or don't like the end result are less likely to contribute (Harkins and Szymanski 1987; Karau and Williams 2001; Kravitz and Martin 1986; Pritchard et al. 1988; Triplett 1898; Zajonc 1968).

How much influence does the group have on a member's or participant's life? Since people in social movements tend to identify with the group's ideology and lifestyle, they are likely to be influenced a lot. Sociologists call this a *diffuse impact*—an influence that affects all aspects of their lives. Interest groups, on the other hand, are likely to have a more *segmented impact* on members' lives.

Social researchers have noted this difference in religious groups. Members of the FLDS (Fundamental Latter-day Saints), for instance, have less freedom in their choice of partners than Methodists or Presbyterians. Similarly, advocate groups exert varying influence on ideology, activities, lifestyle, likes, and dislikes (McGuire 1997).

### Rewards and Equity

People have fixed ideas of fairness when it comes to rewards. There are four main ways rewards are distributed fairly. (1) The most common way is equity. Rewards are distributed in proportion to members' contributions. Equity is the preference of groups that want to avoid conflict and maintain solidarity. (2) Some groups or some situations call for equality (all members receive the same rewards). (3) Equal distribution, or distribution according to relative need, is sometimes considered fair. (4) Specialized tasks may receive particular importance, with those members responsible being more highly rewarded.

When people feel that they are under-rewarded or that rewards are unequally distributed, they become dissatisfied or angry. They may do less, and eventually withdraw. Over-rewarding participants is less troublesome but can create feelings of guilt, which could encourage increased effort (Austin and Walster 1974; Deutsch 1985; Miller and Komorita 1995; Saito 1988).

### Groupthink and Other Group Decision-making Processes

To make a good decision, a group needs good information, and that information needs to be shared with all the members. Members also need to agree on priorities and values.

One well-studied phenomenon is groupthink, when a group of ordinarily reasonable persons makes an irrational and flawed decision. This happens when the group is highly cohesive, composed of members who are fairly homogeneous, somewhat cut off from the environment, and under some amount of stress. The decision, at the time, appears to all group members as being reasonable and appropriate. Group members do not seek alternatives, and usually there is a group norm of avoiding harsh judgments of leaders and other members to prevent disunity. The group members come to feel that they are invulnerable and disregard obvious signs of danger. The leader is likely to take an active role in promoting a particular solution.

An example of groupthink is the 1961 Cuban invasion—the Bay of Pigs—which turned out to be a humiliating failure for the U.S. government. In this case, normally intelligent and informed government advisors suppressed dissension, overvalued certain information, and overlooked situational factors in their eagerness to address the political threat of Castro's growing power.

To avoid such mistakes, researchers recommend that leaders encourage differing views, avoid promoting one particular solution, divide the workgroup into different subgroups to come up with different ideas, allow people to express doubts, and appoint a devil's advocate (Janis 1982; Park 1990; Paulus 1998).

## ▋▋ GROWTH AND DEVELOPMENT OF ADVOCATE GROUPS

Social movements go through four or five stages as they develop from a collection of like-minded individuals into an organized force for change. In general, the same process of development applies to other advocate groups.[18]

The first stage, *emergence,* is a time when the advocate group is forming. One or more persons take up the challenge of advocating for change. They discuss the need and the action, and they organize themselves. For instance, when Elizabeth Fry learned about the appalling conditions of imprisoned women, she decided to visit to see what she could do. She enlisted the help of her friends. They brought clothes and blankets to the prisoners in Newgate, and they convinced the prison authorities to let them teach the women.

The problem is identified in the emergence stage, and a core group of members are assembled. At this stage, the group is not formally organized, although there may be a group that works together.

---

18. The stages identified in advocate group development are slightly different from the stages of social movement development identified by others, such as Smelser (1962), Tilly (1978), and Best (2008). The stages involved in Smelser's structural strain theory have already been discussed above. The four stages identified by Tilly and others are (1) emergence, (2) coalescence (3), formalization, and (4) decline. Best identifies six stages in what he calls the "natural history model of the social problems process": (1) claims making, (2) media coverage, (3) public reaction, (4) policy making, (5) social problems work, and (6) policy outcomes.

In the second stage, *coalescence,* the problem is framed and defined, new members are recruited, resources are gathered, leaders emerge, an organizational structure emerges, and a plan of action is developed.

This happens informally for social movements during public events such as demonstrations. For other advocate groups it may be more formal, with the selection of a leader and development of charter or rules.

All advocate groups need a coherent description of the problem and its resolution. Slogans emerge to focus the group and garner public attention. Plans are developed to attract new members and additional resources, including money. A plan of action is worked out.

The group will need more information to convince others. How many people are affected? How many situations are there like this? Why did these situations come about? What policies, laws, and personnel impact the situation? To address this need for information, communication networks are established and alliances are formed.

The group will convince others formally or informally. Formal methods include advertising, public speaking, magazine and journal articles, and lobbying for political change. Less formal methods include rallies and demonstrations, leafleting, telling family and friends, and holding bake sales and other fundraisers. In the twenty-first century, groups that use both formal and informal methods probably have a web page.

The third stage in the development of an advocate group is *action.* The group is clear on the problem and what needs to be done. All that is left is implementation. Action may include lobbying to get a law passed or embarking on an educational campaign by advertising, public speaking, writing magazine and journal articles, or working to make sure a program is implemented.

Once Elizabeth Fry understood which things needed to change, she and her friends began contacting officials—including members of Parliament—to make prisons more humane. This led to changes in prison laws.

The fourth stage is *bureaucratization.* Not all groups develop to this point, but if they do, they become more formal in order to be successful. At this stage, a movement relies less on the charisma and talent of the original leaders and more on the skills of a capable staff. As it becomes more bureaucratic, the group loses some of its ability to address specific concerns.

The fifth stage, for some, is *decline*, or change. The reasons for decline can be positive or negative. On the positive side, if the goals are met, there is no need for the group to exist. On the negative side, the group may decline for a variety of reasons: poor leadership, loss of interest among members, lack of funds, internal conflict. The goal may have shifted as leaders acquired money and power. Perhaps leaders have "sold out," becoming unwilling to question authorities because of the loss of personal prestige involved. Or, as was the case for the Chinese students at Tiananmen Square, severe repression from outside may cause the movement to wither. Members become fearful and unwilling to risk the loss of prestige, jobs, or even their lives.

Sometimes a new group forms among dedicated members who are not accommodated or intimidated. In that case, the stages start over again.

## ▓ A TYPOLOGY OF ADVOCATE GROUP CHANGE

All advocate groups want to realize social change. But they differ in how many people they attract and how much change they want to see. Some groups promote limited social change, whereas others promote radical change. Some groups promote structural change, whereas others promote change for specific members of society.

The typology presented here was developed by David Aberle (1966) and used by Harper (1993) to identify both the amount of change sought by a group and the level of change. The typology has two levels of change—at the individual level and at the structural level. Change may be partial or total. Combining the level and degree of change gives us four possible kinds of change. Whereas Aberle used the typology to identify social movements, we will use it to understand the type of change sought by all advocate groups.[19]

An *alternative change* is partial (or limited) change on an individual level. This is the type of change sought by a group that wants limited change for a specific group. For example, Promise Keepers promotes more responsible fa-

19. A good discussion of this typology of social movements is found in McAdam and Snow 1997. There are some differences in how the categories are applied to advocate groups here. Another discussion is found in Harper 1993.

thering and husbanding among Christian men. Catholic Anti-abortionists is a group that discourages abortion among Catholic women and others.

A *redemptive change* is radical change on an individual level. This is the type of change sought by a group that wants to see radical change for a select group of people. Alcoholics Anonymous is an example of a group seeking redemptive change as alcoholics radically change their lifestyle.

A *reformative change* is limited change at a structural level. It is a change sought by a group that will likely focus on a single issue, or a group of related issues. Environmental groups, civil rights advocates, gay rights advocates, and women's groups are examples of groups seeking reformative change.

A *transformative* or *revolutionary change* is radical change at the structural level. This is the type of change sought by a group that wants to transform an entire society. The American Revolution, the French Revolution, the Bolshevik Revolution in Russia, and the Communist revolution in China are all examples of groups seeking transformative change. On a less dramatic level, radical feminists are another example of a group seeking transformative change. They believe that only through the restructuring of all of society and all of society's institutions can gender equality be achieved.

## ■■ CONCLUSION

Using social movement, social psychology, and group literature, I have outlined the important characteristics of advocate groups. There are different types of advocate groups, and they form for different reasons. Groups have different objectives and pursue different kinds of change. As we examine the advocate groups for particular problems, this information will help us understand the dynamics of change. We have only scratched the surface of this very interesting subject.

### ■ QUESTIONS FOR REVIEW

1. What are the characteristics of interest groups?
2. What are the characteristics of social movements?
3. What are think tanks, and how do they differ from political parties?

4. Explain the three broad categories of advocate group formation.

5. Explain the four types of change given in the typology of change.

## ■ QUESTIONS FOR FURTHER THOUGHT

1. Give an example of a solution to a social problem using the rational human being worldview.

2. What human nature worldview does MADD have?

3. Think of an advocate group that you have been a part of in the past (e.g., a local advocate group for your school). What kind of change did it advocate? What kind of human nature worldview did it have?

# CHAPTER THREE

# AMELIORATING ACTIONS, REACTIONS, AND CONSEQUENCES

## ■ PART I: Ameliorating Actions

This chapter presents possible ameliorating actions for social problems, as well as reactions and consequences. Six common actions are discussed. Understanding them will help the social researcher realize the complexities involved.

Sociologists often focus on government legislation or government programs. These are important to the social change process. But it is tempting to see them as a quick and simple fix. Although laws assure compliance, they may not resolve the underlying issues. And some problem situations do not respond to regulation, for instance, eating disorders. Doctors or counselors are more effective. In some cases, education is crucial, as in the case of AIDS or STDs. And sometimes government regulation would actually have a negative effect. Strict regulation of violence in the media conflicts with our constitutionally guaranteed freedom of speech. Finally, individual actions are not an insignificant part of ameliorating actions, despite the fact that many often feel that their actions are insignificant and have no impact.

In Section 2, the six common ameliorating actions are used to introduce specific social problems. This allows us to stay focused on the problems and their advocate groups, rather than veering off into discussions of traditional sociological subjects and theories. As will become apparent, many problems have more than one ameliorating action. One action may be appropriate at a particular time, but later another action becomes more productive.

51

Not all actions taken to resolve a problem are successful. Sometimes an ameliorating action creates another problem—with or without resolving the first problem. An example of this is Prohibition in the 1920s. It is important to recognize that not all ameliorating actions work out the way they were intended. People resist change. And opposition groups form. The history of successes and failures of particular ameliorating actions is important to our study.

When is a social problem resolved? Just as a social group recognizes that something is a social problem, so too a social group decides when a problem is resolved. When the advocate group or the public no longer feels compelled to advocate for the target group, the problem ceases to be a social problem. The target group members may be better off than they were originally, or it may be that attention has moved elsewhere. There are two reasons an advocate group no longer advocates—either the situation has improved or the will to act has disappeared for another reason. Even if the situation has improved significantly, that doesn't mean that *all* the persons in the target group are better off. Nor does it mean that all issues have been resolved. In theoretical terms we talk as if life can be categorized, analyzed, and even controlled. But in reality, life is messy! It rarely fits into compartments.

## ■■ LEGAL REFORMS

Legal reform is often an essential part of an advocate group's efforts to effect change, even if other measures are used. Legal reform is particularly important when people resist change—when the well-being of a minority is threatened, or when collective resources (taxes) are needed to finance a new development, or when entrepreneurs or monopolies are making excessive profits. Legal reform is needed when two groups compete for resources or territory.

Many situations may benefit from legal reform, but at least five require it: (1) social discrimination, (2) unequal distribution of resources (government or other), (3) profiteering, (4) conflict between groups with different values, and (5) threats to the physical or social well-being of individuals. (The five situations correspond roughly to reasons social problems occur as stated in Chapter 1: racism and discrimination, inequality, self-interest, and competing interests.) By examining these situations we can understand why this is true. In all cases, national, state, or local authorities form the action group to enforce the laws.

### Social Discrimination

Social discrimination results in social inequality. Both issues are difficult to resolve, particularly when they have to do with race. One minority group in particular has suffered great inequality of opportunity for more than two centuries.
As slaves, African Americans were not given basic human rights: a slave was
counted as three-fifths of a person in the census, and slaves had no voice in
managing daily affairs. Other minorities faced less extreme discrimination but
experienced stressful circumstances. People fleeing the Irish potato famine in
the mid-1800s were regarded as "no-good drunks"; Italian immigrants sub-
jected to IQ tests in the early 1900s were thought to be imbecilic; and so on
(Murdoch 2007). Eliminating discrimination means treating minorities equally
and valuing them fully. It is difficult to change attitudes. Sometimes prejudice
is so ingrained in a group's worldview that only the threat of severe government
penalties changes it.

The civil rights movement concluded in 1964 with legislation that upheld
the right of every person to vote, to participate in a democratic government, to
be treated equally, and to have equal access to social and economic resources.
It provided means to sanction persons who violated those rights—for minorities
and for women (a clause was included that sanctioned gender discrimination
in the workplace). Nearly one hundred years elapsed after the Emancipation
Proclamation before the U.S. government was prepared to protect the rights
of its African American citizens (Hasday 2007).

Could this change have happened without legislation? It seems doubtful.
Some people were averse to change. Their ancestors fought to prevent change
at the cost of their lives. But after one hundred years, the resistance to change
was lower than it had been. Resistance may have softened by the military's integrated units during World War II, where soldiers of all backgrounds worked
together under one command. There is speculation that this forced cooperation
gave soldiers a new appreciation for people from another group and hence they
were less resistant to change (Colley 2003).

Legal reform is also appropriate when discrimination arises by accident.
Racial profiling (targeting members of a racial category as criminal suspects)
became an important issue in the late twentieth century because of the illegal
drug trade. Key drug traffickers were known to be Hispanic, so police targeted

Hispanics in their efforts to stem the flow of drugs. Similarly, after 9/11, because of the ethnicity of known terrorist groups, immigration officials stopped more Middle Easterners than others. In inner-city areas, police are more likely to suspect African American males of illegal activity. Minority advocate groups were quick to point to racial profiling in these situations. All groups claiming discrimination seek legal protections (Withrow 2006).

### Unequal Distribution of Resources and Unintended Consequences

Unequal distribution of resources is often—but not always—related to social discrimination. Minority groups are almost always at a disadvantage in terms of access to physical and social resources. Their life chances are less. Groups such as the National Association for the Advancement of Colored People (NAACP) and the League of United Latin American Citizens (LULAC) advocate for increased economic, educational, political, and health resources.

Schools around the country receive differential funding to the extent that their finances come from property taxes. In Texas wealthy districts have far more money than poor districts have. In 1984, MALDEF (Mexican American Legal Defense and Educational Fund) took legal action against the state of Texas claiming that students in poor school districts were being discriminated against.[1] In 1989 the Texas Supreme Court ruled the system was unconstitutional. A law was passed in 1993 to "recapture" revenue from high-wealth districts and give it to lower-wealth districts (Robin Hood funding). Wealthier districts raised their property taxes and complained (Coalition to Invest in Texas Schools 2004; *Fort Worth Star-Telegram* 2010).

### Profiteering

When an individual, a group of individuals, a company, or an institution profits at the expense or misfortune of others, legal reform is needed. It may be that the profiteers took advantage of a legal loophole or used government funds in unintended ways, or dishonestly exploited an opportunity. Business regu-

---

1. The lawsuit was filed against the Texas commissioner of education.

lations are supposed to avert these situations, but they are not always successful. Sometimes the laws are successfully skirted, so that additional preventative regulations are needed. Problems associated with profiteering that can be addressed by government regulation include fraud, white collar crime, monopolies, corruption in big business and in other organizations, organized crime, identity theft, and lawsuit abuse.

At the turn of the twentieth century, the new middle class feared that the barons of industry and corrupt politicians would dominate our free society. The progressive movement that formed pursued large-scale regulations that wouldn't interfere with American values of individualism and freedom. Government agencies such as the Pure Food and Drug Administration and the Interstate Commerce and Banking Commissions were established, and laws were passed to constrain monopolies (Harper 1993, 167–169).

### Different Values

Countries with homogeneous populations may have fewer divisive issues, but disagreements occur everywhere. When two parties both stake a seemingly legitimate claim, a third party intervention or government legislation is needed.

There are great differences in regard to religion. Often people who feel strongly about something for religious reasons are unwilling to compromise. Abortion is an issue that divides along religious lines: fundamentalist Christians are likely to oppose it, whereas women's groups in general support it. Resolving this dispute requires finding a criterion to use to decide which view, or which part of each view, is acceptable. Even when laws are passed, not everyone is happy.

Regional differences (e.g., gun control) can also be contentious. Those who oppose gun control are largely from the South and Southwest, whereas supporters tend to be based in the Northeast. Other issues that are difficult to resolve include euthanasia, abortion, same-sex marriage, stem cell research/cloning, surrogate mothers, school vouchers, and election reform. Advocate groups for these causes have very different values and views of life. Different politics, membership in different ethnic groups, or generational differences make these contentious issues difficult to resolve. When advocate groups seek contentious ameliorating actions, they become part of the problem.

Government legislation can act as a kind of mediator for these groups, providing a compromise ameliorating action needed for peace to be maintained. Sometimes group differences evaporate over time, as seems to be the case with euthanasia. Opposition today is much weaker than it was a few decades ago. It is possible for a disastrous event to galvanize popular opinion in such a way that an ameliorating action becomes acceptable to all parties.

### Threats to the Physical Well-Being of Individuals

In general, governments create laws to ensure the safety of their citizens. The criminal justice system has been established to address violations. From time to time it becomes clear that the existing laws are not sufficient, hence legal reform is necessary for the protection of particular target groups. Women's groups and others worked to change stalking laws and protect women who were endangered. Similarly people worked for legal change to protect women who were abused. Hate crimes, rape, coyotes, corruption of police and legal officials, prostitution, gangs, and nursing home abuse are some of the problems in this category.

## ▪▪ GOVERNMENT PROGRAMS

Some social problems are so large that only a government program can practically address them. Government programs are established at a national, state or local level. Or there may be cooperation on the national-state level, as in the case of TANF (Temporary Assistance for Needy Families), which is mandated on a national level and administered at a state level.

But advocate groups don't necessarily agree on the amount of responsibility that the government should assume. Some argue that government responsibility deprives individuals of important social roles. One example of this is education. For the first two hundred years of our history, education was the responsibility of parents, though children were encouraged to attend schools that were available. That changed between 1852 and 1918, when all states passed mandatory education laws. Laws were amended in 1925 to allow private schools, as a result of lobbying efforts by Catholics. Laws were again amended in the 1980s and 1990s, when states allowed home schooling. Other changes in education include vouchers, tuition tax credit, scholarship tax credit, education deductions, and charter schools (Coulson 1999).

Another example of government or institutions taking over a role traditionally left to families is care of the elderly. This assistance is welcomed, however, particularly for the oldest and most infirm, because the amount of care and medical attention they need exceeds what most families are able to provide.

A third example is the U.S. welfare system. The AFDC, or Aid to Families with Dependent Children, was created in 1935. Complaints of corruption and recipient dependency led to its reform in 1996. TANF, the assistance program that replaced AFDC, requires recipients to work and provides money for child care (Maryland Budget and Tax Policy Institute 2006).

Those opposed to government social welfare programs argue that they are inefficient and expensive, and encourage dependence. They may actually replace traditional lifestyles, as some argue has happened in Sweden, where the government takes responsibility for many economic roles, including child care, health care, and even funerals. Swedes are less likely to marry and more likely to live alone than adults in other high income countries; 50 percent of all Swedish children are born to unmarried parents (Popenoe 1994).

Others see government assistance as necessary and benevolent. It's the job of government, they argue, to assist its citizens in need. Of course, government money for programs comes ultimately from higher taxes, but that is a price that proponents are willing to pay for things like health care and unemployment benefits. Many European countries take this approach, and in most cases they have higher taxes than the United States.

Some government-run programs have been quite successful, for example, Social Security. Since its inception, destitution among the elderly has been greatly reduced (Social Security Administration 2011). Other programs—Medicaid and Medicare, standardized testing in education, and environmental programs—have been less successful.

## ▓ PROFESSIONAL AGENCIES, NONPROFITS, AND SPECIAL INTEREST GROUPS

Social problems can be successfully addressed by nongovernmental groups, including professional organizations (doctors, teachers, journalists, etc.), nonprofits (churches, philanthropic groups, etc.), and special interest groups. The problems they address include child care, homelessness, drug and substance abuse, spousal and child abuse, and juvenile delinquency. Others include various health-related problems such as eating disorders, AIDs and other sexually transmitted diseases, teen pregnancy, and teen suicide. Some problems may not be resolved with professional agencies or nonprofit groups, but they require their assistance on a continuing basis. Once laws were passed to eliminate discrimination, for instance, several different organizations continued to monitor the results, including the NAACP, Quakers, Southern Poverty Law Center, ACLU, and LULAC.

Until recently, because of separation of church and state issues, any organization that received government money could not be religiously affiliated. That changed in 2004 with President Bush's faith-based initiative, which allowed religious groups with social service programs to compete for government funding (Theocracywatch 2011). One problem successfully addressed by religious organizations is homelessness. Numerous shelters in cities across the country are run by religious organizations, such as the Salvation Army, Presbyterian Night Shelter, Union Gospel Mission, and many others.

### Professional Ethics

Potentially problematic situations that arise in nongovernmental agencies are addressed through professional ethics—standards set by practicing professionals in a particular field. Professionals in any field who fail to adhere to the standards or commit ethical violations are sanctioned by the professional organization. For medical doctors, a sanction might include loss of their license to practice medicine (the AMA, or American Medical Association, works with the government to certify medical practitioners). When professional standards are high, and adhered to, legal regulations are fewer.

An example of how this works is seen in media self-censorship. After 9/11, journalists and media figures recognized that certain issues were sensitive and should not be published. At least for a time, there was little or no opposition to President Bush among the usually critical journalists (Pew Research Center 2000).[2]

---

2. Unfortunately, self-censorship sometimes serves establishment interests, but that is another story.

In contrast, professional ethics are not able to regulate violence and sexual content on the Internet. Private web page publishers do not belong to professional organizations, so they are not bound by professional ethics. Thus laws are needed to prohibit extreme violence and sexual content. But the lines are sometimes murky, and professional organizations have to follow the laws, as well.

Sometimes professional ethics alone does not ensure the safety or well-being of a group of people. Nursing home abuse has become an issue in recent years, leading to new regulations and stronger enforcement (FindLaw 2011). Similarly, in education, when it became clear that students were not reading at the appropriate grade level (and some were graduating from high school unable to read), a government program was instituted to ensure a minimum educational standard (Armario and Turner 2010; Conley and Hinchman 2004).

Sometimes professional ethical codes conflict with each other. This is seen in regard to euthanasia. Because doctors take an oath to protect life (Hippocratic Oath), they are reluctant to publicly endorse assisted suicide, even if it is the compassionate thing to do when a person is terminally ill and in pain.

## ■■ EDUCATION AND PUBLIC AWARENESS CAMPAIGNS

Warning people about the consequences of their choices and the seriousness of certain problems can be the main action or an additional action proposed by an advocate group. Even when problems are addressed through laws or government programs, education may be needed as well. Many of the problems mentioned here can be improved with education or a propaganda campaign. Education can be done through the media, with the use of government publications, through professional agencies such as doctor's offices, or through other government organizations.

When the target group is also the offender, education is a must. This includes eating disorders, AIDS and STDs, teen pregnancy, and teen suicide. Education is also a must when the ameliorating action to a problem involves individual action that is difficult to legislate: spousal and child abuse and environmental issues. Other problems for which education is important are euthanasia, same-sex marriage, immigration, and identity theft.

Dallas city councilman Dwaine Caraway opted for a Pull 'Em Up campaign when he discovered that a city ordinance banning saggy pants was unconstitutional. The Fort Worth city council decided to join in. They found billboard space, enlisted a local artist, got donations from local businesses, and got support from a local mentor group that sponsored a basketball tournament, dance, and other events with a "pull 'em up" theme. The mentor group is planning more events, and former Fort Worth mayor Mike Moncrief encouraged parks, sports venues, and the zoo to support the effort by putting up posters and distributing bumper stickers. The campaign is intended to reach the teens who wear their pants low, often revealing boxer shorts, and also parents, who may not realize the detrimental effect their sons' appearance may have on future opportunities (Dickson 2011).

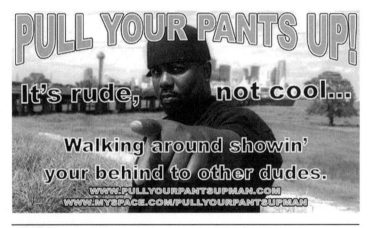

**FIGURE 3.1.** A media campaign started by Dallas City Councilman Dwaine Caraway.

**FIGURE 3.2.** Dwaine Caraway, Dallas City Councilman, started a "Pull 'Em Up" publicity campaign when he discovered that a city ordinance banning saggy pants was unconstitutional.

## ∷ INTERPERSONAL INTERACTION, APOLOGY, REPARATION

### *Interpersonal Interaction*

Interpersonal interaction, apology, and reparation are generally not sufficient in themselves, although they contribute to the success of other actions. Interpersonal interaction (when members of two or more conflicting groups have an opportunity to interact on a personal basis) is particularly apropos when there is discrimination or conflict between two groups. It destroys stereotypes that group members have and helps them judge each other more realistically. This counters a common perceptual bias—the fundamental attribution error, which is attributing mistakes to personal error for people you don't like ("he's just dumb"), and to circumstance for people you like ("the deck was stacked against him"). It also reduces the polarization of opinions (DeLamater and Myers 2007).

Interpersonal interaction is effective when used with legal regulations. A major example of the effectiveness of interpersonal interaction was mentioned above—the integration of the military during World War II. Military personnel interacting in close quarters with members of a different group developed new appreciation for them as individuals.

An experimental residential camp in Northern Ireland is another dramatic example. In the 1970s, Protestants and Catholics lived in different parts of Belfast, often behind protective barriers. Children attended segregated schools, and people in one community knew few people from the other community. There was virtually no trust on any level, reflected in the high security and frequent bombings. In this environment, a countryside camp was established where members of the two different communities could meet and talk with each other for several days at a time, in a safe environment. Persons attending the camp were amazed to discover that people they regarded as their enemy were similar to themselves. It is hard to say how much the camp contributed to the improved relationship between the two groups. Two women, Betty Williams and Mairead Corrigan, were awarded the Nobel Peace Prize in 1976 for their work in founding the Northern Ireland Peace Movement (later renamed Peace

People) to bring Protestants and Catholics together. Politicians John Hume and David Trimble received the prize for their courageous work in 1998 (Buscher and Ling 1999).

This interpersonal integration effort between Catholics and Protestants in Northern Ireland continues in the Dallas–Fort Worth metroplex every summer. Students from the different communities in Ireland come to the United States and interact with each other in a foreign country. Newspaper reports of the value of their experience always describe the surprise of students when they find friends among the members of the other group (Aasen 2010).

### Apology

Apology is an important part of any individual's daily repertoire, and is an important auxiliary ameliorating action for social problems. Apologies on an institutional or governmental scale have not been emphasized as important to solving social problems. But in the past twenty years they have become more common, for example, Japan's apology for its treatment of Koreans during the occupation of Korea, U.S. government apology for slavery, U.S. government apology to African Americans used in medical research, and Germany's apology for the atrocities of Hitler (www.upenn.edu/pnc/politicalapologies.html).

How much do government apologies contribute to a reameliorating action of an issue? In all the examples above, apologies took place many years after the violation, so they were not issued by the same people who committed the offense. Perhaps a better question to ask is, Does the apology lead to better feelings between the target group and the offending government? It doesn't cost anything, in most cases, so it is hard to see how it could hurt. If it makes things just a little better, it is beneficial.

### Reparation

Some people undoubtedly feel that an apology doesn't go far enough. Because of the gravity of the injustice, there must be reparation to restore goodwill. Forty acres and a mule illustrates this idea. After the Civil War, General William Sherman responded to the need in the South by issuing a temporary order giving freed families an excess military mule and forty acres of land along the coast of Georgia and South Carolina. With Lincoln's assassination, the order was rescinded, and the whole incident taken as one of the failures of Reconstruction. However, the idea of the U.S. reparation to former slaves was revived again in 2000, when several thousand taxpayers mistakenly claimed a $43,000 slave tax credit (Darity 2008; Flemming 1906; PBS 2011; Truth or Fiction 2011).

Interpersonal interaction, apology, and reparation are particularly helpful in problems where racial and gender discrimination are involved. More recently, interpersonal interaction has been used somewhat effectively as a criminal punishment: a criminal offender is sentenced to the service of a family or individual similar to those whom he/she offended. It is also used as a means of helping abusers or rapists realize the destructiveness of their actions.

## ▣ INDEPENDENT, INDIVIDUAL ACTIONS

It is not uncommon for people to think that a problem is so great that nothing anyone can do will make a difference. But it is not true that individual action has no effect. Democracy works because people cooperate: our society is based on the idea that individuals make important contributions to society. Some are convinced that if everyone, or at least a lot of people, made a concerted effort to perform acts of kindness the world would be transformed. To that extent the Random Acts of Kindness Foundation and the World Kindness Movement lobby all of us to let our better nature come forward.[3]

Financial contributions are important, since most advocate groups rely on donations. Americans are among the most generous people in the world.[4] They gave a total of $290.9 billion in 2010 (approximately 73 percent from individuals),

3. The Random Acts of Kindness Foundation was established in 1995 as a resource for people committed to spreading kindness. www.actsofkindness.org.
   The World Kindness movement is an outgrowth of the Small Kindness movement of Japan. It emerged from a Tokyo conference in 1997 and took shape in Singapore in 2000. It aims to inspire individuals towards greater kindness and to connect nations to create a kinder world. www.worldkindness.org.sg.
4. According to the World Giving Index, a composite measure of financial giving, time as volunteer, and personal assistance developed by the Charities Aid Foundation, the United States is the fifth most generous country in the world, after Australia, New Zealand, Canada, and Switzerland (*Guardian* 2010).

which is more than twice that of any other country.[5] Giving in the United States is not restricted to the upper classes; the majority of households with incomes less than $100,000 give to charity (Bond 2009, 2011; *USA Today* 2007, 2010; Giving USA Foundation 2010).

Volunteering is another important way to contribute. In the aftermath of Hurricane Katrina, people in nearby cities donated their time, energy, and resources to help those who were evacuated from New Orleans and elsewhere in Louisiana. Many nonprofit organizations—women's shelters, homeless shelters, church service organizations—rely heavily on volunteers, and would not be able to function effectively without them. Schools also rely on parents who volunteer. Some 63.4 million people volunteered their services in 2009 (*USA Today* 2010).

There are other things that individuals can do. They can take the time to become informed on an issue. They can write letters to their legislative representatives or to the local newspaper. They can change their personal consumption of resources or change other aspects of their behavior. They can have discussions with family, friends, and neighbors, and even hold meetings to focus attention on a particular concern. And of course individuals can join advocate groups and help promote social change. Some people actually devote their lives to the promotion of a cause, either paid or unpaid. Many people who are capable and qualified choose to work for less pay because their job contributes to the betterment of others.

A touching example of one person's influence is found in the life of Fanny Kemble, a nineteenth-century British actress who married a Georgia plantation owner. Convinced that her husband treated his slaves kindly, she stayed in the city. When she finally visited the plantation, she discovered the slaves' misery and joined the Underground Railroad, a group of men and women who helped slaves escape. During it all she kept a diary of what she witnessed.

---

5. The Giving Foundation revised its earlier figures downward after its 2010 report conflicted with earlier reports. In 2010 giving to religion was 35 percent of the total, at $100.63 billion; education received 14 percent of the total at $41.67 billion; grant making foundations received 11 percent of the total at $33 billion; public society benefits received 8 percent of the total at $24.24 billion; health received 7.8 percent at $22.83 billion; arts and culture received 4.5 percent of the total at $13.29 billion; health received 7.8 percent at $22.83 billion; international affairs (relief and development) received 5.4 percent of the total at $15.77; and environment/animal organizations received 2 percent of the total at $6.66 billion (Barnes 2011).

The chasm between Fanny and her husband led to a divorce. Later, at a crucial time in England during the Civil War, she published her journals. The Confederacy was not recognized by England as a legitimate government. "Whether or not Kemble's book played any role in England's stand has been debated, but there is no disputing Kemble's willingness to put forward her abolitionist feelings at great personal cost" (Kemble 2000, 6).

## ■ PART II. Reactions and Consequences

*Fatalistic Resignation:* As already noted, people don't always welcome social problems as opportunities. They are frequently reluctant to change, even if it is in their own best interest. People in the target group sometimes have a kind of fatalistic resignation. They are so used to something they don't see it as a problem, or they are resigned to the situation the way it is. In many ways, the slaves helped by Fanny Kemble had this attitude. They didn't believe that they could ever be free of the situation and resigned themselves to their lives. This attitude is found today among people who have little or no political power. Inner-city residents often face seemingly insurmountable racial and economic barriers: they accept that this is their fate—even if they don't like it.

*Blaming the Victim:* People not in the target group do not always welcome reameliorating social problems. They may believe members of the target group are responsible for their own situation. Sociologists call this blaming the victim—such as blaming rape victims for dressing provocatively or being in the wrong place at the wrong time. Another example is the common belief that poor people who live in unfortunate circumstances are lazy. Blaming the victim is a superficial approach that overlooks the complexity of a situation and factors beyond a victim's control. For instance, the unemployed may want to work but are not able to find jobs because of discrimination, lack of transportation, or lack of qualifications.

*Cynicism:* Some people are skeptical that things can change. These cynics see the problem as too big to tackle. Or they have been discouraged by unsuccessful attempts in the past. Cynicism about world poverty, health, or hunger, for instance, is quite common. They shrug their shoulders and shake their heads sadly, concluding that only a large government action or a miracle can change things. There is not much that they personally can do.

*Romanticization:* Sometimes people oppose reform because the target group is romanticized in some way—seeing them as idyllic as they are so change would spoil things. An example would be opposing development for an indigenous people because their traditional way of life would be destroyed.

Marx is sometimes criticized for romanticizing the workers and demonizing the production owners in his theory of revolution. He thought that change would come only if power were taken from the owners. He had no option of negotiation, nor did he entertain the possibility that the owners might be concerned about the workers. On the other hand, he overvalued the workers. Once they overthrow the owners, they will create an idyllic society, where everyone is treated kindly and fairly. He did not entertain the idea that the workers might ever be greedy and selfish like the owners.

## ■■ OPPOSITION GROUPS: CAMPAIGNING AGAINST REFORM

*Ideological Reasons:* People who are against a proposed *ameliorating action* might form an advocate group to oppose the change. This might be because of ideological reasons–they believe that the proposed change is wrong because it does not agree with their worldview. Opposition groups that address religious issues fall into this category.

One of the best examples is the issue of abortion. In the 1960s and before, several groups worked to legalize abortion, particularly in cases of rape. The 1973 Supreme Court decision *Roe v. Wade* made it a constitutional right, at which point groups for and against both became more organized (Lewis 2011; All About 2011). Because groups in support of abortion formed first, the pro-life (originally Right to Life) groups can be seen as opposition groups.

*Well-Being/Identity Is Threatened/Afraid of Change:* Opposition groups form because they are afraid of change, or their group well-being or identity is threatened. Group members also might see themselves differently than others, causing them to act in a discriminatory way.[6]

The Ku Klux Klan discussed in Chapter 1 is more correctly seen as an opposition group. The identity of its members as citizens was challenged; hence, their well-being was threatened by the election of African Americans to political office. They saw themselves not as vigilantes but as protectors of the cultural tradition.

Opposition groups will use many of the same tactics as advocate groups: campaigning, lobbying, pursuing legal action, or engaging in confrontation. The groups will be successful to the extent that they are able to garner resources. Even though people oppose change, they may not be willing to support an opposition group with time, money, or other resources. Successful opposition groups come to have their own identity. Change that threatens the status quo will have opposition groups that have more urgency, and may be confrontational. This is true with the anti-abortion issue. Sadly, people have been killed in these attacks on abortion clinics and on doctors, underscoring the strength of the opposition, although not all members condone the violent tactics.

## ■■ CONSEQUENCES FOR THE TARGET GROUP

Not all ameliorating actions are predictable. Sometimes the action has good results, sometimes not so good. Or there may be some improvement, but more improvement is needed.

Social Security, as mentioned above, is a success. It has reduced the number of elderly poor dramatically. However, it is now a problem in that there are questions about how long it will remain economically viable.

Another successful group is Mothers Against Drunk Driving. It helped pass laws that had severe consequences for offenders. Combined with an educational campaign on the subject, the number of persons killed or injured from drunk driving has significantly declined.

A program that has been partially successful is the Medicare Modernization Act of 2003. It was intended to provide additional assistance for prescription medicines for the elderly, in light of the increases in the cost of medicine over

---

6. For more theory, consult the literature on intergroup conflict.

the years. The new measure required seniors to sign up for one of several different plans, which was confusing for many elderly. In addition, some seniors were scammed by persons pretending to represent a legitimate drug program. Further, after the new regulations went into effect, a donut hole was discovered: assistance for drugs was suspended at a certain point, with no assistance at all until spending reached a higher level. The donut hole was addressed, and the program seems to be working fairly well now, although it still is complicated for seniors signing up.

Another program that has been partially successful is the welfare program called Aid to Families with Dependent Children when it was set up in 1935. As discussed above (and again in later chapters) there were so many complaints of corruption and dependence that it was reformed in 1996. Intended to end dependence on state assistance, a time limit was established for receiving assistance in the new TANF program. Also administration of the program was changed from the federal level to the state level, although money still came from the federal government. Politicians still disagree about how many hours a recipient should work in order to continue receiving assistance, as well as other facets of the plan. Everyone agrees it is better than it was; but still, improvement needs to be made.

Some problems don't seem to improve regardless of what actions are taken. Teen drinking seems to cycle up and down somewhat independently of efforts to reduce this behavior. Prostitution continues in most communities, despite efforts to end it.

Some problems seem to actually get worse. The war on drugs doesn't seem to have lessened the use of illegal substances in our country. In fact, the number of people who are arrested for drug trafficking seems to have increased.

## ▉ UNINTENDED CONSEQUENCES

Sometimes an ameliorating action for one problem can lead to another problem, or create unanticipated results. This happened with Prohibition. When the sale of alcohol was made illegal to stem the social problems associated with excessive drinking—particularly among the lower classes—it led to a rise in organized crime. It also led to deaths of those who drank deadly home brew. In some ways the same thing is happening today with the drug trade. Sale of illegal drugs has become a very high profit business, and with the stakes so high, it has increased the criminal involvement in that sector (Thornton 1991).

Another example of unintended consequences is found in the government's attempts to eliminate the slums of the inner cities during the 1950s. Substandard housing was eventually replaced with public housing projects, which effectively excluded African Americans from the wealth generation (owning homes) for several decades. In addition, the neighborhood fabric was destroyed and replaced with new opportunities for crime (Halpern 1995).

Yet a third example of unintended consequences is affirmative action. The law was passed in the 1960s to eliminate discrimination against qualified minorities in the workplace. In higher education, it came to function as a kind of quota system—a certain number of places were reserved for minorities. The intention was to give minority students who were not as strong academically a break and to ensure a student body that was more racially diversified. But soon nonminorities claimed reverse discrimination. In the 1990s, a student denied admission to UT Austin Law School claimed she was unfairly excluded: her exam scores were higher than minority students who were accepted. The Fifth Circuit Court of Appeals ruled in her favor, prohibiting the use of race as an admission criterion.[7] Minority advocate groups began looking for another way to increase minority enrollment in higher education. Shortly thereafter, the 10 percent law was passed, whereby high school graduates in Texas who ranked in the top 10 percent of their class would automatically be admitted to the state universities. This gave students from the lower performing, primarily minority schools located in lower socioeconomic areas easier access to college admittance, and minorities continued to be educated in similar numbers. Thus this illustrates both unintended consequences and an alternative solution (Eastlant 1996; Sturm and Guinier 1996).

## ▉▉ ASSESSING OVERALL SOCIAL BENEFIT

There are few times when everyone agrees on either the identification of a social problem or its ameliorating action. Yet despite the disagreements, there has been a certain amount of progress in addressing the major social problems of the past. For instance, in this country we no longer have children who work

---

7. Other state courts have subsequently handed down similar rulings.

for very low wages. All children, even those from very poor homes, have access to twelve years of education. We have laws that ensure the safety of our foods and beverages. There are laws that stipulate the minimum wage a company can pay. There is a complex system to regulate traffic and make it safe for everyone (as safe as possible). There is regulation of air travel and other commercial transportation.

All in all, these changes have made our society a better place to live. When the measures were instituted, not everyone agreed about the seriousness of the problems, or how to solve them, or even if they were problems. But because public attention turned to these issues, improvements were forthcoming. This leads us to another observation: ameliorating actions to social problems require some kind of action on the part of more than an individual or a small group. They require thoughtful examination and the cooperation of large numbers of people, institutions, and the government.

■ QUESTIONS FOR REVIEW

1. For what situations are legal reforms needed?

2. What problems are addressed by professional organizations and nonprofit groups?

3. What other kinds of ameliorating actions are there to social problems?

4. What are the common reactions to social problems?

5. What is an opposition group? Why does it form?

6. Do actions that address social problems always turn out as expected? Why or why not?

■ QUESTIONS FOR FURTHER THOUGHT

1. Can you think of laws that have been passed to address a social problem that, in the end, created an additional or different problem?

2. What propaganda campaign can you think of that has had positive results? Why?

3. What are the social problems addressed by the professional organization that you are likely to join when you graduate?

4. Are there people who understand the likelihood of unsatisfactory consequences to the proposed actions before they are implemented? If yes, why isn't their understanding made use of in subsequent actions?

---

■■ ■■ ■■ BOX 3.1.

## OCCUPY WALL STREET

On September 17, 2011, several thousand people began an extended occupation of Zuccotti Park near Wall Street in response to a suggestion by an editor and co-founder of Vancouver-based magazine *Adbusters*. Young and old from New York and elsewhere around the country brought their sleeping gear to protest the economic inequities associated with big corporation. The movement, which one month later had no specific demands, received within that time some $300,000 in donations as well as blankets, sleeping bags, food, and medical and hygienic supplies. Supplies are kept in a donated storage space a block away that is also being used as a make-shift headquarters.

The protest moved across the country with the help of Internet media. Similar protests sprang up in Boston, Washington, Chicago, Los Angeles, and Fort Worth and other cities where Facebook pages and Twitter accounts appealed for local volunteers. More than 900 events were planned on Meetup.com. Blogs and photos were part of the 10–15,000 posts an hour in mid-October. A Website called Occupy Together coordinated some of the activity. The Facebook page Occupy Wallstreet had 138,000 members a few weeks after it started.

*Source:* Ramirez 2011, Caruso 2011, Preston 2011.

*Questions for Further Thought:* Using your knowledge of the formation of social movements, what do you think will develop with this protest? Will it become a full fledged movement like the Civil Rights Movement? Will it disappear after some time? Why are the people participating in the protest? Do they all have the same motivations? Will a specific demand appear at some time? If so, what will it be? What solutions will be sought? What solutions are reasonable to expect to be forthcoming? What impact will this protest have? Who will it impact the most?

# CHAPTER FOUR

# SOCIAL DYNAMICS
## The Change Process and Models of Change

Sociology examines the parts of society, how they are arranged in space, and how they influence each other. Parts of society are usually thought of as individuals, groups, institutions, social structure, roles, norms, power, stratification, tradition, and so on. This approach to understanding society is what August Comte (one of the first sociologists) called *social statics.* It is a continuation of the ancient Greek view (from Parmenides) of the world as "a motionless continuum of matter and space" (Harper 1993, 4).

Another way to examine society is to look at motion. The study of movement is the study of change. Comte called this approach to society *social dynamics.* It is in line with the Greek philosopher Heraclitus, who saw everything as constantly changing. "One never steps into the same river twice," he said. There is a dichotomy between these two approaches. Sociologists have focused on the parts rather than motion because studying movement is more complicated (Sztompka 1993).[1] Examination of structure is more in line with Western thinking. Social research includes some aspects of social dynamics, but it is not

---

1. A traditional correlation of two or more social components draws inferences of the effect of one component on the other based on changes observed at two or more specific points in time. While this is superior to the understanding of the components at a single point in time, it does not take into account feedback loops and other influences on all of the social components. A comprehensive model that accurately captures the confluence of influences in all directions is mathematically very challenging. Some analysts have concluded that the laws of social science can only be of the second stage in deterministic type, hence verification "exceeds by orders of magnitude all previous efforts expended on the natural sciences" (Stent 1978, 57).

a commonly studied area. This chapter is drawn from a variety of sources and addresses factors of change pertinent to the study of social problems. It is not a comprehensive review of the social change literature.

# ■ PART I: Processes/Patterns of Change

There are at least three different ideas about how change moves through human affairs.

## ∷ CHANGE IS LINEAR: PROGRESS AND EVOLUTION

Linear change is directional, as in "things are getting better." It incorporates the idea of agents of change (people) who work to make things better, and often includes the idea of necessary stages or steps toward some desired end state.

Our Western idea of linear progress developed over a long period of time. The Greeks saw the world as existing in a process of growth; the Jews saw history as being guided by divine will or providence. For people of the Middle Ages, knowledge was constantly and gradually increasing. In the seventeenth century, Francis Bacon introduced the idea of progress—the possibility that a group of people with knowledge and purpose can work together to achieve an improved social state of being. By the nineteenth century, everyone talked about progress; all the early sociologists incorporated it into their theories (Sztompka 1993; Tuveson 1995).

Charles Darwin used the idea of directional change in his theory of evolution—an irreversible biological transformation of plant and animal populations (Lenski 1995).[2] Lenski et al. (1995) used the idea in his concept of sociocultural evolution; his early theory of social development was based on the linear acquisition of new technology (Lenski 1966). Karl Marx saw social change as being directional, with the revolution and the establishment of an

---

2. The key elements of classical nineteenth-century evolutionary change are that it is natural, directional, and immanent (comes from inside), and continuous and necessary (Adams and Sydie 2001, 450).

ideal communistic society as an inevitable end point (Marx and Engels 1971; Marx 1967).[3]

Development is another linear term. On a global scale it refers to the economic and social achievement of a society by transformation of conditions of poverty and low productivity. Development goes hand in hand with the adoption of pragmatic, scientific (Western) methods over traditional beliefs and practices (Bernstein 1995).

Modernity is another term that incorporates linear change. Since the Enlightenment, for two hundred years or more, the term has referred to the latest in industrial and scientific developments of Western society. We also talk of "modern" thinking, which is rational, utilitarian, and, of late, global (Kumar 1995).

A term that some use interchangeably with modernity is urbanization—the movement of people to concentrated residential areas. Cities as commercial centers have been developed by competing elites. This was followed by decentralized industrial communities and centers for global interaction with various political jurisdictions and municipal services (Mingione 1995).

Each of these terms incorporates the idea that the latest change is an improvement over what existed before, and that future improvements will supersede the current one.

## ▪▪ CHANGE IS CYCLICAL: GROWTH AND DECAY

This is the idea that history repeats itself, that civilizations first rise and subsequently fall, that there is no golden age toward which all of humankind is progressing. Rather, each civilization passes through its own cycle of growth and decline. Mistakes of one age are repeated in the next age, since each group must learn the lessons itself. Each era has potentials that are developed and then exhausted, and eventually lead to decline and decay, and a return to a beginning point.

---

3. Marx used Hegel's dialectic to describe the process whereby the proletariat overcomes the domination of the bourgeoisie. But he postulates movement or change in one direction only. "Marx was a staunch believer in progress as the overall direction of the historical process. He shared the optimism of the evolutionists, emphasizing the constant betterment of society." (Sztompka 1993, 155)

This idea is more common in the non-Western world. Hindus, for instance, believe that world civilizations have gone through at least four different ages. The Sanskrit word *yuga* refers to an epoch or an age (Watts 1972, 137). The age just ending is Kali Yuga, or age of conflict.[4] Greek philosophers also thought that civilizations went through stages. Hesiod had five different ages; like the book of Ecclesiastes, Aristotle thought that everything had happened before (Symonds 1879). The fourteenth-century Muslim sociologist, Ibn Khaldun, saw a cyclical pattern in conflict and the development and weakening of social bonds. He observed strong feelings of solidarity as a community forms, perhaps because of common threats faced by the group. Later there was a weakening of social ties as the group relaxed into the security of mundane affairs, until finally the social bonds collapsed altogether, and the group dispersed. Then new groups formed (Ibn Khaldun 2004; Sztompka 1993; Harper 1993).

Some Western theorists and historians have incorporated the idea of cycles in their thinking (Sztompka 1993). In the eighteenth century, Giambattista Vico (1961) speculated that all civilizations go through predictable stages to reach their apex; then they decline and decay to be replaced by new civilizations. In the twentieth century, Oswald Spengler (1939) had a similar idea: all great cultures go through a cycle of emergence, growth, fulfillment of their destiny, and then decay and death. According to Spengler, the collective biography of these cultures is what we have come to call history.

Sociologist Vilfredo Pareto (1966) described what he called *cycles of social dominance*.[5] He called the two alternating groups of elites the "foxes" and the "lions." The clever foxes manipulate their way into positions of power. But once there, originality, rationality, and cleverness become a destabilizing force that creates an opening for the lions to regain power. The strong lions appeal to a conservative desire for security; thus, they rule by force rather than cleverness. But the flaws in their rule over time allow the foxes to once again gain

---

4. The ages, in order of their appearance, are the Age of Wisdom (Satya Yuga), the Age of Ritual (Treta Yuga), the Age of Doubt (Dvapara Yuga), and the Age of Conflict (Kali Yuga) (Finney 2010).

5. Pareto viewed society as basically stable, with each social upset, whether political, criminal, or natural, being countered by a conservative reaction that restores the social order to its previous state.

power. Thus power continuously shifts back and forth between rulers who use cleverness and brute force.

Another sociologist, Pitirim Sorokin (1937), thought that cultures cycle back and forth between ideational and sensate.[6] An ideational culture emphasizes an inner spiritual reality of truth and goodness; self-improvement comes from resisting sensuous temptations. A sensate culture, on the other hand, emphasizes the material world; truth and goodness are defined by physical experiences. A third culture is transitional between the other two. An idealistic culture has elements of both; it is both material and spiritual, with self-fulfillment that includes improvement of both the self and the environment (Zimmerman 1968; Sztompka 1993). In Sorokin's assessment, twentieth-century Western civilization was sensate headed for idealistic (Harper 1993).

Some economists have argued that there is a pattern of long wave expansion and contraction of the world economy, with peaks and depressions occurring every fifty years. Others are unconvinced of the existence of these so-called Kondratieff cycles. Nevertheless, human lives are somewhat cyclical: the work week, stages of a person's life, biological cycles, economic cycles of prosperity and recession, and so on. And nature has many cycles: day and night, seasons of the year, growth of plants, and the natural environment.

## ∷ CHANGE IS DIALECTICAL:
## THESIS, ANTITHESIS, SYNTHESIS

Dialectic change is an interactive process whereby the stages and the end result are undetermined. It is similar to linear change in that there is a direction. But it also has recurring patterns, albeit at different levels than previously achieved. The dialectical process is usually credited to the nineteenth-century philosopher Hegel, who tried to capture the dynamics of change in social issues of tradition, religion, and personal freedom. He identified a process of thesis,

---

6. Sorokin thought of societies as continually developing and changing. But because there are only so many possibilities, there are recurring patterns or rhythms of change. Yet because the rhythms are slightly different each time, it is never an exact repeat. He identified early Greece as ideational; Rome as sensate; early European culture as ideational; and Renaissance/ Enlightenment Europe as sensate.

antithesis, synthesis through which cultural ideas and norms pass.[7] An idea arises (the thesis—abortion, for instance). Soon there is an opposing idea (the antithesis—anti-abortion). After some arguing back and forth, a compromise develops that incorporates both points of view. It is a higher, more developed idea than the original due to all the discussion and debate. (As to the synthesis between pro-life and pro-choice, it hasn't exactly happened yet!) (Hegel 1977; Bhaskar 1995; Solomon 1983; Sztompka 1993).

An interesting aspect of the dialectic is that it is impossible to predict where the change will lead, impossible to know what kind of synthesis will be derived— or even if the change will have good or bad results. In that sense, it is not a planned change. Conflicts over ideas and actions can develop at any moment, and at times develop where they are least expected. Change emerges, as it were, from existing conditions. That is, the existing conditions, whatever they are, have within themselves the seeds of something new, as well as the opposition to that new thing and the ability to blossom into something more than it was.[8]

In some ways, Sorokin's theory of cultural change is dialectical. As for Hegel, cultures have immanent and characteristic rhythms that determine which of the three cultural forms will appear. And each culture has within itself the seed of change, once the premises are exhausted (Coser 1977).

Another sociologist doesn't specifically talk about change, but his idea of social development is more or less dialectical. For Etzioni (1988) people are not primarily rational, selfish individuals. Rather, there is a "productive tension" within the individual between self-fulfillment/gratification and fulfillment of the collective purpose in response to the pull from the community. Thus any social change process is a kind of dialectic between these two purposes. (Etzioni

---

7. This is not the same as the concept of the dialectic used by Marx. First and most importantly for this discussion, Marx foresaw a definite end and projected change in a specific direction, whereas Hegel had no particular end or direction in mind. Second, Marx's use of the dialectic characterizes the sides as "right" and "wrong" (the proletariat is "right" whereas the bourgeoisie is "wrong"); hence the end result is not unity of the two but victory of one side over the other. For Marx, it is not a friendly (if serious) exchange of views with possible compromises, but a deadly zero-sum conflict. Marx used the dialectical process to describe the fight over material sources and power, whereas Hegel used it to describe development of invisible social concepts—cultural ideas and norms.
8. Modern theories call this idea *emergence*—a system has the ability to change, to emerge, into something new without outside assistance or direction.

calls this *communitarianism.*) By implication, any social arrangement too far to one side (rational, individualistic) or the other (moralistic, social control) will not be long lasting.

One might think of Sorokin's ideational and sensate cultures as a kind of dialectic, as well. There is a tension in many areas of life: between religious or spiritual goals and material success. There is a tension between conservative, traditional forces striving to preserve that which is good in society versus progressive, liberal forces striving to introduce new and fresh ideas. There is a tension between artistic, creative individuals who crave freedom to express their inner world and the rigorous, controlled scientist who tediously builds ideas one small step at a time. We might even include Marx's observation of tension between the capitalist and the worker (bourgeoisie and proletariat). In each case, the character of life emerges as individuals balance these two opposing pulls.

## ▝ OTHER IDEAS OF SOCIAL CHANGE

Social change has limited appeal as a research area in sociology today. Still, it is an integral part of many social theories. For instance, conflict theorists advocate changes in the social structure to make society more equal and effect more equal distribution of resources; conflict, as the engine of change, can be either destructive or creative. Functional theorists see change as a response to unmet needs arising from within the social system. Interactionists believe the social order is constantly being created, recreated, and negotiated as individuals interact with each other and with the system.

Sociologists who study modernization and national development also study social change. It is not possible to review all the ideas of change in the different theories, but some of the major ones are discussed briefly.

### *Development*

Immanuel Wallerstein sees global level development as systemic and heavily dependent upon economics. The world system is economically and socially unequal and polarized. Class distinctions exist between states because of an emphasis on accumulation of capital. Core nations control the productive activities, and periphery nations struggle to survive. The change accompanying decolonization was positive. So was the fall of Marxist states that didn't live up to their ideology. But change is ultimately continuous and multidirectional, with an undetermined outcome. Increased crowding, poverty, and other tensions around the world make mass destruction a real possibility (Adams and Sydie 2001).

Theda Skocpol takes a more optimistic view of world development because of her study of social revolutions. She concluded that rapid transformation of state and class structure happens when a weak or rigid government is threatened from outside. Revolutions also require that a discontented and fairly independent group of people (communities) exist inside the country who are ready to aggressively challenge the existing system (Adams and Sydie 2001). Populations that are repressed or starving are unlikely to revolt.

Niklas Luhmann sees society as a system, but he is not interested in economics and social power to the same extent as Wallerstein. He is interested in the interrelationship of societies. Each society is a separate autopioetic system (it creates and recreates itself through its own inner reflexive and recursive processes). It interacts with other societies like a dynamic organism. The world system is currently an open one, but that will change. Complex societies tend to create boundaries and strengthen them over time, which divides people into "us" and "them." Modern society, according to Luhmann, is not organized by state or religion, or by nationalism or cultural identity (Allan 2006; Wallace and Wolf 2005).

### Modernization

Anthony Giddens sees modernity as a force created by humans that comes to have a life of its own. Life is increasingly "disembedding" from local or traditional institutions. It becomes a juggernaut, or a "runaway engine of enormous power." Collectively, we as human beings can drive this juggernaut to some extent, but it "threatens to rush out of our control and . . . rend itself asunder" (Giddens 1990, 139). This modernizing force was created by well meaning persons striving to be more practical and efficient, but it has become an irresistible force that demands adherence. And where it will lead is not entirely clear.

Jean Baudrillard (1994) is concerned with the modern tendency to abstract ideas and experiences from the real world. He says that we are creating a society that is a complete illusion, a world in which meaning and reference to reality are disappearing from our social life. Historically people worked and exchanged the products they made. Today people display signs and exchange (purchase) things that have no relation to reality. The Ponzi scheme of Bernard Madoff is an example. Investors bought into the image of wealth, and so long as the illusion was satisfying, no one questioned it. It is a postmodern theory of hyper-reality and simulacrum (Allan 2006).

### Systems Theories

Finally, two systems theories address social change. Both use living organisms as a systems model. Walter Buckley (1968) identified the simplest system as one that is mechanical with no feedback loops and no outside interaction. A complex adaptive system, on the other hand, has feedback loops and is open to external influences. Thus it is self-regulating and self-directing, and can even change its structure if necessary. Being open to external influences means it can adapt to its environment. Psychological and sociocultural systems are a complex adaptive system; society is also morphogenic (can change its structure during development).

Society, for Talcott Parsons, is a set of interrelated systems. A sophisticated culture has systems of language, religion, kinship organization, and technology and further creates systems of social stratification, cultural legitimation, bureaucratic organization, economics, norms, and democratic associations. The relationships between the functional components of the systems (norms, values, roles, etc.) are periodically adjusted to make the system work better. Human motivations (or needs) are a major source of change, although component strains are important from time to time. Parsons identified four change processes: differentiation, adaptive upgrading, inclusion, and value generalization. He did not address fundamental changes in the system itself, only the working of the parts. Regarding social change and the future of humanity, he is cautiously optimistic (Parsons 1966; Wallace and Wolf 2005).

## ∷ CAUSES OF CHANGE

### Materialistic Sources of Change

What starts the change process? Marx was adamant that inequality, or the unequal distribution of resources, was the beginning point of social change. This is materialism—looking to the physical world for the factors that lead to change. This view is seen in the role Marx gave to the economy: the infrastructure, or base that shapes other social institutions (politics, education, religion, family). In other words, from this perspective, it is technology and economic production that shapes the ideas and values of a society. When the means of production change, the social institutions change.

Lenski based his theory of sociocultural evolution on Marx's view. Based on their technology and means of production, societies moved from hunting and gathering societies, to horticultural and pastoral societies, to agrarian societies, to industrialized societies. As the productive technology became more sophisticated, the forms of social organization also became correspondingly more complex.

Another well-known theory of social change and technology is William Ogburn's (1938) concept of *cultural lag*. When technology or our ideas about technology change more quickly than culture, there is a period of tension between the two. An example of this today is stem cell research. Until the moral questions are resolved, some of the many uses of stem cells in modern science have been put on hold.

### Nonmaterialistic Sources of Change

Idealism is the theory that ideas or beliefs are a major factor of social change. Weber (1958) described the way in which religious beliefs shape people's ideas of duty and obligation and how they impact what people do. In *The Protestant Ethic and the Spirit of Capitalism*, he examined the ascetic religious values of European Calvinists that played an important role in the economic development of the Industrial Revolution.[9] The importance that Weber placed on ideas is seen in several of his concepts: *verstehen* (interpretive understanding for social phenomena), *ideal types* (an analytical construct against which real life is compared), *charisma* and *rationalization* (a change in thinking and values from tradition to practicality and efficiency).

---

9. Weber's social analysis is multidimensional. Some of his theory, particularly concerning class and status stratification and bureaucracy, resembles that of Marx.

### People as the Sources of Change

Are exceptional people the causes of change? This is a claim that is debated by sociologists. One view is that yes, great individuals *are* agents of change. People with exceptional knowledge, competence, talent, skill, strength, cunning, or charisma seem to influence the direction of whole societies. These are people who are pushed to do things that result in the creation of new social or cultural awareness. Their influence might be in a positive or negative direction. Consider, for instance, Jesus, Buddha, Mahatma Gandhi, Alexander the Great, Hitler, Stalin, Napoleon, Newton, Columbus, Copernicus, Edison.

Another view is that the people we know as leaders are a product of their time. They are not exceptional, but they *are* in the right place at the right time, and have the abilities needed for the situation—so they are associated with great moments of history. Social determinists would have us believe that the persons we revere captured and reflected the spirit of their time better than others, so they became leaders. Certainly without the social milieu of their time, the most notable historical figures would not have risen to prominence. But all of these persons were able to take advantage of their situation. They may have been ordinary persons, who, in the course of fulfilling their own dreams, became trendsetters and thus influenced culture. Examples are Elvis, Daddy Rice, Madonna, the Beatles, Coco Chanel, Gianni Versace, and numerous others (Sztompka 1993).

Which view is correct is hard to know. But certainly any study of social change has to include the influence of prominent people.

### Innovation and Innovators

Innovation—the discovery or invention of something new—is one kind of social change. It is usually derived from things or ideas that exist in the society already. Innovators are likely to be more autonomous and perhaps less anxious. Anthropologists say that cross-cultural contact is a major source of innovation (Harper 1993).

Diffusion is the adoption of new ideas by others throughout the society, often by hearing about it from someone else who heard about it. When new ideas come from a group, those who first adopt them are often centrally located in society and have high socioeconomic status. But if the innovation comes from outside the group, marginals are likely to be the first adopters. In general, marginals are more likely to be first adopters because they are not as concerned about what others think.

In addition to location in the group, researchers are interested in the characteristics of first adopters. One study found that about 2.5 percent of the population are first adopters, or innovators. They tend to be young, wealthy, cosmopolitan, and possibly opinion leaders. About 13.5 percent are early adopters. They are respected in society and have high status as opinion leaders. About 34 percent are the early majority—people who adopt something new only after others have adopted it. The late majority, about 34 percent of the population, are skeptical and will only adopt something new after being convinced and pressured. The last 16 percent are the laggards, who are tradition oriented and have no desire to change. They tend to be elderly, with lower social status and less income (Rogers 1962).

If adoption of something new is required by law, it presumably has already been sanctioned either by a majority (who voted for it) or by social leaders (lawmakers).

One major reason that good innovations are not adopted is fear. Other reasons are that it may "be out of sync" with what exists, or violate aesthetics or morals, or be a threat to vested interests of money, status, or prestige (Harper 1993).

## ■ PART II. Models for Social Change

A model provides an example of something so the researcher can understand how it works—compare it with what is at hand and see what is missing. For social problems there are several models; one size doesn't fit all. There are different kinds of change and different circumstances. The models here address three different areas of change. The first has to do with convincing people to change, the second has to do with organizational principles of change, and the third has to do with changes associated with technology.

### ■■ HUMAN INTERACTION

These two models present a plan for action when the target group is disadvantaged, and those with power do not want to change. There are two very different approaches, reflecting different assumptions of human nature. One is confrontational and the other is peaceful.

### Marx's Ameliorating Action: Revolution

Karl Marx's model is confrontational. In a nutshell, the suffering group has power in its numbers and should use that power to force the establishment to change—a revolution. Marx lived in England at the beginning of the Industrial Revolution, and was appalled at the mistreatment of the poor, including children, who worked in unsafe conditions for almost nothing. He blamed the factory owners who became wealthy because they didn't pay their workers enough. The workers, for their part, too often accepted their fate; he called it *false consciousness,* or not recognizing their unfair treatment. Marx wanted them to band together to improve their situation. He called this *class consciousness,* or an awareness that they were part of a group, that they were being treated badly, and that they wanted to change their situation.

For Marx, then, the poor workers were both the target group and the action group; they are the ones who suffer and the ones with the will to act to resolve the situation. As a materialist, he focused on economics as the underlying cause of social inequality. The ameliorating action, according to Marx, is for the workers to throw off the oppressive control of the owners. He concluded that the owners would not change, nor give up their wealth without being forced—the rational human being view. The will to act comes from class consciousness.

Marx's analysis of the workers' situation in a capitalist system is insightful. His political theory has been used to inspire revolution and reform around the world: in the Soviet Union, China, countries in eastern Europe, Cuba, North Korea, and some other countries. The communist governments that were subsequently established improved the lives of the poor in terms of education, jobs, housing, and other basic needs. But the human cost was great. In the Soviet Union some 20 million people died in Siberia resisting government attempts to collectivize their farms (White 2011). In Cambodia, some 2 million people died in the Killing Fields, when the government evacuated whole cities in an effort to "reeducate" those who preferred Western capitalist ways (Murphy 2009). Dissenters of the restrictive communist regime in the Soviet Union are legendary, including Solzhenitsyn, who wrote about the gulag (Michaels 2002).

Students opposed to the communist system in China demonstrated in Tiananmen Square, thousands tried to escape from eastern Europe (Harmstone 1984), while boatloads of refugees came to the United States from Cuba.

Conflict theorists who defend Marx's theory insist that true communism was never established in any of these countries.[10] Labor unions and others who used Marx's theory in the United States didn't have enough support for a national revolution, but succeeded in improving their wages and working conditions. Today, Marx's description of inequality appeals to most minority groups, as they work to create better opportunities in our society. Some social theorists use Marx's theory to analyze public consumption of goods and culture; they claim that the producers of cultural artifacts manipulate the pubic into buying what they want them to buy. Thus they create and dominate our culture.

There are many strengths in this model of social change. It has been used in many situations during the last century. However, it is good to keep in mind its inherent flaws. It does not universally value human life. It underestimates the establishment or ruling party's ability to change and overestimates the working class's ability to set up an ideal society.

### Gandhi's Ameliorating Action: Satyagraha

Another model for social change involving human interaction came from Mahatma Gandhi: use of peaceful means, including self-sacrifice to convince others to change. He developed what has become known as nonviolent resistance in order to help India resist the unjust and unwanted rule of the British Empire. It was a method conceived in his early career in South Africa, where he was angered by South African discrimination against the Indian community. He used his considerable legal and personal energies to improve the situation. Returning to India, he became a moral force among a people eager to win independence from the British. Rather than resort to legal or military methods, Gandhi encouraged use of an inner, personal force. He used the term *satyagraha*—the force that is born of truth and love, or nonviolence. (*Satya* means truth with love,

---

10. They also disavow his political theory, which they say is responsible for the atrocities.

and *agraha* means firmness or force.) As Gandhi explains, because truth appears differently to different people, one cannot use violence on one's opponent, but rather should help them to understand that their view of truth is not correct. "He must be weaned from error by patience and sympathy. . . . And patience means self-suffering."

In other words, recognizing that your opponent is wrong, you willingly endure hardships so that your opponent can realize his error and change. Gandhi thought that if you have the strength of your convictions, you can afford to be patient and help others realize a higher truth, even if it means that you will suffer in the process. It was a technique that he claims to have learned from his wife, who patiently endured his erroneous ideas. The idea also grew out of Hindu ideas of *ahimsa*—the nonharming of living things—and *tapasya*—the willingness to sacrifice oneself. He believed that *ahimsa* is the basis of a search for truth, that truth is the substance of morality, and that morality is the basis of all things (Gandhi 1960).

To most Westerners, this is a religious philosophy. Yet many in India regard Gandhi as a politician, not a religious leader. In truth, Gandhi became a significant political force against the British rule in India. The suffering he was willing to endure to achieve his ends was the sacrifice of his life. On several occasions, he pledged to fast until death unless the British relented, giving him a power over events not often seen. Not everyone understood his approach, however, and not all his followers had the same self-discipline. At one point, when resistance turned violent, Gandhi called off the resistance and retreated from public life for a time.

In the end, it is impossible to discuss India's independence without devoting a significant part of the story to Gandhi. His success is an example for other groups facing discrimination and injustice. Indeed, other social reformers have studied his methods and used them in their own struggles, among them Martin Luther King, Nelson Mandela, and Aung San Suu Kyi.

Like Marx, Gandhi sees the ones who suffer as both the target group and the advocate group. As an idealist, he sees an incomplete understanding of truth as the cause of the problem. The ameliorating action is for the advocate group to help those in power to understand; this arises from his view of the compassionate, sacrificing human being. The will to act comes from love and a personal desire for higher truth.

Nonviolent resistance has become a common term, although it can include actions and attitudes that are combative. Gandhi's *satyagraha* is not just a technique to get one's way, but pursuit of a higher truth for both parties. Applied halfheartedly, without the willingness to sacrifice and without genuine concern for the other, it will be less successful. It has sometimes been criticized as weakness.

## ▦ ORGANIZATIONAL PRINCIPLES

The second group of models has to do with organizational principles: how many people are needed to effect change, what principles should be followed to be most effective, and what actions should individuals take. As noted above, not all models fit all situations.

### *Restructuring or Critical Mass Model*

The main idea of this model is that there is a point when something receives sufficient support (a critical mass) for the outcome to change. It comes from David Korten (2006), who believes that human history is at a unique point of change today. Unlike any other time in the past, a massive change in values, organizational structure, and goals in societies around the world is possible. The result would be a more humane, people-centered world order. The reason for this shift is that a critical mass of people who want it will tip the scale. The number of people ready to embrace change has increased to the point where there is a shift in popular thinking. The people who love life rather than money—the cultural creatives—are increasing to a critical point.[11] In the 1960s, they were only 5 percent, but by the late 1990s their numbers swelled

---

11. The first (lowest) of Korten's five levels of awareness is magical consciousness—impulsive and driven by emotion, and self-oriented. The second level, imperial consciousness, is self-oriented, defined by order, regularity, and stability. At the third level, socialized consciousness, cultural norms are internalized: there is a realization that social prosperity is necessary for individual prosperity. Less self-oriented than the previous two levels, people at this level still have a small worldview based on their membership in a particular group. Cultural creatives, people at the fourth level of awareness, are concerned about justice for everyone, not just their own group: it comes with age. Spiritual creatives are a smaller group at the highest level of consciousness; they are evolutionary cocreators who have transcended group loyalty, and are actively seeking to improve things for everyone.

to 26 percent of the U.S. population, and they are growing worldwide (60 percent are women). As they increase their momentum, others will join with this group and social thinking will tip in a new direction. He calls it "the birthing of a new era," a "global cultural and spiritual awakening" (Korten 2006, 21).

Our current environmental and social systems are failing so badly that we *must* reorganize ourselves, according to Korten. We are currently at the end of a five-hundred-year reign of Empire—societies dominated by imperial elites wielding power and privilege. Centralization, hierarchical authority, market competition, violence, greed, and ruthless competition for power and material goods have been the order of the day. Feminine contributions to culture and government are ignored, and "higher order" potentials of love and service are suppressed. It is a profit-driven, corporate-managed society.

Earth Community, which is replacing Empire, will be egalitarian and democratic. Human relationships will be partnerships; everyone's physical needs will be met; feminine and masculine powers will be balanced; and human potential will be developed. Twelve guiding principles characterize Earth Community: (1) economic democracy (equality), (2) local preference (control is maintained at a local level), (3) human scale (not large, inhuman corporations), (4) living indicators (well-being of all), (5) fair-share taxation, (6) responsive markets, (7) responsibility for harms caused, (8) patient capital, (9) generational jubilee (equitable distribution of estates), (10) information and technology sharing, (11) economic self-determination, and (12) fair and balanced trade.

The three stages of this massive change are spiritual or cultural, economic, and political. In spiritual or cultural turning, there is a change in the thinking of people in a society. In economic turning, people with more eco-friendly lives turn away from wealth to embrace stewardship and helping others. In political turning, democracy of money becomes democracy of the people, citizens become more active, competition becomes cooperation, justice changes from retributive to restorative, coercion becomes mutual responsibility and accountability.

There have been other predictions of a great change. Philosopher Teilhard de Chardin (1964) predicted an omega point when the people on earth are able to function like a single living organism. Writer Karen Armstrong (2006) predicts a new axial age—an intense and urgent time of searching and spiritual breakthroughs. Former Czech president Vaclav Havel (1995) predicts "transcendence [as] the only real alternative to extinction." And there are others.

In the critical mass model, the target group is the powerless who have been forced to repress higher ideals. The cause of the problem is self-interest of those in power. Time is one part of the ameliorating action, plus plans of the critical mass. Korten's cultural creatives are the main advocate group. Their will to act comes from both the failing of existing systems and the pursuit of higher ideals. It is unclear what will happen to those in power after the massive changes. Presumably they will be caught up in the changes as well.

### The Synthesis Model

This model promotes the resolution of problems using the world's highest ideals, instead of settling for the lowest common denominators. Spiritual politics, developed by McLaughlin and Davidson (1994), uses universal principles common to all religions, such as compassion, unity, truthfulness, fairness, tolerance, responsibility, and respect for life. Problems come from deep within a society, they say, and consequently draw attention to attitudes and events that need to be changed. Solutions should bring out the best in all parties and make everyone better off and happier in the long run.

The four principles of spiritual politics are reframing, systems thinking, win/win, and synthesis. *Reframing* is looking at a problem in a larger context. For example, the group Common Ground reframed military power as establishing one nation's security without creating insecurity in other nations. *Systems thinking* is looking at the situation in terms of relationships rather than as linear cause and effect. Western medicine, for instance, does not reflect systems thinking as much as Eastern medicine, whose patients include healthy persons who are treated to keep them well. *Win/win* is looking for solutions that give something to everyone, rather than zero-sum, which creates polarizations and makes people choose sides.[12] *Synthesis* is bringing two sides together to create something bigger than either one by itself. On a social level, synthesis in terms of housing, education, or welfare would be combining aspects of government assistance and personal responsibility.

---

12. Zero-sum assumes a fixed number of things, so if one person has more, another automatically has less.

The synthesis model highlights the gap between the two different sets of goals—the personal and the private. A related approach by David Whyte (1994) advocates bringing moral values into the corporate world by means of workshops using poetic images. The goal is to help others to be in touch with their creative inner life that is often at variance with the demands of their profession. His is also a synthesis approach, in that he is attempting to bring together the external, competitive, professional world and the internal, moral, and personal world, with the end result, hopefully, of a more humane professional world.

The target group and the advocate group are unspecified in this model. The ameliorating action is negotiation, rethinking, and compromise—and creating something bigger and better than what existed before. The will to act, at least for the authors, is the desire to have a bigger, better, and more harmonious world (society, group). This model is based on the greater good human being view, or possibly the compassionate/sacrificing human being view.

### The Emergence Model

This model looks to "bottom-up" changes rather than to the more familiar "top-down" organizational structure. It comes from chaos and complexity theories developed in the 1980s to explain the surprising discovery that nonliving systems can organize themselves (Lewin 1992; Gleick 1987; Eve, Horsfall, and Lee 1997; Scott 1991). Order emerges from within (from the bottom) because the system follows some simple rules (and chooses which rules/organizing principles to follow).

Several aspects of this discovery challenged scientists. First, in chaos, or system breakdown, phenomena are not predictable.[13] Second, in choosing its organizing principle, a nonliving system acts like a living organism.[14] Third,

---

13. A simple example is a pile of sand being continuously created by adding one grain at a time at the top. Suddenly the limit is exceeded, and the whole pile gives way to chaos—the sand spreads out in many directions. No one can predict which way the sand will go. This is chaos.

14. "Self-organizing is the capacity of open and living systems, such as we live in and we ourselves are, to generate their own new forms from inner guidelines rather than from the imposition of form from outside" (Loye and Eisler 1987, 56).

the pattern created (the new organization) is repeated at each smaller and smaller (scalar) level.[15] Visually, this is seen in the Mandelbrot set.

Another challenge is that at the choice point (bifurcation, or system change), even systems that are ordinarily closed become open to influences from the external environment (Davies 1988, 83). Also, the way a system chooses is surprising. Mathematically, the system generates two answers, and then chooses one over the other. Or it may go back and forth between the two different answers. Or it may generate other answers.[16] (Prior to bifurcation—choice point—prediction is probabilistic, like living organisms.)

Chaos theory arose spontaneously in several different fields—mathematics, meteorology, molecular chemistry, physics, and others. Researchers realized that new system patterns are predictable if the initial conditions are known precisely. But they are almost impossible to know, and tiny differences at this point make huge differences later on (the so-called butterfly effect). And the math is prohibitively complex.[17]

Emergence has some ramifications to social life. Its "bottom up" process is of interest to people who study social crises, when structures and even rule of law break down. At these times, people are left to their own devices to recreate social harmony, just as a system in chaos uses local rules to recreate system order.

Another application is within social organizations. It may be that social order can emerge from people following simple organizing principles, contradicting the traditional wisdom that a strong leader is needed to bring order to social chaos.

An advocate group that appears in sync with emergence is the random acts of kindness group noted earlier. This group advocates that the world will be a better place if each person does random acts of kindness. This is already seen in the spontaneous donation of money and goods when someone's house is

---

15. Scalar levels are increasingly smaller systems within a larger system, each being fully functional. Tsonis (1992) contends that simple rules and random selection can produce all the intricacies of nature—shape of clouds, snowflakes, trees, and so on. The randomness approximates free will in living things.

16. In chaos and complexity theories, the different directions the system generates and chooses from are called "attractors." This whole process of a system generating new directions and choosing between them is referred to as "self-organization of dissipating systems," or simply emergence.

17. This is complexity theory.

burned in a fire. What if individual acts of kindness were extended to everyone helping a homeless person, or someone in poverty?

One sociologist has incorporated the idea of self-organization, or autopioesis. Niklas Luhmann is interested in communication between people and groups, and his analysis is particularly relevant to the field of law, where interaction is more structured and creates a network unto itself (Allan 2006).

The problem, in the emergence model, is chaos. The advocate group is the system in chaos. The ameliorating action is the emergence process, whereby the system develops its own solution. Practically speaking, that means that rather than trying to organize the chaos from a centralized, hierarchical position, the solution will arise from the people involved. The people involved are the action group. It is important to remember that the emergence model is *not* a code of ethics or morals that people are encouraged to follow, although the simple rules they follow may be moral or ethical. Since emergence applies to nonliving systems as well, it makes us wonder if an outdated organization could generate its own reform.

## ∷ TECHNOLOGY

The last group of models has to do with changes in technology. This is important because of the impact that new technology has on human life and social organizations.

### *The Redesign Model*

This model suggests there are times when it is necessary to rethink *everything*—throw out all the old ways of doing things, and start over. This is seen in the way architect William McDonnough and Michael Braungart (2002) look at pollution: we have a design problem, they say, not a waste problem. Reducing the human ecological footprint will preserve fewer natural resources than reducing the amount of waste produced.[18]

---

18. Brown's (2006) Plan B 2.0 is a detailed examination of problems of poverty, the earth's dwindling resources, health, stabilizing the climate, urban environments, and the economy. Like Korten, he thinks that the problems have become so bad that we must fix them. He has no particular model for doing that, however, other than being aware of the issues, being informed on the details, and working to improve things.

Today's production methods developed during the Industrial Revolution, when natural resources seemed unlimited, and pollution (air, water, and land) was unknown. Environmental concerns were not an issue. Things were made, used until they became broken, and then discarded. Over the years, this led to a buildup of toxins, gigantic amounts of waste, burial of valuable materials in waste, depletion of natural resources, regulations, production of dangerous material, and erosion of the diversity of species. This method of production has led us to create an environment that is often artificial and hybrid: foods that are less nutritious, air that is polluted, floods caused by cemented water-ways, and the discarding of material that is still usable. It is a cradle to grave philosophy.

Current measures are band-aids. Recycling, for instance, is often down cycling—a continual reduction in quality until the material is discarded, such as recycled paper. What is needed is a paradigm shift—a change in the way we think about production. Factories don't have to produce pollutants. Production methods can be developed that don't create waste. Buildings can be designed to produce more energy than they consume and purify their own wastewater. Products can be designed to decompose and feed the soil when they are thrown into the earth, or designed so that the raw materials can be reused at a later date. Transportation can improve the quality of life; we can live in a world of abundance—not limits, pollution, and waste.

> Once we set about designing with such missions in mind . . . We leave aside the old model of product-and-waste, and its dour offspring, "efficiency," and embrace the challenge of being not efficient but effective with respect to a rich mix of considerations and desires. (McDonnough and Braungart 2002, 72)

Their cradle to cradle model identifies things as either biological nutrients or technology. Things that can decompose should go back to nature. Things that don't decompose should be used again to produce other things. Among their successes is a factory in Germany where the wastewater is actually cleaner than the water going in. The "living roof" at the Ford Motor complex in Michigan is another example; it has eleven acres of vegetation that purify storm water and also provide natural air conditioning. The project cost $13 million. But a storm water management system would have cost $48 million for concrete pipes and a chemical treatment system. A third example is a green roof for Gap that blocks the noise from airplanes overhead.

In this model, the problem is pollution and depletion of natural resources. The target group is everyone. The action group is the producers, and ameliorating action is to redesign production to produce less waste.

### The Manure Model

This model proposes that some problems are solved by unforeseen leaps in technological development. This comes from a story about the growth of New York City (Horsfall 1982). In the late 1800s, a respected theorist predicted the extent of growth of New York City based on horse manure. Transportation, he reasoned, was needed to bring food and other goods into the city, take garbage out, and transport people from one place to another. He estimated how many horses were needed per person to sustain life, and how much manure each horse produced daily. By his calculation, there was a limit on the number of horses because of the amount of manure they produced. Thus there was a limit on the number of people who could live in the area. What he did not take into account, of course, was gas-powered engines.

In the same way, there are problems whose solutions will be out of date almost before they can be implemented. This is particularly true in GRIN technologies (genetics [changing our genes], robotics [creating machines that can perform human activities], info technology, and nano technology [smaller and smaller "machines"]).[19] The pace of these new developments has increased to the point where they double every year or two: the number of human genes mapped doubles every few years; the amount of computer memory you can get for $1 doubles every fifteen months or less; there are now motors smaller than a human cell. We will soon be facing a "singularity" (a term borrowed from mathematics)—sudden, dramatic change, graphically represented by a line that shoots up vertically instead of gradually increasing. In terms of human life, it is a time of mind-boggling social change, a time when the normal ways of doing things no longer make sense, the laws break down, and we can't predict the future (Garreau 2004). Here are some examples:

---

19. This research is conducted by DARPA (Defense Sciences Office of US Defense Advanced Research Projects Agency) and others.

1. The telekinetic monkey: a monkey is taught to play a video game. When its neurons are connected to a computer, it can continue to play the game by thought alone, without using the controls.
2. Pain vaccine is being developed that will block intense pain in seconds and last for thirty days without affecting other reactions.
3. A researcher is developing methods to stop bleeding, restore vision, and mend wounds within days, as well as regenerate limbs.
4. A program known as Engineered Tissue Constructs has a goal of re-building people's organs or body parts—within their own body.
5. Researchers are developing a way for humans to sleep like whales—half a brain at a time—and to increase cellular metabolism to the level of strength and endurance of athletes.
6. Others are developing a drug that will cure any virus.
7. Metabolic engineering is exploring the idea of hibernation or sus-pended animation for the wounded, so that they can survive without oxygen until help arrives.
8. Cochlear implants will allow the deaf to hear.
9. An exoskeleton is being developed that will allow a person to run and jump at fantastic levels, and carry heavy loads (500 pounds) effortlessly.
10. A brain machine interface is being developed—a wireless modem in-serted into a person's skull.

Will these fantastic abilities to alter our lives so dramatically be used for good or ill? Some researchers confidently predict a better world, whereas others more pessimistically predict a Frankenstein scenario. In either case, they point to changes few of us can imagine. The social problem and target group are unspecified in this model. The ameliorating action is technological develop-ment. The action group would be the innovators, or the first persons to adopt new change.

## ■■ CONCLUSION

These seven models present very different ideas of change. Each has practical applications. The Marxian and Gandhian models have been used to bring about social change around the world. The restructuring, synthesis, and emergence models represent some of the best current thinking about our world today. The redesign and manure models point to changes in the future that we may not imagine at this time. This is by no means a comprehensive survey of all the possible theoretical or practical ameliorating actions.

■ **QUESTIONS FOR REVIEW**

1. Explain the differences in the three directions of change—linear, cyclical, and dialectic.

2. What are the three common causes of change?

3. How many people are likely to adopt a new change before it becomes widespread?

4. What are the models for change involving human interaction?

5. What are the models for change involving organizational principles?

6. What are the models for change involving technology?

■ **QUESTIONS FOR FURTHER THOUGHT**

1. Think of things that have changed in your life over the years. Are these changes linear, cyclical, or dialectic?

2. Which cause of change do you think is more important—material (economics) or nonmaterial (ideas, beliefs)? Why?

3. Are you part of the innovators, early adopters, early majority, late majority, or laggards when it comes to adopting new ideas and technology?

4. Which model for change involving human interaction do you believe is most effective? Why?

5. In which situations would each of the models for change involving organizational principles be best suited?

6. Have there been times in our cultural past when we ignored the models for change involving technology, but we shouldn't have? What were the results?

# Section II

## THE PROBLEMS

# CHAPTER FIVE

# PROBLEMS ADDRESSED
# THROUGH GOVERNMENT PROGRAMS

As noted in Chapter 3, some problems are so large that they can only be addressed by a government-run program—health care, welfare, Social Security, Medicaid, and Medicare. Biases and political platforms can make these complex problems more difficult to understand. Issues may be oversimplified, and supporting facts may be selected to support a particular view. One must take care not to be "swallowed up" by rhetoric. Because the proposed changes take a long time to implement, they are also frustrating problems.

Government programs are not necessarily the solution everyone wants. There are different answers to the question, Who is responsible? Some favor socialized programs: they argue that government involvement in daily life leads to long-term social gain for everyone. Others insist that the essence of democracy is individual responsibility and choice, which is threatened by mandatory government programs.

Money is also an issue. Not everyone believes that funding these programs is money well spent. Some costs can be passed on to state or local authorities, or the user (as in medical copays), or donations (nonprofits). Still, each program adds to the national deficit, which has grown so large that it is almost meaningless to the common person. What are the consequences of the deficit? Whatever they are, the government has, so far, been able to continue.

There is a satisfaction in "digesting" the problems and examining the stand of the various players. That is my goal here in presenting these issues. For each problem that is addressed, a solution suggested by one advocate group is presented. All the solutions examined favor large-scale government programs. This does not imply that these are the best or only solutions. They were selected because they add something to the discussion. (1) Physicians for a National Health Program highlights the fact that doctors too face difficulties in the health care system; hence, they favor a nationalized program. (2) The National Committee to Preserve Social Security and Medicare is one of the optimistic voices on the scene at the moment, arguing for the viability of Social Security—a view that sometimes gets drowned out. (3) Legal Momentum advocates for those who fell through the cracks in the current welfare system (TANF). Because their need is so great, one can almost forgive Legal Momentum's dramatization of the extreme poverty rates. (4) Also recommended is the Gray Panthers. They take an insightful if not strident defense of the federally run Medicare program. Their ardent lobbying has earned them a place at the negotiating table.

No ultimate solutions are given. Negotiations will continue beyond the particulars presented here. Readers are encouraged to research other solutions, and to discuss their strengths and weaknesses. The chapter also includes an analysis (with an aim to understand, not judge the success) of the solution of one health care advocate group, Physicians for a National Health Program, using the analytical tools presented in Section I. Additional advocate groups are given for each of the four problems.

## ∷ HEALTH CARE

*Health is a state of complete physical, mental and*
*social well-being and not merely the absence of disease or infirmity.*

PREAMBLE TO THE CONSTITUTION OF THE WORLD HEALTH ORGANIZATION
AS ADOPTED BY THE INTERNATIONAL HEALTH CONFERENCE, NEW YORK,
SIGNED ON JULY 22, 1946, BY THE REPRESENTATIVES OF SIXTY-ONE STATES
AND ENTERED INTO FORCE ON APRIL 7, 1948.

The definition has not been amended since 1948.

Around the world people today are healthier and wealthier, and live longer than thirty years ago (World Health Organization 2008). The improvements are even more dramatic when compared with the early 1900s, when the average American lived only forty-seven years. Today the average life span is 77.9 (CDC 2010). However, when the health of people in the United States is compared to those elsewhere, the picture is not so good. Regarding life expectancy, the United States ranks fiftieth, putting it in the lower third of developed countries.

In the Virgin Islands it is 79.05 years, in Canada it is 81.23 years, and in Macau—which has the highest life expectancy—it is 84.36 years (CIA 2009a).

Another indicator of a nation's health is its infant mortality rate.[1] At 6.29 per year, the United States is forty-fourth.[2] In comparison, Cuba's rate is 5.82, United Kingdom's is 4.85, Korea's is 4.26. In Singapore—the country with the lowest infant mortality—it is 2.31 per year (CIA 2009b).

### Medical Tourism

Despite this low international ranking, many Americans believe that we have the best medical care in the world—the most highly skilled doctors, the best-equipped hospitals, and the most advanced medical treatments. In the past, people around the world came to prestigious U.S. health facilities, such as the Mayo Clinic, to get treatments they couldn't get anywhere else. But today, Americans are traveling to lower-income countries for medical treatment. Medical tourism is a growing industry, featuring less expensive dental, medical, or surgical treatment in places such as Mexico, India, Thailand, Costa Rica, or Turkey. Despite travel costs, lack of insurance, and increased health risks, this is an attractive option (Hareyan 2009).[3]

### Cost of Health Care

Medical tourism points to the biggest health care problem today—expense. Costs have more than doubled since 1990, becoming approximately 16 percent of the economy (Kirkpatrick 2009). Since the 1960s, the average increase per year is more than 10 percent. Half of that increase comes from the complexities of medicine (Greenburg 1982) and new technologies (CT, MRI, organ transplants, and new drugs). The other half comes from increased needs of an aging population, fraudulent claims, malpractice lawsuits, and unnecessary tests recommended by doctors practicing defensive medicine (McBride 2002). Other

---

1. The number of deaths per 1,000 live births.

2. According to calculations by the WHO, the United States is thirty-seventh.

3. Increased health risks include lower standards of health care, increased risks from alternative health care practices, plus the increased travel risk to some countries.

analysts blame the for-profit system, which leads to rising insurance prices (Brownstein 2009), unpaid medical bills (Hunt 2009), and lack of competition among hospitals (Dafny 2008; Nelson 2009; Thomasson 2002).

### Insurance Industry

Rising costs have made the insurance industry a dominant force in health care. The first health insurance was a prepaid hospital plan offered by Baylor University in Dallas in 1929. Health insurance benefits became popular during World War II as compensation for wage controls. Ten years after the war, nearly 70 percent of the country had some form of health insurance (Blue Cross Blue Shield Association 2009; McBride 2002).

Today the cost of insurance is itself an issue. In 2008, the average cost for private health insurance, which 66.7 percent of the population had, was $12,680 per family (U.S. Census). Most families (58.5 percent) have employer-paid insurance, but even so, costs are rising. High deductibles that lower insurance costs for companies are commonly $1,000 or more annually. Out-of-pocket expenses have also increased and insurance covers less and less (Abelson 2008).

Some analysts believe that insurance companies are actually causing the rise in health costs. A total of $300 billion a year, or approximately 15 percent of all medical expenditures, goes to payment processing (LeCuyer and Singhal 2007). The lack of competition is also a problem. There are about 1,300 companies nationwide, but in sixteen states, one company has half (or more) of the insurance policies (Brownstein 2009). Industry peculiarities are another factor. Managed care systems were introduced in the 1970s to control medical costs, but increased administration actually added costs. Income tax exemptions are a third factor. They led to increased premiums and, again, increased costs (McBride 2002).

### Uncollected Bills and For-Profit Hospitals

A total of 46.3 million people in the United States, or 15.4 percent of the population, had no health insurance at all in 2008 (U.S. Census).[4] In Texas the

---

4. There are three government programs for adults who need assistance. Medicaid is for the poor, Medicare is for the elderly, and veterans programs are for former military per-

figure was even higher—one-quarter of state residents were uninsured in 2009 (Spangler 2009). An estimated 22 percent of those without health insurance were illegal immigrants (U.S. Census). Even worse off were those with serious health problems or chronic illnesses whose conditions made insurance prohibitively expensive, and yet, prior to the health care reform, they didn't qualify for government assistance. As a result, they tended to forgo or delay medical treatment, which often exacerbated their condition (Tu and Cohen 2009).

In 2007, about 20 percent of the families in the United States couldn't pay their medical bills, and 20 percent of them considered bankruptcy as a solution (Cunningham 2008). Sixty-two percent of the bankruptcies that year were due to illness and medical bills (Himmelstein et al. 2009). In 2009, health care costs were a contributing factor in an estimated 800,000 bankruptcies.

**TABLE 5.1. FAMILIES WITH MEDICAL BILL PROBLEMS, 2003–2007***

|  | *2003 (%)* | *2007 (%)* |
|---|---|---|
| Total US | 15.1 | 19.4 |
| Age 65+ | 6.9 | 7.9 |
| Insured <65 | 14.3 | 18.3 |
| Uninsured <65 | 27.2 | 34.4 |

*Difference between 2003 and 2007 is statistically significant at p <.05.

*Sources*: HSC 2003 Community Tracking Study Household Survey; HSC 2007 Health Tracking Household Survey.

When people can't pay, the costs are borne by others. Doctors and hospitals say the number of unpaid bills is increasing. For instance, in 2007, Texas doctors averaged $85,000 in uncollected bills and gave out an additional $48,000 in charity services. Texas hospitals were unable to collect $5.3 billion (out of $130 billion in total patient charges) and gave out $7 billion in charity services (Hunt 2009). Increased fees commonly offset that revenue.

---

sonnel. There are also state-run programs for children, SCHIP (State Children's Health Insurance Program). These programs serve 29 percent of the population, or 87.4 million people. Medicaid serves 14.1 percent of the population (42.6 million), and Medicare serves 13.8 percent of the population (41.4 million) (U.S. Census).

Hospitals have become dominant players, as well. Some analysts argue that as businesses, they don't have the competition they need. Sixty percent of the for-profit hospitals with little or no competition generate up to three times more profit. A higher profit comes from higher patient costs and more insurance (Dafny 2008; Nelson 2009; Thomasson 2002).

### Complementary Medicine and New Directions in Health Care

The medical system in this country is, by and large, regulated by the American Medical Association (AMA), a professional organization of doctors that was founded in 1847. The AMA works with the state to license practicing physicians and other medical practices.

A lot of the world's traditional medicine would be considered complementary or alternative medicine in the United States. For instance, the dominant Western model is that a patient is a sick person, whereas other approaches focus on keeping people well. In the West, healing practitioners such as herbalists, midwives, chiropractors, osteopathic physicians, and masseurs were squeezed out as the medical profession developed (Eskinazi 1998). Today, however, many in the United States are dissatisfied with the Western approach, and some 33 percent of Americans seek out complementary or alternative medicines.

In 2007, Americans spent a total of $33.9 billion (11.2 percent of their out-of-pocket medical spending) for alternative practices such as meditation, yoga, chiropractic care, and alternative therapies, as well as herbal supplements. The amount spent on natural products such as fish oil, glucosamine, and Echinacea was $14.8 billion, or more than 33 percent of out-of-pocket prescription drug spending. The amount spent on alternative practitioners such as acupuncturists, chiropractors, massage therapists, homeopaths, and hypnotists was $11.9 billion—a quarter of what was spent on doctors. The 38 million people who visited alternative practitioners spent an average of $122 on their visits (NCCAM 2009; Marchione and Stobbe 2009).

Western doctors have come to accept these treatments as effective in particular situations. In some cases, insurance companies will pay for them (Jonas 1996). Recognizing the importance of alternative approaches to health care, Congress created the Office of Alternative Medicine in 1992, which is housed in the National Institutes of Health.

### Quality of U.S. Health Care

The quality of health care in the United States compared to its cost is a major concern. We pay more for health care than people in other countries—twice as much in many cases. The average American spent $6,714 on health care in 2008, which is 15.3 percent of the U.S. GDP (WHO 2009). And yet the United States ranks thirty-seventh (out of 191 countries) in overall health, after Europe, four Latin American countries, and five Middle Eastern countries (WHO 2000). Those top ranked are France, Italy, Spain, Oman, Austria, and Japan. (Please see Table 5.2 for more comparisons.)

**TABLE 5.2.  HEALTH CARE STATISTICS OF THE TOP COUNTRIES, CANADA AND THE UNITED STATES**

| | Population | Gross National Income per person | M/F Life Expectancy at birth | Prob dying <5 (per 1000 live births) | M/F Prob dying age 15-60 (per 1000) | Spending on health per person | Spending on health % of GDP |
|---|---|---|---|---|---|---|---|
| France | 61,330,000 | $32,240 | 77/84 | 5 | 124/57 | $3,554 | 11.1% |
| Italy | 58,779,000 | $28,970 | 78/84 | 4 | 83/44 | $2,623 | 9.0% |
| Spain | 43,887,000 | $28,200 | 78/84 | 4 | 105/44 | $2,388 | 8.1% |
| Oman | 2,546,000 | $19,740 | 72/77 | 11 | 160/90 | $ 382 | 2.3% |
| Austria | 8,327,000 | $36,040 | 77/83 | 4 | 105/51 | $3,545 | 9.9% |
| Japan | 127,953,000 | $32,840 | 79/86 | 4 | 89/44 | $2,514 | 7.9% |
| Canada | 32,577,000 | $36,280 | 78/83 | 6 | 89/55 | $3,672 | 10.0% |
| US | 302,841,000 | $44,070 | 75/80 | 8 | 137/80 | $6,714 | 15.3% |

*Source:* World Health Organization, 2008.

### Health Care Problems Worldwide

Interestingly, other countries face many of the same problems found in the United States. The health economy is growing faster than GDP everywhere—a 35 percent increase in health expenditures between 2000 and 2005 (WHO 2008). Patient poverty—because of health care bills—affects some 100 million people annually. Worldwide, there is also an increase in hospital acquired infections, and care that is too specialized, too short-term, or too commercial. Some problems common elsewhere are *not* found in the United States. The black market, corruption, and bribery are not big issues here, and medical professionals do not seek other income because they are underpaid (WHO 2000). WHO emphasizes preventive health and primary health care, and recommends universal health care coverage worldwide (WHO 2008).

### Medical Systems

Countries around the world have different systems to provide health care. Most systems have some level of government involvement, although one must be careful about overgeneralizing government participation in health care. One extreme is health care that is government owned and operated with all medical practitioners being government employees. These were originally found in socialist societies, such as China, Cuba, and the former Soviet Union. The other extreme is private health care institutions and providers, with little or no government involvement. This has been the situation in the United States until recently. Most systems are somewhere in between, with some government involvement and some market forces. We will look at four different systems.[5]

---

5. The typology here is roughly equivalent to that of T. R. Reid in *The Healing of America: A Global Quest for Better, Cheaper, and Fairer Health Care*, although the countries associated with each differ slightly.

 1. The Beveridge model, named after William Beveridge, a social reformer who inspired the UK National Health Service. In this system health care is financed and provided by the government through taxes. There are no medical bills. Hospitals are owned by the government and doctors are government employees. There are also private doctors. Countries with this system are the United Kingdom, Spain, Italy, Scandinavia, and Hong Kong.
 2. The national health insurance model found in Canada. The providers of health care are private, and the payer is the government-run insurance program, which collects premiums and pays the bills.
 3. The Bismarck model, named after Otto von Bismarck, who invented the welfare state as part of the unification of Germany in the nineteenth century. Health care providers and payers are private. Private health insurance is nonprofit and everyone is covered. It is financed by employers and employees. Doctors have their own private business and hospitals are privately run, but medical services and fees are regulated as a cost control measure.
 4. The out-of-pocket model found in undeveloped countries—Africa, India, China, and South America. The rich get good care, the poor stay sick or die.

Reid contends that the U.S. system has elements of all four systems: the Bismarck model for working people with health insurance provided by employers; the Beveridge model for Native Americans, military personnel, and veterans; the National Health Insurance model for those on Medicare; and the out-of-pocket model for the 45 million or so uninsured.

### Government Owned and Managed Systems

Sometimes called socialized medicine, these systems were once found in the former Soviet Union and China, although market systems now operate in both. Problems encountered in a government owned and managed health care system include wait times, rationing, restrictions on physician choice, and treatment choices (Tanner 2008).

Prior to the 1980s, China provided health care for rural areas by means of "barefoot" doctors—school graduates with some first aid training. This program dramatically increased the country's life expectancy in the 1950s, 1960s, and 1970s. Economic reforms moved China's health care system to a free market model. The burden of paying for health care then fell to local governments, rural hospitals, and clinics. They passed the fees on to individual patients, who, in turn, found it difficult to pay (Fourney 2003). Lack of coordination of government pricing and other organizational policies led to substantial problems across the country in the 1990s. However, the overall health status of the Chinese people did not decline, possibly as a result of improved nutrition, clean water, and education (Hsiao 1995). In 2009 the Chinese government announced a major new plan to reform its health care system with a goal of providing coverage to 90 percent of the population by 2011 (Wang 2009).

The former Soviet Union established a state-run health care system in all of its eighty-nine associated states, with the government paying for medical school, health facilities, and health services. It never actually achieved its goal of universal, free access to equal quality basic health services in each state. The rural areas, in particular, were underserved, but still basic care was provided. Since the break-up of the Soviet Union, the newly independent countries have struggled to maintain existing services (Balabanova et al. 2004). Russia itself has not maintained the same level of health care as indicated by life expectancy and so on. Its current system is underfunded and disorganized, with a shortage of general practitioners. Russians used to the government-run program don't have faith in the current system, but must pay 30–50 percent of the costs. Badly needed reforms are unlikely to occur in the near future (Vienonen and Vohlonen 2001; Rosenfeld 1995).

Cuba is one country that still has a government owned and run health care system. It has raised the health standards in general. Today it ranks fourth among Latin American countries, but ranked thirty-ninth on the WHO world health index in 2000 (the United States ranked thirty-seventh). Its successes come from a focus on public health interventions. There is mandatory HIV testing and treatment, education of children about HIV and sexually transmitted diseases, as well as a vaccination program for TB and other common diseases. As a result of these measures it has a relatively low incidence of HIV and TB, and a low birth rate. It has one of the best doctor/patient ratios in the world, which means each patient gets attention, including doctor visits to the home. The country also focuses on nonmedical determinants of health, especially sanitation and literacy among women, which has reduced infant and maternal mortality (Dosani 2009).

### Single Payer System

A single payer system is more common than government owned and run health care. In this approach, the government pays for everyone's health, a kind of government insurance. Doctor bills and health care needs are paid with revenue from taxes and fees collected from the patient. The government also sets prices for services. Some single payer systems have a way for individuals to opt out.

The United Kingdom has a more centralized health care system than most. The British government pays most health care costs with small copays for prescription drugs and dental care. Doctors and nurses are government employees. But in recent years, UK health care costs have exceeded the National Health Service budget. Hospitals have fixed spending levels that determine the number of patients they can serve. As a result, there are long waiting lists for admission, and the government has imposed a mandatory wait time for treatment in an attempt to control costs and to ensure that efficient hospitals are not overrun. There are also waiting lists for specialists, most of whom are not available nights or weekends because of salary cuts. Expensive procedures and technologies are rationed, with the result that some people are denied treatment. About 10 percent of Britons have health insurance that gives them access to speedier service and greater choice of doctors (Tanner 2008).

Canada also has a single payer system. The government acts like an insurance company funneling money through the provincial (or state) governments that pay bills. Provinces have different health care programs, but all must meet certain conditions, such as universality, portability, accessibility, and nonprofit administration, to get federal money. Waiting lists are a major problem. There is less technology per person than in the United States and fewer doctors; Canadians spend $1 billion annually in the U.S. health care system. Many also have employer-provided private insurance, and most believe their system needs major revision (Tanner 2008). Still, according to analysts, the Canadian system is not better or worse than our own, but performs differently (Docteur and Berenson 2009). Neither country ranks in WHO's top 10 (Canada is thirtieth and the United States is thirty-seventh).

### Managed Competition

Many European countries and Japan have a system whereby health care is private but regulated by the government. Individuals choose their own insurance providers (Tanner 2008).

France, ranked number one in health care according to WHO in 2000, has basic universal health insurance. Mostly this is provided at work, but benefits and reimbursements are regulated.[6] (The unemployed have a separate fund.) Patients pay the bills and are reimbursed, but those with debilitating conditions such as cancer, heart disease, and diabetes pay nothing. Health care provider charges are regulated, so doctors earn less in France than in the United States ($55,000 versus $146,000 for a primary care physician). But medical school is free, malpractice suits are strictly controlled, and the state pays two-thirds of a doctor's social security tax (up to 40 percent of income). French citizens are largely happy with their health care system, but the rising costs may present problems in the future (Tanner 2008).

Japan, also highly ranked by WHO, has a similar system, with four different groups. Two employer programs (one for large companies and another for small, particular industry companies) pay premiums through reduced wages. Plans for the self-employed and retirees are administered by municipal governments. The elderly have a special fund that draws from the other three. Benefits are generous, but there are significant copays. The average out-of-pocket family cost is $2,300 annually.[7] Hospitals are private but regulated and have salaried doctors. Nonhospital doctors are regulated. Analysts conclude that healthy

---

6. Employers pay 12.8 percent of the wages for each employee, and the employee pays another 0.75 percent, for a total cost of 13.55 percent of wages.

7. This is 17 percent of total health care spending.

lifestyles account for the 25 percent lower health care spending per capita than in the United States. Another 15 percent is attributable to aggressive U.S. practices (too many unnecessary tests) (Tanner 2008).

### Free Market Competition

Until recently, the U.S. system was a consumer driven, direct fee for service system, where the patient selected the services he or she wanted and was responsible for payment. Insurance companies have taken over much of the cost, but ultimate responsibility lies with the individual. In most cases, insurance companies paid the doctor or the hospital directly, avoiding a reimbursement process. The U.S. system grew in the free market environment favored by many Americans. The underlying assumption was that the best way to distribute quality goods was to let the market regulate itself—have people pay for a desirable product. However, market forces have not created an optimal or even acceptable health care industry in the United States.

### *Discussion*

Rising health costs are a challenge everywhere. It is not clear if the systems that function well at present will be able to continue without changes. It is also worth noting that most systems have large nonprofit components, and the health care industry is regulated to keep the costs down. Many systems have centralized records that are more efficient than record keeping in the U.S. and reduce the possibility of treatment error. France's Carte Vitale is the best example so far: it is a card with a memory chip that the patient keeps to be read and added to by health care providers (Reid 2009). Finally, universal coverage and preventive care make a health care system cheaper and more effective.

### *Health Reform*

U.S. government programs such as Medicare, Medicaid, and health care for Native Americans, military personnel, and veterans function somewhat like the government run programs or single payer systems described above (see footnote 5). But the majority of the population faces high costs and, prior to the health care reform, many were uninsured. Other needed reforms include improved preventive care, improved record keeping, increased market access, prescription drug control, and medical malpractice reform. There are also the costs of maintaining a for-profit system, and a strong health industry presence in Washington, D.C. Pharmaceutical companies and others spent $263.9 million in the first half of 2009 (Center for Responsive Politics 2009).

The health industry played a role in defeating the managed care reform proposed by Hillary Clinton (then First Lady) and her team in the 1990s.[8] Some of the same players opposed the health care reform bill that finally passed in 2010. But Americans want reform, and some report that two-thirds want universal coverage (Rasmussen Reports 2009). More people are beginning to notice that we spend twice as much on health care and receive less than those in most other developed countries (Reid 2009).

In 2009 several health care reform bills came before the House and Senate, and in March 2010 the Affordable Care Act was finally passed.[9] Some of the major reforms are:

1. Everyone must have insurance. Those without insurance will not be covered until Medicare changes go into effect in 2014, the date that penalties for not having insurance also take effect.
2. Subsidies will be provided to help low-income persons pay for insurance.

---

8."The health insurance industry committed tens of millions of dollars to the famously effective 'Harry and Louise' TV ads, which began denouncing the 'Hillarycare' plan months before it was completed. The hospital industry, the drug industry, and many physicians groups joined the insurers in opposition. Business support began to crumble. Organized labor, angry at the Clinton White House because of the NAFTA free-trade agreement, was lukewarm at best. Liberal backing was tepid, because the compromise plan the Clintons came up with fell short of the single payer universal coverage plan that the left had expected from a Democratic president. Meanwhile, an important Republican strategist, Bill Kristol, circulated an influential memo saying that GOP political interests dictated defeat of the Clinton plan.By early 1994, when the Clintons abandoned their plan, the central ethical argument for universal health care coverage was nowhere to be heard" (Reid 2009, 182–183).

9. The Obama-Biden health care plan emphasized the following:

1. Lower costs using the following measures: increase competition in the insurance industry, prevent insurance waste and Medicare abuse, allow cheaper imported medicine and generic drugs, allow Medicare to negotiate drug costs, establish and use an electronic health information technology system, establish transparency of costs, reduce costs of catastrophic illnesses, emphasize disease prevention and management, ensure quality care, and reform medical malpractice.

3. No one is denied insurance due to a preexisting condition.
4. Young people can remain on their parents' policy until age twenty-six. This went into effect in 2011, as did ending lifetime caps and increasing coverage of preventive care.
5. Preventive services will have no copays, deductibles, or coinsurance.
6. An insurance marketplace exchange will be set up to allow people to compare rates. In the meantime, some local comparisons are on www .healthcare.gov.

But cost—to both individuals and government—remains a challenge. Government costs for the new health care bill are estimated to be $938 billion, adding to national deficit concerns (Smith 2009; Levey 2010).[10] And insurance companies became nervous about profits. Late in 2010, there were threats of higher premiums: 12–18 percent in Virginia, Wisconsin, and Iowa; 21 percent in New Mexico; 39 percent in California; and a whopping 56 percent in Michigan. But under the new law, at least 80 percent of the collected premiums must be spent on health care rather than on administrative expenses, salaries, or overhead (Jarvis 2010), and starting in 2011 insurance companies must publish rate increase justifications on their websites.

Not everyone is in favor of the Affordable Care Act. Republicans have vowed to repeal it, although it is unlikely they can under a Democratic president with veto power. Tactics include lawsuits filed by several states challenging the federal authority to require everyone to buy health insurance.[11] On

---

2. Provide affordable coverage for everyone by using the following measures: guaranteed eligibility, an exchange that offers insurance options (and provides comprehensive benefits, affordable premiums, simplified paperwork, easy enrollment, portability, quality and efficiency), tax credits for families and small businesses, employer contribution, required coverage for children, expansion of Medicaid and SCHIP, flexibility for state plans.

3. Promote prevention and strengthen public health by the following measures: worksite intervention to prevent illness, school-based health screening to address obesity, emergency response at workplace, individual and family activities/actions, coordination at federal, state, and local levels (Obama-Biden 2009).

10. Earlier estimates ranged from $829 billion to $2.5 trillion, or 17.3 percent of all spending in the United States.

11. The states include Alabama, Alaska, Arizona, Colorado, Georgia, Indiana, Idaho, Florida, Louisiana, Michigan, Mississippi, Nebraska, Nevada, North Dakota, Pennsylvania, South Carolina, South Dakota, Texas, Utah, and Washington.

the first step of the measure's journey through the court system, several state-level judges have ruled it unconstitutional. In late September 2011, the Obama administration filed an appeal with the Supreme Court to uphold the measure as being constitutional. The Justice Department (which filed the appeal) argued that similar challenges were made to the Social Security Act, the Civil Rights Act, and the Voting Rights Act. In each case, the challenges were unsuccessful. A ruling is expected in late 2012 (Vicini 2011).

### National Health Insurance: A Solution Proposed by the Physicians for a National Health Program

The health care bill does not specify a national health program, but some see it as the first step in that direction. It is worth looking at the arguments for such a program as a solution to some of the problems in the U.S. health care system today. One group that favors this alternative is the Physicians for a National Health Program (PNHP). Organized in 1987, it has more than 17,000 members and chapters. It advocates a single payer national health insurance, in which the public or a quasi-public agency organizes health financing, but delivery of care remains largely private. Access to comprehensive health care is a human right, it says, and should be provided to everyone in the United States whether employed or not, and regardless of previous medical conditions. Under its proposal, everyone would be covered for doctor, hospital, preventive, long-term care, mental health, reproductive health care, dental, vision, prescription drug, and medical supply costs. All patients would have their choice of doctors and hospitals, and doctors would "regain autonomy over patient care."

The PNCP faults our current for-profit, patchwork system of insurers, doctors, hospitals, and others in the medical industry. One-third of the money spent goes to the bureaucracy, which is so vast that doctors and hospitals need a staff to deal with it. Especially in the insurance industry, many expenses have nothing to do with health care: overhead, underwriting, billing, sales and marketing, huge profits, and exorbitant executive pay. Pursuit of profit should not be a part of the care-giving industry, it says. The complexities and expense of billing and administration can be minimized only with a government-run national health insurance, which will also eliminate disparities of race, ethnicity, social class, and region. Copayments and deductibles increase costs and endanger the health of the poor, decrease the use of vital services, discourage preventive care, and increase administrative costs. Eliminating this redundant paperwork would save $350 billion a year, it says. But allowing a private insurance industry to continue to function undermines the success of a nationalized program.

The model that it advocates is Medicare, which is currently more efficient than commercial insurers. Hospitals would be paid a monthly sum to cover operating expenses, the amount negotiated annually. The sum would be based on community need and would not cover marketing or excessive executive incomes. Major equipment purchases and renovation or construction of health facilities would come from the national health insurance budget, to be overseen by regional health planning boards composed of experts and community representatives.

In the PNHP proposal, long-term health care of disabled persons in nursing homes and elsewhere would be coordinated by a local agency with an annual budgetary allotment. Home and community-based services would be encouraged. All drugs and medical supplies would be paid for, based on a national formula. The government would negotiate with the drug companies and manufacturers. Whenever possible, the lowest cost medication would be selected. The PNHP would want additional reforms to address other problems in the pharmaceutical industry and prescribing practices.

All Americans would be issued an NHI card entitling them to receive care without copayments or deductibles (HMO option). Or they could use their card at a fee for-service practitioner, or any institution receiving a global budget.

The PNHP proposes that doctors be paid in one of three ways: (1) fee for service, set by a negotiated fee schedule; (2) salary from institutions such as hospitals, health centers, group practices, home care agencies; (3) salary from HMOs, group practices, and other institutions that are paid for outpatient, physician, and medical home care. It contends that a simple fee for service would reduce physicians' office overhead and simplify billing.

The PNHP claims that the total cost of its program would be a modest increase over what the government already spends. By its estimates, the government already pays for two-thirds of the total health spending in the United States when payment for public employees' private health coverage and tax subsidies to private insurance are included. The percentage of current spending by the government under its plan would be 85 percent. Additional funds would be raised through income taxes. Tax increases "would be more than offset by the elimination of insurance premiums and out-of-pocket costs."

The effect on corporate America would be a savings because its tax contribution to NHI would be less than current health costs. Hospital functioning would be more stable; nurses and other health workers would have a more humane and professional environment in which to work. The PNHP believes the end result would be improved health across the board.

Advocacy of the PNHP is mainly education, including speakers, forums, conferences, scholarly articles, and appearances on national television and news programs. The full proposal was published in *JAMA*, August 30, 2008 (290, 6). It can also be found at www//pnhp.org/publications/pnhp.proposals.php.

### Analysis

Analyzing health care from the point of view of PHNP, an advocate group, the six ingredients of the social problem are:

*Target Group/Situation:* The PNHP sees at least three victim groups and situations: First, the uninsured who do not have access to adequate health care.

Second, those with health insurance who pay exorbitant prices for inadequate care, with much of what is paid going to overhead and other non-health costs.

Third, physicians and health care workers who, in the current system, are not happy with their work because they have to spend unnecessary time on administrative work, and thus cannot treat patients the way they think best.

*Ameliorating Action:* Its solution is to establish a single payer system (probably the government), which would redress problems faced by all three target groups. Those who do not currently have access to affordable health care would have access. And doctors and health care workers would be free to practice their own profession.

*Action Group:* Implementation of its program would obviously fall to the government. Legislation is implied on a very broad scale. The steps needed to implement this solution are not specified. One big omission is the fate of the many persons currently employed by the insurance industry. While it advocates against insurance involvement in health care, to eliminate a whole segment of an industry in one fell swoop would be dramatic and likely involve additional governmental costs as well. Another omission is any sort of time frame. Once its solution were enacted into law, how long would it take to be set in motion? And how would the changes be made? These are not insurmountable omissions, but not including them makes the proposal somewhat less realistic.

*Will to Act:* There is obviously a problem with the will to act. The group itself (PNHP) has been inspired sufficiently to lobby for this course of action. But whether there would be enough support for this proposal to be enacted into law is doubtful, at least at this time. There are many who would support this plan, but many others would strongly oppose it. Its proposed solution—a single payer system—is at one end of the spectrum of possible solutions, which largely explains the opposition. Still, bringing this approach into the arena of public debate helps clarify the issues and shift public opinion toward government involvement.

*Why Did the Problem Develop?* The PNHP appears to point to development as a major reason. It characterizes the current health care system as "patchwork," implying that there is no overall coordination to fit the individual pieces together harmoniously. Excessive bureaucracy and administration come from development. But "huge profits and exorbitant executive pay" would fall under self-interest—a second reason.

*Level of Social Problem:* The PNHP is obviously tackling this at a national level, although it advocates local agencies and community-based solutions, particularly for the disabled.[12]

## About the Group

*Type of Advocate Group:* The PNHP is a special interest group in that it is well organized and seeks action through institutional means. Its diverse members and

12. U.S. health care reform is national. But an examination of health care systems worldwide suggests that it is an issue that will soon need to be addressed on a larger scale.

supporters are unlikely to personally identify with the advocate group. Rather, it is likely to be something that they believe in and contribute to furthering.

*Why Did the Advocate Group Form?* Desire for structural reform describes the doctors who are frustrated with the health care system. Their solution contains elements of deprivation or relative deprivation in that they are advocating for the welfare of those without health insurance. Reformation capacity also explains the efforts that this advocate group has made so far to present itself and its cause to a larger public. It has a well organized web page, many well researched papers, and high status speakers available to those who are interested. This group has both money and expertise available to be effective.

*View of Human Nature:* Assumes both greater good human being and a rational human being. It sees the government and powerful parties currently pulling the strings in the health care system as rational humans: changes don't happen without laws being passed. In other words, those in power are not going to give up their advantages unless they are forced to do so. The recipients of the health care services, on the other hand, are more characterized as the greater good human beings, in that they would want what they can get but are willing to adjust to what is available so that others can also get what they need. This is also how the group sees itself—not excessively self-interested nor overly altruistic, although its position—that the health care industry should not be for profit, and that doctors should be paid a salary or fixed fees—requires some amount of sacrifice. This view of human nature is common among those who favor the Marxian model of change.

*Dynamics of the Advocate Group:* The PNHP appears to be a traditionally led and organized group, with a strong leadership. It appears to have clear goals and is effective in the results, although in this case a nationalized health care system may be beyond its reach.

*Stage of Development of the Advocate Group:* The PNHP appears to be in the coalescence stage of development. It has formulated its program, presented its cause, and is pursuing its goals. Either because it has not yet achieved its goal or it simply has not been organized long enough, it does not yet appear to be bureaucratic. But it has a fairly organized structure, in terms of both lobbying and finances. It has existed long enough to clarify its positions and establish methods of promoting its cause.


### Other Factors

*Claims Making:* The arguments of the PNHP are fairly convincing, and its information and data seem reliable and accurate. Given that its membership represents a very educated group (a high percentage of members are physicians and medical professionals), accurate information is to be expected. One obvious bias in its argument is use of the bandwagon technique—it makes it seem as if everyone feels as it does, which exaggerates its statements. It is impossible to know whether its cost calculations are correct or not.

As to opposition groups, there certainly are those. Despite indications that public opinion favors health reform and a majority want universal health coverage, a nationalized program is still controversial. In particular, conservative politicians are unlikely to appreciate its merits. Even though President Obama's health care bill was moderate, the Republicans vowed to repeal it. However, after that happened, there was a new move to work together with Democrats to develop alternatives.

*Consequences/Unintended Consequences:* Even though the health care reform bill has been passed, some of it may be reversed by future governments. Even with no major changes, it is not clear if implementation will bring the desired results. As mentioned, some see the bill as a first step toward a national health insurance that would cover *everyone* who does not receive assistance with health care costs. Whether national insurance is just a dream or a reality is to be seen.

*Type of Reform Sought:* Whether the reform sought is seen as reformative or transformative depends upon how one views the existing health care system. The best argument is probably for a transformative change, since it is seeking a significant change in the way that the whole health system is structured and run.

The model for social change that best fits its approach is probably a redesign model. Again, its proposal will require people to look at things and define things differently, in particular, the idea that the health care industry should not be for profit. This seems to be pointed at the insurance industry and the drug companies. But there are others in various sectors of health care who currently make a profit who would also be affected.

*Assessing the Overall Benefit:* The overall benefits of health care reform are positive despite the controversies and problems that sti exist. Since the PNHP proposal was not enacted into law, it is impossible to assess the results of that.

### ■ QUESTIONS FOR REVIEW

1. What are the main problems in the health care system of the United States?

2. Which of the four kinds of medical systems (government controlled and managed system, single payer, managed competition, free market competition) exists in the United States? Which groups of Americans have which kind of system?

3. How does the PNHP solution solve the problems in the U.S. health care system?

### ■ QUESTIONS FOR FURTHER THOUGHT

1. Why do you think the doctors in PNHP support a national health care system?

2. What ameliorating actions are proposed by other groups?

3. Who are the big winners and losers in the proposals?

4. What government legislation is required for the different proposals?

5. What are the financial investments of the different proposals?

6. Which proposal do you favor? Why?

### ■ OTHER ADVOCATE GROUPS

Alliance for Health Reform
American Association of Retired Persons (AARP)
Center for Studying Health System Change
Health Care for America Now (HCAN)
Health Care Now
Kaiser Family Foundation

## ▓▓ SOCIAL SECURITY

Social Security is the government stipend paid to 58.7 million people—retired people, surviving spouses and minor children, and disabled.[13] It is the primary source of income for 64 percent of the recipients, and the only income for about 33 percent of the recipients. Since its inception in 1935, it has successfully reduced poverty among those over age sixty-five from 30 percent in 1965 to 10 percent or less (about 3.6 million). It has also reduced poverty among the disabled and young children of deceased workers (Sloan 2000).

Social Security was started in response to severe nationwide poverty. It was one of several government programs enacted by Franklin D. Roosevelt during the Great Depression. Its enactment was controversial with many doubting they would ever see anything of the $60 a year they paid. Today the average annual contribution is about $4,000, and the average monthly benefit is $1,072.[14] At an annual $600 billion, Social Security has one of the biggest budgets in the government.[15] (Over 420 million different Social Security numbers have been issued, with no numbers repeated.)

To avoid being seen as a government handout, Social Security was set up to look like a government trust fund created from funds paid into it.[16] But its

---

13. 5.2 million are nonretired, disabled recipients who receive Supplemental Security Income (Social Security Administration, www.ssa.gov, October 2010). In 2009, there were 36 million retired workers and their dependents, 6 million survivors of deceased workers, and 10 million disabled workers and their families (www.ncpssm.org/ss_primer).

14. Social Security taxes are 6.2 percent of a person's wages matched by an equal amount from the employer, or 12.4 percent for self-employed, with a maximum of approximately $12,000.

15. The cost to run the program since 1935 has been $1.2 trillion. Total collections over the years have amounted to $13.8 trillion; total payouts, $11.3 trillion. Amount of reserves held in government bonds today is $1.3 trillion (Social Security Administration, www.ssa.gov, October 2010).

16. "Almost everything about Social Security is an accident. Even something as fundamental as where the program is headquartered is a historical fluke. Social Security, the country's biggest domestic program, is in Baltimore rather than in Washington because when the Social Security Act was passed in 1935, federal bureaucrats couldn't find big enough digs to track the lifetime wage history of every American worker. But a former Coca-Cola bottling plant in downtown Baltimore was available. So Social Security set up its massive operations center there. Plans to move the whole show to Washington fell through in 1939

**FIGURE 5.1.** An early Social Security flyer.

*Source:* http://www.ssa.gov/history/check.html.

when its spanking-new headquarters building was commandeered by the War Department as part of the World War II buildup. So Social Security never left Baltimore, even though computers have long since superseded the filing cabinets.Understanding Social Security's quirky history is critical to understanding the program's current travails" (Sloan 2000).

assets—$1.3 trillion—are held in government Treasury bonds redeemed by borrowing or through other increasing revenue measures. In other words, practically speaking, the government has already spent the money collected, so that each year benefits are paid from Social Security taxes collected concurrently (Moynihan and Kerry 2000; Social Security Administration 2011).[17] The number of payers per single recipient has steadily declined from 41.9 in 1945 to 3.4 in 2000 and a projected 2.8 in 2015 and only 1.9 in 2075. Three factors contribute to the decline: a third of the recipients are survivors or disabled, people live longer today than they did in 1935, and baby boomers are beginning to retire. The fear is that in the future the amount collected from Social Security taxes will not be sufficient to pay the benefits.

There are different predictions as to how long the Social Security system will continue to pay benefits. It was an election issue in 2000, just as it was in 1936, with a popular, pessimistic view that by 2015 the government would have to borrow to pay benefits, and by 2020, there would be a $200 billion cash shortfall. But since then things seem to have improved. The Social Security trustees report in 2004 stated that benefits could be paid in full until 2044, and after that paid at 75 percent, allowing for inflation rises.

There have been changes over the years. In 1965, Medicare was added. In 1983, Social Security taxes were increased, the retirement age was set to gradually rise to sixty-seven, and benefits paid to high income retirees were taxed. In 2010 and in 2011 no automatic cost of living adjustments were given for the first time since the 1970s, when the measure to counter inflation was passed.

The optimistic view is that with these measures, Social Security is basically sound. The fewer numbers of payers into the Social Security system is offset by the fact that people today earn more. And tweaking tax and benefit levels, by increasing the age of retirement and perhaps trimming benefits to upper income persons, will keep the program working for many years.

Conservative, free market reformers would like to see a move toward privatization, putting all or some of Social Security taxes into individual savings/investment accounts. The most common proposal is that 2 percent of the taxes paid each year would go into an investment account. Similar to existing federal employee programs, individual taxpayers would choose between government

---

17. See another account from NCPSSM below.

bonds, corporate bonds, or a stock market index. The argument is that this will protect the system by encouraging young workers who would otherwise be pessimistic about their benefits.

Under the current system, benefits for high income workers are not that much more than for lower income workers, since it is the latter who most need additional retirement income. Opponents of privatizing measures point out that it benefits upper income workers more (2 percent of $150,000 is $3,000, whereas 2 percent of $30,000 is only $600). Other worries about privatization are that if anyone other than the government handles the accounts, too much would be paid in brokers' fees; in addition, the complexity of keeping records of all those accounts would be prohibitive. But even those who oppose privatization of Social Security are generally in favor of reforms such as raising the retirement age, lowering benefits, and/or taxing the benefits of the rich more heavily. In sum, liberals oppose privatization, conservatives favor it. Moderates accept some market investment but want to see reforms that will increase benefits.

### Medicare and Medicaid

Both Medicare and Medicaid were established by the Social Security Act of 1965. Medicare provides medical care for the elderly. It functions like a national health insurance program. The recipients pay a premium and copays. It does not cover glasses, dental care, or long-term nursing home care, but the hospital insurance program is free (with a deductible and copay). About half of a recipient's total medical bills are paid by Medicare. Another 20 percent is covered by private insurance, and an estimated 20 percent is an out-of-pocket expense. Medicare is also available for people with disabilities. About 14 percent of the 42 million Americans receiving Medicare have disabilities (Kaiser Family Foundation 2005).

Medicaid provides medical care for lower income persons. It is funded by the federal government and state governments. There are five basic low income groups (some 25 different categories): children, pregnant women, adults in families with dependent children, individuals with disabilities, and individuals over sixty-five. Each state determines eligibility (with federal guidelines), and the amount and length of assistance available. There is another health care program for low income children not eligible for Medicaid: SCHIP, or State Children's Health Insurance Program. Set up in 1997, it too is funded by both federal and state governments and administered at the state level.

Both programs were initially administered by the Social Security Administration. In 1977, they were transferred to the Health Care Financing Administration, which in 2001 became the Centers for Medicare and Medicaid Services (CMS). Today, the CMS, still based in Baltimore, administers three other programs as well: SCHIP, HIPAA (Health Insurance Portability and Accountability Act of 1996: health insurance for people who lose their jobs), and CLIA (Clinical Laboratory Improvement Amendments, which regulates laboratory testing on humans).

More than 87 million people received Medicaid and Medicare in 2004, at a total cost of $602 billion. Approximately half the total amount goes to Medicare—$297 billion—and half to Medicaid—$305 billion (Kaiser Family Foundation 2005).[18]

### Medicaid Issues

The financial burden of Medicaid on state budgets has grown over the years. It is the second largest budget item in many states.[19] Increasing numbers of persons with economic difficulties make states fearful of being able to cover rising Medicaid costs. In seventeen states, 25 percent or more of the population receives Medicaid (Kaiser Family Foundation 2005). The 2010 health care bill set performance standards to receive federal money (HHS 2010; Schwartz 2011), including enrolling all uninsured and nonelderly in or near poverty. This has led some governors to seek more federal responsibility. Twenty states have joined in a lawsuit to protest what some analysts call an "unmanageable financial burden" (Anrig 2010).

After the 1996 reform to welfare (the Personal Responsibility and Work Opportunity Reconciliation Act), legal resident aliens were barred from receiving Medicaid for the first five years in this country (except for emergency services).

---

18. A third of Medicaid patients are elderly or disabled. They account for two-thirds of its annual expenditures. They are too poor to pay for their medicine, even with assistance from Medicare.

19. In Colorado in 2011, it will be 10 percent of the state budget (Schwartz 2011).

There were also concerns about eligible persons not enrolling in Medicaid. In 2008, about 12 million eligible people were not enrolled in either Medicaid or SCHIP. Some argued that administering Medicaid, like Medicare, on the federal level would resolve many issues (Anrig 2010). The government would be expected to spend $1.6 trillion on Medicaid from 2014 to 2019, and more excess would be eliminated from central administration than the current system mandates.

### Medicare Issues

There have been several changes to Medicare since it was instituted.[20] The Medicare Modernization Act of 2003 addressed the issue of prescription drugs. The elderly spend more on drugs than other segments of the population.[21] Prior to 2003, they paid up to five times the rate of inflation for prescription medicines (Walsh 1999).[22] Even those with private insurance were paying $1,000 to $2,500 a year for medicine (Issues 2000). Many seniors and others resorted to buying their medicines in Canada. Minnesota Senior Federation, founded in 1973, arranged visits to Canadian doctors and pharmacies. Internet pharmacies were also set up. The U.S. Customs Service reported in 2001 that $1 million of medicine was shipped to the United States from Canada (Teichert 2002). This traffic declined after 2003 (Weil 2004; Wolfe 2010).

The Medicare Modernization Act was not flawless, however. The so-called donut hole (gap in drug coverage) has been corrected (Bihari 2010).[23] But the difficulty of selecting a drug coverage company from approximately forty different, competing companies is confusing. Still, drug costs for seniors have

---

20. An unpopular reform, the Medicare Catastrophic Coverage Act (MCCA) concerning hospitalization and hospice care, was passed in 1988 and soon repealed.

21. The elderly consume 30 percent of prescription drugs and make up 14 percent of the population (Walsh 1999).

22. Pharmaceuticals have a profit margin of 28 percent—three times that of other industries. Generic drugs, which account for about half of the prescriptions, make up only 10 percent of total drug spending. Drug companies counter generic drug sales with advertising to get brand loyalty (Walsh 1999).

23. Prescription drugs are covered up to a total copay of $2,840. At that point, the recipient pays 100 percent of the drugs to $4,550. After that, Medicare pays most of the cost. This flaw made many critical of the legislation, but it has been addressed and will be corrected in a few years. In 2010, people in the donut hole were given a $250 rebate. In 2011, they will be given a 50 percent discount on drugs purchased "in the gap." In future years they will pay only 25 percent of the cost of drugs "in the gap" (Bihari 2010).

been reduced to an average premium of $30 a month. And the competition has saved the government some $261 billion in five years (Matz 2010).

Proponents are nervous about the ramifications of the effect of the 2010 health care bill on Medicare. Part of the overall increased health costs are to be covered in part by decreased Medicare spending. If Medicare payments are lower than those of Medicaid, doctors and hospitals will withdraw from the Medicare program and reduce recipients' access to high cost technology such as PET scans (Goodman 2011).

### Keep Social Security As Is: A Solution Proposed by the National Committee to Preserve Social Security and Medicare

Formed in 1982 by the grandson of Theodore Roosevelt, the National Committee to Preserve Social Security and Medicare (NCPSSM) argues that Social Security will be increasingly important to America's well-being in the future; only half of the population has a 401(k) or other retirement fund, and the average savings account is only $70,000.[24] The group maintains a strong lobby presence in Washington and actively involves any and all who want to participate in its educational and lobbying efforts.

The Social Security Administration has met its obligations for seventy-five years, at a cost of less than 2 percent. It is not in crisis, the group argues. With "modest changes" it can continue indefinitely. Even without changes, it can pay full benefits until 2037, and 78 percent benefits for several decades thereafter.[25] The baby boomer bulge was adjusted for in 1983, and costs to Social Security will grow slightly. "As a proposition of the Gross Domestic Product (GDP), Social Security costs are projected to rise from under 5 percent in 2009 to just over 6 percent in 2034, and then drop back down to only 5.8 percent by 2050" (www.ncpssm.org).

---

24. www.ncpssm.org.

25. "Total income to the Social Security Trust Fund from payroll taxes in 2009 was $819 billion and total expenditures (benefits and other expenses) were $683 billion, resulting in a surplus of $137 billion. The Trust Funds were credited with $116 billion in interest from earnings, which represented an effective annual rate of return of 5.1 percent. Surpluses over the past two decades built up the assets in the trust funds to $2.2 trillion at the end of 2009. These surpluses will continue for the next decade, increasing the asset amount to more than $3.9 trillion by 2018" (www.ncpssm.org/ss_prime).

The group also takes issue with the idea that revenue to pay Social Security benefits is increasingly coming from fewer and fewer workers. Government bonds, where most of the surplus is being held, are sound and amount to $2.6 trillion. The government has never failed to repay bonds to an investor when they come due. So the Social Security Administration has reason to believe its money is secure.

The NCPSSM notes that Social Security is particularly important to women: they live longer, work for lower wages, have fewer years in the workforce, and are less likely to have pensions and other savings. The group also opposes raising the retirement age, since lower income persons, who need Social Security the most, have not increased in longevity as much as higher income persons. And those with physically demanding jobs—nursing care, janitorial jobs, outdoor service jobs, waitressing, or other jobs that involve standing on one's feet all day—may not be physically able to continue past a certain age. Further, there are fewer job openings for an elderly blue collar or service worker.

The NCPSSM opposes privatization of Social Security because it would give higher income persons more benefits and would increase administrative costs, since Wall Street would charge much more than the 2 percent the Social Security Administration has used to run the program. It notes that 96 percent of Americans believe the money they contributed to Social Security is "their" money, and that Social Security is not a major cause of the current deficit. Hence, its argument is that privatizing Social Security would divert funds from benefits and create a need for higher taxes in the long run.

The NCPSSM opposes most of the proposed changes suggested in the December 2010 report from the National Commission on Fiscal Responsibility and Reform.

1. *A 2011 Payroll Social Security Tax Holiday*: The NCPSSM opposes it on the grounds that it is better not to change the way Social Security works, while admitting that there is enough money to make such a cut and still pay full benefits in 2011.[26]

---

26. By their figures, estimated income to Social Security in 2011 is $732 billion; total cost of the program, benefits and administration, is $729.6 billion. There is an additional $118 billion interest income to Social Security.

2. *Reduce the Cost of Living Adjustments (COLAs)*: The NCPSSM does not think COLAs should be indexed to spending substitutions. Such linkage would reduce benefits by 0.3 percent a year. Because of rising health care costs, retired persons' cost of living increases are actually underestimated already.[27]

3. *Raise the Retirement Age*: The NCPSSM does not want to see the retirement age raised from its current level of sixty-six (to rise to 67 by 2022). The longevity of lower income men has not increased to the same extent as it has for upper income men, and has actually gone down for lower income women. Further, lower income jobs are often physically demanding, and such workers are less able to continue past the current retirement age, if jobs for them even exist.[28]

4. *Change the Benefit Formula*: Currently the monthly Social Security benefit is 90 percent of the average monthly income up to $761.32, 32 percent on additional earnings up to $4,586, and then 15 percent on earnings over that. The proposal is to change the formula to 90 percent, 30 percent, 10 percent, and 5 percent. "This proposal is a benefit reduction pure and simple," the NCPSSM argues, and no one will benefit from the change.

5. *Eliminate All State And Local Government Programs* that currently exempt their workers from receiving Social Security.[29]

---

27. To offset this, the commission proposal includes a 5 percent boost to older retirees to begin twenty years after eligibility (age 85 or later). NCPSSM estimates that after twenty years Social Security benefits would be reduced by more than 6 percent.

28. Proposal is to raise it to 68 by 2050, and 69 by 2075; with early retirement raised to 63, and then 64. The commission proposed a hardship waiver for no more than 20 percent of retirees for those in physically demanding jobs. The NCPSSM believes that this would be difficult to administer.

29. In Ohio, Massachusetts, Louisiana, Nevada, Colorado, California, Alaska, Maine. Three other proposed changes are:

1. Index taxable maximum to 90 percent of wages. It has been set at 90 percent, but those in the upper income group had more growth in earnings, so now it is 82 percent. The NCPSSM doesn't seem to object to this one.

2. Increase the amount of the special minimum PIA. Today the minimum is $763.20. The proposed minimum would be kept above the poverty threshold at 125 percent of poverty level, or $1,128 in 2009. Those with low wages would benefit.

3. Increase flexibility in applying for benefits: Proposed choice of collecting half benefits early and the other half later (for early retirees).

## ■ QUESTIONS FOR REVIEW

1. When was Social Security established, and why?

2. What early Social Security Administration change led to the problem of Social Security today?

3. What does it mean to privatize Social Security?

4. What is the argument to preserve Social Security as it is?

## ■ QUESTIONS FOR FURTHER THOUGHT

1. If there were no Social Security system in place, how would our society be different?

2. The wealthy pay more in Social Security tax; what benefits do they receive?

3. What are the dangers of privatizing Social Security?

4. What other ways does society have to take care of the elderly?

## ■ OTHER ADVOCATE GROUPS

Alliance for Retired Americans (ARA)

American Association of Retired Persons (AARP)

American Association of University Women (AAUW)

American Federation of Labor (AFL-CIO)

Cato Institute

Century Foundation

Commonwealth Fund

Democratic Party

Families USA

Gray Panthers

Heritage Foundation

Pharmaceutical Research and Manufacturers of America (PHRMA)

Public Citizen

Republican Party

The Seniors Coalition

## ⠿ WELFARE

Government assistance for the less fortunate has increased and changed in the last hundred years. Prior to the twentieth century, the needy relied on family, the local community, churches, and other charity groups. During the Depression, Franklin Roosevelt established the first big government assistance program in this country. The New Deal (1935) included Social Security and Aid to Dependent Children (ADC), a modest welfare program that later became Aid to Families with Dependent Children (AFDC). Medicare, Medicaid, and public housing were added in the 1960s.

By the late 1980s, it was obvious that the so-called welfare program needed reform. The system encouraged dependence on government assistance, critics said, and women had more children to get more money (assistance was given per child). There were other abuses. Reform measures were extensively debated. Congress finally agreed on a bipartisan effort in 1996: the Personal Responsibility and Work Opportunity Reconciliation Act. TANF (Temporary Assistance for Needy Families) replaced the earlier AFDC program. This new federally funded assistance program was to be administered at the state rather than federal level. Another change limited the amount of time a person could receive assistance to a total of five years over a lifetime. Further, states were mandated to assist recipients to find jobs and provide childcare for those who needed it.

TANF recipients are not automatically eligible for Medicaid.[30] Uninsured working parents who don't qualify can receive health care for their children through SCHIP, or State Children's Health Insurance Program, a program set up in 1997. Together with Medicaid, SCHIP covers close to 75 percent of uninsured children, including those in families with income above the poverty line (Dubay et al. 2007).

Some results of welfare reform are encouraging. States administer the programs that provide income security, health care, social services, and job training programs to low income persons.[31] Caseloads were cut in half by 2002

---

30. Only 14 percent of uninsured adults qualify for Medicaid, according to the Urban Institute. Unless otherwise noted, information in this section is taken from the three extensive follow-up studies conducted by the Urban Institute.

31. States collectively received $1.8 trillion in revenues and spent $2.1 trillion in fiscal year 2002.

(4.6 to 2.1 million families) and continued to decline (1.7 million in 2008, according to Legal Momentum). More than 50 percent of welfare recipients reported they were working in 2002, and deep poverty (income below 50 percent of federal poverty level) declined from 60 percent to 42 percent of the recipients. Child poverty rates dropped, with the percentage of poor children receiving welfare declining from 62 percent in 1995 to 24 percent in 2007 (US Census Bureau 2007). Similarly, the percentage of U.S. poverty declined from 15.1 percent (1993) to 12.7 percent (2004), but increased again to 14.3 percent in 2009 (Lower-Basch 2011).

Today, the government spends more than $130 billion a year on SCHIP, Medicaid, child care subsidies, and other support programs, including food stamps and the earned income tax credit (EITC), designed to help families stay off welfare. About 25 percent of those who were on welfare at one time continue to make use of these programs. Those who take advantage of the supports are less likely to return to welfare. But an estimated 33 percent of low income families receive none of these government supports. The reasons for not receiving assistance include not knowing the support is available or how to get it, and the stigma associated with receiving welfare assistance.

Not all the issues have been resolved and reform still has its critics. The bill's reauthorization in 2002 and again in 2005 required work stipulations for the welfare caseload (half of the recipients should work at least 30 hours a week, if there is adequate child care). But this increases paperwork for everyone and reduces flexibility (Lower-Basch 2011). Further, nearly half of the recipients (44 percent) have two or more barriers to work, including no high school diploma, language barriers, poor health, an infant or a disabled child at home, or no work experience in the recent past. Critics argue that there is not enough funding for vocational training, so the problems of those who lack education and work experience and have health problems are not addressed. Also, many of those who work have menial, low-paying jobs and may need assistance again in the future.

Further, child care subsidies for low income families have been problematic. Some states have long waiting lists for child care subsidy vouchers or certificates for the private market. In some cases, the subsidized care available doesn't meet developmental child care standards. There are also questions about the five-year time limit, and about families falling through the cracks. Those who leave the TANF program (after 5 years) are no longer tracked since they are out of the system. If they have no job or other support, they could be reduced to begging or crime, or become reliant on churches and other faith-based organizations that pick up the slack left by government programs.

Some faith-based organizations are concerned about extending the Emergency Fund, set up to cover additional needs during a recession.[32] Some question the cost motivations coming from state administrators, but the National Association of State TANF Administrators (NASTA) has published similar concerns. They recommend increasing recession money and increasing TANF generally in order to cover inflation costs. They also prefer more flexibility in administering the program, and other measures rather than work to assess their efforts (Casey 2011).

Congress did not reauthorize the bill as scheduled in 2010, but postponed action and discussion to September 2011.

### Reauthorize and Improve TANF:
### A Solution Proposed by Legal Momentum

Legal Momentum, an advocate group, is dedicated to the legal defense of the rights for women and girls.[33] It was started in 1970 as NOW (National Organization for Women) Legal Defense and Education Fund. Its New York and Washington, D.C., offices are mainly staffed by women. As stated in its objective, Legal Momentum pursues five areas of public policy relating to women: equal employment opportunities, workplace rights, strengthening the safety net for women, protecting victims of violence, and promoting gender equality.

The group would like to extend or eliminate the five year time limit and raise the financial eligibility criteria—currently set at 29 percent of the official poverty level. As it exists, TANF does not provide an adequate safety net for women who need assistance. The program success, measured by decreasing

---

32. The original 1996 bill provided $2.5 billion, which was used up in 2008–2009. An additional $5 billion was given under the American Recovery and Reinvestment Act of 2009, but it expired in September 2010 (Sisters of Charity Foundation of South Carolina 2010).
33. Information for this section comes from "The Bitter Fruit of Welfare Reform: A Sharp Drop in the Percentage of Eligible Women and Children Receiving Welfare," www.legal momentum.org/assets/pdfs/lm-tanf-bitter-fruit.pdf. Accessed January 20, 2011.

numbers on the welfare roles, is misleading. It claims that twelve out of fifteen welfare leavers earn less than poverty level, and 30–50 percent are unemployed within a few months after exiting. People are not "graduating" out of the program into financial stability. Rather they are falling into the street because of reduced eligibility. The number of single mother families (1.7 million) with incomes of less than $3,000 was 56 percent higher in 2004 than in 1995. An estimated 2.3 million families did not receive needed assistance in 2005, which has led to an increase in extreme poverty.

To increase success, Legal Momentum recommends increased federal oversight for state TANF administrators. Federal incentives for a reduced caseload encourage state administrators to push people out of the program and avoid the mandated work quotas. Many states have barriers for receiving TANF, including procedural requirements, misinformation, and denials unrelated to family need. Further, some state governments use the federal TANF money that comes unmarked with percent usage for the services that have public appeal (and win votes).

Legal Momentum also recommends changes in child care. Currently nonworking mothers are sanctioned when "appropriate" child care is available. But what is "appropriate" child care? Also, it would like to see all disabled children included in child care, as well as school age children during the summer months.

Legal Momentum would like to remove the denial of benefits to children, especially to those born into a TANF family, or whose mother is noncompliant. The combined benefits (including food stamps) should be raised to poverty level, at least. Immigrant victims of violence should be included, and "marriage promotions" that do not apply to parents who don't want to get married or to same-sex couples should be eliminated.

■ QUESTIONS FOR REVIEW

1. When was the first welfare program established in the United States? What was it called?

2. What were the criticisms of the welfare program prior to its reform in the 1980s?

3. How is TANF different from AFDC? Who receives aid? Who pays for it? Who administers the program?

## ■ QUESTIONS FOR FURTHER STUDY

1. What is the alternative to federal or state programs to assist people in need?

2. What are the problems of a welfare program?

3. Legal Momentum argues that women are "falling" into the street instead of "graduating" into responsible, working citizens. How can this be verified? If so, why are state and federal officials not taking note of this failure? If so, how can it be changed? Is there any exaggeration in Legal Momentum's claim? If so, why would the group exaggerate?

4. How do state and federal authorities have to work together in TANF? What are the difficulties of this cooperation? What are the advantages?

5. Do you think there are still people who take advantage of the system?

## ■ OTHER ADVOCATE GROUPS

Brookings Institution
Cato Institute
Heritage Foundation
National Center for Policy Analysis
Sisters of Charity Foundation of South Carolina
Urban Institute

# CHAPTER SIX

# PROBLEMS ADDRESSED THROUGH GOVERNMENT LEGISLATION

Laws are an important part of a peaceful society, and they play a role in addressing social problems, albeit often only *part* of a resolution. There is a danger of relying on laws over other means of social control (the means by which actions of individuals are controlled). Threat of punishment or physical force may bring order to a situation, but it doesn't necessarily bring peace or resolve the underlying issues. Sociologists would be quick to point out that social norms are another effective means of social control. Social norms are the unwritten rules of behavior found in every group or society. Convincing a person "it" is the right thing to do—whether by logic or by social acceptance—is sometimes more effective. Another important factor is individual self-restraint and discipline. Because of religion's effect on individual actions, early sociologist Emile Durkheim thought it was an important means of social control.

Not all problems can be addressed by government legislation. For example, eating disorders and alcoholism, as noted earlier, cannot be legislated, although contributing factors may be controlled. Additionally, sometimes passing a law actually creates additional problems, as happened during Prohibition.

With these caveats, then, we turn to problems that legislation can solve. As discussed in Chapter 3, laws are necessary to resolve the following situations: (1) when people resist change, (2) when the physical or social well-being of some part of the population is threatened, (3) when two or more groups have a conflict over values or territory, (4) when there is unequal distribution of resources, (5) when a group is discriminated against, (6) when there is profiteering. In some ways, all of these situations apply to discrimination and to illegal immigration. There has been more progress resolving discrimination than illegal immigration.

## ⠿ DISCRIMINATION

Discrimination—an action—can happen when two or more categories of people come together; members of one category (group) are treated differently. This usually means that one group has more resources, advantages, and power. Discrimination is associated with stereotypes and prejudice—which are attitudes. A *stereotype* is broad generalization about a category of people. It is usually exaggerated, is often derogatory (although there can be positive stereotypes, too), and evokes emotion. The belief that all African Americans are good at sports or music is a stereotype, for instance. So is the belief that all Asians are smart. A *prejudice* is an irrational judgment about individuals based on one or more stereotypes about the category of people to which he or she belongs. It is irrational because there is little or no empirical evidence to support the judgment of the individual, or to support the stereotype (Allport 1979). It is important to remember that, while discrimination and prejudice are found together, it is possible to be prejudiced and not discriminate. Similarly, it is possible to discriminate and not be prejudiced.

Discrimination and prejudice exist throughout society, but for some of the population it is a significant problem. Women, handicapped, religious and ethnic groups, gays and lesbians often receive differential treatment. Sociologists call these groups *minorities*—people with some physically distinguishing characteristics and a subordinate status in society (Wirth 1945). *Racism* is the belief that one racial category is superior. *Sexism* is the belief that one gender is superior. A category of people can be a minority even if they compose a majority of the population.

There are several theories about why stereotypes and prejudice develop. According to the scapegoat theory, people who are themselves disadvantaged may blame minorities for their problems (Dollard et al. 1939; Douglas 1995). Immigrants, for example, are often blamed for a variety of social ills (Scheer 2006).

A similar theory, the authoritarian personality, was developed by Adorno and colleagues (1950), who noticed that people who are prejudiced are often intolerant and rigid as well. They conform to conventional norms and authorities, and insist that others do the same. The theory is that these persons over-compensate for personal insecurity and project their own faults onto an "inferior" minority group.

A third theory is that stereotypes and prejudice come from the existing culture. The understanding and intimacy between groups differs (Park 1924). This social distance between groups can be measured. The Social Distance Scale (Bogardus 1933) ranges from 1 (complete acceptance of a group, including marriage) to 7 (complete rejection of a group, including barring members from entering the country). When the scale was first developed in 1926, the average social distance score between all groups was 2.14. In 1991, it was 1.76, indicating we are less prejudiced today as a society than we were eighty-five years ago (Bogardus 1958; Kleg and Yamamoto 1998).[1]

Last, the conflict theory explains prejudice in terms of societal stratification. People who are powerful and privileged are likely to use disadvantaged minorities for their own benefit and tend not to see their own role in their situation (Rothenberg 2008). For example, in Texas, and elsewhere, people hire illegal Mexican workers knowing they don't have to pay as much for their services.

To understand discrimination today, we need to look at the different types of discrimination.

### Institutional Discrimination

Prejudice is not desirable, but we cannot legislate against it. Discrimination, on the other hand, is illegal in some, but not all, situations; a society we are not yet fully aware of all the different kinds of discrimination (Wildman et al. 1996). One kind that is important to be aware of is institutional discrimination. This is when the traditions or regulations of an institution (legal system, criminal justice system, economy, educational system, etc.) discriminate without specifically mentioning a particular group. Although this differential treatment may not be intentional, sometimes it is a subtle way to bar members of an

---

1. Kleg and Yamamoto do not unequivocally state that ethno-racial attitudes have improved, however. They point to methodological limitations—different wordings, different instructions—as well as the well-known discrepancy between expressed attitudes and demonstrated actions.

unwanted group. Women on the police force, for example, had to meet higher standards and accept lower job status to compete with male officers. In some cases officer height and weight requirements excluded most women. Only 2 percent of all police officers were women in 1970. But by the mid-1990s, 15 percent of the New York police officers were women (Price 1996). Another example is the literacy requirements in the pre–Civil War South that prevented African American men from voting.

### Racial and Ethnic Discrimination

Racial groups have distinguishing physical characteristics, but most scientists today concur that these distinctions are primarily social rather than biological. There are no sets of physical characteristics that definitively distinguish one group from another biologically (Gould 1981). Further, qualifications such as being one-thirty-second of a race as an identifier, as existed in Louisiana for many years, is acknowledged as meaningless today (Robbin 1999). Ethnic groups have a shared cultural heritage, and may or may not have a racial distinction, as well.

Most racial and ethnic minorities in our society are disadvantaged in terms of education and income. In 2009, the median family income in the United States was almost $50,000. But for African Americans it was $32,584, and for Hispanics it was $38,039 (U.S. Census Bureau 2010). Close to 30 percent of the U.S. population has a college education. But only 19.3 percent of African Americans and 13.2 percent of Hispanics have completed college (U.S. Census Bureau 2010a).

In 2009, the U.S. poverty rate, which means a family of four living on $21,954 or less, was 14.3 percent. But that same year, more than a quarter of African Americans and Hispanics lived in poverty (U.S. Census Bureau 2010).

Most minorities also have less net worth (wealth is what you own minus what you owe), so they are less able to weather economic downturns. In 2002, the median net worth for a non-Hispanic white household was nearly eleven times more than that of Hispanics, and there was an even greater disparity for African Americans (Pew Hispanic Center 2004). Some argue that wealth is a measure of advantage, and the disparity reflects a "history of discrimination" (*New York Times* 2004).

Each racial and ethnic group has its own history in this country, and in most cases, that includes some outstanding incidents of discrimination. For

**TABLE 6.1. MEDIAN FAMILY INCOME 2009**

| | |
|---|---|
| Asian | $65,469 |
| White (non-Hispanic) | $54,461 |
| African American | $32,584 |
| Hispanic (all races) | $38,039 |
| All US | $49,777 |

*Source:* US Census Bureau 2010.

**TABLE 6.2. US POVERTY RATE 2009**

| | | |
|---|---|---|
| All US | 43.6 million | 14.6% |
| African Americans | 9.9 million | 25.8% |
| Hispanic (all races) | 12.0 million | 25.3% |
| White (non-Hispanic) | 18.5 million | 9.4% |
| Asian | 1.7 million | 12.5% |

*Source:* US Census Bureau 2010.

**TABLE 6.3. MEDIAN WEALTH 2009**

| | |
|---|---|
| White (non-Hispanic) | $113,149 |
| Hispanic (all races) | $ 6,325 |
| African American | $ 5,677 |

*Source:* US Census Bureau 2011; Kochhar, Fry and Taylor 2011.

the American Indians, one unforgettable incident was the "trail of tears" in 1839, when the Cherokee nation was forcibly removed from the southeastern United States and traveled on foot to what is now Oklahoma (Perdue 1989). All of the various Native American tribes underwent forced assimilation in the late 1800s, and were relocated to reservations.[2] They did not become U.S. citizens until 1924 (Deyhle and Swisher 1997; McCarty 1998; Tyler 1973).

After the war with Mexico in 1846, some 75,000 Mexicans living north of the border became U.S. citizens. The Treaty of Guadalupe Hidalgo granted them the right to keep their culture and property. But over time, much of their land was lost, either because it was sold at a disadvantage, claimed by others, or through

2. Native American children were sent to boarding schools where they were dressed in Western clothes and taught English.

nonpayment of taxes (Alonzo 2011; del Castillo 1990). And there are other issues of discrimination in the southern United States. In the early 1900s, Mexican workers came to the United States on a seasonal basis, and many settled permanently. But during the Depression, some 400,000 immigrants and approximately 600,000 U.S.-born children were forcibly repatriated to Mexico (Hoffman 1974).

The ancestors of most African Americans were brought to this country as slaves. They were uprooted, forced to endure miserable conditions at sea, and, if they survived, sold to the highest bidder on the auction block. Thereafter, they had no civil rights, inadequate food and clothing, were frequently abused physically, and many women were abused sexually. After the Civil War, with the right to vote, they wasted no time in electing African Americans into positions of leadership. There were African American lieutenant governors and members of both houses of Congress. Their success was threatening to the communities where they lived, and soon the Jim Crow laws and segregation were established. Lynchings were the means of enforcing these laws. Well-known advocate groups—the NAACP and the Leadership Council on Civil and Human Rights—were formed in the early 1900s by educated African American leaders, including W. E. B. DuBois and Philip Randolph. The civil rights era began in the 1950s. Separate but equal was soon ruled unconstitutional, and integration was mandated (Sowell 1981; Klarman 2004).

This is just a very brief summary of some of the histories. The significance is that, unfortunately, there are many incidents of discrimination—personal and institutional—in our history. Legislation has helped to better the situation for minorities. But not all the laws have been beneficial.

### Discrimination in Education

We have not yet shaken the legacy of segregation in education.[3] In the 1970s, busing was an important part of integration focused on addressing racially segregated neighborhoods.[4] But parents objected to the long bus rides. They claimed

---

3. In 1954, the Supreme Court ruled in *Brown v. Board of Education* that segregated schools are unconstitutional.
4. The Supreme Court ruled in 1971 that busing was a constitutionally approved way to desegregate schools.

busing destroyed neighborhood schools and increased discipline problems. Many whites moved to other school districts in the suburbs or sent their children to private schools. By the 1980s, inner-city schools were largely nonminority (Frum 2000; Kozol 2005, 2006). As a result, there is more segregation in American schools today than in the 1960s (Lockette 2010; Kozol 2006). Forty percent of all U.S. students are minority and 30 percent attend schools in neighborhoods with 90 percent minority population—schools where 75 percent of the students receive free or reduced-cost lunch. Experts agree that schools that are 90 percent minority are "fundamentally different from other schools," in terms of availability of AP classes, number of veteran teachers, graduation rates, and so on (Lockette 2010). Some have pressed for magnet schools[5] and charter schools[6] as a solution. But magnet schools can create a two-tier system within one school, and charter schools end up being primarily minority, since they are located in primarily minority school districts.[7]

More importantly, desegregation efforts have not contributed to improved educational opportunities for most minorities (Armor 1995). The discussion was taken to the larger public with the release of a critical movie, *Waiting for Superman,* which charges that the school system today fails students who are not high achievers (Guggenheim 2010). The movie has stirred critics. A movie website urges supporters to work toward the laudable goals of great teachers, prepared students, excellent schools, and increased literacy.

The popular debate was also stirred by a controversial figure, Michelle Rhee, who served as chancellor of the Washington, D.C., public schools from 2007 to 2010. She blamed teachers and the school system for D.C.'s record as the "worst performing school district in the country" (Chu 2011). Her approach was to turn "the system on its head by closing dozens of failing schools and firing

---

5. Magnet schools specialize in some subject, such as science or art. They are often in minority areas, so nonminority students are bused to the school.

6. Charter schools are an alternative to the regular public schools. They are set up by contract or charter through a state agency, are funded by the government, but do not have to follow the guidelines of the traditional public schools. There are some 3,000 charter schools in forty states. www.uscharterschools.org/pub/uscs_docs/o/faq.html#8.

7. Students at magnet schools are tested for the appropriate classes. Minority, low-performing students are in different classes than the high-performing, nonminority students, although they are all in the same school building.

more than 1000 ineffective educators" (Winfrey 2010). Public school teachers were unsettled when she advocated merit-based salaries instead of tenure, and parents were angered when they had to find new schools. So, although she succeeded in raising both reading and math scores in the district dramatically and improved graduation rates, her radical approach made her too controversial. She has since formed her own advocate group, Students First, with the intention to reform the current education system, which, she claims, "works for the school bureaucracies and the teachers but not for the children" (Denby 2010).

### Discrimination in Housing

During the first half of the twentieth century, most minorities were unable to buy houses or live in predominantly white neighborhoods. They faced *redlining*, or mortgage discrimination. Lenders identified neighborhoods as high risk areas and refused loans to residents, or charged higher interest rates, and/or demanded higher down payments. Minorities also faced *racial steering*—not being given full realtor information and/or steered toward minority neighborhoods when looking for housing. This led to largely minority residential areas at risk for *absentee landlordism, neighborhood disinvestments,* and *gentrification.* Minorities without means or financial assistance had to rent from landlords who charged a lot and were not likely to keep the property in good repair—perhaps because of low property values, but to the detriment of the neighborhood. Some cities neglected public services in minority neighborhoods—whether because of low income from taxes or blatant discrimination: lack of maintenance on schools, streets, parks; inadequate garbage collection; and inadequate transportation. Some minority communities experienced gentrification—purchase of large areas of the neighborhood by investors who built upscale housing that the original residents couldn't afford, forcing them to move elsewhere.

The Fair Housing Act of 1968 made overt housing discrimination illegal, and the Federal Home Mortgage Disclosure Act of 1975 prohibited discriminatory redlining.[8] But the *white flight* of the 1960s and 1970s, mentioned above,

---

8. It prohibited refusing to rent or sell to anyone on the basis of race. It has subsequently been expanded to include religion, nationality, gender, family status, and disability. www.justice .gov/crt/about/hce/housing_coverage.php.

led to large minority populations in many inner cities, with tendencies toward increased crime, gangs, and dilapidated housing (Massey and Denton 1998).[9]

Whether because of past discrimination practices, or simply preference, segregation of residential neighborhoods in the United States is still the norm, although it is not as complete as in the past. The average white person today lives in a neighborhood that is approximately 75 percent white. African Americans and Hispanics live in neighborhoods that are close to half black or Hispanic, respectively. Five major cities have a dissimilarity index of 80 (100 indicates complete segregation): New York, Milwaukee, Newark, Detroit, and Chicago. Seven cities have an index of 70, although sixty-one cities are less segregated than they were ten years ago (El-Nasser 2010; Frey 2010).

Discrimination today primarily centers on these inner-city, lower socioeconomic areas, which are primarily minority. Legislation regarding housing discrimination pertaining to disabilities was passed in 1991. In July 2007, the National Association for the Advancement of Colored People (NAACP) filed a suit against fifteen large U.S. mortgage companies, claiming unfair practices—in particular, the high cost of subprime loans to African Americans who qualify for prime loans. The organization seeks elimination of lender discrimination and better borrower information in regard to fees, practices, and product choices (NAACP 2009–2011).

### Job Discrimination

Until the 1960s there were few restrictions on hiring practices. Stereotypes and prejudice often made it difficult for minorities to find work, other than in the lowest paid sector of the economy. Employment difficulties were compounded by lack of education. Since 1963, seven laws have been passed in an effort to provide all groups access to the same level of employment. The laws affect hiring, firing, compensation, job assignment or classification, promotion, job advertisements, recruitment, testing, use of company facilities, training, benefits, and disability leave.

---

9. White flight is large-scale migration of whites from racially mixed inner-city areas to more racially homogeneous suburban areas. As indicated above, education was a major factor.

Briefly, the seven laws are as follows. (1) The Equal Protection Act (EPA) made wage discrimination based on sex illegal. (2) Title VII of the Civil Rights Act of 1964 made it illegal to discriminate in the workplace against persons of a different race, color, religion, sex, or national origin. (3) The elderly (40 years of age or older) were protected by the Age Discrimination in Employment Act of 1967 (ADEA). (4) Disabled federal workers were protected by Sections 501 and 505 of the Rehabilitation Act of 1973. (5) Disabled in both private and government jobs were protected from discrimination by Title I and V of the Americans with Disabilities Act of 1990 (ADA). (6) Employer discrimination based on genetic information was protected by Title II of the Genetic Information Nondiscrimination Act of 2008 (GINA). (7) Since 1991 it has been possible to collect monetary damages in cases of intentional employment discrimination (U.S. EEOC 2009).

So, has job discrimination been eliminated? According to two Rutgers law professors, the answer is no—it is alive and well in every region of the country, and in all occupational levels (managers to service jobs) (Blumrosen and Blumrosen 1999). Their four-year study using company reports found that as many as half of the companies examined had been discriminating for at least nine years.[10] Medical, drug, and health-related industries account for 20 percent of all discrimination. The other top discriminatory industries are eating and drinking places, department stores, grocery stores, computer and data processing services, hotels and motels, telephone communications, commercial banks, and motor vehicles and equipment manufacturing. The studies discount employer explanations that minorities were not interested in the work or were not available, and conclude that African Americans are discriminated against more than other minorities.

"Intentional discrimination is still so pervasive that affirmative action programs continue to be necessary," the researchers conclude (Blumrosen and Blumrosen 1999, xviii). Enforcement of existing laws will not change the situation.

---

10. The study looked for a statistical imbalance in composition of employees. In 1977 the Supreme Court stated that a statistical imbalance is a "telltale sign of purposeful discrimination. In many cases the only available avenue of proof is to use racial statistics to uncover clandestine and covert discrimination" (Blumrosen and Blumrosen 1999, xiv). In other words they compared the number of each minority employed by a company to the number qualified for employment. Each industry and occupation has a different average. Their findings were highly significant.

They also recommend that the federal government keep discrimination statistics and make them available to employers. Also fair arbitration systems should be developed.

TABLE 6.4. **RISK OF MINORITY DISCRIMINATION EACH TIME A JOB OPPORTUNITY IS SOUGHT IN THE OCCUPATION**

|  | *Blacks* | *Hispanics* | *Asian* | *Women* |
|---|---|---|---|---|
| Officials and managers | 26.6% | 21.8% | 24.6% | 18% |
| Professionals | 27.6% | 20.7% | 30.8% | 23% |
| Technical workers | 29.1% | 21.9% | 30.2% | 23% |
| Sales | 39.5% | 28.1% | 27.3% | 20% |
| Office and clerical | 31.8% | 21.8% | 26.4% | 19% |
| Craft workers (skilled) | 28.7% | 27.1% | 35.0% | 37% |
| Operatives (semi skilled) | 33.2% | 33.4% | 42.8% | 38% |
| Laborers | 34.9% | 34.4% | 43.6% | 30% |
| Service workers | 40.3% | 34.0% | 38.1% | 19% |
| All comparisons | 34.1% | 35.0% | 39.0% | 23% |

*Source:* Blumrosen and Blumrosen 1999.

### Hate Groups and Hate Crimes

Racial discrimination can turn violent. One of the most infamous hate crimes in recent years was the killing of a black man near Jasper, Texas, in 1998. James Byrd was beaten and then dragged behind a truck; parts of his body were found in various places along the road (King 2002).

Sometimes violent racial or minority discrimination is denied or hidden. Some forty years after the initial incidents, offenders from the civil rights era are only now being prosecuted. In 2001, Thomas Blanton was convicted for his involvement in an Alabama church bombing that killed four young African American girls in 1963. In 2005, Edgar Ray Killen was sentenced for his collaboration with the Ku Klux Klan to murder three civil rights workers in Mississippi in 1964. Whole communities sometimes silently conspire not to talk about an event. Until recently, many were unaware that the racial violence of the 1921 Tulsa race riot was among the worst ever. A commission was set up in 1997 by the Oklahoma state legislature to bring this sad past into our recorded history (Ellsworth 2007; Goble 2000; Tulsa Reparations Committee 2000).

Some groups have faced hate crimes for many years. Attacks against Jews have gone on for centuries and continue today (LCCR 2011). Others, such as gender violence, are newly acknowledged (it was not included in the Hate Crime Statistics Act of 1990) (LCCR 2011a).

Hate crimes are defined as crimes motivated by biases of race, color, religion, national origin, gender, sexual orientation, gender identity, or disability.[11] The Hate Crime Statistics Act of 1990 made it mandatory to collect and report hate crime data from around the country separate from other crimes. In 2009, there were 6,604 reported hate crimes incidents, with vandalism and intimidation accounting for more than half. Twenty-two percent of all hate crimes were simple assault, and during that year there were eight murders and nine forcible rapes identified as hate crimes (FBI 2010).[12] Racial discrimination was the motivation for nearly half of the hate crimes (African Americans were victims in 35 percent of the crimes). Religious discrimination accounted for almost 20 percent of the crimes, sexual orientation for 18.5 percent, and the remainder ethnicity and disability.

Many hate crimes are not reported, so the number of incidents is thought to be much higher. Fear of reprisal and fear that the justice system is prejudiced are the main reasons for nonreporting. Yet the damage is considerable to the persons involved—psychological as well as physical. After a second notorious hate crime in 1998 (a gay Wyoming college student, Matthew Shepard, was robbed, beaten, and killed) legislators proposed additional measures. The Matthew Shepard and James Byrd Jr. Hate Crimes Prevention Act (HCPA) of 2008 gives the federal government more authority to investigate hate crimes and provide grants for programs to prevent hate crimes.

---

11. Crimes against persons are murder and nonnegligent manslaughter, forcible rape, aggravated assault, simple assault, and intimidation. Crimes against property are robbery, burglary, larceny-theft, motor vehicle theft, arson, and destruction/damage/vandalism.
12. This data comes from the FBI's Uniform Crime Reporting Program, which collects data from other law enforcement agencies. See method page for note on biases. www2.fbi.gov/ucr/hc2009/index.html

## Hate Groups

A hate group is a group of individuals who collectively have an extreme, even violent prejudice against another group, to the extent that they feel hate crimes are justified.[13] According to the Southern Poverty Law Center (2011), the number of hate groups in the United States has increased over the last decade.[14] (Interestingly, almost all group leaders are men.) Grouping them by ideology, the SPLC has identified approximately eight different types of hate groups (see box).

---

**■■ ■■ ■■ BOX 6.1.** ————————————————

### PROFILE OF HATE GROUPS BY IDEOLOGY

1. **Antigay**: Opposition to equal rights for gays and lesbians has been a central theme of the Christian right's organizing and fund-raising for the past three decades—a period that parallels the fundamentalist movement's rise to political power.
2. **Anti-immigrant** hate groups are the most extreme of the hundreds of nativist and vigilante groups that have proliferated since the late 1990s, when anti-immigration xenophobia began to rise to levels not seen in the United States since the 1920s.
3. **Anti-Muslim** hate groups are a relatively new phenomenon in the United States, most of them appearing in the aftermath of the World Trade Center terrorist attacks on Sept. 11, 2001. Earlier anti-Muslim groups tended to be religious in orientation and disputed Islam's status as a respectable religion.
4. **Black separatists** typically oppose integration and racial intermarriage, and they want separate institutions—or even a separate nation—for blacks. Most forms of black separatism are strongly anti-white and anti-Semitic, and a number of religious versions assert that blacks are the biblical "chosen people" of God.

*(continues)*

---

13. There is an overlap between hate groups and opposition groups (see also the discussion of opposition groups in Chapter 8). Because it deals specifically with discrimination, the discussion of hate groups is kept in this chapter.
14. SPLC identified 1,002 hate groups in 2011. It defines a hate group as having one of its main functions to destroy or persecute another group (usually for ideological reasons). As noted below in the Solution section under claims making (page 156), this definition is too political and not tied closely enough to hate crimes.

┌─ ▇▇ ▇▇ ▇▇ BOX 6.1. ────────────────────────────────────

**PROFILE OF HATE GROUPS BY IDEOLOGY** *(continued)*

5. **Deniers of the Holocaust,** the systematic murder of around 6 million Jews in World War II, either deny that such a genocide took place or minimize its extent. These groups (and individuals) often cloak themselves in the sober language of serious scholarship, call themselves "historical revisionists" instead of deniers, and accuse their critics of trying to squelch open-minded inquiries into historical truth.

6. **Radical traditionalist Catholics,** who may make up the largest single group of serious anti-Semites in America, subscribe to an ideology that is rejected by the Vatican and some 70 million mainstream American Catholics.

7. **Sovereign citizens movement:** The strange subculture of the sovereign citizens movement, whose adherents hold truly bizarre, complex antigovernment beliefs, has been growing at a fast pace since the late 2000s. Sovereigns believe that they get to decide which laws to obey and which to ignore, and they don't think they should have to pay taxes.

8. **White nationalist** groups espouse white supremacist or white separatist ideologies, often focusing on the alleged inferiority of nonwhites. Groups listed in a variety of other categories—Ku Klux Klan, neo-Confederate, neo-Nazi, racist skinhead, and Christian Identity—could also be fairly described as white nationalist.

   a. **Christian Identity** is a unique anti-Semitic and racist theology that rose to a position of commanding influence on the racist right in the 1980s. "Christian" in name only, the movement's relationship with evangelicals and fundamentalists has generally been hostile due to the latters' belief that the return of Jews to Israel is essential to the fulfillment of end time prophecy.

   b. **Ku Klux Klan,** with its long history of violence, is the most infamous—and oldest—of American hate groups. Although black Americans have typically been the Klan's primary target, it also has attacked Jews, immigrants, gays and lesbians, and, until recently, Catholics.

   c. **Neo-Confederate:** The term is used to describe twentieth- and twenty-first-century revivals of pro-Confederate sentiment in the United States. Strongly nativist, neo-Confederacy claims to pursue Christianity and heritage and other supposedly fundamental values that modern Americans are seen to have abandoned.

*(continues)*

---

■■ ■■ ■■ BOX 6.1.

**PROFILE OF HATE GROUPS BY IDEOLOGY** *(continued)*

    **d. Neo-Nazi** groups share a hatred for Jews and a love for Adolf Hitler and Nazi Germany. While they also hate other minorities, gays and lesbians, and even sometimes Christians, they perceive "the Jew" as their cardinal enemy.

    **e. Racist music groups** are typically white power music labels that record, publish, and distribute racist music in a variety of genres.

    **f. Racist skinheads** form a particularly violent element of the white supremacist movement, and have often been referred to as the "shock troops" of the hoped for revolution. The classic skinhead look is a shaved head, black Doc Martens boots, jeans with suspenders, and an array of typically racist tattoos.

---

*Source:* Southern Poverty Law Center 2011a (www.splcenter.org/get-informed/intelligence -files/ideology).

---

### Racial Profiling

Minorities have long complained that they face discrimination in the criminal justice system. During the 1990s there were increased complaints that police were targeting minorities for traffic stops, searches, tickets, and arrests. (Increased stops were associated with the use of a drug courier profile to apprehend drug traffickers, according to the Racial Profiling Data Center.) This led to declining confidence in law enforcement across the country. Both anecdotal and statistical evidence confirmed that minorities were disproportionately targeted (Ramirez, McDevitt, and Farrell 2000).

Racial profiling is the use of race, ethnic origin, or nationality as an identifier to stop or arrest criminal suspects. The 1990s situation brought the issue to the attention of the highest government officials. Racial profiling was declared "wrong" in 2001 by then President George W. Bush, who called on law enforcement agencies to end its practice (DOJ 2003). Data collection was recommended as a means of combating both the practice and the public perception of the practice (Data Collection Resource Center n.d.; Ramirez, McDevitt, and Farrell 2000).

Since the attack on the Twin Towers on September 11, 2001, Middle Easterners have become a new target for racial profiling, especially at airports (ACLU

2009). Some people object to the increased powers of officials to monitor Internet and telephone traffic and hold terrorist suspects under the Patriot (Uniting and Strengthening America by Providing Appropriate Tools Required to Intercept and Obstruct Terrorism) Act of 2001. Nevertheless, certain provisions were renewed for four years in 2011 (Mascaro 2011).

So, has racial profiling been reduced? Maybe, but it has not been eradicated. The Department of Justice reportedly expressed continued concern about "biased policing" among officers in the Los Angeles Police Department. The department has been under federal oversight since 2001, when it was ordered to make sweeping reforms on the issue (Rubin 2010).

### Affirmative Action:
### A Brief Look at a Solution to Discrimination

Affirmative action is the practice of giving minorities preferential treatment to compensate for the historical disadvantages they experienced, in order to put them on an equal footing in competing for jobs and admittance to institutions of higher education. American presidents have noted the unfair competition faced by minorities since the 1950s. Kennedy was first to use the term "affirmative action," and Johnson mandated against minority discrimination by employers (SOSU 2011; Wilcher 2003; Fitzpatrick 2009).

The ruling has been controversial—sometimes supported by the Supreme Court, sometimes not. Colleges and universities used affirmative action in the 1970s to encourage minority students and to make their campuses more diverse. It came to be perceived as a quota system, which the Supreme Court ruled illegal (while encouraging preferential treatment of minorities) in 1978. In the 1990s, the *Hopwood* case[15] and others got a lot of attention. White students claimed reverse discrimination (they were discriminated against because they were *not* minority). State and national rulings said race could not be a criterion for admission.

---

15. In *Hopwood v. State of Texas,* 1994, Cheryl Hopwood, who was denied admission to the UT law school, argued her scores were higher than many minorities, hence claiming reverse discrimination (Kauffman and Gonzalez 1997). See also discussion in Chapter 3, "Unintended Consequences."

Concerned that minority enrollment in colleges would drop, states instituted various alternative policies.[16] In 2003 the Supreme Court ruled that the University of Michigan could not use a point system that allocated bonus points for race in their admission process, but they could use racial considerations to ensure a racially diverse student body. Studies show that without some preferential treatment, some colleges and universities across the country have a very low minority enrollment (Espenshade and Radford 2009). Schools are convinced that the quality of minority education has improved because of affirmative action, as has minority participation in higher paying professions (SOSU 2011). But some racial advocate groups, like the NAACP, have become ambivalent. While its leaders have supported it in the past (Fletcher 1998), the NAACP does not completely support the measure today, although its website is careful to document studies showing public approval between 50 and 60 percent (NAACP 2009–2011a).[17]

## Take 'Em to Court:
## A Solution Proposed by the Southern Poverty Law Center

Discrimination is a big issue, and there are many proposed solutions—too many to discuss or even list. There are advocate groups for each minority. The person who wants to understand the dynamics of our culture will find these claims and proposals a good source of material. We will consider a solution to racial discrimination taken by an advocate group that, in many ways, functions like a think tank: it spends a lot of effort collecting information and makes that information available to others. But the Southern Poverty Law Center also has a specific advocacy program, which it pursues even more energetically. Founded by two Alabama lawyers in 1971, its goal is to see the "promises of the civil rights movement become a reality." It claims its "lawsuits have toppled institutional racism in the

---

16. Texas used the 10 percent policy: students who were in the top 10 percent of their high school graduating class would be admitted by state colleges and universities.
17. A 2003 Gallup Poll found 49 percent favored affirmative action; a 2001 Gallup Poll showed 61 percent favored keeping it or increasing it. A Pew Research Center study in 2003 found 63 percent favor affirmative action that helps blacks, women, and other minorities get better jobs and education (NAACP 2009–2011a). http://leadership500.naacp.org/advocacy/research/affaction/aa4.html.

South, bankrupted some of the nation's most violent white supremacist groups and won justice for exploited workers, abused prison inmates, disabled children and other victims of discrimination."

One of the features of this advocate group is the heavy involvement of lawyers: a majority of the staff members and half of the six senior staff members. Fighting racism and injustice in court is its major advocacy. It regularly sues hate group members and others on behalf of the victims—for murder, violence, and other acts of discrimination. As a result of these cases, at least four hate groups have become defunct.[18] Second, the SPLC tracks activities of hate groups in order to expose their activities to law enforcement agencies, the media, and the public. Third, it provides educators, law enforcement officers, and others with educational materials promoting tolerance. The Teaching Tolerance program is geared toward reducing intergroup hostility and developing a public that is more tolerant of all groups. One of its school campaigns, The Mix It Up At Lunch Day, is an annual effort to get students to sit with someone new at lunch.

The SPLC is also concerned about immigrants, the LGBT community, and juveniles. It has filed lawsuits on behalf of immigrants and works to expose violations of their civil rights, especially workplace exploitation. It educates the public on the issue and lobbies the government. It works to ensure LGBT rights are protected in the southeastern United States. It is concerned about minority youth who are "needlessly pushed out of schools into the juvenile justice system."

The group maintains a lot of information on its website and has numerous print publications, including a monthly magazine, *Intelligence Report.*

### Analysis

Using the theory presented in the first four chapters, the six ingredients of the social problem of discrimination from the point of view of the advocate group SPLC (Southern Poverty Law Center) are as follows:

*Target Group/Situation:* The SPLC sees minorities and other vulnerable members of society as victims. These are people who need the protection of the law against those who would discriminate against them.

---

18. White Aryan Resistance, the United Klans of America, the White Patriot Party militia, and the Aryan Nation. www.splcenter.org/what-we-do/hate-and-extremism.

*Ameliorating Action:* Its solution is to use the legal system to force those who have caused suffering to be accountable for their actions (and obey the law). This primarily means suing offenders for punitive damages or other settlements. It also promotes action by the criminal justice system through its efforts to highlight the illegal activity of hate groups. Finally, it promotes future tolerance between groups through educational programs for children.

*Action Group:* The SPLC is itself the action group, to the extent that it takes someone to court. The legal system is also an action group enforcing the laws of the land, which are supposed to mean equality for everyone. The criminal justice system is the action group for illegal actions committed by hate groups.

*Will to Act:* The will to act comes from the force of the law. Laws have already been passed that guarantee equal treatment for all people.

*Why Did the Problem Develop?* The view of the SPLC as to why there is discrimination is not entirely clear, except that much of it is historical. Growing out of the civil rights era, it would undoubtedly point to the inequities of segregation and the resulting power structure as the cause of much discrimination and many injustices.

*Level of Social Problem:* Discrimination, from the point of view of the SPLC, is national and even international. However, it is tackling the problem at the local and state levels, primarily (lower courts). On occasion, the cases go to the Supreme Court—which would be on a national level.

## About the Group

*Kind of Advocate Group:* The SPLC is a special interest group in that it is well organized, focused, and effective. It is not very large, but has considerable social resources and support. Especially notable is the social standing advocate members have as lawyers, and as a result, the social standing that the group acquires through its legal activity.

*Why Did the Advocate Group Form?* All three categories of group formation apply to this group. The civil rights legacy definitely points to a desire for structural reform—changing society so that all people have equal rights. Second, the group's social resources and status, as mentioned above, point to reformation capacity: it is composed of people able and willing to fight for the rights of those not able to speak so eloquently for themselves. And finally, as one reads through the SPLC material, it is clear that the motivation of the staff at all levels is to make the world a better place. Perhaps we could say that the members have a need to work for a cause beyond themselves: a belief that they as individuals are needed to improve the world.

*View of Human Nature:* The SPLC is somewhere between the greater good human being and compassionate sacrificing human being. Or perhaps it embraces both at different times. Staff members seem dedicated to their work and invest long hours to see their cause succeed. It is likely that they see the victims as compassionate, sacrificing persons—imputing the highest values on them. It may be that, like Marx, they see victims and perpetrators of injustice differently. The perpetrators of discrimination are more likely to be seen as greater good human beings—once they realize they can't get what they want, they will settle for peaceful coexistence.

*Dynamics of the Advocate Group:* The SPLC makes use of traditional social functioning. It is organized; its leadership style appears to be collegial and democratic, yet authoritarian on occasion. It seems to be fair in its methods, although one presumes that as lawyers, there is a certain amount of personal financial reward in the activities.

*Stage of Development of the Advocate Group:* The SPLC is in the bureaucratization stage. It has formed, organized, and established a structure and works to achieve its goals. Whether it will face decline in the future remains to be seen.

### Other Factors

*Claims Making:* Surprisingly, the SPLC's claims making is not entirely unbiased. While it is very insightful in its observations, its classification of hate groups is not entirely satisfactory. Some groups appear to be of a different political persuasion rather than groups that are likely to commit hate crimes. As mentioned above, attitudes cannot be legislated—nor a point of view. The key distinction between an advocate group and a hate group is willingness to cause harm and a failure to "play by the rules." A group that engages in criminal activity, especially in the interest of denigrating others, it is rightly considered a hate group. This author would exclude some groups in the SPLC's list of hate groups.

*Opposition Groups:* They certainly exist. All the groups that the SPLC identifies as hate groups are automatically opposition groups. These opposition groups are threatened—both in ideology and in well-being.

Public reaction to the problem of hate groups is often ignorance, or anger followed by fatalistic resignation ("That shouldn't happen, but what can you do?").

*Consequences/Unintended Consequences:* Consequences of SPLC actions are positive. It is using the law and legal system to benefit persons who are being discriminated against. Because of its actions, others who might discriminate in the future will not be so eager to do so because of the consequences.

*Type of Change Sought:* The SPLC seeks redemptive change for the members of the hate groups—hate groups should be stopped from acting in a destructive manner in the future.

*Model for Social Change:* The critical mass (restructuring) model. The SPLC seems to take the stance that once enough people are prohibited from taking advantage of others and realize the consequences of their actions, society will be better for everyone.

*Assessing the Overall Benefit:* All in all, the SPLC has a positive effect on our society. It assists when help is needed and makes everyone rise to a higher standard of applying justice.

### ■ QUESTIONS FOR REVIEW

1. What is discrimination? Which groups are particularly at risk for discrimination?
2. What kind of discrimination has been common in our society?
3. What laws have been passed to combat discrimination?

## ■ QUESTIONS FOR FURTHER THOUGHT

1. If you could imagine a different historical scenario, one in which Native Americans did not die off in large numbers but became the dominant group in the United States, how would our society be different today?

2. If the southern states had not succeeded in passing and enforcing the Jim Crow laws, how would the life of African Americans as a group be different than it is today? How would our society differ?

3. When thinking of the 1980s *Star Wars* movie series, what kind of comment was the producer making about our society in terms of racial and minority discrimination?

4. What is the difference between hate groups, as defined and identified by the Southern Poverty Law Center, and mud-slinging, hardball politics?

5. Why do you think the Matthew Shepard and James Byrd Jr. Hate Crimes Prevention Act (HCPA) of 2008 was passed? How is it intended to end discrimination?

## ■ OTHER ADVOCATE GROUPS

### African American Advocate Groups

Black Leadership Forum

Joint Center for Political and Economic Studies

Leadership Conference on Civil and Human Rights

National Association for the Advancement of Colored Persons (NAACP)

National Urban League

Rainbow/PUSH Coalition

Southern Christian Leadership Conference (SCLC)

### Hispanic Advocate Groups

League of United Latin American Citizens (LULAC)

Mexican American Legal Defense and Education Fund

National Council of La Raza

## ■ OTHER MINORITY GROUPS

Organization of Chinese Americans

American Indian Movement (AIM)
Anti-Defamation League (ADL)
American-Arab Anti-Discrimination Committee

## ■ OTHER ORGANIZATIONS

American Association for Affirmative Action (AAAA)
American Civil Liberties Union
Amnesty International
Coalition Against Hate Crimes
Coalition to Defend Affirmative Action, Immigration, and Immigrant Rights, and Fight for Equality by Any Means Necessary (BAMN)
Ethnic Majority
Families United Against Hate
Human Rights Watch
Institute on Race and Justice, Northern Illinois University
Lamberth Consulting
Simon Wiesenthal Center
Urban Institute

## ■ ILLEGAL IMMIGRATION

It is often said that the United States is a land of immigrants. Most of the 311,855,931 people living here as of July 2011 are immigrants or descendants of immigrants.[19] Before turning to the problem of illegal immigration, we will consider U.S. immigration policies and patterns.

More than 150,000 people came to the United States in the seventeenth century. They were predominantly from northern Europe. The newly formed U.S. government passed the Naturalization Act in 1790, limiting citizenship to free white residents and their children.[20] The steady stream of immigrants

---

19. U.S. Census Bureau, www.census.gov/main/www/popclock.html.
20. For wording, go to http://web.me.com/joelarkin/MontereyDemographicHistory /Naturalization_1790.html.

who came to the new country throughout the eighteenth and nineteenth centuries peaked between 1847 and 1854. Concerns about who was entering the country led to the Chinese Exclusion Act of 1882, which barred Chinese immigrants and some others. By 1900, the average number of immigrants per year was 891,000. Again concerned about the identity of the immigrants, the Asiatic Barred Zone Act was passed in 1917, restricting Asians and certain undesirables.[21] To address the increasing numbers coming from southern and eastern Europe, the Emergency Quota Act was passed in 1921, followed by the Immigration Act in 1924. The latter limited immigrants from any given country or ethnic origin to 2 percent of their presence in the 1890 census (LeMay 2004; Cohn 2010; Migration Policy Institute 2011).

Mexican immigration increased in the early 1900s as well. Some estimate that as many as 1.5 million Mexicans came to the southern states from 1900 to 1930 (Ahlborn et al.). U.S. labor needs coincided with immigrants' desire to leave the turmoil of the Mexican Revolution. "No one knows how many Mexicans entered the United States after 1910, or how many of those who came stayed, but in 1916 the Commissioner of Immigration said that more than 1 million Mexicans were in the United States. Many Mexicans came on their own, but thousands of others were recruited to fill labor shortages and break strikes" (Ahlborn et al., 8). When the U.S. Border Patrol was established in 1924 (CBP 2010), Mexicans could no longer go back and forth so freely. But the government was not eager to restrict Mexican immigrants because at that point they were 75 percent of the labor force for southwest vegetable, fruit, and truck-delivered crops, and employers had testified to Congress in their favor (Ahlborn et al.).

From 1930 to 1946, there were fewer immigrants to the United States than there had been one hundred years earlier. In addition, 500,000 to 1 million Mexicans (including U.S.-born children) were repatriated during the Depression (Cohn 2010; Ahlborn et al.; Hoffman 1974).[22] But in the 1940s, workers were again needed, so a guest worker program was set up. Workers could stay for only nine months of the year. An estimated 5 million people took part in the Bracero program from 1949 to 1964 (LeMay 2007).

---

21. http://library.uwb.edu/guides/USimmigration/1917_immigration_act.html.
22. Most estimates are about 500,000, but, as discussed in the previous section, Hoffman puts the figure at 400,000 adults and 600,000 U.S.-born children.

The 1940s brought more openness. In 1943, several immigration statutes were repealed, allowing Chinese immigration and naturalization. After World War II, objections to the quota system led to the Immigration and Nationality Act of 1952, when Japanese were allowed to become citizens for the first time.[23] But it was the 1965 Immigration Act that replaced the quota system with the preference system: immigrants were approved based on individual, not national, qualifications (Daniels 2008).[24]

American opposition to Castro made the government more sympathetic to the large number of Cubans seeking asylum in the 1960s. Refugees were also assisted with housing and jobs. But the welcome mat began rolling up when 20,000 criminals and mentally ill persons came with the 125,000 Marielitos (persons imprisoned or suffering because they opposed Castro) in 1980. They were subsequently apprehended and repatriated. The U.S. government refused entry to thousands who tried to enter in 1994, giving rise to the "wet foot, dry foot" nickname for America's immigration policy: those who arrive safely can stay, but those caught in the water (between Cuba and the United States) are sent back (LeMay 2004; LeoGrande 1998).

### Illegal Aliens

When it comes to undocumented immigrants, the main concern is Mexico: 60 percent of all illegal residents are from Mexico (Preston 2010; Passell and Cohn 2011).[25] This is in part because of the immigration patterns that developed after the Bracero program was replaced by the 1965 Immigration Act. The guest worker program ended, but the need for jobs did not, and after twenty-five years, Mexicans knew where to find jobs and homes, and other things they needed in the United States. The difference was that now they were employed illegally, and they didn't go back after nine months (LeMay 2007). In the 1980s, the average

---

23. http://library.uwb.edu/guides/USimmigration/1952_immigration_and_nationality _act.html.

24. http://library.uwb.edu/guides/USimmigration/1965_immigration_and_nationality _act.html.

25. Twenty percent are from other Latin American countries, 11 percent from Asia, 4 per- cent from Canada and Europe, 4 percent from Africa and other areas (Pew Hispanic Center 2011).

annual number of illegal immigrants was about 225,000, 20 percent of all immigrants (National Research Council 1997). An attempt to address the growing numbers of illegal immigrants was made in the 1986 Immigration Reform and Control Act (IRCA), which granted amnesty to approximately 3.1 million illegal residents. A second measure passed in 1990 granted amnesty to their relatives. Still, approximately 6 million more entered illegally from 2000 to 2008.

In 2010, U.S. illegal residents declined slightly to 11.1 million (which is 3.7 percent of the population), but there were still three times more than in 1990, and a third more than in 2000 (Passell and Cohn 2011). Not all entered illegally, however. An estimated 40 percent of illegal residents (including those from non-Mexican countries) came on a tourist or student visa and overstayed (National Research Council 1997). The fact that illegal immigration has not declined more with the economic downturn indicates that other migration factors are as important as economics: social networks of friends and families, political freedom, and generous public services (CIS 2011).

Some analysts call it a "battle for the border," which will be lost. According to this view, the large government agencies—Immigration and Naturalization Service, Border Patrol, National Security Council Working Group on Illegal Immigration, National Guard, Army Reserve, and others—cannot stop the transnational communities that continue to function as if the border didn't exist. People in these communities "circulate resources." Despite their illegal status and the opposition they face, they create neighborhoods, organize themselves, and link themselves to society through schools and businesses, all the while maintaining electronic communication with relatives at a distance. They have created an informal guest worker program that is supported by many U.S. employers. Their existence is tacitly supported legally, locally, and by institutions such as schools and churches, and yet they are given no recognition or assistance (Rodriguez 1999).

The main concentrations of illegal residents are in Texas, California, Florida, New York, Illinois, and New Jersey (Pew Hispanic Center 2011). During the last three years their numbers increased in Louisiana, Oklahoma, and Texas, but elsewhere they declined (Passell and Cohn 2011).

Since 2001, some $90 billion has been spent by the federal government on measures to secure the border—on law officers, predator drones, remote surveillance cameras, and the fence. Still the Border Patrol says that only one in five is caught. Others say it is more like one in ten, and studies reveal they catch less than a third of the illegal immigrants today than they did ten years ago (Mendoza 2011).

The U.S. border with Mexico is 1,959 miles long. The entire 1,254 miles of border in Texas is along the Rio Grande River. The other three states have land borders, except for twenty-four miles in western Arizona. Arizona has 351 miles of land border, New Mexico 199 miles, California 141 miles. In 2006, the federal government announced plans to build a fence along the border to help with security. Texas now has 650 miles of fence or concrete walls, but mayors and other officials in the area where more fence was to be built urged the government *not* to build it because the money could be better spent elsewhere (Martin 2009). The entire fence idea, even the virtual fence, was abandoned in 2010 because of the cost and other problems (Hsu 2010; Brandenburg 2010).

However, the idea of a fence remains popular in Arizona. The state has a 375 mile border with Mexico and ranchers have complained about damage to their

**FIGURE 6.1.** Just how easy is it to cross into the U.S. from Mexico? This boat, burro, and truck on the Mexican side of the Rio Grande River in the Boquillas Canyon, Big Bend National Park, Texas, indicates it is not hard at all. The river is some 30 feet across at this point. Taken March 2010. Photo by Sara Towe Horsfall.

**FIGURE 6.2.** At Hot Springs in Big Bend National Park, Texas, it is possible to wade across the Rio Grande River. Land in the foreground is in Texas; land on the other side of the river is in Mexico. March 2010. Photo by Sara Towe Horsfall.

property by illegals passing through. One rancher claims they "tore up water pumps, killed calves, destroyed fences and gates, stole trucks and broke into his home." He was sued by a group of illegals that he held briefly at gunpoint (Seper 2009).[26] In March 2010, an Arizona rancher was killed ostensibly because of border-related crime in the area (Malkin 2010). Arizona governor Jan Brewer defended an April 2010 state law that allowed police to ask for proof of citizenship if they stopped someone. More recently, the state authorized a fund-raising project to build a fence in Arizona (Davenport 2011). Alabama also passed an immigration law, most of which was over-ruled by a federal court in 2011. But police officers are allowed to check immigration status of persons in a traffic stop (Bluestein and Reeves 2011).

Other communities are taking matters into their own hands as well, because, they claim, the federal authorities are not taking sufficient action. In 2006, the city

26. They were represented by the Mexican American Legal Defense and Educational Fund (MALDEF).

council in Farmers Branch, Dallas County, passed an ordinance prohibiting property owners from renting to illegal immigrants. Today the town of 30,000 has a Hispanic population of 47 percent—a more than 300 percent increase over 1990. Council members claim the drain on the public services—schools, streets, utilities, parks, and so on—is more than the community can withstand (Tinsley 2006; Solis 2010). Even though district judges have so far ruled the ordinance unconstitutional (immigration is a federal, not a local, issue), several other communities, such as Hazelton, Pennsylvania, Freemont, Nebraska (CNN 2010), Temecula, Lancaster, and Lake Elsinore, California (Rosen 2011), have passed similar ordinances.

One tricky question regards the fate of the children who were very young when their parents came here as illegal immigrants. These youth are denied many citizenship rights, and yet they are more at home here than in Mexico. The Dream Act, proposed in 2010, and again in 2011, was intended to open the door to citizenship for these youth (Demirjian 2011).

Experts have debated whether illegal immigrants cost more than they contribute to the economy for decades. They no doubt add to the cost of state and local social services. But they pay a lot in taxes, and they are a vital part of the labor force. And they add something culturally. Some oppose the costly bilingual education programs, and about twenty-five states have passed official language laws. But in the meantime, the use of Spanish has grown, particularly in the southern states. There are now two Spanish national television networks, and many Spanish radio stations, newspapers, magazines, and journals.

Immigration reform is an "economic imperative," President Obama told people in El Paso in May 2011. He called for increased enforcement of existing laws and procedural reform to make it easier for immigrants to become legal (CNN 2011). Liberals favor fewer immigration restrictions and argue that illegal aliens should have access to basic services, including schooling, medical assistance, and welfare. Meanwhile, conservative lawmakers are calling for more border security, and some want to see another guest worker program. Other proposals for reform include separating the functions of INS and Border Patrol.

### Money Transfers

A high percentage of Hispanic immigrant earnings are often sent back to their home country. In 1998, 26 percent of all Latino households in the United States sent an average of $221 a month home to relatives (deSipio 2000). Remittances increased every year by an average of 17 percent until 2009, when they dropped back to the 2000 level, and were the same in 2010. But even still, for some countries, such as Haiti, Guatamala, Honduras, Nicaragua, and El Salvador, the remittances are more than 10 percent of the gross domestic product (IDB 2010).

Mexico received more remittances than other countries in Central America in 2010, at $21.1 billion. Almost all of them came from people living in the United States. In 2007, the total of the remittances sent to Mexico were $24 billion, the second largest source of foreign income in Mexico, after oil exports (*Fort Worth Star-Telegram* 2008).

---

**■■ ■■ ■■ BOX 6.2.**

**MEXICAN POVERTY**

In 2010, 46 percent of the people in Mexico were poor, according to a study by the National Council for the Evaluation of Social Development Policy (CONEVAL). Slightly more than 10 percent of those in poverty live in extreme poverty. That means that 52 million people in Mexico are poor, and more than 5 million people live in extreme poverty. These rates have increased in the past two years (Associated Press 2011).

---

**Coyotes**

No one knows exactly how many people cross the long U.S.-Mexican border illegally each year, but the dangers they face are known: drowning, rape, physical attack, starvation, dehydration, being forced to smuggle drugs or money, and death. For this risk, the charge is $1 to $3,000 for a Mexican, and up to $60,000 for people from other countries (Beaubien 2011; Gazzar 2005).

There are many published personal accounts from those who made it. But there are also accounts of those who don't make it. In 2002, the bodies of eleven illegal immigrants were found locked in a grain car in Iowa; they had been put on the wrong train (Gazzar 2005). In 2004, one hundred undocumented immigrants were found locked in a small, decrepit house in Los Angeles with no light and little food waiting for relatives to pay ransom. Police also found a brothel of teenage girls who were forced to work to pay their debt (Sanchez 2004). In Texas, undocumented Mexicans were found locked in the back of an unventilated truck, near death and abandoned on the road (Sedeno 2004). So many have tried unsuccessfully to cross the Arizona desert on foot that the

U.S. government has established water stations for them. In 2005, the Border Patrol rescued seventy-seven people walking across the desert west of Tucson, Arizona, who were severely dehydrated. They overpowered the smuggler and called 911 (Gazzar 2005).

Even so, the crossings continue. Border areas easily crossed are heavily patrolled with helicopters, weapons, and motion detectors. Warning signs are posted in English and Spanish. Many who try to cross in the nonmilitarized areas where the crossing is more treacherous don't make it. Crime on the Mexican side has increased the dangers there. Drug cartels that earn millions of dollars a year from smuggling fees are now major players (Beaubien 2011; Gazzar 2005).

The Border Patrol can't afford to do autopsies on all the bodies it finds, so unless the body has a knife or gunshot wound, it is buried nearby. Many Mexican families have relatives who left for the United States and were never heard from again. Both the Mexican and the U.S. governments have publicity campaigns to encourage Mexican residents not to try to cross illegally into the

**FIGURE 6.3.** In southern Arizona, encounters with illegal immigrants in remote mountainous recreational areas is not uncommon, as evidenced by this sign entering Carr Canyon a few miles from the border with Mexico. A blimp commonly observes all movement in the area. June 2009. Photo by Sara Towe Horsfall.

United States. They warn of the life-threatening dangers of illegal crossing—of the militarized zone, of the desert where they will die without water, of the coyotes and others who take advantage of them.

But not all coyotes (people who transport illegal immigrants from Mexico to the United States for a fee) are ruthless criminals. Some say they do it to help, and, while they make a good living, they take care to ensure the safety of their customers—and look to repeat business and referrals (Gazzar 2005).

### Comprehensive Immigration Reform: A Solution Proposed by the League of United Latin American Citizens (LULAC)

LULAC was founded in 1929, a time when Hispanics in some areas were facing social discrimination issues.[27] Since then it has been an important advocate for Hispanic issues, including legal issues.

On immigration, including illegal immigration, LULAC's view is that the United States is a land of immigrants. Each group has contributed to the culture and to economy, bringing their energy and values that melded together into a society that is uniquely American. Similarly, hardworking Hispanic immigrants and their families—legal or not—have much to contribute. The country will be richer culturally, more prosperous economically, and have a bigger and better outlook on life by openly accepting this group.

Immigration reform should include restructuring the naturalization process, according to LULAC. It would cost more to deport the 11 million illegals seeking documentation than to make them legal. And polls indicate people in the United States are not against immigrant groups, so long as they obey the laws, learn English, and integrate. Family unification should be a guiding principle in legalization.

In terms of a guest worker program, LULAC recommends making sure there are strong worker protections before implementing it. And the guest worker laws should be consistently and justly enforced without violating anyone's civil rights.

---

27. www.lulac.org/ and http://lulac.org/advocacy/issues/immigration_comprehesive_reform.

**FIGURE 6.4.** Mexican craftsmen left items "for donation" on the trail at Hot Springs in Big Bend National Park, Texas. They watched with great interest when someone looked at their items, and waved with relief when money was deposited in the container for the items taken. They undoubtedly waded across the Rio Grande River to put the items there in the morning and will wade across to collect the money after a sale. No law enforcement agents were to be seen but a sign on the trail warned that buying from Mexicans was illegal. March 2010. Photo by Sara Towe Horsfall.

Of particular concern to LULAC are the 65,000 high school graduates annually who don't have legal status. It would not cost the United States anything to grant citizenship to these children who came with their parents as illegals and grew up here. They could then get an education, develop professions, and contribute to society like other youth. "A very conservative estimate finds that the average DREAM Act student will make $1 million more over his or her lifetime."

As to current immigration policies, LULAC notes that the proposal to build a wall (the U.S. government calls it a fence) along the border sends the wrong message to the countries in Latin America. Trade and political cooperation requires trust and goodwill. Stringent and awkward border restrictions also have a negative impact on economics, in terms of additional transportation costs and procedures. And it keeps out a needed workforce. More worrying to Mexico, it provides a way for drug traffickers and organized crime to entrench themselves in Mexican society.

There are several myths about illegal immigrants that LULAC is careful to counter. Most importantly, they contribute to the economy. They do not take jobs; rather, their skills and labor are complementary. And they will fill the gap in the workforce as baby boomers retire. Their lower wages do not decrease anyone else's wages, but to the contrary increases them slightly because of the boost in productivity.

Second, they contribute to the social fabric. More than half of undocumented workers have counterfeit identity documents, so they collectively contribute substantially through their taxes. On the other hand, they will never receive the benefits, so their windfall Social Security payments come at a good time. As to other social services, illegal immigrants are generally not eligible, but they do assimilate by buying homes and becoming citizens. As a group, they have a low rate of criminal convictions.

While not endorsing the bill in its entirety, LULAC supports the Secure America and Orderly Immigration Act (SAOIA), first proposed by Senator John McCain and Senator Edward Kennedy in 2006. Although never passed, the bill has been discussed and amended in the years since. A summary of the measures follows:

- A plan to enhance border security will be developed and funded, and will include better coordination between federal, state, and local authorities, and between federal departments (Immigration, Customs, Border Protection). Financial and technical assistance will be given to Mexico to "dismantle human smuggling operations" and establish better border control on its southern border. Also, a cooperative program with Mexico and Central American countries will be established to track gang and other criminal activities.

- A new H-5A temporary three-year (renewable) visa for guest workers who maintain residence in their home country and don't violate U.S. laws. Guest workers are entitled to all U.S. labor protections and taxes. Employers cannot withdraw their visas. Foreign labor contractors can't charge for their services, and any transportation charges should be reasonable. The cap on guest workers is 400,000, with some adjustments and minimum 10 percent increases per year; 50,000 visas are reserved for rural countries that have a drop in population. Guest workers are only eligible for jobs posted in America's job bank for thirty days.

- Visas will be machine readable and tamper resistant. Information about employment, and so on, will be encrypted. The same system will be used for other immigrant visas. Employment based green cards increased from 140,000 to 290,000 per year, and unused numbers roll over from year to year.
- A H-5B nonimmigrant visa for illegals (and their families) who have been in the United States since 2005 and are employed. With a H-5B visa they can apply for permanent residency. Only authorized persons can represent an immigrant on legal concerns (for their protection).
- Hospitals will be reimbursed for emergency care of undocumented immigrants.

## ■ QUESTIONS FOR REVIEW

1. Describe the effect of the following immigration laws: Chinese Exclusion Act, Immigration Act of 1924, Immigration and Naturalization Act of 1952, and the amendment of that act in 1965?

2. What was the Braceros program and how did ending it contribute to the large number of illegal immigrants today?

3. What is the cost of maintaining the U.S. borders, particularly the U.S.-Mexican border?

4. Who enforces immigration policies?

## ■ QUESTIONS FOR FURTHER THOUGHT

1. This section has focused more on illegal immigrants from Mexico than other parts of the world. How are Mexican immigrants different from the others? How are they the same?

2. What problems would be encountered if the border with Mexico was more open?

3. Could there ever be a Unified North America (Canada, United States, Mexico) that functions like the European Union? Why or why not?

4. Why are some communities passing city ordinances restricting illegal immigrants? Will this have ramifications for relationships between local, state, and federal government?

5. How can concerns about undocumented workers be balanced with concerns for drug smuggling, human trafficking, and migration of international terrorists?

## ■ OTHER ADVOCATE GROUPS

### Advocates for Immigrant Rights

American Civil Liberties Union (ACLU)
Center for Human Rights and Constitutional Law
Council on Hemispheric Affairs
Inter-American Dialogue
Leadership Conference on Civil and Human Rights
League of the United Latin American Citizens (LULAC)
National Association for Bilingual Education
National Immigration Forum
Urban Institute

### Advocates for Limited Immigration or Immigration Controls

Americans for Legal Immigration
American Immigration Control Foundation
Center for Immigration Studies
Center for Individual Rights
Heritage Foundation
Sachem Quality of Life Organization

---

■■ ■■ ■■ BOX 6.3.

### DISCRIMINATION AGAINST MUSLIMS

A Gallup poll found that 9 out of 10 American Muslims are loyal to the US even though they faced more recent incidents of discrimination than other groups. American Muslims are also more confident in the fairness of the American political system than other groups, but were critical of its foreign policy.

---

*Source:* Goodstein 2001.

# CHAPTER SEVEN

# PROBLEMS ADDRESSED THROUGH PROFESSIONAL ORGANIZATIONS, NONPROFIT GROUPS, AND SPECIAL INTEREST GROUPS

Not all social problems can be resolved with government programs or by laws, although both are very important. Many problems need the assistance of professional groups. Problems involving youth are often addressed through schools. Health problems are often addressed by doctors or other health care providers. Assistance to those in need often comes from churches or religious organizations. Sometimes the government provides financial assistance, but not always. Americans are traditionally very generous people, and many programs are funded through private giving or through a combination of government and private funding.

President George W. Bush's faith-based initiative allowed federal agencies to fund churches and other religious groups. His argument was that in some areas, religious groups could serve the needs better than government programs. In 2003, the federal government gave $1.17 billion to faith-based groups, with states being encouraged to do the same. Not only has Obama not abandoned Bush's initiative, he has expanded it. A report in 2009 found that thirty-six states had faith-based initiatives, and one hundred cities had offices or liaisons to religious communities (Steinfels 2009).

Whether it is religious groups, professionals, nonprofits, or special interest groups, clearly people outside the government can work together to address social problems.

## ▚ DRUGS AND ALCOHOL

The main problem with drugs and alcohol is that they are addictive, which can lead to destructive behaviors, and long-term addiction has serious health risks. There is a heavy social cost to the individual, to families, and to communities. Addiction is dependency on a substance to maintain a normal sense of well-being. Drug addiction involves biological, psychological, social, economic, and cultural factors. Physical dependence includes withdrawal symptoms. Psychological dependence includes a willingness to sacrifice other things for the sake of the drug experience. The word *addiction* comes from a Latin word meaning to admire or surrender to a master. It was first used for alcohol, but then more commonly for drugs (Goode 2004). People who use drugs commonly refer to themselves as users, druggies, or junkies, and the term *hooked* refers to those who have taken the drug long enough to get withdrawal symptoms when they try to stop.

Researchers do not agree about what causes drug addiction. Some argue that people who use drugs do so to escape the reality of the world they live in. The DSM, a handbook for psychiatrists, and the World Health Organization use the terms *addiction* and *substance dependence* synonymously, referring to loss of freedom (inability to quit) as well as physiological and behavioral aspects.[1] This argument for addiction as a disease includes the fact that even after remission of several years, "the threat of relapse is always real" (Goode 2004, 30–31).

Others argue that addiction begins when users realize that they can avoid the pain and discomfort of withdrawal by taking another dose—however they came to take the drug in the first place. Along with this view is the observation that when the drug is difficult to obtain, excessive amounts are likely to be used once it is available (Lindesmith 2004).

Researchers also do not agree as to whether alcohol and marijuana should be included among addictive drugs. Clearly they can be addictive, but should they be controlled substances with possession treated as a criminal offense?

During the last century, the perspective has alternated between one of treating drug and alcohol abuse as a disease (treated by professionals) to one of

---

1. *Diagnostic and Statistical Manual.*

treating the abuse as a punishable criminal offense. When seen as a crime, it was assumed that lack of drug supply would "dry out" the offenders and the problem would be eradicated. When seen as a disease, addicts were treated in some way, most commonly some form of drug maintenance.

### Types of Drugs

There are many different types of drugs, but the focus here will be on narcotics and alcohol. By law, narcotics include "opium and its derivatives, the coca leaf and its active ingredient cocaine, and the cannabis plant, the source of marijuana and the powerful resin hashish" (Musto 1999, xiii). Other controlled substances include LSD, amphetamines, methamphetamines, barbiturates, and other chemically designed or designer drugs.

Opium comes from the opium poppy. One of the biggest producers in the twentieth century was Turkey, then Mexico and Afghanistan. It is used for pain, coughs, and other conditions. Its derivatives include codeine, morphine, and heroine. The coca plant grows in the Andes Mountains of South America. Locals use it as a digestive and circulatory aid. Cocaine, a powder derived from the leaves, is an analgesic (pain reliever). Amphetamines are chemically produced drugs that were first used to treat personality disorders. They are known as crystal meth, crank, speed, or ice. Barbiturates are also chemically produced and used as an anticonvulsant, especially for epilepsy. LSD, or lysergic acid diethylamide, is a chemically produced hallucinogenic. It was popular in the 1960s, thought to simulate spiritual experiences, and commonly called acid. Marijuana and hashish were also popular in the 1960s when they were also called weed. Today marijuana is used in chronic illnesses, and to counter the nausea caused by chemotherapy treatment for cancer.

### Modern Use of Alcohol and Drugs

The consumption of liquor and beer in the United States doubled each year from 1960 to 1980, and the use of wine trebled. From 1980 to 1994, however, it fell 20 percent per capita (Barr 1998, 17, 223). The alcohol content varies from beer—5 percent or less—to hard liquor—40 percent or more. The designation "proof" is double the percentage of alcohol by volume, so that 86 proof is equal to 43 percent alcohol. Most alcohol has nutritional value, especially calories. There is evidence that moderate wine drinking contributes to good health and longevity, but excessive drinking overloads and damages the liver, as well as the central nervous system. Heavy drinking is associated with cardiovascular problems. Someone with a blood alcohol content (BAC) of 0.1 or more has reduced coordination and is considered unable to make good judgments. Most would receive a DUI (driving while under the influence) charge if driving. In 1995, there were an estimated 10 million alcoholics in the United States, and approximately 20 million problem drinkers, which cost the country more than $100 billion in terms of loss, health care, and decreased productivity (Siegal and Inciardi 2004).

According to the CDC, in 2009, about 9 percent of the population used illicit drugs, approximately 7 percent used marijuana, and 3 percent used psychotherapeutic drugs (CDC 2011b).

Before seeking solutions to the drug and alcohol problem today, it is helpful to look at the history of drug and alcohol use in the United States, and its regulation.

### Alcohol

Many of the first settlers in North America—including the Pilgrims—drank water only if other beverages ran out; water was considered unhealthy (Barr 1998). Other drinks included beer and rum in the northern colonies, and in the south rum and whiskey, as well as wine, if they could afford it. In an effort to improve productivity by having workers drink beer instead of rum, James Oglethorpe persuaded the British Parliament to prohibit rum sales in the Georgia colony; the measure was repealed in 1749. Drinks like the mint julep, made with locally produced whiskey (or imported brandy), remained popular (Barr 1998).

And it was not just men who had a problem with alcohol. In the 1800s, women from all classes were known to drink. Common prescription "medicines" taken four or more times a day, were 18–42 percent alcohol by volume—comparable to sherry or whiskey. An upper class woman might have been a cologne drunk, while a working class woman had her "growler" filled while she waited by the side door of the saloon. Some turned to a nonalcoholic medicine, such as Coca-Cola, which originally contained cocaine (the cocaine was removed from Coca-Cola in 1903) (Barr 1998, 135–140).

The first temperance societies that formed in 1820s encouraged people to drink plain water instead of fortifying it with alcohol. Several who did died from the contaminated water, since no water treatment system was developed until after the Civil War (Barr 1998, 209). The first water purification system in New York was unsuccessful. But eventually it was worked out, and water, not alcohol, became the common drink.

Prior to Prohibition, several states tried to control alcohol sales, notably Maine and Massachusetts, although cider, beer, and wine were often exempted. One concern of the temperance campaigners was the immigrant workers who spent their meager salaries in the saloon rather than feeding their families. In 1916, 47 percent of tax revenues came from alcohol (Musto 1999).

### Prohibition

The Eighteenth Amendment (1920) banned alcohol sales. Whether or not its intent was to integrate heavy drinking immigrants into American life (Barr 1998, 248), it dried up legal sources of alcohol—but not the demand for it. Alcohol was brewed in private stills and imported illegally from Canada. Those who couldn't find anything else used undrinkable forms of alcohol. One result was the growth of an organized underworld. Anyone willing to risk the penalties had an economic opportunity. Some $2 billion a year that had previously gone to legal suppliers now went to organized crime. Crime increased in the large cities by 24 percent the first year (Gray 2000).

"In 1925, agents for the Prohibition Enforcement Bureau seized 172,537 illegal stills, but for every still captured, nine continued to operate" (Barr 240). The inability of the legal system to stop alcohol production (and sales) led to tougher penalties, disrespect for the law, and eventually to corrupt law officers. Government spending tripled. Sentences escalated to five years and $10,000 for a first offense. By 1929, some 25 percent of federal agents had been dismissed for things like bribery, extortion, conspiracy, embezzlement, and submission of false reports (Gray 2000, 67). Thousands died every year from drinking industrial alcohol, and by 1930 some 15,000 persons were paralyzed from drinking "jake," a dangerous combination of Jamaica ginger and methanol (Barr 1998, 241).

Prohibition didn't mean that alcohol wasn't available; it just changed venues. Wine could not be served in restaurants, so before dinner cocktails in a more clandestine location became customary—even in the White House. Doctors could still prescribe alcohol, albeit in limited quantities (1 pint per person per 10 days) (Barr 1998).

After close to ten years, even formerly staunch prohibitionists wanted it to end. Pauline Morton Sabin formed the Women's Organization for National Prohibition Reform in May 1929. William Randolph Hearst said Prohibition had "set the cause of temperance back 20 years" because it didn't educate people, so the effect was that drinking had actually increased. Even John D. Rockefeller, a major supporter of the Anti-Saloon League, condemned Prohibition because it recruited "a vast army of lawbreakers" (Barr 1998, 239, 249).

Several states kept Prohibition after 1933 (the Twenty-first Amendment overturned Prohibition). The last holdout was Mississippi, where alcohol sales weren't legal until 1966. Fifteen states prohibited sale of drinks in bars or restaurants, and three states allowed only 3.2 percent beer to be sold. In Oklahoma individual drinks couldn't be sold legally until 1985, and in Kansas until 1987. Dry counties remained common across the United States (Barr 1998, 252).

### After Prohibition

Alcohol can be addictive, but is it a drug? After Prohibition some people classified it as such to get tighter controls. In the 1970s, psychiatrist Morris Chafetz, director of the National Institute on Alcohol Abuse and Alcoholism, called it a drug so that its abuse would be taken seriously. Former surgeon-general Dr. Everett Koop called it a "toxic, potentially addictive drug." Betty Ford stated that it was the "number one drug of addiction" in the United States (Barr 1998, 18–19).

Others disagree, saying that alcohol's biggest effect is learned—it is an expected result. A study from the 1970s found that those told they were drinking alcohol but given water felt an effect, whereas those given hard liquor but told it was water felt nothing (Barr 1998, 24).

Another view is that alcoholism is a disease. Many nineteenth-century doctors thought of it as an illness. When it is regarded as a disease rather than a moral failing, social condemnation and stigma are neutralized, and the alcoholic becomes blameless—an approach taken by Alcoholics Anonymous in 1935 (Barr 1998). But the disease view served the government too. Officials could claim that the alcoholic and the drug addict could only be "cured" when they consumed no alcohol or drugs (Musto 1999, 214). But there is no known pathogen (physical cause) for it as a disease, and no antidote (physical cure). Curiously, only 21 percent of doctors today regard it as a disease. As one researcher argues:

> The disease concept of alcoholism is destroyed by its own internal contradiction. Any alcoholic who seeks treatment is told that by drinking alcohol he sets off an irrepressible desire for the substance and that he must therefore agree as a condition of his treatment to abstain from drinking. Yet if he does as he is told and abstains during treatment, he is disproving the theory that alcoholism is a disease that causes an inability to abstain from drinking. (Barr 1998, 23)

The medical view of alcoholism is not accepted in the armed forces. In a 1980 study, 16 percent of military personnel admitted to having been involved in a situation with serious consequences because of alcohol. Fear of reprisals typically prevents drinkers from seeking help (Barr 1998).

Yet another model is the European one—learn to drink responsibly. People with this view point to Mediterranean countries where wine is consumed with food. There are no drinking restrictions and few abusers.

In most states, the drinking age is twenty-one, but during the Vietnam War, it was lowered to eighteen or nineteen in some places. In recent years binge drinking has become a concern (five or more drinks in a row for men, four for women) of college students. Young people, freed from parental restraints, attend parties where large amounts of alcohol are consumed. As many as 40 percent of college students drink to get drunk, with fraternity and sorority members most at risk (Weschler et al. 2004). In most cases, however, this level of drinking does not continue later in life.

### Opium, Cocaine, and Their Derivatives

In the nineteenth century, considerable quantities of opium were imported to America, most of it legally. It was used for medicinal purposes—for stomach pains, coughs, insomnia, diarrhea, and as a calming antidote for other diseases. The attitude toward opium changed, however, with the spread of opium dens frequented by deviant underworld figures and Chinese (Barr 1998). An ordinance against opium in San Francisco in 1875 was one of the country's first drug laws.

Meanwhile, patent medicines, readily available around the country, commonly included heroin, morphine, and cocaine. Cocaine was popular because it was inexpensive and readily available. It was used in medicines, taken as a tonic, and touted as an addiction cure. In the South, however, it was erroneously feared as giving superior strength to African Americans. Morphine was commonly given for pain. Heroin, like cocaine, was introduced by clinical laboratories as a relatively harmless treatment for common ailments (Musto 1999).[2]

At the turn of the twentieth century, researchers estimate there were 250,000 addicts, but drug imports were rising. A 1902 report stated that in five years cocaine imports had increased by 40 percent, opium imports by 500 percent, and morphine imports by 600 percent, but doctors were prescribing them less than before (Gray 2000; Musto 1999).

Concerns about the opium trade led to a U.S. call for restrictions at the International Conference on Opium in The Hague in 1911. In 1914, the U.S. Congress passed a tax law, the Harrison Narcotic Act, to control the distribution of narcotics. The next year, 184,000 physicians, pharmacists, dentists, veterinarians, and traders registered (Musto 1999). At that time, physicians commonly treated addicts by drug maintenance—providing the lowest possible dosage of the addicting drug so the person can function normally in society and does not resort to the criminal underworld. Dr. Charles Terry of Florida insisted there was only a 5 percent cure rate, but 80 percent of the addicts he saw lived normal lives. In Louisiana, Dr. Willis Butler successfully stabilized the drug dosage of addicts and sent them back into the community. Around his Shreveport clinic crime was reduced and drugs were not sold, but crime increased and heroin and morphine were sold when the clinic was closed in 1923 (Gray 2000; Musto 1999).

---

2. The popularity of these medicines declined once people realized what was in them. "The Pure Food and Drug Act of 1906 required that any quantity of cannabis, as well as several other dangerous drug substances be clearly marked on the label of any drug or food sold to the public" (Musto 1999, 216).

A 1919 government report on drug use recommended more federal and local medical care for drug users.[3] The report claimed 1 million addicts, a figure considered to be exaggerated then and now. Approximately 238,000 addicts were being treated by doctors, and others were treated at government facilities around the country. The report claimed 61 percent of the treated addicts were "permanently cured" (Musto 1999, 137).

### Drug Users as Criminal Offenders

By the 1930s, drug addicts, like alcoholics, were regarded as immoral and criminal. Doctors who provided drugs were believed to be part of the problem. Maintenance clinics had been shut down and doctors were prosecuted for prescribing drugs. A bill for a national program to combat drug addiction failed in Congress. Another report claimed that only 10 percent of addicts were cured by medical treatment and that abrupt withdrawal worked just as well as maintenance.[4]

Government control of drugs increased when eight pharmaceutical companies were approved to manufacture narcotic painkillers (these companies now have a dominant market presence) (Gray 2000). In 1929, the Narcotic Division, working within the Prohibition Unit, had a $1.6 million budget. Two narcotic "farms" to house convicted addicts separately from others were approved, but not set up until 1935 and 1938 (in Fort Worth and Lexington) (Musto 1999). In 1930, the Federal Bureau of Narcotics (FBN) was formed to operate on its own apart from alcohol enforcement. It was a major drug enforcer during the 1930s and 1940s.

### Move Toward Drug Use as a Disease, Again

After World War II, Congress became concerned about the role of organized crime in the narcotics traffic. Other organizations preferred the earlier medical approach

---

3. By the Special Narcotics Committee of the U.S. Treasury Department.

4. Early heroin users in New York were entertainers, gangsters, and street people. After World War II, use spread among African Americans and Puerto Ricans. In the 1950s it became popular among young people. For a brief period in the 1970s supplies ran out, after President Nixon threatened and cajoled Turkey to prevent supplies from leaving that country. Soon supplies resumed from Mexico (Preble and Casey 2004; Musto 1999).

to drugs. The Joint Committee of the American Bar Association and the American Medical Association called for relaxed restrictions for doctors and more lenient sentences for offenders in the 1950s. The FBN condemned the approach as dangerously soft-hearted (Musto 1999). Still, in 1962 the Supreme Court declared addiction was a disease, not a crime. Courts became critical of prosecuting petty dealers who were addicts; methadone came to be seen as a substitute for heroin. By the end of the 1960s, the view of addiction as a disease had become popular again. In 1969, the National Institute of Mental Health, which regarded addiction as either a psychological problem or a physical disease, had a budget of $250 million compared with only $6 million for the FBN. The NIMH took the bars off the windows of the narcotic farms and turned them into hospitals.

Meantime, the drug abuse control amendments of 1965 added amphetamines, barbiturates, and LSD to the list of dangerous drugs. A presidential study of 1967 found that considerable amounts of drugs were being smuggled into the country and recommended customs enforcement to counter drug habits.

### The DEA and Nixon's War on Drugs

There were several successive changes in the federal drug agencies. The Bureau of Drug Abuse Control was formed in the Department of Health, Education, and Welfare, but it soon joined with the FBN to become the Bureau of Narcotics and Dangerous Drugs (BNDD) housed in the Justice Department (Musto 1999). In 1970, the Comprehensive Drug Abuse Prevention and Control Act led to the formation of the Drug Enforcement Administration (DEA) within the Justice Department. It left defining health risks and dependence to the Department of Health, Education, and Welfare.[5] The 1970 act also ranked drugs according to their dangerousness, and established a special commission to study government response to drugs (it recommended decriminalizing marijuana). The commission recommended consolidating all government agencies into one that would oversee enforcement, treatment, and research. It also recommended education efforts be stopped because they were ineffective and uncoordinated (Musto 1999). The National Institute on Drug Abuse (NIDA) was formed in 1973, which consolidated several government prevention programs (but not enforcement).

---

5. An array of presidential and government drug offices, reports, commissions, committees, programs, and agencies functioned during the last half of the twentieth century.

## Drug Users as Criminal Offenders, Again

After the tolerance of the 1970s, in the 1980s officials returned to criminal prosecution to treat drugs and alcohol. Almost all states had mandatory minimum sentences for drug offenses by 1983, and additional federal laws were passed to deal with dealers, to increase law enforcement, and to put warnings on alcohol containers. The prison population grew from the 1980s to 2000, with at least half of the increase due to drug offenses (Musto 1999, 279). Further, from 1985 to 2000, the war on drugs cost the United States some $300 billion, and many lives (Gray 2000). Some suggest that the drug trade has produced similar organized crime groups as did Prohibition. The map of Chicago today is "chillingly similar" to the gangland map of Chicago in the 1920s.

> On the near North Side where the O'Banion gang once slugged it out with the Terrible Gennas, you now find the Vice Lords facing off with the Latin Kings. And where Terry Druggan and Frankie Lake once peddled synthetic scotch whiskey and needled beer, the Mexican Mafia now provides cocaine and heroin. And there can be no doubt who is the successor to Big Al [Capone]. The vast territory that sweeps from the South Side and arcs around the Loop to the west is owned and operated by Larry Hoover and the Gangster Disciples. (Gray 2000, 21)

---

■■ ■■ ■■ BOX 7.1.

### U.S. EXPANDS ITS ROLE IN HELPING MEXICO FIGHT THE WAR ON DRUGS

By Ginger Thompson, *New York Times*
SUNDAY, AUGUST 7, 2011

Washington–The US is expanding its role in Mexico's bloody fight against drug-trafficking organizations, sending new CIA operatives and retired military personnel to the country and considering plans to deploy private security contractors in hopes of turning around a multibillion-dollar effort that has shown few results.

In recent weeks, small numbers of CIA operatives and US civilian military employees have been posted at a Mexican military base, where, for the first time, security officials from both countries are working side by side to collect information about drug cartels and help plan operations.

Officials also look into embedding a team of US contractors inside a specially vetted Mexican counternarcotics police unit.

*(continues)*

---

**:: :: :: BOX 7.1.** ―――――――――――――――――――――――

**U.S. EXPANDS ITS ROLE IN HELPING MEXICO FIGHT THE WAR ON DRUGS**
*(continued)*

Officials from both sides have said the new efforts have been designed to get around Mexican laws that prohibit foreign military and police from operating on its soil and to prevent advanced US surveillance technology from falling under the control of Mexican security agencies with long histories of corruption.

"A sea change has occurred over the past years in how effective Mexico and US intelligence exchanges have become," said Arturo Sarukhan, Mexico's ambassador to the US. "It is underpinned by the understanding that transnational organized crime can only be successfully confronted by working hand in hand and that the outcome is as simple as it is compelling: We will together succeed or together fail."

The latest steps come three years after the US began increasing its security assistance to Mexico with the $1.4 billion Merida Initiative and tens of millions of dollars from the Defense Department.

They also come a year before elections in both countries, when President Barack Obama may face questions about the threat of violence spilling over the border and Mexican President Felipe Calderon's political party faces an electorate that is almost certainly going to ask why it should stick with a fight that has left nearly 45,000 people dead.

---

Some prevention programs have been started in schools. Drug Abuse Resistance Education (DARE) involves meeting with police officers to learn about the dangers of drug use. Another program is Students Taught Awareness and Resistance (STAR) and Life Skills Training (LST). The latter is said to receive a more positive evaluation than the others.

### Marijuana

#### Marijuana as a Controlled Substance

During the first part of the twentieth century, marijuana was not considered as dangerous as other drugs and was not proscribed until 1937. During Prohibition, marijuana was legal and consumed in tea rooms. But after 1933, it became the focus of government action, being portrayed in an exaggerated way as a drug that caused wild, even violent behavior, especially among Mexicans on the southern border. One official declared it was a national crisis. The 1937 Marijuana Tax Act taxed grower, distributor, seller, and buyer. After that it was not illegal but was hard to get (Gray 2000; Musto 1999).

Since then various people have repeatedly lobbied and testified to its usefulness and safety. A report from the New York Academy of Medicine in 1945 stated that marijuana did not lead to insanity or violence, was neither addictive nor a gateway to other drugs, and was in fact less dangerous than alcohol. But the perception of it as a dangerous drug remained.

### Marijuana as a Dangerous Drug

Marijuana became a favorite during the 1960s. It was a time of youth rebellion against the establishment and protests against U.S. involvement in Vietnam. Perhaps because of the seemingly unjustified sentences for using marijuana, young people ignored the warnings about other drugs during this time, as well (Musto 1999).

Under the 1970 Drug Abuse and Control Act, marijuana was categorized as a dangerous drug, but in 1972 the commission set up to study it recommended that it be decriminalized, making it a finable offense. President Nixon didn't agree, so possession and use remained a punishable crime (Musto 1999; Gray 2000). A 1971 poll found that 24 million people used marijuana, with 40 percent between the ages of eighteen and twenty-one (Musto 1999, 248).

By 1975 only 35 percent of the population thought marijuana was a dangerous drug (Musto 1999, 258). In 1988, after two years of DEA hearings and deliberation, the DEA's administrative judge ruled that "marijuana in its natural form is one of the safest therapeutically active substances known to man." Still, the DEA rejected the idea of medical marijuana (Gray 2000, 176).

### Marijuana as a Medicine

By the 1990s, marijuana use was found among twelve- to seventeen-year-olds, with approximately one in five high school seniors having used it. As of 2011, twenty-four states[6] have decriminalized marijuana, making it similar to a minor

---

6. Alaska, Arkansas, Colorado, California, Connecticut, Hawaii, Illinois, Kansas, Maine, Massachusetts, Michigan, Minnesota, Missouri, Mississippi, Montana, Nebraska, Nevada, New York, North Carolina, Ohio, Oregon, Pennsylvania, Texas, Washington.

traffic violation (no prison time, criminal record), and fifteen states[7] have approved the medical use of marijuana. But it is still illegal at the federal level, so violators could be prosecuted even though no state laws were broken. In 2008, a World Health Organization study found that 42 percent of the U.S. population had tried marijuana at least once and a high percentage had tried it by age 15 (Lynch 2008).

## Understanding the Drug Problem

### Who Becomes an Abuser?

Clearly drugs, alcohol, and marijuana are addictive. But not everyone uses them, and not all who use them abuse them. The fact that general use of drugs declined after the Pure Food and Drug Act of 1906 shows that most people can recognize the dangers. Young people, however, may not have the ability to distinguish. This is why we have age limits on alcohol. Alternatively, some argue that rebellious youth use alcohol precisely because it *is* illegal, and in some European countries young people are not restricted but rather are taught how to drink responsibly. In any case, reports are that less than 10 percent of the population use drugs and marijuana consistently.

### Who Controls the Supply?

If a substance is illegal, the government controls the supply, and the legal authority punishes offenders. If a substance is illegal but there is demand for it, the persons who control the supply are, by definition, criminals. In that case, all laws concerning fair trade and taxes to the government are inapplicable. In fact, as we all know, criminal suppliers can be ruthless because they have nothing to lose and everything to gain by their ruthlessness.

If a substance is controlled, only certain qualifying persons can supply the substance under approved conditions. This is sometimes called the public health approach: physicians are allowed to prescribe certain drugs so their use is

---

7. Virginia allowed physicians to prescribe marijuana in 1979; California legalized marijuana in 1996; Alaska, Oregon, and Washington in 1998; Maine in 1999; Colorado, Hawaii, and Nevada in 2000; Maryland in 2003; Montana in 2004; Rhode Island in 2006; New Mexico in 2007; Michigan in 2008; Arizona and New Jersey in 2010; and Delaware in 2011.

controlled and crime eliminated. If a substance is not illegal and not controlled, the individual is responsible to monitor its use and guard against addiction.

Alcohol actually fits in all three of these categories. It is illegal for minors, legal for adults in most places, and controlled in venues where alcohol is served but minors are present. Alcohol is also controlled, in that containers must contain a warning label, and in some places, the person serving the drinks bears some responsibility if there is an accident caused by overdrinking.

### Should Drugs Be Allowed for Recreational Purposes?

The problems that develop with drug use are primarily concerned with nonmedical use. In most cases alcohol use is recreational rather than medicinal. Marijuana is being approved for medicinal use in several states, although clearly it also has a recreational use.

### How to Treat Addicts

What kind of help do addicts need? Most agree that even alcohol addiction is hard, if not impossible, to counter alone. When drugs are illegal, the user is drawn deeper into the criminal world to fulfill his or her need. What is an acceptable punishment for users who become pushers to support their habit? Is drug maintenance an alternative? How should treatment centers be financed and run? Should alcohol be included? For alcohol, at what point does acceptable use become a criminal offense? Who should treat juvenile offenders and juvenile addicts?

In 1903, pharmacist James H. Beal, who assisted the Committee on the Acquirement of the Drug Habit, concluded, "The principal object of the law must be to prevent the creation of drug habits, rather than to reform those who are already enslaved, however desirable the latter might be." A second statement is by President Jimmy Carter, who in 1977 said, "Penalties against possession of a drug should not be more damaging to an individual than the use of the drug itself; and where they are, they should be changed" (Musto 1999, 18, 261).

### Who Benefits?

Everyone benefited when alcohol was legalized after Prohibition: crime went down, people did not die or become paralyzed from bad alcohol, tax revenues went up, alcohol producers went into business, social drinkers no longer had to break the law. Those who did not benefit were bootleggers whose customers disappeared.

Today, those who benefit from illegal drugs are those involved with the drug cartels. On the other hand, the cost to the government to prevent drug sales is considerable. And the cost in loss of human life is also considerable. The cost in Mexico, a major route for drug supplies to the United States, is political instability; politicians or law officials who take a stand against the illegal drug trade risk their lives.

Most people (80–90 percent) in the United States, however, are not directly affected—except that their taxes are consumed by the exorbitant costs of policing the drug traffic and housing criminal offenders.

### What Is the Goal for Society?

An alternative model of sorts is found in Europe. In the Netherlands, small amounts of marijuana are sold legally in shops near the center of Amsterdam. In Britain heroin is available, and hence there is no illicit market for the drug. Users are given medical guidance.

Clearly strict controls, while intended to keep dangerous substances out of the hands of abusers, have unintended consequences. It is unlikely that drug use and abuse will go away anytime soon, so we must decide what kind of society we want. How do we balance the dangers with the freedom that we cherish? How do we protect youth and others who are susceptible? How do we treat those who have fallen into addiction?

### End Drug Prohibition; Regulate and Control Drugs: A Solution Proposed by Law Enforcement Against Prohibition (LEAP)

Founded in 2002, LEAP is made up of former law enforcement officers or lawyers, judges, and others involved in the war on drugs. They are speaking out against the failure of the current system, saying it has not reduced drug use, addiction, or crime.

For four decades the US has fueled its policy of a "war on drugs" with over a trillion tax dollars and increasingly punitive policies. More than 39 million arrests

---

**:: :: :: BOX 7.2.** ————————————————————————

## DRUG DEATHS PASS TRAFFIC FATALITIES

By Lisa Girion, Scott Glover, and Doug Smith, *Los Angeles Times*

SEPTEMBER 18, 2011

Los Angeles–Propelled by an increase in prescription narcotic overdoses, drug deaths now outnumber traffic fatalities in the US, a Los Angeles Times analysis of government data shows.

Drugs exceeded motor vehicle accidents as a cause of death in 2009, killing at least 37,485 people nationwide, according to preliminary data from the US Centers for Disease Control and Prevention.

Though most major causes of preventable death are declining, drugs are an exception. The death toll has doubled in the last decade, now claiming a life every 14 minutes. This is the first time that drugs have accounted for more fatalities than traffic accidents since the government started tracking drug-induced deaths in 1979.

Fueling the surge in deaths are prescription pain and anxiety drugs that are potent, highly addictive and especially dangerous when combined with one another or with other drugs or alcohol. Among the most commonly abused are OxyContin, Vicodin, Xanax and Soma. One relative newcomer is Fentanyl, a painkiller that comes in the form of patches and lollipops and is 100 times more powerful than morphine.

---

for nonviolent drug offenses have been made. The incarcerated population quadrupled over a 20-year period, making building prisons the nation's fastest growing industry. More than 2.3 million U.S. citizens are currently in prison or jail, far more per capita than any country in the world. The United States has 4.6 percent of the population of the world but 22.5 percent of the world's prisoners. Each year this war costs the United States another 70 billion dollars. Despite all the lives destroyed and all the money so ill spent, today illicit drugs are cheaper, more potent, and much easier to access than they were at the beginning of the war on drugs, 40 years ago. Meanwhile, people continue dying on the streets while drug barons and terrorists continue to grow richer, more powerful, better armed.

Not one of the stated U.S. drug policy goals of lowering the incidence of crime, addiction, drug availability, or juvenile drug use, has been achieved.

Instead, our approach has magnified these problems by creating a self-perpetuating, ever-expanding policy of destruction, yet the United States still insists on continuing the war and pressuring other governments to perpetuate these same unworkable policies. The drug war wreaks havoc, funds terrorism, and causes major corruption around the globe. This is the very definition of a failed public policy. This madness must cease!

With this in mind, current and former members of law enforcement have created a drug policy reform group called LEAP. Supporters of LEAP believe that to save lives and lower the rates of disease, crime and addiction, as well as to conserve tax dollars, we must end drug prohibition. LEAP believes a system of regulation and control is far more effective than one of prohibition.

### Racial Discrimination of Current Drug Policy

In terms of racial apprehensions, according to LEAP 72 percent of drug users are white, and only 13 percent are African American. Yet 81 percent of the federally prosecuted drug offenders are African American. The current drug policy keeps "a massive segment" of black men in prison. LEAP members want persons incarcerated for violation of zero tolerance to be released and have their record expunged. But those convicted of additional crimes should not be exonerated.

### Current Drug Policy Encourages Illegal Activities

The current drug policy also feeds the drug cartels and criminal gangs that make $500 billion a year. These illegal activities flourish when drugs are prohibited, just as they did during Prohibition.

### Current Drug Policy Does Not Educate

The amount of money spent on arresting drug offenders would have greater impact if it were used to educate teens and others about drug use. Also, those who suffer from drug addiction should be provided help in drug treatment centers or by drug maintenance. The government could treat these people at a fraction of the current cost of the drug war.

### A Fair Drug Policy Should Balance Freedom and Potential Harm

Adult drug abuse is a health problem and a matter of individual freedom, so long as others are not harmed. Because drugs are dangerous and addictive,

━━ ■■ ■■ ■■ BOX 7.3. ━━━━━━━━━━━━━━━━━━━━━━━━━━━━━

**BRUTAL DRUG GANG TAKES OVER MIGRANT SMUGGLING**

By Tim Johnson, McClatchy Newspapers

FRIDAY, AUGUST 12, 2011

Arriaga, Mexico–One of Mexico's most powerful criminal gangs has muscled into the migrant smuggling racket, changing what had been a relatively benign, if risky, industry of independent operators into a centralized business that often has deadly consequences for those who try to operate outside it.

Los Zetas, who earned a reputation for brutality by gunning down thousands of Mexicans in the battle for drug-smuggling routes to the US, now control much of the illicit trade of moving migrant workers toward the US border, experts in the trade say.

They've brought logistical know-how, using tractor-trailer trucks to carry ever larger loads of people and charging higher prices, as much as $30,000 per head for migrants from Asia and Africa who seek to get to the US.

They've also brought an unprecedented level of intimidation and violence to the trade. Los Zetas or their allies often kidnap and hold for ransom poor migrants who try to operate outside the system. If relatives don't wire payment, the migrants are sometimes executed and dumped in mass graves or forced into jobs with the criminal group.

Nearly a year ago, Zetas gunmen were implicated in the slaughter of 72 migrants at a ranch near San Fernando in Tamaulipas state, barely a 1½ hour drive from Brownsville.

Other mass graves discovered in northern Mexico may also be the work of Los Zetas pushing to control smuggling to the US.

Alejandro Solalinde, an activist Roman Catholic priest who runs a migrant shelter in the town of Ixtepec, in Mexico's Oaxaca state, said Los Zetas had been merciless with migrants.

"Los Zetas control the trafficking of persons," he said. "They are crueler and kill more easily. . . . They are voracious. They ask for more and more and more money."

The ascendancy of Los Zetas in migrant smuggling, formerly the preserve of relatively small independent operators known as "coyotes," who smuggled groups of 20 or fewer migrants north, has transformed the business.

Mexican officials report regularly finding tractor-trailer trucks loaded with as many as 250 migrants. The heavily armed drivers, who travel with escort vehicles, make payoffs at police and immigration checkpoints.

they require regulation and control. Restrictions should include age restrictions on the sale and use of drugs. Different drugs have different risks, so each would have appropriate controls. Government can assess the risks associated with each drug, and issue warnings.

Their recommendation is that drugs should be legalized and government should take over procuring drugs (to ensure quality control) and offer free distribution to addicts, free treatment centers, and education for users and the public. In this way, overdoses would be eliminated, the government would earn money taxing the sales, and there would be no deaths associated with drugs, and also fewer AIDS cases. Four European countries do this with success: Switzerland, the Netherlands, Germany, and Denmark.

## Analysis

*Target Group/Situation:* For LEAP, the target group—the victim—is everyone who experiences the violence associated with the drug wars.

*Ameliorating Action:* The action is to make drugs legal, albeit with controls.

*Action Group:* The action group in this case would be the government, as a law would need to be passed.

*Will to Act:* At the moment (2011) the will to act is not sufficient. The idea that drugs are dangerous and must be eliminated is still popular. However, increasing violence and the obvious inability of law enforcement agents to stop the flow of drugs may increase the will to act before long.

*Why Did the Problem Develop?* For LEAP, the problem developed because of a misinformed belief that a stricter policy would eliminate the drug problem, in essence, ignorance.

*Level of Social Problem:* This problem exists at all levels: local, regional, national, international.

## About the Group

*Type of Advocate Group:* LEAP is a special interest group. It has legal standing and has a purpose to change the laws that make drugs illegal, putting appropriate controls and regulations in their place.

*Why Did the Advocate Group Form?* LEAP formed because of a desire for structural reform—the current way of addressing drug issues does not work. Arresting people for no reason other than drug possession fills the prison system at a cost to the taxpayer, diverts law enforcement away from more important problems, and does not prevent drug abuse. But it does increase crime and the amount of money that goes to drug cartels or drug gangs.

*View of Human Nature:* The view of human nature that this group takes seems consistent with the greater good human being: if people realize the dangers and work together, the problems can be resolved without resorting to restrictive policies and punishments. Perhaps in regard to drug treatment, the view of human nature is more the compassionate, sacrificing human being. This group wants drug addicts to be treated and helped, not faced with a criminal record.

*Dynamics of the Advocate Group:* The group appears to be loosely organized, with some formal structure but not particularly hierarchical. The central organization seems to function more as a coordinating group for its activities, while individuals pursue the goal of eliminating drug prohibition as they see fit.

*Stage of Development of the Advocate Group:* It started in 2002, so it is a fairly new organization. It has some sophistication but has not developed a central authority of single point of view, exactly. Perhaps the coalescence stage best describes this group.

## Other Factors

*Claims Making:* While the arguments made by LEAP representatives are very enthusiastic, they appear to be quite factual. The figures used are intended to shock and drive home the point. The data given on the website is not sourced and is somewhat glossy. But still it is believable. The bias they have is the enthusiasm, which can skew the presentations.

*Opposition Groups:* There is definitely opposition to this viewpoint. LEAP is one of the few groups, and a minority of those in law enforcement, that want to end drug prohibition. No doubt some of the opposition to their viewpoint would be vigorous. It is a controversial issue.

*Consequences/Unintended Consequences:* The point of LEAP's argument is that the results of the war on drugs are unintended. No one intended to spend so much to fight drugs, and yet be unable to make a dent, or perhaps even increase the violence, and certainly increase the crime organizations. As to the unintended consequences of making drugs legal but controlled, the organization doesn't see any. There would definitely be a period of adjustment, while people got used to and discovered the best way to control and regulate the drugs and treat addicts.

One consequence of making drugs legal would be a reduction of persons in prisons across the country. Another would be the reduction in law enforcement agents, and activity in the court system.

*Type of Reform Sought:* The change sought is reformative: it wants a relatively small change (making drugs legal) for everyone. In terms of the type of change, it wants a legal change, but also perhaps a government program (treatment) and/or allocation of treatment to professional groups (doctors or others who can administer drugs in a controlled way).

*Model for Social Change:* Either restructuring or redesign. It could be restructuring in that the current way of controlling drugs will need to be revamped. Different laws will apply (presumably something about doctors or professionals administering drugs to addicts), and so it is unlikely that police officers would be the ones apprehending those who don't follow the restrictions. It could be redesign model in that a whole new way of addressing the situation needs to be worked out. It will take some creative thinking, and in a way, it is a new paradigm.

*Show Them What Will Happen to Them:*
*A Solution Proposed by the Montana*
*Meth Project's* Not Even Once *Campaign)*

Please see Box 9.2 (in Chapter 9) for a seemingly successful media campaign against meth.

## ■ QUESTIONS FOR REVIEW

1. What are the different controlled substances in the United States?
2. How did drug use first develop in the United States?
3. What was Prohibition? Why was it instituted, and what was the result?
4. What is the government agency that regulates drugs today?

## ■ QUESTIONS FOR FURTHER THOUGHT

1. Why were so many women addicted to drugs and alcohol in the nineteenth century?

2. Are there unregulated substances today, similar to those contained in patent drugs in the nineteenth century?

3. What is the difference between alcohol, narcotics, and marijuana in terms of use? In terms of addiction? In terms of legal ramifications? In terms of use by young people?

4. Given that so many states have approved of marijuana for medical use, what do you think will happen to the federal law that classifies it as a dangerous drug? Who will oppose changing it? Will the Supreme Court play a role?

## ■ OTHER ADVOCATE GROUPS

### Decriminalize Drugs
American Civil Liberties Union (ACLU)
Cato Institute
The National Organization for the Reform of Marijuana Laws (NORML)

*Lesser Punishment and/or Treatment*

Alcoholics Anonymous (AA)
Drug Policy Alliance
Drug Strategies
National Association of Drug Court Professionals (NADCP)
Partnership at Drug Free

*Traditional Approach*

Center on Addiction and Substance Abuse (CASA)
Center for Drug Abuse Prevention and Center for Drug Abuse Treatment
Drug Abuse Resistance Education (DARE)
Drug Free America Foundation (DFAF)

*Another Helpful Site*

National Drug Strategy Network: Criminal Justice Policy Foundation

## ∷ HOMELESSNESS

A homeless person, as defined by the McKinney-Vento Act of 1994, is someone who has no regular, adequate nighttime residence and consequently sleeps in someone else's house, in a motel or hotel, a campground, a shelter or another institution, a car, a park, or an abandoned building.

No one knows exactly how many homeless people there are. The best estimates come from a count of the people in shelters and on the street on a specific night around the country—671,859 at the last count.[8] To that figure, some would add anyone who was homeless for any length of time throughout a given year. They argue this is a more accurate count. Using that method, the National Law Center on Homelessness and Poverty estimates that more than 3 million people were homeless in 2010.

---

8. A count of the number of homeless around the country on one night in January is taken by various agencies every other year and submitted to the Department of Housing and Urban Development to qualify for housing assistance funds (NAEH 2011).

Men are the majority of homeless (64 percent in 2008). There are about the same number of blacks as whites (42 percent black, 40 percent white, and 11.6 percent Hispanic in 2008). In terms of age, most are between thirty-one and fifty (40 percent in 2008), although many are fifty-one or older (15 percent in 2008), and many are younger than eighteen (20 percent in 2008) (NAEH 2011).

Most of the homeless are in large urban areas, but rural areas also have homeless. They are likely to be transients, staying with friends or relatives, or sleeping in a car. Residents may be unaware of the homeless in their community because there are so few shelters or support programs in rural areas.

### *Why Are People Homeless?*

Some homeless are normal families who are temporarily unable to afford regular housing. They are unable to meet mortgage payments or rent. Some are without work, but those who are employed likely faced a financial crisis of some sort—bankruptcy from health care bills is not uncommon. (NCH reports that 19 percent of the homeless are employed, the NLCHP reports almost half: NCH 2009; NLCHP 2010.) A study of the homeless in Fort Worth, Texas, found a family of four living in the shelter although the husband worked for the city. They had lost their home and had nowhere else to go (Pate 2002). At least one well-known actress was at one time a homeless person. Debbie Reynolds revealed that she once lived in her car and used public bathrooms on a daily basis.

The current high unemployment rate and home foreclosures from the recent recession have impacted homelessness. Nearly 40 percent of foreclosure evictees were renters. HUD has reported a shortage of housing available for people with low incomes (NCH 2009b). Those who couldn't find other accommodations and/or assistance became homeless. Families include children. Sixty percent of the children (under 18) who are homeless are with families. They live doubled-up with family or friends (34 percent in 2000) or in motels or elsewhere (23 percent in 2000) (NCH 2009). Still, with minimal assistance, these families are usually able to "bounce back" (NAEH 2011b).

Veterans are another recognizable group of homeless (11.6–13 percent). They often have physical or mental disabilities as well as substance abuse problems and/or inclinations toward violence stemming from difficulties returning to civilian life (NAEH 2011b; NCH 2009).

About half of the homeless have mental health issues, and about one-quarter are seriously mentally ill. Many of these are the chronic homeless (18 percent in 2008), with physical or mental disabilities. This is the public face of homelessness—what people imagine when they think of the homeless. This group also consumes a majority of the assistance resources. Prior to the 1990s, some of the mentally ill were patients in mental hospitals, but the deinstitutionalization of treatment closed many state hospitals. Officials today state that most are able to function within the community as long as they have supportive housing and services. Forty-three percent of the adult homeless are disabled, 13 percent are physically disabled (NAEH 2011b; NCH 2009).

Youths who run away from home due to family conflict, divorce, neglect, or abuse are a fourth group of homeless. An estimated 1 million youth a year are homeless for some time during the year. About 36 percent of the youth (7 percent of all homeless) are long-term homeless (NAEH 2011b).

Another reason for homelessness is domestic violence. In 2008 it was reported that 15 percent of the homeless were victims of violence, and some researchers estimate that half of the women and children who are homeless have experienced domestic violence (NCH 2009).

### Cost of Homelessness

Advocates contend that the current shelter approach is the most costly option. Providing emergency shelter for a homeless family costs more than it would to arrange for transitional or permanent housing for the family. The emergency room, which the homeless typically use, is the most expensive health care; and because they delay care, homeless typically have longer hospital stays. Ordinances against loitering put many homeless in jail repeatedly, at a cost to the city. Recent studies indicate that the overall cost of providing permanent housing and support services would be much less (NAEH 2011c).

### Funding for Assistance Programs

The McKinney-Vento Assistance Grants program, first established in 1985, provides the bulk of government assistance. It distributes funds to assistance providers who work together in a local area. It was updated in 2009 in the HEARTH Act

(Homeless Emergency Assistance and Rapid Transition to Housing), which emphasizes families, prevention, permanent housing, and rural communities.

The 2009 Homelessness Prevention and Rapid Re-Housing Program (HPRP) allocated $1.5 billion to help people stay in permanent housing. It pays security deposits, utility or moving bills, rent to avoid eviction, and helps families move to their own apartments. A big difference is that now people on the verge of homelessness qualify and can receive assistance for three to eighteen months (O'Leary 2010).

The government agency SAMHSA (Substance Abuse and Mental Health Services Administration) provides substance abuse and mental health services. It also provides services for those going into permanent housing. This ten-year government plan to combat homelessness, announced in 2010, focuses on education, employment, housing, and health care. It was developed by a partnership of four agencies—Housing and Urban Development, Labor, Health and Human Services, and Veterans Affairs.

Private funding for homelessness comes from many sources. Big donors are the United Way and the John D. and Catherine T. MacArthur Foundation. Religious groups and churches also provide assistance in various forms.

### Local Agencies

Government funding stipulates cooperation between local agencies to coordinate services. The Tarrant County Homeless Coalition, for instance, includes seven different agencies that provide assistance to the homeless in the area: (1) Presbyterian Night Shelter, (2) Fort Worth Day Resource Center for the Homeless, (3) Union Gospel Mission of Tarrant County, (4) Salvation Army, (5) Safe Haven of Tarrant County (family violence victims), (6) ACH Child and Family Services' Emergency Youth Shelter (for runaway youth), and (7) Arlington Life Shelter. Four of them are located within a small area near downtown Fort Worth, where homeless are known to hang out, not far from a large highway underpass. Day shelters usually provide meals and other amenities such as showers. Night shelters can house limited numbers of people, who are allowed to come inside only after a certain hour and are asked to leave by a fixed time in the morning. Because the homeless have no residential address, they lack many of the privileges others take for granted, including voting rights, education for children, and health care. Some shelters allow the homeless to use the shelter address, so they can apply for jobs or government benefits.

### A Comprehensive Ten-Year Plan: A Solution Proposed by the National Alliance to End Homelessness

In 1983 a group of concerned leaders who formed the Committee for Food and Shelter soon found that the problem was much bigger and more complex than they first imagined.[9] In 1987 it became the current organization. Currently there are 2,000 providers and 10,000 partners affiliated with the alliance. A nonprofit group, it analyzes policy and develops pragmatic solutions, working with public, private, and nonprofit sectors. Part of its mission is to provide data that can inform policy makers and educate the public.

The alliance works to end homelessness mainly by assisting communities to develop local plans. The data about homelessness that they make available emphasizes the four populations of homeless who need specific kinds of assistance. (1) Chronic homeless need housing with no time limits, and supportive assistance, also with no time limits. (2) Families need help with prevention strategies and rapid rehousing. Rent assistance, help with security deposits or services can prevent people from becoming homeless in the first place. Help with employment, TANF services, and counseling can help others to stabilize. This assistance is available from the government through the HPRP of 2009. (3) Veterans need permanent housing and services, without limits. (4) Youth need intervention services, housing, and transitional support for foster care.

The alliance has a checklist for local communities that are developing a plan for homelessness in their area. The plan should be comprehensive and systematic, making sure to address all the facets of homelessness. The plan should be based on reliable data about the number of homeless. Emergency services and other assistance should be easily accessible to the vulnerable population. Certain homeless persons—released felons, foster children, and those released from mental health facilities—will have special needs, such as case management, services, and housing. Homeless housing should not have mandates for sobriety or treatment, since many have a mental illness, substance

---

9. www.endhomelessness.org.

addiction, or negative behavior patterns. Cash assistance programs through the federal or state government can help people become more stable.

The group's plan includes four principles. (1) Everyone should cooperate to identify those who are homeless. State and local agencies and organizations whose clients are homeless should be included in the planning. (2) To prevent homelessness, those who already receive public assistance—from the mental health, welfare, veterans, criminal justice, and child protective services systems—should be held accountable, and given incentives for positive client outcomes. (Close the front door.) (3) Help those who are not chronically ill and chronically homeless to exit the system as quickly as possible. (Open the back door.) (4) Make sure that affordable housing is available, and that the poor have adequate income to pay for necessities; otherwise, in the long run, the cycle will begin again. (Build the infrastructure.)

So far the alliance has helped 243 communities to develop ten-year plans to end homelessness. The group optimistically reports that progress is being made in ending homelessness.

■ **QUESTIONS FOR REVIEW**

1. What are the five different populations of homeless, and why did they become so?

2. How many of the homeless are men? Women? Children? Mentally ill?

3. How are homeless people helped? Who pays for the shelters and services?

■ **QUESTIONS FOR FURTHER THOUGHT**

1. Which figure do you think is a more accurate count of the homeless—the point in time count or the annual estimate of people who have been homeless at some point in the year? Why?

2. How are the groups of homeless different? How are their needs different?

3. The McKinney-Vento Act requires that local providers work together and that they take a count every other year. Has this helped the overall assistance of the homeless? Why or why not?

4. Why does the National Alliance to End Homelessness focus on local communities rather than lobby the government for more funding?

5. Have you ever visited a homeless shelter? Plan a visit, perhaps volunteer. See if you can identify the different groups of homeless.

## ■ OTHER ADVOCATE GROUPS

Health Care for the Homeless
Home for the Homeless
Interagency Council on the Homeless
International Union of Gospel Missions
National Alliance of HUD Tenants
National Alliance to End Homelessness
National Center for Homeless Education
National Coalition for the Homeless
National Coalition for Homeless Veterans
National Law Center on Homelessness and Poverty
National Student Campaign Against Hunger and Homelessness
Presbyterian Network to End Homelessness
The Salvation Army

## ▓ DOMESTIC VIOLENCE (SPOUSAL/PARTNER AND CHILD ABUSE)

### Spousal or Intimate Partner Abuse

An estimated 960,000 to 6 million incidents of intimate partner violence occur each year, including current or former spouse, boyfriend or girlfriend.[10] Although some men are victims, 85 percent of the victims are women. Half of the women report physical injuries and 20 percent seek medical assistance. Young women (ages 20–24) and those who are separated or divorced are most at risk, although 25 percent of all women of all races are estimated to experience domestic violence at some point in their lives. It is 80 percent more likely in urban areas; those with incomes less than $50,000 are three times more

---

10. The large range of the number of victims is because different studies use different measures and estimate in different ways. No one really knows for sure.

likely to experience it. Thirty percent of the women killed and 5 percent of the men killed are intimate partner homicides, mostly spouses. In 2000, that was 1,237 women and 440 men.[11] More than 75 percent of the women were stalked before they were killed (Domestic Violence Resource Center 2011).

In 2004, close to 2.2 million people called a violence crisis or hot line. Some of the calls came from a friend or family member; nearly 75 percent of the people know someone who has been abused. Shelter assistance reduces the number of incidents and the severity by 60–70 percent. Still, medical and mental health costs related to intimate partner violence are nearly $4.1 billion annually. Less than 25 percent of the abused (21 percent females, 10 percent males) turn to an outside agency for assistance. Studies have found that 30 percent or more of the abusive incidences are not reported, mainly because they considered it a private matter, or women are afraid (15 percent), or the abused wants to protect her partner (12 percent) (Domestic Violence Resource Center 2011).

### Social History of Abuse in the United States

Domestic violence has long been recognized as problem, but until the 1960s and 1970s there were few measures to address women as victims. Puritan laws prohibited wife beating, but a woman accused of witchcraft had little protection. The temperance movement raised the issue in the 1800s but soon switched to a woman's right to divorce a drunkard. Toward the turn of the century, investigation of child abuse in poor immigrant communities led to the discovery of wife abuse as well. In the 1920s, concern shifted to abused women as the problem when married women were abandoned or had left abusive husbands. They were morally suspect as single mothers and it was difficult for them to provide for their children. Finally, in the 1960s, the feminist movement took up violence against women as one of their issues. Two shelters opened in the United States in 1972; NOW (National Organization for Women) lobbied for government assistance; several states passed family rape laws. By 1977 there were eighty-nine shelters and many crisis hotlines. Feminists also lobbied for the stalking laws.

---

11. Some, but not all, of the men killed by a spouse were abusers. The case of Francine Hughes illustrates this situation. An abused woman who feared for her life and the lives of her children, in 1977 she set fire to her house which killed her husband. She was acquitted. Her case, and the movie portraying her story, *The Burning Bed,* starring Farrah Fawcett, is proclaimed a "turning point" in the fight against domestic violence (Ahern 2009).

Today shelters provide emergency assistance, counseling, legal assistance, and often assistance with children, jobs, and housing (Eigenberg 2001).

### Legal Response to Domestic Violence

Response to domestic violence situations by the police in the 1960s and 1970s was mostly ineffectual. Such calls were often given low priority, and if the police did respond, they had no power to arrest anyone unless someone pressed charges. Abuse victims were often unwilling to do that, out of fear of retaliation, or other reasons. "The failure of the police to make arrests was seen as a graphic demonstration to both offender and victim that her injury was not important to society" (Buzawa and Buzawa 1993, 341). Laws were changed to allow police to arrest without witnessing a misdemeanor assault, and/or mandated arrest if an officer confirmed it was a domestic assault situation. Twenty-five states have laws against domestic violence (as opposed to being charged with homicide, assault, criminal trespass, or other offenses). Forty-nine states allow women to file marital rape. In some places today, police must arrest someone if they answer a domestic violence call, and the arrest cannot be dropped (Eigenberg 2011).

### Theories of Intimate Partner Violence

The view of domestic violence as an issue of coercive control grew out of experience of working with battered women in shelters. The power and control wheel developed by the Domestic Abuse Intervention Project in Duluth, Minnesota, has been used in batterers' groups and training sessions around the country. The control tactics include intimidation (smashing things, abusing pets, showing weapons), emotional abuse isolation (calling her names, making her feel guilty, playing mind games, humiliating her), isolating (controlling who she sees, where she goes), minimizing, denying, and blaming (making light of abuse, saying she caused it), using children (using children to relay messages, making her feel guilty about children), using male privilege (making decisions, treating her as a servant), using economic abuse (preventing her from getting a job, making her ask for money), coercion and threats (threatening harmful acts, threatening to leave or to commit suicide, making her drop charges, making her do illegal things) (Yllo 2011).

The feminist view of domestic violence is that it is the result of patriarchal tradition of male power and privilege, and the resulting gender inequality. Psychological approaches emphasize personality traits such as low self-esteem of the abuser, passive-aggressive behavior, and the desire to control someone. Another approach stresses social learning—abusers learn their behavior in their family and in society. Violence theories stress that when the cost is not great, a person will use violence. In any case, unsatisfying relationships and stress are common triggers (Strong et al. 2008).

Early theories had it that the woman had a personality type that made her susceptible to abuse, but researchers now believe that learned helplessness more likely developed as a result of repeated abuse (Walker 1993). Despite all the upset, fear, and danger, abused women do not easily leave the abuser, even after repeated incidents, for a variety of reasons including fear, economics, beliefs, and love. Counselors generally do not encourage a woman to leave, but wait for her to choose that course.

Influenced by the feminist views, early views of intimate partner violence mostly blamed the man as the perpetrator of violence, but recent studies show that women use violence as often as men, although their motives are different (defense versus control) (Frieze 2005). Substance abuse is associated with abuse 25 percent of the time but is usually not a cause (Gelles 1993).

### Recent Concerns of Intimate Partner Violence

Awareness has developed of violence in gay and lesbian couples. It occurs at about the same level of frequency as in heterosexual couples. It is especially likely in couples who are dependent upon each other. It is more difficult for them to get help, and they face additional discrimination from officials who might otherwise help them (Renzetti 2011).

Another concern is dating violence, which can include physical violence, emotional or verbal abuse. Recent use of alcohol and history of family violence are two common factors, although it is often precipitated by jealousy or rejection. When it occurs, partners are not quick to leave the relationship (Katz, Kuffel, and Coblentz 2002; Shook et al. 2000).

Another concern is domestic violence perpetrated by police. The numbers are unknown; most police involved are reassigned or otherwise punished lightly. Still, the 1996 Lautenberg Act prevents anyone who has been convicted of domestic violence from owning a firearm. Some researchers conclude police regard it largely as a symbolic statement (Eigenberg and Kappeler 2011).

### Child Abuse

The American Society for the Prevention of Cruelty to Animals was formed in 1866. The first society to protect children (New York Society for the Prevention of Cruelty to Children) was formed eight years later, in 1874. Even with an organization, not much attention was given to child abuse until 1962, when C. Henry Kempe and his colleagues coined the term *battered child syndrome*, a condition of serious, chronic abuse that can cause permanent injury or death. Using X rays, Kempe claimed that "the most dramatic and telling of the signs and symptoms are multiple fractures of bones in varying degrees of healing. If physicians find in the X rays multiple breaks in varying degrees of healing they can conclude with a reasonable degree of certainty the presence of severe child abuse" (Kemp 1998, 42).

Because of Kempe and his colleagues, within three years all states had laws requiring doctors to report cases of suspected child abuse (Swinton 2005). The federal Child Abuse Prevention and Treatment Act of 1974 expanded the reporting to relevant professionals and government officials: it required states to have laws for reporting and procedures to investigate. Child Protective Services, or similar agencies, were established in the states. The act defined child abuse as physical or mental injury, sexual abuse, exploitation, neglect, or maltreatment of a child under eighteen, or an age specified by the state in terms of sexual abuse (Kemp 1998).

There were 3.3 million reports of suspected child abuse in 2009 (involving 6 million children), and 24 percent were substantiated. Neglect was the major form of abuse (78.3 percent), with physical abuse at 17.8 percent, sexual abuse at 9.5 percent, and psychological abuse at 7.6 percent (ACF 2009). About 9 children in 1,000 are abused; 20 percent of the abused are less than a year old. More than 3 million children received preventive services, including 21 percent who were placed in foster care.

Many children die from abuse and neglect. In 2009, the estimated number was 1,770; 35.8 percent died from neglect exclusively; 81 percent were less than four years old. Women were the perpetrators in 53.8 percent of the cases, but considering that children spend more time with women than with men, it does not imply that women are more inclined to abuse than men (ACF 2009). Head injuries, such as *shaken infant syndrome* which causes damage to the brain because of shaking, are the most common fatalities. Visceral injuries (injuries to smooth muscles or organs), bone fractures, and burns are other common injuries (Kempe 1993).

Characteristics of the child can contribute to abuse, including if a child is the wrong sex, was unwanted, was born outside of marriage, or is abnormal or difficult. Parental characteristics also contribute to abuse, such as if the parent was abused as a child, or has low self-esteem, or has a bad marital relationship, or has unrealistic expectations for the child. Family characteristics include unemployment, social isolation, low income, unsafe neighborhood, single parent, and health problems (Strong et al. 2008).

Sexual abuse is defined in different ways, but generally refers to sexual activity or exposure. In most cases the abusers are men, and most are known to the child. Young girls between seven and thirteen are especially at risk. Some other risk factors are a distant relationship with parents, living with a stepparent, or heavy alcohol consumption in the home. What is so devastating about child abuse, and any abuse, is that children are dependent on the adults around them. Incest between father and daughter, or stepfather and stepdaughter, is the most traumatic. Results of sexual abuse are both emotional and physical (Strong et al. 2008).

### *Help Children Negotiate the System: A Solution Proposed by Court Appointed Special Advocates (CASA)*

The National CASA Association recruits, trains, and supports volunteers to represent abused and neglected children in the courtroom and elsewhere.[12] They are appointed by the court to advocate for the most difficult of the 700,000 children assigned to foster care each year, children who have been taken from their homes because of abuse or neglect. The job of the CASA volunteer is "to make sure [the children] don't get lost in the overburdened legal and social service system or languish in inappropriate group or foster homes." The CASA volunteer is the only adult consistently present for many children.

---

12. www.casaforchildren.org/site/c.mtJSJ7MPIsE/b.5301303/k.6FB1/About_Us__CASA
_for_Children.htm.

In 2010, 240,000 children were helped by 75,000 CASA volunteers. Research indicates that CASA volunteers contribute to less time in foster care and a greater likelihood of a permanent home for abused children.

The program began in 1977 with a Seattle juvenile court judge who was concerned about the lack of information about these children when they appeared in court. For more information, go to http://nc.casaforchildren.org/files/public/site/publications/theconnection/Connection_Spring2007.pdf.

## ■ QUESTIONS FOR REVIEW

1. How many intimate partners are abused annually? How many of them are women?

2. What changes in police procedures and laws have improved the response to intimate partner violence?

3. Approximately how many children are abused each year?

4. When did child abuse become a more public issue, and why?

## ■ QUESTIONS FOR FURTHER THOUGHT

1. What are the difficulties faced by a woman who is abused by her intimate partner?

2. What are the difficulties faced by a man who is abused by his intimate partner?

3. What are the difficulties associated with spousal abuse by police? By gays or lesbians?

4. Why is neglect the most common form of abuse?

## ■ OTHER ADVOCATE GROUPS

Children's Assessment Center (CAC)
Court Appointed Special Advocate Association
Domestic Violence Resource Center
Emerge: Counseling and Education to Stop Domestic Violence
Gay Men's Domestic Violence Project (GMDVP)
My Army One Source (Family Advocacy Program—FAP)
National Coalition Against Domestic Violence
Prevent Child Abuse America

## ⠿ TEEN SUICIDE AND GANGS

### *Teen Suicide*

Approximately 2,000 teens between ten and nineteen kill themselves each year. Although the teen suicide rate has declined by more than 25 percent since 1990, for adolescents between ten and twenty-four, it is the third most common cause of death. Over half kill themselves with a firearm. Males commit suicide four times more often than females, but females attempt suicide three times more often than males. More than half of those who kill themselves are substance abusers. For every successful teen suicide, twenty-five more have attempted suicide, and many need medical attention (NAMI 2011; OSU Medical Center 2011; APA 2005).

Teen years are a time of change, and some adolescents find it more difficult to adjust than others. Teens who feel alone, rejected, or hopeless are more likely to see suicide as a solution, particularly if they have suffered loss, humiliation, or trauma. Risk factors include depression, substance abuse, aggressive or disruptive behaviors, and a prior suicide attempt. Some other indicators are withdrawal, neglect of personal appearance, marked personality change, persistent boredom, and intolerance of praise or rewards. Teens planning suicide may become cheerful after giving or throwing away their possessions (APA 2005).

Teen suicide is especially difficult for parents. Death of a child for any reason is difficult, but suicide brings out other factors and guilt. Other family members also suffer, as do friends, classmates, and community members.

### *Gangs*

In 2009 there were an estimated 28,000 gangs and some 731,000 gang members in the United States. They are mostly located in larger cities and suburban areas (more than 90 percent of the gangs) where, according to law enforcement agents, adult gang members dominate; teen gangs predominate in rural areas. Gang activity has gone up since 2003, after a notable decline during the last few years of the twentieth century. Today, all states report gang activity, although youth participation around the country varies. Milwaukee, Wisconsin, has high youth involvement (15.4 percent) whereas Will County, Illinois, has low youth involvement (3.8 percent) (Esbensen et al. 2010). Some cities have notable gang membership: Pittsburgh, for instance (24 percent), and Rochester, New York (32 percent). Government studies identify gang members as 80–90 percent minority; however, self-report studies indicate similar numbers of white participants as participants from different minority groups. Similarly, some studies indicate twice as many male members, but others say females are equally represented (Howell 2010; NGC 2009; Howell et al. 2011).

### Gang Violence

More than 1,000 gang-related homicides occurred annually between 2002 and 2009. One-third of them were in two cities—Chicago and Los Angeles.[13] On the other hand, more than half of the larger cities had very little or no identified gang-related homicides. Most gang violence has to do with intergang conflict and drugs. Other causes are migration of gangs within the United States and from outside the United States, and emergence of new gangs, as well as return of gang members from prison. A smaller portion of gang violence is caused by conflict within gangs (NGC 2009; Howell et al. 2011).

Not all cities record gang-related crimes, but those that do include aggravated assault, drug sales and robberies, as well as larceny, motor vehicle theft, and burglary/breaking and entering (NGC 2009).

### Joining Gangs

Contrary to the perception of coerced membership, studies show that gang membership is appealing to youth. It meets their needs for protection, fun, respect, and money, as well as companionship. These social functions, combined with the popularization of gangs in gangsta rap and elsewhere in American culture, have made the gang "look" very familiar to most young people. Some studies have found up to half of the teens participating on occasion, or having friends who are gang members. Many young girls have boyfriends who are gang members (Howell 2010).

Risk factors for joining gangs include individual characteristics, family, school, peer group, and the community. Naturally youth in environments

13. The top counties with high gang homicides are Nash, North Carolina; San Francisco, California; Baltimore, Maryland; Montgomery, Ohio; Saginaw, Michigan; Oakland, California; Cumberland, Maine; Bibb, Georgia; Allen, Indiana (Howell et al. 2011).

where there are high levels of criminal or gang activity are more likely to become involved, particularly if they have few ties to community, church, or school. Family difficulties are another obvious factor in gang involvement, with single parent households, poverty, abuse, or neglect being particularly significant. Most gang members have low academic achievement and do not value school associations. This is in part because of the negative conditions in difficult schools that many gang members attend. Having friends who are aggressive and antisocial is one of the strongest predictors of gang membership, as are a personal inclination toward alcohol or drug use, having been victimized in some way, or having problems such as hyperactivity or depression (Howell 2010).

### Prevention and Intervention for At-Risk Youth

Researchers stress that any program to address gang activity needs to separate out the different groups of teens and not assume that all who are involved should be treated the same. There are at least four different levels of programs.

1. Some programs should be addressed to all youth in a community. These awareness campaigns, centers for public services, school-based life skills programs, community cleanup and organizing can be provided by schools, churches, or other community organizations.
2. High-risk youth who have delinquency inclinations but are not yet involved in gangs are a top prevention priority. Programs for this group need to help teens find attractive alternatives to gang involvement. They also need effective support systems to meet their social, emotional, and psychological needs while helping them learn social responsibility.
3. Gang intervention programs target youth who are involved in a gang but have not yet become criminal offenders. This group needs intensive treatment services and supervision, including group and family therapy, and mentoring.
4. It is the small number of chronic, violent gang and nongang offenders that the police should focus on in terms of law enforcement and prosecution. Because this group is responsible for most of the illegal activities in the communities, criminal treatment rather than restorative programs is appropriate (Howell 2010).

### Ten Existing Programs

Several programs have been implemented to address gang-related youth. The most effective has been scientifically assessed but was not intended as gang intervention, but simply to improve antisocial behavior in young boys between seven and nine. Five programs seem successful but have not yet been scientifically verified.

(1) The Preventive Treatment Program in Montreal improved school performance and reduced delinquency and substance abuse through involvement of parents. (2) Gang Resistance Education and Training (GREAT) is a program of presentations about gangs presented by police officers in schools. (3) Aggression Replacement Training (ART) in New York focuses on anger control and moral reasoning. (4) CeaseFire, in Chicago, educates the public away from norms of violence through public media. (5) The OJJDP Comprehensive Gang Prevention, Intervention, and Suppression model has been effective in reducing gang violence. It uses outreach (including mentoring) services and surveillance. (6) Striving Together to Achieve Rewarding Tomorrows (CASASTART) works with schools, police, and others to reduce drug use and delinquency in schools.

Four programs seem successful, use original methods, and have not been evaluated scientifically. (7) Boys and Girls Gang Intervention Through Targeted Outreach recruits gang members for activities in an effort to reduce criminal activities. (8) Broader Urban Involvement and Leadership Development Detention Program works with youth in detention as well as other gang members. (9) Movimiento Ascendencia (Upward Movement) works to keep young girls from joining gangs. (10) Mountlake Terrace Neutral Zone serves as a safe place for at-risk youth to gather.

### Direct Intervention: A Solution Proposed by the Gang Prevention/Intervention Through Targeted Outreach: Boys and Girls Clubs of America

In operation since 1865 to serve disadvantaged youth around the country, the Boys and Girls Clubs of America formally organized in 1906.[14] In the early 1990s with funding from the Office of Juvenile Justice and Delinquency Pre-

---

14. www.bgcnj.org/main_sublinks.asp?id=6&sid=97.

vention two programs were started to address gang membership—one for prevention and one for intervention. The programs aimed to recruit from thirty to fifty youth who are either at risk for gang membership or already gang members and provide them with positive experiences that meet their needs. The program was also to provide individual attention and assistance in dealing with law enforcement, school, family and club activities and encouraging academic achievement. The goal was to provide youth with what they receive in gangs—supportive adults, challenging activities, a place where they feel safe.

Services in the intervention program include drug treatment, tattoo removal, job training, and educational services. A major component is recruiting hard to reach youth. Club staffers develop strategies to involve youth not normally involved in their programs or other youth programs. They are recruited directly and through referrals from school, social services, police, and probation. Although staffed by Boys and Girls Clubs, the intervention program is run separately. Because the clubs are different, there is no one way the program is implemented. Clubs decide the target population, the community agencies they will work with, and the programming they offer based on the interests of those who participate.

Program evaluators concluded that the Boys and Girls Club were successful in recruiting both at risk youth and gang members. The programs have high retention and participation rates in the programs over time. Further, youth did receive adult support and guidance, and most youth said they felt a sense of belonging to the club. The activities were generally interesting and challenging. Most of the youth who participated rated safety at the club highly, whereas their school was not rated so highly. Challenges of the program included frequent staff changes. Not all clubs had enough relationships with the schools or police to document and or monitor the students' progress. The program costs much less than gang suppression.

Comin' Up Gang Prevention program in Fort Worth is a Boys and Girls Club Intervention program run in cooperation with the city of Fort Worth. It has been working with gang related youth since 1996, and has programs in several of the Boys and Girls Clubs around the city, particularly in the north and west sides. All program youth are identified gang members. The clubs provide activities, counseling, assistance in education, and life skills development to encourage alternatives to gang life. It also works to establish truces among rival gangs and reduce gang violence. It employs successful former gang members as outreach workers. Several Texas Wesleyan interns to the program were subsequently hired as full-time gang workers. The program was featured at the National Gang Symposium in June 2011, in Orlando, Florida (Wood 2011).

---

**■■ ■■ ■■ BOX 7.4.**

### GREAT PROGRAM TO COMBAT GANG MEMBERSHIP AMONG YOUTH

The Gang Resistance Education and Training Program (GREAT) was created in 1991 by Phoenix law enforcement agencies and soon came into use around the country. It consists of a set of thirteen lessons taught by police officers in the schools, with two goals: (1) avoid gang membership, violence, and criminal activity and (2) develop a positive relationship with law enforcement. The lessons focus on skills to avoid gang involvement and behavior, including refusal skills, communication, conflict resolution, and anger management.

The initial evaluation of the program indicated that attitudinal changes had occurred but no behavioral goals had been achieved. So a revised program has been used since 2003. It is taught in sixth and seventh grades by officers who certified to teach after a one- to two-week training period. Response to the program has been generally positive among students, parents, teachers, and school officials. Initial evaluation of the revised program indicates behavioral as well as attitudinal improvements.

---

*Source:* Esbensen et al. 2011; NGC 2009a.

---

### ■ QUESTIONS FOR REVIEW

1. Which teens, and how many, are at risk of suicide?
2. Which teens, and how many, are at risk of gang activity?
3. Where does most gang activity take place?

### ■ QUESTIONS FOR FURTHER THOUGHT

1. How does the method of suicide chosen by males impact the overall gender rate of teen suicide?

2. What kinds of things can families and friends do to prevent suicide of a loved one?

3. Why do you think that government studies of gang membership record fewer white gang members than self-report studies? Which do you think is correct? Why?

4. Why do you think there is more gang activity in some cities than in others?

5. What criteria should be used to evaluate a gang intervention or prevention program? What kinds of behavior and/or attitudes are important to change?

## ■ OTHER ADVOCATE GROUPS

### *Teen Suicide*
American Academy of Pediatrics
American Association of Suicidology
American Psychiatric Association
Glendon Association
KidsHealth
National Alliance on Mental Illness (NAMI)
Teen Suicide

### *Gangs*
Arise
Boys and Girls Clubs: Targeted Outreach
GangFree
National Gang Center
Panzou Project
Safe Neighborhood Project
Street Gangs

# CHAPTER EIGHT

# PROBLEMS WITH ACTIVE OPPOSITION GROUPS

Opposition groups form in response to changing traditions. There are two possible situations—a tradition is being changed or a tradition is being extended. In the first case, an advocate group proposes or enacts a measure that changes the status quo—making abortion legal, for instance. The opposition group forms to protect the status quo. In the second case, the proposed change will extend the power and status (or other rewards) of those already in control. The opposition group forms to prevent, limit, or undo the status quo.

Internal motivations involved in the formation of opposition groups were discussed in Chapter 3. There may be a difference of ideology, or the group's well-being is threatened, or there is fear of losing identity or fear of change. In most cases, however, were it not for the original advocate group proposal or action, there would be no opposition group. Once formed, the group functions like any other advocate group, with some caveats.

An active opposition group will likely change the final resolution of the problem. There will likely be some kind of a compromise. This may weaken the solution. Or, on the other hand, it may be a better solution: addressing an issue from multiple perspectives can bring more clarity to an issue.

The philosopher Hegel addressed this process in his idea of development—thesis, antithesis, synthesis. In brief, he observed that when an issue arises, it contains within it the "seeds" of its opposition: the original argument may be overstated, oversimplified, too general, too exclusive. In short, something is missing. Thus opposition—the antithesis (anti-thesis)—develops to fill in the gaps. As the two positions interact (through public debate), there is a gradual melding together of the views into a synthesis. Presumably, the synthesis contains the best of both the thesis and the antithesis, although since it is a social process there is no assurance that the best elements are kept, only the most acceptable.

Applying this scenario to social problems tells us that the original proposal for action by an advocate group may be missing something. The missing elements are clear to the opposition group. Through the resulting public debate, issues are clarified, and the resolution is more accommodating and agreeable. At its best, opposition groups are a sign of a healthy democracy.

A word of caution: opposition can be messy. Persons who want change often take an extreme view. The more entrenched the conventions are, the more extreme and emotional is the proposal for change. An extreme proposal may not be realistic, but it becomes a means of pulling society away from entrenched conventions or traditions. Once the advocate group expounding the extreme view becomes an accepted part of the public discussion, its very presence changes the way others think about the situation.

Another difference between opposition groups and other advocate groups is the likelihood of a personal dislike of persons from the original advocate group. At times, it is reciprocal. This personal dislike is evidenced in the rhetoric between groups, the stereotypes that develop about persons from the other group— based on the way they dress, on where they live, on their personal habits. Carried to an extreme, this characteristic can make the opposition group dangerous, as has been the case in the abortion conflict. Many of the hate groups identified by the Southern Poverty Law Center, discussed in Chapter 6, are opposition groups.

To summarize, an active opposition group is an advocate group that formed because it opposed an action or proposed action by another advocate group. The action either changes some tradition within society or extends the authority of those in power. Opposition groups that oppose changes to the status quo tend to be more extreme as a means of bringing change to the establishment. If the opposition group acquires sufficient power, it will force compromises to the original resolution. There is often a personal dislike between members of the opposition group and the original advocate group.

## ■■ ABORTION

As the 1800s began, abortions were legal and a large part of what midwives and some others (homeopaths, apothecaries) did. The move to make abortion a criminal act came from at least two sources—a backlash against suffrage and birth control movements and from doctors working to legitimize the medical field. The AMA argued that, in addition to being immoral, abortion was a health risk if not performed by medical doctors. When upheld, this eliminated the competition from traditional health practitioners (Sanford 1998; NAF 2010). By 1880 every state had criminal abortion laws (except when done by a doctor to save a woman's life) (Reagan 1998).

Criminalizing abortions did not prevent women from having them, but it did make them more life threatening. An estimated 2 million abortions per year were performed in the 1890s, most of them on married women. By the 1950s, that number had fallen to 1 million a year. Throughout most of the twentieth century, abortions were self-induced or performed illegally in anonymous facilities, with few precautions for infection or hemorrhaging. The poor were especially at risk. In 1969, 75 percent of those who died from abortions were minority women (Reagan 1998; Sanford 1998).

In the 1960s, the women's movement took up the issue of legalizing abortion, with support from some others. Known as pro-choice, advocates basically argued that a woman's body and health is her own business, and she has exclusive rights as to what happens to it. (They usually believe that life begins when a child is born and that the fetus's rights are secondary.) Legal abortions prevent unsafe practices and are therefore better for both baby and mother. Some pro-choice advocates are concerned about population growth, arguing that overpopulation causes poverty and other problems. Some endorse sterilization of women in poor countries—with or without their knowledge or consent. This is not a view supported by most pro-choice advocates, however.

By 1967, there had been some relaxing of the abortion laws. One-third of the states allowed it in some form. In 1970 it was legal in several states, including New York. The 1973 Supreme Court ruling in *Roe v. Wade* made abortion available to all women. The Court ruled that during the first trimester of pregnancy, only a woman and her doctor could make the decision to end a pregnancy. In the second trimester, it could only be done in the interest of the woman's safety; in the third trimester, only if the woman's life is threatened by the pregnancy (Sanford 1998). In years immediately following, it was legal but costly and not available everywhere. Access was limited for some women, particularly poor and minority.

Before 1973, public opposition to abortion came primarily from Catholic professionals and organizations. After the Court decision, the National Right to Life Committee (NRLC) formed to make abortion illegal again. After a few years, non-Catholic religious conservatives joined the cause (Munson 2002; Balmer 2006). Together they referred to themselves as pro-life, emphasizing their belief that life begins at conception, so abortion at any stage is killing of a human. Many pro-life advocates—but not all—derive their beliefs from their religious views and subscribe to traditional gender roles (Munson 2002).

Pro-life activism of the NRLC and others soon took a recognizable form. First, there were marches on Washington, with an annual March for Life in January. Then there were Life Chain demonstrations: participants with pro-life signs stood in a row on the sidewalk. During "rescue operations" participants blocked an abortion clinic entrance hoping to shut it down for the day. "Truth displays" showed magnified pictures of aborted fetuses to shock viewers into condemning abortion. Abortion workers' homes and other personal locations were picked. In addition, pro-life activism often included sidewalk counseling and crisis pregnancy centers (Munson 2002).

As a result of pro-life activism, the Hyde Amendment was passed in 1976, exempting abortions from Medicaid, which led some states to stop "medically unnecessary" abortions. Thirty-six states now require parental notification or consent for a teen wanting an abortion (Guttmacher Institute 2011b; Sanford 1998). Some restrictions were placed on first trimester abortions in 1992, and many states now require mandatory waiting periods and counseling. According to one report, 162 new measures restricting abortion were introduced in one year, including banning abortion after twenty weeks because the fetus can feel pain or after a fetal heartbeat is detected. Some states have banned abortion from insurance exchanges or restricted medical abortions (Guttmacher 2011).

Violence at abortion centers started in the 1980s. It peaked in the 1990s, and several people were killed before the FACE (Freedom of Access to Clinic Entrances) Act was passed in 1993. It continues on a lesser scale today. A group known as Operation Rescue was blamed for much of the violence—a charge it denies. Still in 2009, after a concerted picketing of an abortion clinic in Kansas, George Tiller, who performed late-term abortions, was killed at church. Doctors in abortion clinics today accept danger as part of the job (Sanford 1998).

Meanwhile, most pro-life groups, including NRTL, condemn the use of violence. (A pro-life demonstrator, James Pouillon from Owosso, Michigan, was also killed in 2009.)

Much of the abortion debate today stems from religious beliefs, but official church views on abortion vary widely. The public stance of Catholic, Eastern Orthodox, Methodist, and Baptist churches is that abortion is acceptable only if the mother's life is in danger. Evangelicals and Mormons accept abortion when there is deformity, or if the mother's life is threatened, or if the pregnancy was the result of rape or incest. Other mainstream churches—Episcopal, Lutheran, Presbyterian, United Church of Christ—are pro-choice (Pew Forum 2010).

In 2010, 1.24 million women in the United States had abortions. This includes 682,000 white women and 464,000 African American women (U.S. Census Bureau 2011). A similar number—1.21 million—got abortions in 2008. That year white and African American women together had 72 percent of abortions (36 percent each), and Hispanic women 25 percent; 18 percent of the abortions were had by teens; 37 percent by Protestants, and 28 percent by Catholics. There were some 1,790 abortion providers in 2008, most of whom treated women up to eight weeks, 64 percent who treated women in the second trimester, 23 percent who treated them after twenty weeks, and 11 percent at twenty-four weeks. In 2008 the average cost for a woman at ten weeks in a nonhospital setting was $451 (Guttmacher 2011a).

As to reasons for abortion, the following were given by 75 percent of the women: couldn't afford the child, it would interfere with work, school, or caring for other dependents, or they had questionable ability to care for it. Half of the women gave family issues or not wanting to be a single parent as a reason. Fifty-four percent of the women had been using contraception. Researchers estimate that 22 percent of all pregnancies end in abortion and that half of all pregnancies are unwanted (Guttmacher 2011a).

### Direct Action to Oppose Abortion:
### A Solution Proposed by Operation Rescue

Operation Rescue has been blamed for much of the violence (including several murders) against those performing abortions, and damage to abortion clinics, although the extent of its responsibility for specific incidents is not clear.[1] The organization now emphasizes peaceful and legal means and disavows some of its past leaders.

Founded in 1986 as an outspoken activist group opposed to abortion, it originally encouraged peaceful disobedience as a means of discouraging women from getting abortions. Its early actions are described on its web page: "Thousands of men and women sat in front of abortion [clinics]" and were arrested and prosecuted. Not centrally coordinated or organized, however, each sit-in was autonomous.

A letter from Operation Rescue spokesperson Robert Brothers, published in the *New York Times* in 1993, gave more details: "There were 50,000 arrests during blockades of abortion clinics since 1998. But no one was ever found guilty of assault" (Roberts 1993).

After the Federal Freedom of Access to Clinic Entrances Act was passed in 1993, the group adopted new tactics, primarily media campaigns. It exposed known abortionists, particularly in California, with the result of many closed clinics and some doctors giving up doing abortions.

The best-known incident involves George Tiller, an abortion doctor in Kansas. Operation Rescue and others continued a prolonged demonstration outside his clinic and employed undercover techniques to try to catch him violating the Kansas abortion law. Before they had gathered sufficient evidence, however, he was killed while ushering at church in 2009. An anti-abortion activist was convicted, but most anti-abortionist groups condemned the action. However, one anti-abortionist leader, Randall Terry, said he was glad that the "mass murderer" had been killed. Curiously, Operation Rescue subsequently bought the abortion clinic where Tiller worked and made it its national headquarters.

Another indication of changed tactics by Operation Rescue is the description of its senior policy adviser, Cheryl Sullenger. She served a two-year federal prison sentence for conspiring to damage an abortion clinic—something she now "regrets." She now favors peaceful activism and denounces violence. She works, instead, to uncover "the seedy underbelly of the abortion industry."

---

1.www.operationrescue.org.

In addition to sit-ins and peaceful demonstrations, Operation Rescue uses truth trucks laden with graphic pictures of fetal deaths, driving them in strategic places. The intention is to shock viewers into changing their mind about abortion.

### Analysis

From the point of view of the advocate group Operation Rescue, the six ingredients of the social problem are:

*Target Group/Situation:* The victims are the unborn children, and secondly, the mothers.

*Ameliorating Action:* Its solution is to (1) help the mother realize her error and change her mind, (2) make it so uncomfortable for doctors performing abortions they decide to stop, (3) expose and prosecute abortion doctors who violate any legal restrictions, (4) cause a decline in abortion patients and doctors so abortion clinics will close.

*Action Group:* In some ways it considers itself an action group, which implies that it does not have faith that the system will change.

*Will to Act:* The will to act for members of this group comes from the members' religious convictions. The distressing photos of fetuses and stories of women whose abortions don't go well create a will to act among others.

*Why Did the Problem Develop?* Operation Rescue doesn't really get into the history of abortion, but if asked, its members would probably cite the women's movement and *Roe v. Wade,* with perhaps some blame going to liberal lawmakers and liberal societal values (as reasons for the 1973 Court decision). From such a perspective, the problem involves self-interest (those involved are more interested in their own affairs than larger issues of God's justice) and ignorance (those in favor of abortion don't realize the pain abortion causes).

*Level of Social Problem:* The problem for Operation Rescue varies from state to state, but occurs throughout the country.

**About the Group**

*Type of Advocate Group:* Operation Rescue started more like a social movement—with little or no coordination between local groups taking independent but similar actions. Characteristic of social movements, it is likely that early activists also identified with the group (as Christians). It has become (it seems) more like a special interest group, with a national headquarters, paid leaders, and an organizational structure. There may be less identification with the group today, since those aware of its violent reputation may distance themselves.

*Why Did the Advocate Group Form?* Reformer motivation is probably the most important reason for the group forming. Group members disliked the current situation, and were able and willing to put their time, energy, and other resources into the group efforts. They likely felt compelled to do what they could do to change things.

*View of Human Nature:* Perhaps not surprisingly, Operation Rescue members' view of human nature is compassionate and sacrificing. This is revealed in the group's tactic of showing graphic pictures of abortion in an effort to get people to change their mind about the procedure. In some ways, however, group members may also adopt the rational human being view, particularly for the abortion doctors, who won't give up their practice unless it becomes uncomfortable not to.

*Dynamics of the Advocate Group:* Operation Rescue seems like a fairly loosely organized group. Perhaps because of the illegal violence, it disavows individual member statements and actions.

*Stage of Development of the Advocate Group:* Operation Rescue appears to be in the coalescence stage. It has established itself as an entity and has some persons it works with (whether or not they are members is not clear), but its window to the world (e.g., Internet page) is slim and focused. The controversy surrounding its actions forced it to regroup and change its tactics.

**Other Factors**

*Claims Making:* The abortion information on the Operation Rescue page is an accurate summary taken from good sources. It doesn't really make other claims in writing. News reports of demonstrations include extreme statements by spokespersons, however.

*Opposition Groups:* This is the pro-life group that liberals revile, rightly or wrongly.

*Consequences/Unintended Consequences:* The unintended consequences of its earlier sit-ins were laws passed barring them from obstructing abortion clinics. The intended consequences of closing abortion clinics have happened as well. Whether it contributes to a culture in which fewer women seek abortion is not clear. But it certainly has stirred the pot.

*Type of Reform Sought:* The reform that it is seeking is that women will decide not to get an abortion—a redemptive change. It also wants doctors to decide not to perform abortions, which would also be redemptive change. The best description of the solution that Operation Rescue seeks is education—it assumes that if people are made aware of the situation, they will change their minds.

*Model for Social Change:* Probably critical mass (not so much restructuring, however). That is, there seems to be an assumption that at a certain point the public opinion will create a shift from one view to another—pro-choice to pro-life.

*Assessing the Overall Benefit:* Whether this group creates an overall positive benefit is difficult to say. Certainly its opponents would claim that harm is done by the abortion clinics that are closed, forcing women to go elsewhere or not have abortions, which could be to their detriment.

## ■ QUESTIONS FOR REVIEW

1. What Supreme Court decision made abortion legal in the United States? In what year?

2. What are the arguments of pro-choice groups?

3. What are the arguments of pro-life groups?

## ■ QUESTIONS FOR FURTHER THOUGHT

1. Which of the groups—pro-life or pro-choice—are opposition groups?

2. What do you think would make a doctor decide to perform abortions?

3. Why do you think the number of women getting abortions in the United States in the late 1800s was more than the number getting abortions today?

4. Why do you think the number of women getting abortions in the United States today is so high?

5. Why do you think that Operation Rescue initially resorted to civil disobedience?

## ■ OTHER ADVOCATE GROUPS

### Pro-Life Groups

American Family Association
American Life League
Concerned Women for America
Family Research Institute
Focus on the Family
Live Action
National Right to Life Committee

### Pro-Choice Groups

American Civil Liberties Union (ACLU)
Catholics for Choice (CFC)
National Abortion Federation (NAF)
National Abortion Rights Action League (NARAL) or Pro-choice America
National Organization for Women (NOW)
Planned Parenthood

┌─ ■■ ■■ ■■ **BOX 8.1.** ──────────────────────────────┐

**ABORTION IN KANSAS**

Two doctors who perform abortions in Kansas filed a federal lawsuit Tuesday to
block a new licensing law and regulations that abortion rights advocates fear will
make Kansas the first state in the country without an abortion provider. Dr. Herbert
Hodes and his daughter, Dr. Traci Nauser, argue . . . the law and accompanying
regulations are designed to stop the state's three abortion providers, all of which are
in the Kansas City area. Supporters of the law say it protects patients from substandard care. (Associated Press)

└──────────────────────────────────────────────────────┘

## ■■ GENDER DISCRIMINATION

Next we turn to gender discrimination, primarily discrimination against
women. As defined earlier, discrimination is an action (treating categories of
people differently) based on prejudice (irrational judgment based on a stereotype). *Sexism* is the belief that men are better than women. Men are, on average, taller, heavier, and stronger than women, but they are not more intelligent
(Tavris and Wade 2001). Nor does the data indicate that women are better
caretakers (Kaye 1990), less inclined to war (Elshtain 1987), more intuitive
(Snodgrass 1985), or more spiritual. These stereotypes developed because it
suits the cultural roles in our society.

Most societies around the world and throughout history are and have been
dominated by men (patriarchal).[2] The worst discrimination against women in
the ancient world occurred in Greece. Highly regarded today as the birthplace
of democracy, in Greek society women were not to be seen and had no voice
in public affairs.[3] Women in ancient Rome fared marginally better, although

---

1. www.operationrescue.org.

2. There is a controversy as to whether matriarchies ever existed historically. Many discount
ancient Crete. Although women were prominent, it is not clear they had dominant social
roles. There is some support for Amazon women warriors, however, in the work of Jeannine
Davis-Kimball.

3. One early sociologist's comment is apropos: "In their conception of women and of the
whole marital relation the Greeks showed a blindness, even a stupidity, which is in striking
contrast to the intellectual brilliancy they brought to bear upon other phases of life" (Goodsell 1915, 92).

in late Rome, they had freedoms similar to modern times (Balsdon 1990; Lefkowitz and Fant 1992). In western Europe, women's economic and political rights varied over the years. Until the Middle Ages, upper-class women were often married off for political gain, but common women were needed and valued for their economic contributions.[4]

In some ways, women of the nineteenth century had fewer rights. In the United States, women were not recognized explicitly in the U.S. Constitution. They had no property rights, could not sign contracts, and had no right to their earnings, inheritance, or children should they divorce. Women who opposed slavery were criticized for speaking about it in public, and when Lucretia Mott and Elizabeth Cady Stanton were barred from attending the World Anti-Slavery Convention in 1840 (Nicholson 1986), they organized the first Woman's Rights Convention, held in Seneca Falls, New York, in 1848. Some three hundred women heard proposals for gender equality that were so controversial that Stanton's husband left the gathering in protest (Macionis 2011). After the Civil War, African American men were given the right to vote, but not women, which strengthened the fervor of those who worked for women's suffrage (Nicholson 1986, 49).[5]

In 1920 the narrowly passed Nineteenth Amendment to the Constitution gave women the right to vote (Amar 2007). Women then turned their attention to other issues, like property, marriage, and reproductive rights. Margaret Sanger had already started her push for birth control. In 1916 she opened a birth control clinic that was closed down a few days later, but caused considerable public debate. In 1923 an amendment to the Constitution was drafted (Equal Rights Amendment) barring discrimination against women on any constitutional right, but it was not approved by Congress for fifty years, and still has not been ratified into law.

---

4. In medieval Europe, some women were allowed to own and conduct a business and all women were entitled to their earnings should they divorce (Coontz 2005, 105, 115).
5. In contrast, Wyoming Territory gave women the right to vote in 1869. When it became a state in 1889, it was the first state with women's suffrage. Three other states soon followed: Colorado, Utah, and Idaho. By 1919, twenty-nine states had full or partial women's suffrage. New Zealand gave women the right to vote in 1893, Australia in 1902, and many European countries just before the United States in 1920 (Amar 2007).

During World War I and World War II, women worked outside the home in large numbers. In 1900, only 20 percent of women worked. By 1945, that number increased to 36 percent, as some 6 million women took jobs in the war industry left vacant by men joining the military. The popular new working woman even had a name—Rosie the Riveter (Sorensen 2004).[6] Unfortunately, when the war ended, men received their jobs back, so many women became homemakers again. Others refused to stop working and found other jobs.

**FIGURE 8.1.** Rosie the Riveter was featured in a government campaign to encourage women to take men's jobs to keep the economy moving during World War II.

*Source:* By J. Howard Miller, 1942. http://www.vahistorical.org /visions/images.htm (Virginia Historical Society).

6. In 1943, 2 million more workers were urgently needed. Magazines, newspapers, radio, store displays, museums all joined in to encourage women who were not used to working outside the home to take up war industry jobs and other jobs necessary to national defense (Thompson, undated). www.rosietheriveter.org/rosiemusic.htm.

In 1961, the Presidential Commission on the Status of Women found that women faced discrimination in every area of American life. This touched off the so-called second wave of feminism.

Again efforts to overcome discrimination against women coincided with efforts to overcome discrimination against African Americans. This time, however, women were included in the 1964 Civil Rights Act. Title VII guarantees women protection from discrimination in the workplace. The Equal Employment Opportunity Commission was set up and soon received 50,000 sex discrimination complaints. Women activists were not satisfied with the way these complaints were investigated and formed the National Organization for Women (NOW) in 1966—to be more proactive regarding workplace equality (Eisenberg and Ruthsdotter 1998).

At the local level, women addressed sexual abuse and domestic violence by establishing women's shelters and rape crisis hotlines. Child care centers were established to support working women. Birth control, family planning, and abortion were addressed. The argument was that control of reproduction is necessary for a woman to have economic independence. Feminists of this era also addressed the so-called double standard: why is it okay for men to have multiple partners, and not women? The birth control pill was seen as a way to provide women more freedom and more control over their own lives.

Another important measure was passed in 1972. Title IX of the Education Code protected women from discrimination in education. This gave women more access to higher education and professional schools, and gave female athletes more funding in sports programs. As a result, more women than men graduate today at all academic levels. In 2008, women received 57 percent of all college degrees and accounted for 59 percent of graduate school enrollment (U.S. Dept of Commerce et al. 2011).

Women's earnings have improved but are not yet equal to men's. In 2009, the average woman earned 80 percent of what the average man earned. This was a great improvement from 1979, when it was 62 percent. But inequities remain (see below). The number of women in the workforce has increased dramatically in the past sixty years. Only 33 percent of adult women worked in 1950, whereas in 2009, 61 percent did. *Glass ceiling* refers to barring women from the highest management positions in a company. Women occupy only

14 percent of management, business, and finance positions (U.S. Dept of Commerce et al. 2011). Only 6.4 percent of top executives in the Financial Post 500 companies were women (Catalyst 2011). *Pink collar* refers to lower paid occupations dominated by women, "women's jobs." In 2009, nearly 20 percent of all women worked in five jobs: as secretaries, registered nurses, elementary school teachers, cashiers, and nursing aides (U.S. Dept of Commerce et al. 2011). Finally, *mommy track* refers to women who drop out of the workforce to raise their children. By the time they return to the workforce, they have missed several promotion opportunities and will end their careers at a lower pay scale than others who continued without hiatus.

Feminism is supporting equal women's rights in society and opposing discrimination against women in all areas. Many of the things denied to women a hundred years ago are commonplace today. Women can vote, have more employment opportunities, can obtain credit cards in their own name, can get a bank loan without a male cosigner, and can buy a house or a car or own a business. A widow receives full Social Security benefits from a working spouse, and classified ads no longer separate men's and women's jobs. There are women in the military and they attend military academies. Women have leadership roles in religion (Eisenberg and Ruthsdotter 1998). Women are protected from sexual harassment in the workplace, and can receive help for situations of domestic violence. Women have equal access to education and (closer to equal) sports opportunities. Even our language has changed: flight attendants not stewardesses, chairperson not chairman, mail carrier not postman.

### Opposition to Feminism

Most women are aware of these changes and acknowledge these accomplishments. And yet some women are critical of the feminist movement, primarily of the strident tone taken in some arenas. There are objections to the present day angry scenarios presented by some feminists.

> American women owe an incalculable debt to the classically liberal feminists who came before us and fought long and hard, and ultimately with spectacular success, to gain for women the rights that the men of this country had taken

for granted for over two hundred years.[However] the large majority of women, including the majority of college women, are distancing themselves from this anger and resentfulness. (Sommers 1994, 17–18)

Another group of women critical of the feminist movement are those who embrace conventional gender roles, primarily because of their religious beliefs. Attacked by early second wave feminists, they came to view both the style and actions of feminists as distasteful. For their part, most feminists viewed these stay-at-home women derogatorily, assuming they must experience gross gender inequity while innocently and ignorantly defending the oppressors (their husbands). The women critical of feminism also disliked the emphasis on sexual freedom, particularly to the extent that it seems to endorse liberal sexual values, which they oppose—in men or in women. Their argument today is that the family is endangered by these claims. They do not want to undercut the male authority; rather, all family members—men and women—need to improve themselves.

This view was evidenced in the opposition to the ERA in 1972. Led by Phyllis Schlafly, they argued that this law would open the door to changes detrimental to women, including men abandoning their families, gay marriage, and a female draft. On her web page, Schlafly quotes extensively from a study by former Chief Justice Ruth Bader Ginsberg (*Sex Bias in the U.S. Code*) highlighting necessary changes if women were treated equally: men would have paternity leave for childbearing, women would be drafted, prostitution would be legalized because there is no sex neutral language, and rape laws would have to be rewritten (Schlafly 2011).

This argument is perhaps best illustrated by public bathroom facilities. When men and women have equal numbers of bathrooms and stalls, women line up to use the facilities whereas there is no wait for men. Equality is not equity because men take less time and hence need fewer facilities.

Some of the women who oppose feminism go on to charge that statistical data are presented and used in a misleading way. Further, they charge that once they become labeled antifeminist, they are shut out of the public debate. The discussion about whether Sarah Palin is a feminist exemplifies this. As one commentator said, "It starts to make feminism look as exclusive as a country club" (O'Grady 2008).

Another group opposes feminism for very different reasons. The men's movement is a response to the tendency to blame men for the discrimination of women throughout society. Certainly some of the male privileges were lost to the gains made the women's movement, but the men's movement contends that it has gone too far. As a group, they are apolitical and not particularly religious. Much of its resistance centers on family court situations, which it says discriminate against men. Far more women than men get custody of children in a divorce, and fathers are often not seen as a resource if something happens to the mother. Further, they are often barred from seeing their children, with little legal recourse.

The men's movement advocates fairness in child support, equal parenting rights, including penalties for being denied access to their children. It would also like to see better handling of false claims by women about abuse in divorce proceedings, and male advocates want more control of reproductive rights (deciding whether or not to abort a fetus). Some argue that women's role in domestic violence is overlooked, and note that there is little government funding for men who are abused. They are concerned about the way that men are portrayed in public, for example, as deadbeat dads, or all men are rapists and pedophiles. In reality, rape laws often exclude men as victims. Some in the movement challenge what they see as feminist dominated media, culture, and society. The personal nature of the opposition sometimes takes a more strident tone, as seen in the terms used: misandry (hatred of men or boys), feminazi, and slogans like "Feminism is the notion that men are not people."

One men's group recently did an informal poll of the ten most important issues. Father's rights topped the list: seeing children, accusations should be verified, fair child care payments. Second on the list was the harm of feminism to men: less attention to boys in schools, unfair rape accusations, and fathers' rights group demonized (Good Men Project).

### Protect Men and Women in the Family:
### A Solution Proposed by Concerned Women for America

Founded in 1979, Concerned Women for America claims to be the "largest public policy women's organization."[7] It focuses on policy research and activism

---

7. www.cwfa.org/main.asp.

with a goal to protect and promote biblical values. The six core values that guide its activities are belief in family and the gift of children, the sanctity of human life, parental educational authority, fighting pornography, religious liberty, and national sovereignty.[8]

The emphasis on family leads to a concern about modern morality. The group notes that sexual experimentation is more widespread today than in the 1960s, with both moral and health ramifications. Similarly, it is concerned about pornography on the Internet, which it says is replacing *Playboy* as an easily available, popular, and destructive pastime.

The group expresses concern about rape as a serious crime but takes the view that feminist "slut walks," demonstrations by scantily clad women who claim that they should be able to dress any way they want and still not be attacked, is not an effective way to make their point. Women should be responsible in their dress. Slut walks are "in your face" about "women's rights."

Regarding current legislation about violence against women, the group claims that while it sounds good—Who is not opposed to violence against women?—it is misleading. In reality, the proposal promotes antifamily policies, gender quotas, and abortion on demand. Regarding child abuse, the group claims that it is often the fault of a live-in boyfriend, rather than parent, which complicates an already complex issue.

The group opposes the UN Convention on Elimination of All Forms of Discrimination Against Women (CEDAW) because, again, it is misleading. Elements of the convention go against the U.S. constitution, in particular, freedom of religion and association. American women already receive legal protection in the Fourteenth Amendment (used in *Roe v. Wade*) and in Title VII of the 1964 Civil Rights Law. And regarding women's equality in other countries, the United States has done more to help women internationally than what CEDAW can do. It has given money to development programs, estab-

---

8. The reader should be aware that each of these is a kind of "code" for the causes it promotes. Belief in the family, for instance, usually implies a man as the head and provider with a woman in a subordinate, caretaking role. "Gift of children" is a reference to its stance opposing abortion. Sanctity of human life refers to its opposition to euthanasia. Parental educational authority refers to homeschooling. And so on.

lished micro credit loans, built schools, provided teachers. On the other hand, an example of CEDAW's ineffectiveness is seen in the fact that the Taliban—whose own record of treatment of women is appalling—signed CEDAW.

On the issue of feminists, Concerned Women see them as women who put personal goals and career above family. Feminists are characterized as women who have it all but are not happy. Further, feminist demands might undercut the happiness and well-being of the men in families. The key to creating a happy home is to have both men and women putting family goals above personal and career goals.

It is defensive of male rights. For instance, there is a concern about the disappearing educated male. The reason appears to be less recess and sports in schools. Title IX has taken away some of the sports activities in university, and with it some men.

Finally, the group notes studies that say 51 percent of Americans are pro-life, 42 percent are pro-choice.

### ■ QUESTIONS FOR REVIEW

1. What rights were denied to women in the 1800s?
2. When and how did women in the United States acquire those rights?
3. What is the basis of opposition to the feminist movement?

### ■ QUESTIONS FOR FURTHER THOUGHT

1. What are the most important gains of the women's rights movement? Why?
2. Are the opposition arguments of the Christian women legitimate? If yes, in what way? If no, why not?
3. Are the opposition arguments of the men's movement legitimate? If yes, in what way? If no, why not?
4. Could second wave feminists have presented their cause without creating opposition groups? What would be different?
5. When you look into the future, how do you think the public opposition between these groups will end?

## ■ OTHER ADVOCATE GROUPS

Some of the organizations that oppose abortion also oppose feminists.
Eagle Forum
Family Research Council
Family Research Institute
Real Women of Canada

### Men's Movement
Fathers4Justice
The Good Men Project
Men's Activism
The Men's Center
National Coalition for Men

### Women's Rights Groups
American Civil Liberties
Amnesty International
Committee on Women in Science and Engineering
Feminist Majority Foundation
Feminist Majority
Human Rights Watch
Institute for Women's Policy
National Organization for Women

### Antifeminist Blogs
Ladies Against Feminism, www.ladiesagainstfeminism.com/about
National Organization of Anti-Feminism, http://groups.yahoo.com/group
/Anti-Feminism
Pro-Male/Anti-Feminist Technology, www.antifemisttech,info.about

### Lawyers' Pages Focusing on Fathers' Rights
Father's Rights, www.fathersrightsinc.com
Fathers and Dads for Equal Custody Rights, www.fathersrights.org

## ■ TWO OTHER PROBLEMS WITH ACTIVE OPPOSITION GROUPS

Abortion and gender discrimination are not the only social problems with active opposition groups. There are many others. The social importance of particular social problems ebbs and flows over time, so that some years they seem important, whereas a few years later they do not. Euthanasia is an example of a social problem that has been more of an issue in the past. The debate today is less about whether it is acceptable and more about why it is still illegal. Within the medical profession it is still an issue of concern. In some ways, same-sex marriage has also become more acceptable, although an intransigent remnant of opposition remains. These two problems will be discussed briefly, and advocate groups will be given, but no solution group will be discussed.

## ■ EUTHANASIA

The word *euthanasia* is derived from ancient Greek philosophers who argued that helping terminally ill persons end their life was a compassionate action if it would make their death more peaceful and less painful. Early Christians, however, declared that only God can determine the time and place of a person's death. This view predominated in western Europe up to the Renaissance. A renewed interest in Greek thought led to reexamination of euthanasia, and by the Enlightenment it was once again a popular solution (Gorman and Roberts 1996). Most of those who oppose euthanasia today, like the early Christians, argue that life is sacred and beyond human right to end.

Today the debate is not just academic. People are kept alive by high-tech medicine, creating the need to redefine the meaning of life. Is someone alive who is brain dead and cannot move or interact with others? For one year in the 1970s, the courts would not allow doctors to withdraw life support from a young woman named Karen Ann Quinlan who was brain dead from a lethal combination of alcohol and pills. The question was again raised in the 1980s when Nancy Cruzan lapsed into a permanent vegetative state after a car accident and was kept alive for five years. And again in the 1990s, Terry Shiavo was kept alive for fourteen years by her parents against the wishes of her husband, who claimed she did not want to be kept alive artificially. His appeal to the Florida Supreme Court was finally granted after a ruling by then Governor Jeb Bush.

Medical doctors publicly reject the idea of euthanasia because it is contrary to the Hippocratic Oath (a vow to preserve life and not cause harm) taken by most medical professionals. They are also uneasy about the "slippery slope"— legalizing euthanasia may lead to rationalizing the death of patients for economic or other reasons. Further, there is the question of authority, as illustrated by the Terry Shiavo case. Who decides?

However, many doctors quietly assist the death process of terminally ill patients who are suffering. One study found that a majority of doctors wanted euthanasia, but only a third would actually participate in it (Boyko et al. 1994). Other doctors admit their participation, and researchers estimate that 70 percent or more of the deaths each day in the United States are timed or negotiated (Clarridge et al. 1996; Malcolm 1990). Unlike doctors, most nurses are openly in favor of euthanasia.

One doctor believed in euthanasia so strongly that he risked his career and his life to advocate for it. For ten years, Jack Kevorkian, a Michigan doctor, openly assisted people who requested his help to die: by his count, 130 terminally ill and suffering persons. But no legal action was taken against him until he assisted someone on the TV program *60 Minutes* in 1998. He was then tried, convicted, and sentenced to twenty-five years in prison. After serving eight years he was released when he was seventy-nine years old. Although euthanasia is legal in only three states, he is one of the few doctors to be legally sanctioned for it (Schneider 2011).

The general public appeared to be increasingly approving of euthanasia in the 1990s. As opposed to the 37 percent who favored it in 1947, close to 75 percent approved some form of euthanasia in 1995, with 80 percent believing that it is a personal decision (Caddell and Newton 1995; Huber et al. 1992; Logue 1991). But according to more recent polls, there are more reservations about its misuse, particularly the protection of vulnerable people. One poll found that only 42 percent favor legalizing euthanasia whereas 36 percent opposed (*US News* 2010). A Gallup Poll found that 45 percent approve of doctor assisted suicide, and 48 percent disapprove (Ertelt 2011a; Gallup 2011).

A distinction has been made between different kinds of euthanasia. Passive euthanasia is when medical treatment (feeding tubes or respirator) is withdrawn. Most people regard passive euthanasia as an enhancement of the natural dying process, particularly of brain dead patients with no hope of recovery. Active euthanasia, on the other hand, involves an intentional action that results in death, such as a lethal injection or breathing carbon monoxide. It is associated with terminally ill patients who are likely to live for some time.

Most states have living will legislation that allows patients to stipulate that they do not want their life to be prolonged by medical technology. Court decisions usually support an individual's or family's right to decide when life support should be removed. But there is some confusion because of a Supreme Court ruling in 1997 that people do not have a right to die. States that have put the issue to vote and not approved it are Michigan, Maine, California, and Hawaii. Court cases in at least three states ruled against euthanasia: New York, Florida, and Colorado. As of 2011, assisted suicide is legal in three states. It became legal, with some caveats, in Oregon in 1997, Washington in 2008, and Montana in 2009 (by a court decision). Active euthanasia is still illegal (Marker and Hamlon 2010). Washington requires the patient to make two oral requests and a written request witnessed by two persons, one of which is a nonrelative. Oregon has similar conditions.

Euthanasia is legal in three countries: the Netherlands (2001), Belgium (2002), and Luxembourg (Marker and Hamlon 2010). In 1981 the Netherlands allowed euthanasia for patients who had no hope of recovery and who requested it. In 2002 the country legalized physician assisted suicide. Critics point to the seeming reality of the slippery slope that has developed there in the ensuing years: 20 percent of the 4,500 cases of suicide each year are decided by doctors without the consent or request of the patient. However, more recently doctors seem to be turning to deep sedation until death because it does not require judicial supervision (Arehart-Treichel 2008; La Corte 2008).

■ QUESTIONS FOR REVIEW

1. What is euthanasia?
2. Which states have legalized euthanasia?
3. How often does euthanasia occur in the United States?

■ QUESTIONS FOR FURTHER THOUGHT

1. Polls show that most people favor some form of euthanasia. Why isn't it legal in more states?

2. Why do doctors and the AMA formally oppose euthanasia?

3. Why do nurses favor euthanasia more than doctors do?

4. If euthanasia were legalized, what are the chances that hospitals would euthanize terminally ill patients because they need the bed for another patient?

■ OTHER ADVOCATE GROUPS

Compassion and Choices
Death with Dignity
Final Exit Network

*Opposed to Euthanasia*

American Medical Association
Euthanasia Prevention Coalition
Focus on the Family
National Right to Life Committee
Patients Rights Council

## ▦ HOMOSEXUALITY

Sexual behavior occurs in private, and not everyone reveals their sexual preference publicly, so it is impossible to know precisely the percentage of same-sex oriented persons in the United States. More than sixty years ago, Kinsey (1948) concluded that 4 percent of males and 2 percent of females are exclusively homosexual, although a majority had at least one homosexual experience. Fifty years later, another extensive study of sexual behavior concluded that 2.8 percent of males and 1.4 percent of females are exclusively homosexual (Laumann et al. 1995) The number of people identifying themselves as homosexual publicly has increased in recent years in the trend toward "outing," and others put the figure as high as 10 percent of the population. Some still choose to keep their sexual preference to themselves, so it is impossible to count. The best estimates are that approximately 3–4 percent of the population (7–10 million people of the total 320 million in the 2010 census) has an exclusive homosexual orientation.

There is convincing evidence that homosexuality is biologically determined, and convincing evidence that it is socially determined, so the question of cause is debated. Homosexuality is found in most societies around the world, and throughout history. Native Americans referred to homosexuals as "two-spirit" (Gilly 2006). It was not accepted in American society in the early twentieth century and was seen as deviant behavior by some professions (the American Psychiatric Association defined it as a mental disorder until 1973; Tyler 1997, 156). Most gays and lesbians believe it is based in biology and argue that it is not a behavior choice. Those who oppose gay marriage believe it is a lifestyle preference that can be altered.

Lesbians are less public and less noticed than gay men, and their sexual behavior was mostly not included in the sodomy laws (ruled unconstitutional in 2003) that remained on the books in some states. They also tend to have fewer sex partners and are more likely to establish committed relationships than male homosexuals. Gay men, on the other hand, are more likely to frequent known social venues and seek brief sexual encounters (Laumann et al. 1994).

Gays and lesbians face discrimination and persecution around the country. In several instances people have been harassed and even killed simply because they are homosexual. In a well-reported incident October 1998, Matthew Shepherd, a twenty-one-year-old student from the University of Wyoming, was lured into a car by two young men posing as homosexuals who then drove outside town, robbed and beat him, and tied him to a fence. He was found after eighteen hours but died several days later (Matthew Shepard Foundation 2010). A 2009 study by Gay, Lesbian, and Straight Education Network found that 67 percent of those with a different sexual orientation felt unsafe at school, 19 percent reported being assaulted, and one-third had skipped a day of school because of safety concerns. The number of homophobic remarks has decreased in the last ten years, but still 85 percent reported being verbally abused (Presgraves 2010).

In part to address this situation, the gay rights groups first organized in 1924. Gays and lesbians have become increasingly vocal in seeking legal protections and social acceptance. They have successfully redefined their social situation as discrimination rather than abnormality (Macionis 2005, 198). The Stonewall riot of 1969, in which resistance to a police raid on a known homosexual establishment continued for two days, led to the new term *homophobia*—an aversion to homosexuals (*New York Times* 2009).

There has been an increasing acceptance of the homosexual lifestyle in the United States. Most college students believe that homosexuals have a right to live as they choose, and partners should have the same rights as those who are married. There is less acceptance of homosexuals in small towns and rural areas, and many homosexuals who are open about their sexual orientation congregate in the larger cities where businesses cater to homosexual customers. Some of the areas are supported by a sizable enough homosexual population that individuals can live their lives associating only with others from their own subculture.

### Same-Sex Marrriage

The current debate about homosexuality is focused on same-sex marriage. Same-sex couples want the legal and economic benefits that a legal marriage provides, including health, home, and auto insurance, adoption, foster case and visitation rights, immigration and residency rights, inheritance, Social Security benefits, and income tax benefits. Other benefits are decision making power over a deceased partner, decision making power over an incapacitated partner, and domestic violence protection orders.

Beginning in 1992 some cities allowed homosexual partners to register themselves as domestic partners, and several U.S. companies allowed for domestic partner benefits, which were similar to spousal benefits. Some states moved toward recognizing gay and lesbian couples as marriage partners. Vermont granted same-sex couples legal rights in 2000. The Massachusetts Supreme Court ruled in 2003 that same-sex couples are entitled to the same rights as other couples. In February 2004, San Francisco mayor Gavin Newsom allowed marriage licenses to be issued to homosexual couples. Some 4,000 gay and lesbian couples from California and around the country subsequently came to San Francisco to be married. In August of the same year, California's high court ruled that Newsom had exceeded his authority and the marriages were nullified. They were briefly legal again, but the 2008 general election rejected a measure to allow same-sex marriages.

Currently, six states have legalized same-sex marriage: Massachusetts in 2004, Connecticut in 2008, Vermont, Iowa, and New Hampshire in 2009, and New

York in 2010. Five more states recognize civil unions with the same rights as married couples: Delaware, Hawaii, Illinois, New Jersey, and Rhode Island. Four more grant nearly all spousal rights to domestic partnerships: California, Oregon, Nevada, and Washington (National Conference of State Legislatures 2011).

State legalization of gay marriage has ramifications. The U.S. Constitution provides that laws of one state must be recognized in another state. Consequently if gay marriages are legal in one state they must be recognized in every state. During the 1990s opponents of gay marriage worked to prevent that from happening. The Defense of Marriage Act (DOMA) was passed by Congress in 1996. It barred federal recognition of same-sex marriage and allowed states to enact similar measures. Since then, thirty-nine states have passed some kind of DOMA law, with over half adding it to their state constitution. Lawmakers also proposed a DOMA amendment to the U.S. Constitution, but since such a measure would require a two-thirds majority in Congress and three-quarters majority of states to ratify it, most consider it unlikely to ever pass (National Conference of State Legislatures 2011). President Obama has stated that DOMA laws are unconstitutional but will enforce them until repealed. Under the law, same-sex couples cannot file joint tax returns or collect Social Security survivor payments and other benefits (Egelko 2011).

Conservative Christians are the most recognizable opposition, primarily on religious grounds. Gays and lesbians, on the other hand, argue that they want social recognition of their commitment, as well as the security, protection, and financial advantages of marriage. Public opinion, particularly among young people, has become more approving of gay marriage. A Gallup Poll reported that 53 percent of Americans now support it. In 1996, 67 percent of Americans were opposed to legalized same-sex marriages. Seventy percent of Democrats supported it in 2011, as opposed to 28 percent of Republicans. Similarly, 70 percent of young adults between eighteen and thirty-four support it, as opposed to 39 percent of those fifty-five or older (Newport 2011).

Internationally, ten countries have passed laws allowing same-sex marriages: Netherlands in 2001, Belgium in 2003, Spain in 2005, Canada in 2005, South Africa in 2006, Norway in 2008, and Portugal, Iceland, and Argentina in 2010. Some other countries have domestic partner registration, giving them some of the traditional marriage benefits: Denmark, Iceland, Sweden, France, Germany, and Hungary (Associated Press 2011a; Williams 2010).

## ■ QUESTIONS FOR REVIEW

1. What percentage of the population is homosexual?

2. What kind of discrimination do homosexuals face?

3. What significance does it have that individual states have legalized same-sex marriage?

4. Why do same-sex couples want their unions to be legalized?

## ■ QUESTIONS FOR FURTHER THOUGHT

1. Do you think that states which have passed DOMA legislation will eventually legalize same-sex marriages?

2. What is the difference between same-sex marriage, civil unions, and domestic partnerships?

3. Do you think there will be a time when same-sex marriages will be legal all around the world?

4. How successful have the gay and lesbian advocate groups been in promoting their cause?

## ■ OTHER ADVOCATE GROUPS

Freedom to Marry

Human Rights Campaign

International Gay and Lesbian Human Rights Commission

National Organization for Women (NOW)

National Gay and Lesbian Task Force

### Opposed to Same-Sex Marriage

Institute for American Values

Institute for Marriage and Public Policy

Marriage Law Project (Marriage Watch)

National Fatherhood Initiative

National Organization for Marriage

# PROBLEMS ADDRESSED THROUGH EDUCATION AND PUBLIC AWARENESS, INTERPERSONAL INTERACTION, REPARATION, APOLOGY, AND INDEPENDENT INDIVIDUAL ACTION

Social order in a peaceful society is based on the voluntary behavior of its citizens—whether out of responsibility, courtesy, conviction, or other reasons.[1] Convincing people to act in the interest of social harmony and their own well-being requires dissemination of information that is framed in a positive and convincing way. Education and public awareness are important to the resolution of social problems, even if they are not the only ameliorating action.

Laws can be an important part of voluntary behavior, such as regulating what is available—taking soda vending machines out of schools or prohibiting the sale of alcohol to minors. They can sanction consequences to some extent—ticketing drunk drivers or charging drug users. But excessive regulation, which is characteristic of a police state, generally leads to dissatisfaction.

To get full cooperation from a community, its members need to be informed of the consequences, or, to the contrary, of situations where their assistance is needed. A simple example of a public awareness measure occurred in Texas during the summer of 2011, when temperatures stayed above 100 degrees for more than forty days. The excessive heat caused electricity use to peak, and providers appealed to residents and businesses to cut back on usage to prevent outages. The appeal was made primarily through the news media,

---

1. The environmental sections of this chapter were written with Candace Halliburton.

with the result that large companies and government facilities immediately turned their air-conditioning up several degrees.

Another example of a media campaign to inform people of an issue is the seatbelt campaign in the 1980s. For the first time since cars were invented, seatbelts were mandatory, to reduce accident fatalities and severe injuries. But many people had not yet gotten in the habit of using them, having gone many years without using them. They had to be informed, hence the Click It or Ticket campaign.

Yet another example is the situation of women during World War II. There were hundreds of vacancies in the war industries and in other essential areas after the men went off to the military. But most women were not accustomed to working outside the home. So the government organized a campaign appealing to women to help the war effort by taking those jobs. Magazines, museums, and other public institutions all participated. Rosie the Riveter—icon of the campaign—is still popular (Sorensen 2004; Thompson n.d.).[2]

For most of the problems discussed in this chapter, information campaigns and individual independent action are important to their resolution. Both are very important to environmental concerns. Without information, people would not be compelled to act. However, as important as legislation is in some areas—the Clean Water Act or Clean Air Act, for instance—it takes concerted effort on the part of many individuals to make a change. People must be conscious of the problems and do their part in avoiding actions that contribute to pollution, or refraining from wasting precious natural resources. Without cooperation from a large segment of the population, environmental concerns cannot be addressed successfully.

Similarly, media campaigns to inform people are essential to any attempt to address the problems of STDs and AIDS. An extensive AIDS campaign began in the 1980s, when a lot of misinformation surfaced as the disease first became known to the public. This resulted in unnecessary discrimination and fear of people with AIDS and HIV. Gradually, over close to a decade, people learned what behaviors to avoid and which situations were "safe." The level of fear went down, discrimination against AIDS patients went down, people took more precautions, and the number of AIDS cases decreased as well. One

2. More details of this campaign can be found at www.adcouncil.org/default.aspx?id+128.

tangible result is the routine use of rubber gloves and face masks by medical practitioners around the country.

Rape and prostitution are also problems that media campaigns can help resolve. History indicates that prostitution can only be addressed through individual action. Other actions included in this category are interpersonal interaction, apology, and reparation. They don't play as significant a role in the problems discussed here but in other problems can be important aspects of a total solution.

## ⠿ GLOBAL WARMING AND POLLUTION

There are many interconnected issues affecting the environment, so it is sometimes hard to know where to start. We have broken them down into two areas—the problem of global warming, which includes pollution, and the problem of depletion of natural resources, or rather, the preserving of natural resources. Most of the current debates fall in these two categories.

### Global Warming

*Global warming,* rising temperatures worldwide because of increased greenhouse gases, is in the forefront of environmental concerns in the twenty-first century. Sometimes referred to as *climate change* (although that term is less specific), it became an issue in the 1980s but died down until the release of Al Gore's successful 2006 documentary *An Inconvenient Truth.* The film was so compelling that in 2007 Gore not only won an Oscar in the documentary category but shared the Nobel Peace Prize with an environmental organization also focused on global warming, the Intergovernmental Panel on Climate Change (IPCC).

The goal of Gore's film was to educate the public about the consequences of climate change, including increased and more destructive hurricanes, more fires and droughts from soil evaporation, rising ocean levels from melting ice sheets at the poles, and endangered low-lying (coastal) regions from rising ocean levels. The film also predicts the spread of pests and disease vectors (mosquitoes, ticks, and fleas) and the extinction of some animal species. There are current situations that point to global warming: twenty of the twenty-one hottest years in history occurred between 1980 and 2005; Mount Kilimanjaro and Glacier National Park are losing snow and glaciers; the ice shelf in Antarctica is breaking up; coral reefs are dying because the ocean is so warm; polar bears have to swim much longer distances because of the melting ice and consequently are drowning; and the Emperor penguin population is declining (Kakutani 2006).

IPCC formed to collect scientific, technical, and socioeconomic information from around the world to develop a complete picture of climate change. Thousands of scientists participate and contribute their research to the reports issued by the UN-based organization on a regular basis. Like Gore, the organization is concerned, as the chairman recently told the press: "By overwhelming consensus, the scientific community agrees that climate change is real. Greenhouse gases have increased markedly as a result of human activities and now far exceed pre-industrial values" (Pachauri 2010).

Most environmental advocate groups see global warming as a major and urgent problem today. It is major because of the disastrous consequences, and urgent because unless we act soon, it will be too late. It is caused by excess carbon dioxide and other gases that keep the heat in the atmosphere, much like glass in a greenhouse—the greenhouse effect.[3] Trees and other plant vegetation that absorb carbon dioxide and give off oxygen have been depleted by deforestation and land clearing for agriculture and urban development, resulting in an imbalance in nature. The predominant view is that global warming is man-made—the carbon emissions have increased since industrialization because of an increased burning of fossil fuels—natural gas, oil, and coal (National Geographic 2011; NASA n.d.).

Another attempt to understand the seriousness of the situation is NASA's Glory satellite, launched in 2011 to study the causes of global warming by observing and documenting particles floating in the air, such as natural dust and volcanic ash, as well as carbon that comes from human coal burning activities. NASA's aerosol polarimetry sensor and total irradiance monitor will identify which particulates predominate (Wall 2011).

### Global Warming Skeptics

But not everyone agrees that the evidence points to global warming or, if it does, that it is caused by human activities. Some claim that global warming is

---

3. The main greenhouse gases are carbon dioxide ($CO_2$), methane, nitrous oxide ($N_2O$), chlorofluorocarbons (CFCs), and water vapor ($H_2O$).

the result of natural causes, such as sun spots, volcanic eruptions, and the wobbly spin on the earth's rotation (Ravilious 2007). The oceans are the biggest producer of carbon dioxide, and some researchers claim there was more of it in the air during the ice age. They point to a medieval warm period to illustrate that dramatic cycles of weather change occurred in the past. Further, many of the weather changes we are experiencing are evidence of a pole reversal—a change in the magnetic fields of the earth—something that happened many times in the earth's distant past. Some skeptics are critical of a small clique of climate scientists who, they say, have dominated the data and have become heavily invested in the global warming theory, thus misinterpreting the data. To the contrary, they say, temperatures have not risen for fifteen years and have been falling for nine years (Monckton 2009).

In July 2011, the sixth annual International Conference on Climate Change was held for the skeptics with the theme of restoring the scientific method.[4] The Heartland Institute states that man-made climate change is a "failed hypothesis" (www.heartland.org). Even some IPCC-associated scientists have taken issue with the conclusion that extreme weather events are caused by global warming (Leake 2010).

### Global Protocols

In 1992 international talks to reduce greenhouse emissions began at the Earth Summit, a UN meeting that produced the climate change treaty—in essence, an agreement to agree. Agreeing on what action to take was harder. The Kyoto Protocol, finalized in 1997, called for reductions in greenhouse gases by 2012. Most countries signed and some will reach their goals. The United States did not sign. It objects to China being held to a different standard as a developing nation. Currently China and the United States are the two largest producers of greenhouse gases, with China exceeding the West in its use of coal. Extending the Kyoto Protocol is dependent on resolving this and several other international issues. In the meantime, worldwide emissions increased 40 percent from 1990 to 2009 according to the Netherlands Environmental Assessment Agency (Friedman 2011; Burleson 2011; Henson 2011).

---

4. http://climateconference.heartland.org.

President Obama has vowed to reduce U.S. greenhouse gases, despite congressional refusal to pass the necessary regulations. As of January 2011, the EPA (Environmental Protection Agency) will require major modifications for new industry facilities. Earlier in the year the government claimed it was on target to reduce its carbon levels to 17 percent below its 2005 levels by 2020 (Friedman 2011; *New York Times* 2011).

Meanwhile a Gallup Poll found that global warming is the environmental issue that people worry about the least—only 51 percent worry about it. This is in contrast to 87 percent who thought the government should encourage or require lowering of power plant emissions in 2006, in a poll by Time, ABC, and Stanford University (Kakutani 2006).

**TABLE 9.1. PERCENTAGE WHO WORRY A GREAT DEAL OR A FAIR AMOUNT ABOUT ENVIRONMENTAL ISSUES**

| | |
|---|---|
| Contamination of soil and water | 79 percent |
| Pollution of drinking water | 77 percent |
| Maintaining fresh water | 75 percent |
| Air pollution | 72 percent |
| Extinction of plant and animals | 64 percent |
| Loss of tropical rain forests | 63 percent |
| Urban sprawl/loss of open spaces | 57 percent |
| Global warming | 51 percent |

*Source:* Gallup Poll, March 26, 2011, www.gallup.com/poll.146810/water-issues-worry-americans-global-warming-least.aspx.

### Air Pollution

One of the factors in global warming is air pollution. Burning of wood and fossil fuels, including oil for cars, coal and natural gas for producing electricity and manufactured goods, is the major cause of air pollution.

Perhaps the most dramatic example of the harmful effect of air pollution in recent memory was the 1952 Great Smog of London, which covered the city for nearly a week. Thousands died. The smog was so thick that visibility was reduced to three feet at night and sixty feet during the day. Since the 1300s people in London have burned wood or coal to heat their homes, so residents, particularly those with respiratory conditions, faced health risks for many years. In

December of 1952, however, in addition to the smog from homes, factories, and diesel powered buses, it was particularly cold and humid, with no wind to blow the smog away (WWTG 2011).

Another city with a severe pollution problem is Athens, Greece. At one time reports indicated that up to six people a day died because of the pollution, caused primarily by 1 million cars and the fact that the city is in a valley, which allows pollution to remain for days without being blown away. In addition to the cars, half of Greece's industry is located in the Athens area. Many are concerned about the damage pollution causes to stone and marble antiquities, such as the Parthenon. Among measures taken to address the situation are giving cars and taxis alternate days to be in the city, using additional filters on buses and factories, and keeping shops open all day (eliminating an afternoon siesta) to reduce traffic (Cowell 1988).

In the United States, the Clean Air Act of 1970 mandated 80 parts per billion ozone standards, which many today say should be reduced to 60 parts per billion. Meanwhile, the health risks of air pollution are becoming more apparent. Mercury, which builds up in the food chain, affects the brain and nervous system and causes birth defects and developmental problems in humans. Breathing difficulties come from particulate matter in the air, which affects asthmatics and can contribute to heart conditions. Hydrogen chloride causes both respiratory and heart problems (ENS 2011; *New York Times* 2011a).

Tighter EPA regulations took effect in 2011, despite objections and serious lobbying from the petroleum industry, which argues that stationary greenhouse emissions (factories, power plants) should be treated differently. The new restrictions affect power plants and oil refineries, and in 2012 cars and light trucks. But some worry that the tension between the White House and Republican controlled Congress may derail these efforts. A *New York Times* editorial states: "The White House is nervous about critics who claim that the EPA is issuing too many new rules—on greenhouse gases, fuel economy standards and toxic pollutants like mercury. All of these rules are overdue, and protecting the environment and public health is the agency's job. President Obama cannot allow politics to trump science" (*New York Times* 2011a).

One concern is chlorofluorocarbons (CFCs), an organic compound developed in the 1930s for refrigeration and aerosol cans. They release chlorine into the ozone layer which, it is thought, is responsible for the hole in the ozone layer that was discovered over Antarctica and led to the 1987 Montreal Protocols—the first treaty on global environment. The United Nations subsequently announced general compliance to the treaty, and receding levels of emissions in recent years (Ungar 2008).

Addressing air pollution has not been easy, since it requires more research and development of alternative sources of energy and alternative methods of operation. There have been some industry restrictions, banning of certain heating methods, and requirement to use unleaded gasoline. The Clean Air Act was originally passed in 1970 and has been amended several times, the last in 1990, with several minor changes since then (EPA 2011a). But the effects of air pollution remain a health and environmental concern.

### Acid Rain

Another concern is *acid rain*. This is any atmospheric moisture that contains high levels of nitric and sulfuric acids which then combine with water, oxygen, and other chemicals to form an acidic compound. It develops naturally from volcanoes and decaying vegetation, but of particular concern is acid rain produced from the fossil fuels burned in power plants. This pollution has been blown hundreds of miles from its source (EPA 2007). Although it doesn't directly harm humans, it has adverse effects on vegetation and can damage buildings and monuments. In 1991 the National Acidic Precipitation Assessment Program (NAPAP) reported that 5 percent of New England lakes were acidic and many could not support fish. Action taken since then has reduced emissions considerably: a 60 percent reduction in sulfur dioxide since 2000, and a 50 percent drop in nitrogen oxide. Overall, air pollution emissions from manufacturers have been reduced by 60 percent in the same period (Pipes 2008).

### Water Pollution

The story is not as positive for *water pollution*, however. Reducing power plant air pollution has resulted in more water pollution. Power plants use water to trap pollutants and have subsequently become the biggest producers of toxic waste in lakes, rivers, and landfills. Pollution that used to go into the air now goes into the water. Water pollution from power plants is not always regulated because some substances, like arsenic and lead, are not mentioned in the Clean Water Act of 1977 which regulates pollutants in U.S. water (Duhigg 2009; EPA 2011).

Around the world, people face serious health concerns from contaminated water, including waterborne intestinal worms, typhoid, cholera, and dysentery. Fortunately, these are not problems in the United States. In most cases, however, enforcement of water regulations falls to state agencies, and industries are not always fined for their violations (Duhigg 2009). More recently trace amounts of prescription medicines have been making their way into our water supply (Kluger 2010). Yet another concern is the contamination of ground water from gas drilling. Water used in hydraulic fracturing, a method of releasing gas from earth formations, is pumped back up full of toxins and various chemicals. In areas where gas drilling is common, there have been numerous reports of damage to the environment and health concerns (Sapien 2009). According to EPA reports, 44 percent of the rivers and streams, 64 percent of the lakes, and 30 percent of estuaries do not meet minimum water quality standards; some 19.5 million Americans become ill each year from drinking contaminated water (Dye 2010).

### Waste

And what to do with all the waste? A total of 230 tons of solid waste was generated in 1999, which means 4.6 pounds per person per day (and about 8 tons in 10 years). Most of that waste goes to landfills—57 percent—but 28 percent is recycled or composted, and 15 percent is burned (EPA 2011b).

**TABLE 9.2. WHAT DO PEOPLE THROW AWAY?**

| | |
|---|---|
| Paper | 38 percent |
| Yard trimmings | 12 |
| Food waste | 10.9 |
| Plastic | 10.5 |
| Metal | 7.8 |
| Glass | 5.5 |
| Wood waste | 5.3 |
| Other | 9.8 |

*Source:* EPA 2011b.

There are some 1,700 landfills around the country. But as they fill up, we are running out of new sites. Also, when waste breaks down, it produces methane, which traps heat more efficiently than carbon dioxide does. And chemicals from the decomposing waste can leak into our water sources. Some countries have invested more heavily in modern waste management technologies. Germany, for instance, has low polluting incinerators that actually produce heat used by residents nearby. The Netherlands has a pay-as-you-throw scheme whereby people pay for garbage collection at the time of purchasing containers, with larger garbage bags more expensive than smaller ones, encouraging less trash (Kallman 2007).

A related issue is what to do with nuclear waste. It remains radioactive for thousands of years, is highly toxic, and can contaminate nearby water. The volume of radioactive waste is growing. Currently it is being buried in containers in Nevada, and of course no one wants it in their backyard.

### Production Paradigm Shift:
### A Solution Proposed by Cradle to Cradle
### Innovation Products Institute

This nonprofit group, founded on the ideas of William McDonnough and Michael Braungart, has the goal of transforming the manufacturing process in the Western world.[5] The founders believe that products can be produced in such a way that the production process contributes to the overall good of society. Rather than polluting the air and water, factories can be redesigned to clean the air and water, so that the whole community benefits.

As explained in Chapter 4, the methods of production we use were developed during a time when pollution and declining resources were not problems. Today most companies resist changing to more environmentally friendly production methods because of cost. But this view of production and cost is outdated. It comes from a paradigm that no longer fits the modern world. What is needed is a complete shift in thinking, to look at resources, production, and costs very differently. Manufacturers do not have to choose between lesser

---

5. www.c2ccertified.org.

evils; they can be a positive good in society. The group promotes "innovation oriented models for eliminating toxic chemicals and other negative environmental impacts."

The institute was based on the success of its founders, who use five principles in the design and assessment process: (1) renewable energy, (2) release of clean water, (3) use of safe and appropriate source materials, (4) social fairness and/or responsibility, and (5) material reutilization. The goal is to create products that meet new levels of environment and human health and safety. To encourage manufacturers to adopt these methods, they issue certificates of recognition to companies or products that meet their standard of "green." The institute now awards the certificates. To be recognized, a company works with the institute to redesign production, to rethink the design, manufacture, use, and reuse of materials and to create products that are safe.

Another measure to encourage environmentally friendly companies and products is its open source information. Cradle to Cradle insists on transparency and sharing—of information, lessons learned, and ingredients. It has developed a public database of preferred alternative chemicals, materials, and processes to help companies reformulate or retool their production. Everyone benefits from sharing a common "palette" of healthy and safe ingredients. "We are better, smarter, and faster at making intelligent changes if we do, and because we simply do not have the time to go it alone."

Cradle to Cradle sees itself as an agent of change. It is not looking for zero emissions or a zero footprint. "Zero is not our hero," it says. Rather it promotes giving something back to the community and the environment, like a tree that emits oxygen and nutrients for soil, purifies water, and provides habitat for multiple species. Everything is designed to be food for something else—food for natural systems or food for industry. When material or processes or emissions are food for another system, everyone benefits.

So far four hundred products and ninety companies have been certified as C2C—which means that they meet an environmental and humanitarian standard. The institute trains the partners, or companies, that are interested in this approach. Currently the institute is run by donations from organizations and individuals, but in the future it will be funded through training, product registration, and certification fees.

### Analysis

*Target Group/Situation:* Cradle to Cradle sees at least two victims: those who suffer from environmental maladies such as pollution and the producers/manufacturers who are caught in an old way of thinking.

*Ameliorating Action:* The group's action is to help producers and manufacturers think in new and creative ways to produce things while contributing positively to the environment and to the social well being of those involved.

*Action Group:* The action group for Cradle to Cradle is the group itself. Or perhaps the group is a catalyst for the producers and manufacturers to figure out what to do.

*Will to Act:* The will to act comes from two sources—a carrot and a stick. The stick is the shortage of resources that the world is facing, along with current and future government regulations on the businesses or industry. The carrot is the joy of finding new ways of doing things.

*Why Did the Problem Develop?* In the group's view, this is a development problem. Production methods that developed during the industrial age are not appropriate today, so new and creative rethinking is needed.

*Level of Social Problem:* The group sees the problem as existing on every level throughout society—wherever things are being produced.

### About the Group

*Type of Advocate Group:* It is a special interest group, bordering on commercial company. However, it is nonprofit.

*Why Did the Advocate Group Form?* It formed as a result of McDonnough and Braungart's resources and creative thinking. So reformer motivation comes into play here. Their desire (motivation) was to make the world a better place—and to have a successful career.

*View of Human Nature:* Probably greater good human being describes their view of humans. It presumes that people will want to do the right thing in their business if they can understand how to do it and make a profit at the same time.

*Dynamics of the Advocate Group:* It seemed to be organized like a company— it is very structured. There is a board and a president, and each person on staff has a title. Presumably staff members are paid well.

*Stage of Development of the Advocate Group:* They are in the emergence stage, although they are quite well organized. They started as an organized group, so that is not an issue. What will be interesting to watch is if they can convince other companies or manufacturers that they have a method that is worth investing in. Another point to watch is whether they become too structured to be effective.

### Other Factors

*Claims Making:* The group seems quite modest in its claims, on the one hand. It freely admits that it does not have all the answers, that companies and staff will search together to find the best alternative methods of production. On the other hand it set itself up to be *the* standard by issuing certificates. Whether that works out as hoped remains to be seen.

*Opposition Groups:* There are no opposition groups so far.

*Consequences/Unintended Consequences:* The group looks to the consequences of the manufacturing processes it helps redesign, and its aim is to have only positive outcomes. So, on the whole, there are no negative consequences. The only negative consequences might be if the group becomes too commercial and loses some of its inspiration. No other unintended or negative consequences are foreseen.

*Type of Reform Sought:* The group is advocating transformative change. Coincidentally it uses the same word to describe itself. It seeks complete change for the whole system, a change in paradigm, the adoption of a whole new way of doing and thinking about things.

*Model for Social Change:* The redesign model.

*Assessing the Overall Benefit:* The group's contribution to the way things are done and to a better future is positive. Even if it doesn't become the leading group in the future, it has made a positive contribution to the thinking and individual lives.

### ■ QUESTIONS FOR REVIEW

1. What is global warming and why is it an issue of concern?
2. What are the international protocols about global warming and who has signed them?
3. What are the consequences of air pollution?
4. What are the consequences of water pollution?

### ■ QUESTIONS FOR FURTHER THOUGHT

1. Given the disagreements regarding the Kyoto Protocol, what is the likelihood of it being extended?
2. Why do you think people are more concerned about water pollution today than global warming—according to the Gallup Poll?
3. If power plants were to seek C2C certification, how might the Cradle to Cradle Institute help them resolve their water pollution and emission problems?
4. Do you think that the Cradle to Cradle Institute will become more important to the manufacturing industry in the future? Why or why not?
5. What will happen when no more landfill sites are available?

### ■ OTHER ADVOCATE GROUPS

American Coalition for Clean Coal Electricity (ACCCE)
American Lung Association
Beyond Coal
Beyond Pesticides
Downwinders at Risk
Earth Justice
Sierra Club

Standing up to Texas' Biggest Polluters
Union of Concerned Scientists (UCS)
350.org

## ▓ NATURAL RESOURCES:
## WATER, LAND, ENERGY, ENDANGERED SPECIES,
## AND RAIN FORESTS

An average American consumes two hundred pounds of natural resources daily (a European consumes close to 100 pounds, and Africans 22 pounds). Many of the resources are renewable, like food, but some, like oil, are nonrenewable. Although we have considerable reserves of oil at the moment, once those reserves are gone, thousands of years will pass before there will be oil again. Some 58 tons of material is extracted from the earth each year (Giljum 2009). And even some renewable resources are endangered, such as the rain forests.

People in rich countries consume ten times more natural resources than people in poor countries do. Our consumption has increased 50 percent in thirty years. This leads to concerns about other issues as well, such as human rights violations and poor working conditions in places like Africa, Latin America, and Asia (Giljum 2009). *Environmental injustice* refers to the fact that minorities and poor people who live in low income communities and countries are more likely to be exposed to pollution and other harmful environmental factors or exploited for the benefit of others. At the same time, they are less likely to be aware of the risks, and even if they were, they would have fewer resources to object to the situation.

At the same time, there has been a dramatic rise in the consumption of natural resources in a few countries. Ten years ago, China's consumption of energy was half of what it is today. At an equivalent of 2.25 billion tons of oil, China consumed 4 percent more energy in 2009 than the United States (equivalent of 2.170 billion tons of oil).[6] And because most of China's energy comes from coal, it has higher emissions of carbon dioxide and other greenhouse gases than the United States (Spencer and Oster 2010).

---

6. Actual energy sources include crude oil, nuclear power, coal, natural gas, and renewable sources, particularly hydropower. The report on China's energy use came from the International Energy Agency (IEA).

Conservation of natural resources in the United States began with President Teddy Roosevelt, who established the U.S. Forest Service, five national parks, fifty-one bird reserves, four game preserves, and 150 national forests. Approximately 230 million acres were protected (NPS 2010). One person who influenced Roosevelt was naturalist John Muir, founder of the Sierra Club—a grassroots environmental organization (NPS 2011). But while Roosevelt advocated using the protected land for production, Muir wanted to preserve it for its natural beauty. In 1970 Richard Nixon established the EPA (Environmental Protection Agency), which also works to preserve natural resources but is subject to the ideology of presidents and Congress.

### Water

Water as a natural resource is important to preserve because all life, including human life, depends on water. The hydrologic cycle describes the evaporation of water from the oceans; it collects as clouds, drops to earth as rain, is transpired by plants or collects in bodies of water or seeps underneath as groundwater and eventually flows back into the ocean (Hubbart and Pidwirny 2011). Runoff from farmland, city streets and parking lots, and lawns is a primary source of pollution (altenergy.com). Only about 2.5 percent of the water is fresh water, and excluding polar icecaps, only 1 percent of it is available for human consumption.

In addition to drinking water, Americans use an estimated 150 gallons of water a day (compared with 40 gallons in the United Kingdom and 22 gallons in China). While we always had plenty of water in the past, there is concern about future water shortages in thirty-six states. Of particular concern are places like Las Vegas and the shrinking Great Lakes (Strassmann 2010; Dye 2011). Also the Ogallala aquifer, an underground water supply for seven states (South Dakota, Colorado, Nebraska, Kansas, Oklahoma, New Mexico, and Texas), is being pumped dry (Adams 2011). Many other countries already have water shortages, and some of them are severe.

Water is important for other reasons. Bodies of surface water (lakes, rivers, etc.) in the United States are protected by the Clean Water Act, but in recent years there has been debate about whether that extends to wetlands, because they are not navigable. *Wetlands,* areas with surface or groundwater and water vegetation— such as swamps, marshes, and bogs—are important to the *ecosystem* (the system of interacting, living organisms and their natural environment). They reduce pollutants, act as buffer to flooding, recharge groundwater, add moisture to the atmosphere, protect shorelines, and prevent erosion. The concern is that they are declining to the point where their functions are threatened (Dye 2011).

## Rain Forests

Much of the earth is covered with forests, but just 2 percent of the surface has rain forests. Found on every continent, they are home to half of the different species of plants and animals. They are important to everyone because of their valuable contributions to the ecosystem. They are a major source of oxygen. They regulate temperatures and weather patterns and are critical in maintaining fresh water. In addition, they provide many important products, such as timber, coffee, cocoa, and plants with medicinal properties. Many cancer medicines are only found in the rain forest. It is estimated that half the animal and plant species of the world are found in the rain forests (Nature Conservancy 2011).

More than 56,000 square miles of rain forest are lost each year to logging, crops and cattle, dams and roads, mining and oil. Environmentalists worry about the effects that activity will have on the planet and the loss of biological environments, medical resources, and animal species. Today the rain forest is half of its original size.

## Energy

Since industrialization, the Western world has consumed increasing amounts of energy, mainly oil, coal and more recently, natural gas. In 2005, 40 percent of U.S. energy needs came from oil, 23 percent each from coal and gas, 8.4 percent from nuclear power, and 7.3 percent from renewable energy (hydropower).[7] Although gas and renewable energy will increase, oil will continue to be the main energy source for some time, primarily because it is cheaper and more available (GEP 2005). We consume more oil than we produce, so we have to import it. But how long will oil supplies last? Earlier predictions were twenty to forty years, but that was extended recently with the discovery of new reserves in Iraq and Central Asia,

---

7. In 2009, the amount of renewable energy from biomass increased substantially.

and because U.S. oil use seems to have leveled off due to the economic downturn, less driving, and cars with higher fuel efficiency (Martin 2010). Our dependence on cars is a major reason that U.S. energy consumption is so high.

Another reason is our dependence on electricity. The main fuel for power plants is coal, although there has been a slight switch to natural gas and renewable energy, mainly wind power (which increased from 11 to 14 percent) (EIA 2011). Nuclear power plants fill approximately 17 percent of the electricity needs worldwide, but uranium is also a nonrenewable source of fuel. It is predicted to last about forty years as well. And there are very real dangers in nuclear power plants, as Japan found out when the 2011 earthquake and tsunami crippled its leading nuclear plant to the point it threatened to blow up (BBC 2011). Nuclear waste is also problematic. And nuclear power plants are less efficient than coal— 2 million tons of coal produces the same amount of electricity as 21 million tons of spent uranium fuel (altenergy.com). Another new energy source is shale gas, production of which rose 48 percent between 2006 and 2010 (EIA 2011).

Use of alternative energy sources has increased in recent years. Although controversial, dams currently provide most of the alternative energy for power plants. Wind power is also promising. A step up from the windmills used by early homesteaders to draw water, today's turbines are popping up in many places. Oilman T. Boone Pickens has invested heavily in the new technology and plans to build a $10 billion wind farm in Texas. Some predict it could fill as much as 20 percent of our future electricity needs (Krauss 2008).

Solar energy is another viable alternative. It is already being used effectively in some remote places, and is likely to become more common for household needs in the future. Geothermal power (heating or cooling from the earth) is already being used to heat most homes in Iceland. Biomass holds some promise but has some downsides. All of these technologies are more expensive than fossil fuels, and hence there has not been as much progress as there might have been. Some researchers insist we will need to have a third of our energy needs come from renewables by 2050 (altenergy.com).

### Land and Wildlife

Increasing urbanization has brought increasing concern about the loss of natural habitats—nature reserves, public beaches and riverfronts, and wilderness areas, among other things. There is also concern about the ability to use the land to grow food or timber, having it available for recreation or wildlife habitats, and as a producer of clean water. Conserving land and protecting the natural environment is important for the health of everyone. Several government agencies work to preserve the environment: U.S. Forest Service, Fish and Wildlife Service, National Park Service, Bureau of Land Management, and other state and local organizations. There are also private organizations dedicated to preserving natural lands.

Similarly, many are concerned about the preservation of natural wildlife and various habitats. There has been a decline in both plant and animal species in modern time, and many wild animals are endangered by the lumber industry, encroaching urbanization, or modern disasters, such as oil spills. The Endangered Species Act (ESA), passed in 1973, protects plants, animals, and habitats that are threatened by extinction.

One nature problem that has arisen in modern times is the transporting of plants and living organisms from an ecosystem in which there are other balancing factors to a new ecosystem in which there are no predators to keep it in check. Lake Caddo in Texas, for instance, is being taken over by the giant salvinia plant that spread into Texas and Louisiana waterways. Native to Brazil, the giant

**FIGURE 9.1.** Sign explaining the Salvinia Weevil at Caddo Lake in Texas. The salvinia is native to Brazil, and can double in size in 3-5 days. It chokes out native vegetation, gets caught in outboard motors, and the large, green, weedy mats that it forms on top of the water are harmful to fish and detrimental to swimming areas. It is spread to other bodies of water on the bottom of boats and trailers not cleaned properly. Photo by Candace Halliburton. (used with permission)

**FIGURE 9.2.** Caddo Lake, Texas. Salvinia weevil can be seen in the foreground, and again in the middle of the lake. Photo by Candace Halliburton. (used with permission)

salvinia was brought to the United States as an aquarium plant. Fast growing, it doubles in size every three to five days, and is now choking out native vegetation. It gets caught in outboard motors and is detrimental to swimming areas. It spreads to other lakes if boats and boat trailers are not well cleaned. The Texas Water Resources Institute is growing a salvinia weevil that eats the plant as a natural way of cleaning up the problem in Lake Caddo (Richardson 2010; Mendoza 2011).

### Celebrate the Beauty of Nature:
### A Solution Proposed by Sierra Club

Founded in 1892 by naturalist John Muir, the Sierra Club aims to preserve communities, wild places, and the planet itself through its work at a grassroots level.[8] It is a large, well organized group that has affiliate organizations around the country and around the world. Its current goals are focused on energy—reduce our reliance on coal and oil through the Beyond Coal and Beyond Oil campaigns, reform natural gas drilling, and protect America's waterways and natural habitats.

---

8. www.sierraclub.org.

Its numerous campaigns address various local environmental concerns. It actively lobbies for federal regulations that safeguard the natural environment and prevent industries from damaging them. It inspires local chapters, especially young people, to work for a cleaner environment locally and nationally. It maintains an extensive, interactive website, and makes a lot of information available to the public, including historic photographs of nature. It is also well-known for its beautiful calendars, books, and seasonal greeting cards carried by bookstores across the country.

Members are also invited to participate in hikes and outings—a tradition established by the founder, who liked to hike in the California mountains. The legal arm, founded as the Sierra Club Legal Defense Fund, is now totally separate and was renamed Earthjustice in 1997.

■ **QUESTIONS FOR REVIEW**

1. How much of the daily consumption of natural resources is by the Western world, specifically Americans?

2. Why are environmentalists concerned about the rain forests?

3. What percentage of our energy needs will likely come from alternative sources in the future and what are those alternative sources?

■ **QUESTIONS FOR FURTHER THOUGHT**

1. In what ways can people in Africa, Latin America, and Asia become involved in preserving our natural resources?

2. Are existing government programs sufficient to address water concerns in America—both drinking water and bodies of water? Why or why not?

3. Since electricity production consumes so much energy, why hasn't there been more focus on reducing electricity use as an environmentally friendly move?

4. How can the United States reduce its dependence on gasoline?

5. What public lands have you enjoyed recently?

■ **OTHER ADVOCATE GROUPS**

American Rivers
Caddo Lake Institute

Center for Biological Diversity
Earth First!
Environmental Defense Fund (EDF)
Environment Texas
Galveston Bay Foundation
Greenpeace
International Rivers
National Wildlife Federation
Natural Resources Defense Council (NRDC)
Nature Conservancy
Oceana
Trust for Public Land (TPL)
Waterkeeper Alliance
World Wildlife Fund (WWF)

## ■■ SEXUALLY TRANSMITTED DISEASES/AIDS

STDs, or sexually transmitted diseases, commonly pass from person to person in blood, semen, or bodily fluids, usually by sexual contact. But they can also be transmitted in other ways, such as blood transfusions, shared needles, or from mother to infant. They have been a public health concern since the 1940s, when the government started tracking the number of cases throughout the country.

In 2009, there were 19 million new STD infections, which cost the U.S. health care system $16.4 billion. Three diseases are tracked by the CDC (Centers for Disease Control and Prevention). Chlamydia cases numbered 1.2 million, although experts estimate the real figure is 2.8 million. This is an increase over last year, in part because of expanded screening. Gonorrhea, on the other hand, is at an all time low, with 301,174 reported cases. Less prevalent, but still of concern, is syphilis, with 13,997 reported cases in 2009 (CDC 2010).

African Americans are at greater risk for all three diseases. They have gonorrhea at a rate twenty time, that of whites, and ten times that of Hispanics; chlamydia at eight times white rates and three times Hispanic rates; syphilis at nine times white rates and four times Hispanic rates. Experts speculatively attribute this to high rates of poverty among African Americans and the already high prevalence of the diseases. Health officials believe that high rates of HIV infection are also related to high rates of STDs in the African American community, as the presence of STDs increases the risk of HIV infection (CDC 2010).

Adolescents and young adults are also at increased risk for STDs. Hispanic men and women in the twenty- to twenty-four-year-old bracket have twice the rates of gonorrhea and chlamydia as white youth, but African American women are even more at risk for both. Syphilis is increasing among gay males, who had two-thirds of all the reported cases in 2009 (CDC 2010).

Gonorrhea, chlamydia, and syphilis are all caused by bacteria, and can be treated with antibiotics, particularly in the early stages. However, they are serious infections and can cause sterility, blindness, mental disorders, and even death if left untreated. However, symptoms can be overlooked, and sometimes there are no symptoms and people are unaware of the infection.

STDs caused by viruses, on the other hand, are incurable. According to some estimates, 20 percent of the U.S. population has genital herpes, and there are some 500,000 new cases each year. The usual symptom is recurrent painful blisters on the genitals, which are highly contagious, and sometimes fever or headache. The newest concern for viral infection is HPV or human papilloma virus, which can cause genital warts and has been linked to certain kinds of cancers. An estimated 0.5 to 1 million people are infected each year with HPV (Women's Health n.d.; NIH 2011).

People from all races, classes, and ages get STDs, although, as mentioned, some sectors are more at risk than others. There are estimates that one in four people in the United States will get an STD in their lifetime. Using condoms and limiting the number of sexual partners reduce the risk. On the other hand, STDs are often associated with risky behaviors that impair judgment. Drug users who share needles are at risk, and those who have had an STD are more likely to be infected again. The government regards it as a "public health challenge," and has recently awarded $5.4 million to four agencies to develop community approaches to STD prevention (CDC 2011).

One STD of particular concern is HIV, or human immunodeficiency virus, which destroys the body's immune system. An estimated 1,178,350 people were infected with HIV at the end of 2009, 20 percent of them undiagnosed.

An average of 50,000 people are infected each year, most of them gay men. Minorities are infected at higher rates than others. African Americans alone make up 44 percent of the new infections: African American men are infected at a rate six times higher than white men. African American women are also at risk, infected at a rate fifteen times higher than white women. Twenty percent of the new HIV infections occur among Hispanics, with Hispanic men twice as likely to get HIV as white men, and Hispanic women four times more likely than white women. Officials call the high rate of minority infection "the most glaring health disparity in this country" (CDC 2011a).

HIV causes the fatal disease AIDS (Acquired Immunodeficiency Syndrome), although it is possible to live with HIV for many years before it becomes AIDS. For the first year with HIV, there are few symptoms, but within ten years, half of those infected with HIV have AIDS, and in twenty years almost all have AIDS. With modern medicines, it is possible to live for years with AIDS, although treatment is expensive. Nevertheless, the disease has taken its toll. Since it was first identified in 1981, a total of 1,107,721 Americans have been infected, and by the end of 2008, 617,025 had died of AIDS related causes (CDC 2011a).

While HIV infections are not increasing in the United States and AIDS patients are living longer, more productive lives, it is a major problem in sub-Saharan Africa, where there were 1.3 million AIDS related deaths in 2009 and an estimated 22.5 million people are infected with HIV—68 percent of all HIV infections in the world. Worldwide some 33.3 million people live with HIV, and in 2009 there were 1.8 million AIDS related deaths. One of the associated tragedies is the large number of children whose parents die from AIDS. In 2009 there were 16.6 million AIDS orphans (children under 18) (Avert 2010, from UN data).

### Educate: A Solution Proposed by the Ryan White Foundation

A young boy, Ryan White, was a hemophiliac who contracted AIDS, and his situation educated the American public about the disease. He was diagnosed with AIDS in 1984, as a result of regular blood transfusions. Very little was known about AIDS at that time, so it was regarded with fear and ignorance. Ryan was not allowed to return to his school because parents feared he would infect their children. Ryan and his family faced threats and accusations. AIDS was associated with homosexual behavior, and many thought that was how he contracted it. After an eighth-month legal battle with school authorities, he was allowed to return to school. But then other students stayed home or transferred to different schools.

The trial made Ryan a public figure, and soon he was a spokesperson for the disease, teaching people about AIDS. His media appearances helped to destigmatize AIDS, and he actively participated in fund-raising and educational campaigns. He stressed the importance of educating people about the disease when he spoke to the President's AIDS Commission, something he did through a 1989 TV movie of his story. Many famous people attended his funeral in Indiana, and several singers dedicated the proceeds of particular songs in his name.

His mother founded the Ryan White Foundation after he died, to increase public awareness of HIV and AIDS. The foundation was active in the 1990s, and in 2000 it merged with AIDS Action, which in turn merged with another organization more recently. This illustrates the rise and demise of advocate organizations. Perhaps its original purpose was fulfilled, and the will to shift to other purposes wasn't there.

However, Ryan White contributed to the AIDS cause in another way. A government program was named after him. Just after he died the federally funded Ryan White Program was signed into law, making $220 million available to persons with AIDS or families who don't have other means of health care. It is the third largest source of federal funding for HIV care. It works with cities, states, and local community-based organizations to provide services. It serves over half a million people a year and in 2009 was extended by President Obama with a budget of approximately $2 million (Kaiser Foundation 2009).

### ■ QUESTIONS FOR REVIEW

1. How many new cases of STDs are there a year in the United States?
2. How do STDs caused by bacteria differ from STDs caused by viruses?
3. Which sectors of the population are most affected by STDs?

### ■ QUESTIONS FOR FURTHER THOUGHT

1. Why is AIDS less of a problem in the United States than in sub-Saharan Africa?

2. Why do you think that African Americans are more at risk for HIV than other racial groups?

3. What kind of things can the government do to reduce STDs? What kind of things can a local community do to reduce STDs? What kind of things can individuals do to reduce STDs in the community? What kind of things can professional organizations do to reduce STDs?

4. How do women contract HIV and AIDS?

5. Who has responsibility to care for AIDS orphans?

## ■ OTHER ADVOCATE GROUPS

AIDS Drugs Assistance Program Advocacy Association (AAA+)
AIDS Healthcare Foundation (AHF)
Aids Vaccine Advocacy Coalition (AVAC)
International AIDS Vaccine Initiative (IAVI)
International AIDS Society (IAS)
International HIV/AIDS Alliance (the Alliance)
Ryan White HIV/AIDS Program
The AIDS Institute (TAI)

## ▪▪ RAPE, DATE RAPE, AND SPOUSAL RAPE

Early rape laws protected men from false accusations but did not protect women. Second wave feminists lobbied to include a female perspective, so that rape is now defined as "carnal knowledge of a female forcibly and against her will." *Statutory rape* is nonforcible sexual intercourse with someone who is younger than the statutory age of consent (FBI 2009). Today women don't have to prove they did not provoke the attack, and prior sexual history or relationship history with the offender cannot be used as a defense for the accused.

In 2009, there were 125,910 reports of rape or sexual assault (down almost 57 percent since 2000). Of the victims, 84.2 percent were women and most of them (79 percent) knew the offender. Of the 19,820 male victims, however, most (74 percent) did *not* know the offender (BJS 2010). As to forcible rapes in 2009, the FBI reported 88,097, a 3.4 percent decrease from 2008. In terms of race, rape victims were three times more likely to be African American than white, and slightly more likely to be Hispanic than white. Many victims were twelve- to fifteen-year-olds, although most were in their twenties (BJS 2010).

It is thought that only half of the rapes that occur are reported each year, although some claim it is only one in fifty (NCVC 2008). Rapes are not reported because victims may not even know rape is a crime or they may fear retaliation or being blamed, or they just don't want to go through the legal hassle. Researchers stress that rape is not a sexually motivated crime but a violent act using sex as a tool of empowerment—something experienced by 13 percent of women in their lifetime. Effects of rape include depression, anger, guilt, self-blame, sexual dysfunction, flashbacks, and suicidal feelings, as well as increased vulnerability, damaged self-image and emotional distancing. In addition, rape victims are much more likely to develop problems with alcohol or drugs (NCVC 2008; NCVC 2009).

*Acquaintance rape* is a forcible sexual encounter between two people who meet in a social setting (excluding family members and incestuous situations). It has become an important problem among young people, especially college students. Sometimes called date rape, it often involves the use of drugs mixed into drinks that make the woman unaware of what is happening. It is less likely to be reported—perhaps only 16–20 percent of the time. Among the drugs commonly associated with acquaintance rape are rohypnol (commonly called roach, roofies, rope, forget pill, Mexican valium, or circles), an illegal white or green pill that makes clear drinks blue and other drinks cloudy. Also common are GBH (called charry meth, bedtime soap, energy drink, or G), a pill or odorless powder that can be obtained legally, or a liquid with odor; and Ketamine (black hole, bump, cat valium, kit kat), a liquid or powder, also legal, that works quickly. College officials are increasingly warning students about the conditions associated with sexual violence (NCVC 2008a; MedicineNet 2011).

Men are not included in the legal definition of rape, and so government rape figures reflect violence against men as sexual assault. This is a problem among youth as well as in the prison population. It affects an estimated 3 percent of men in the United States, with a first experience for most (71 percent) between twelve and eighteen. Gang rape, the use of weapons, and physical injuries are not uncommon (NCVC 2008).

Laws against marital rape were passed in the 1990s. Prior to that, in many places it was accepted that a married man was entitled to sex with his wife. In fact, most marital rape is part of an abusive relationship. Nearly 2.5 million cases are reported each year, with African American women at greater risk than others. It became a crime in all states in 1993, but most states have some exceptions. It occurs in all types of marriages, affecting all races, ethnicities, social classes, and ages. It also occurs in gay and lesbian couples, although less visibly. As in other instances of domestic violence, victims fear reprisals; often police treat marital rape calls differently than other cases of rape (NCVC).

*Stalking* is another serious phenomenon, defined as persistent efforts to establish or reestablish a relationship against the will of the victim. Between 1 and 2 percent of the population are stalked, 75 percent of them by someone they know and 10 percent by a stranger. Nearly half have at least one unwanted contact per week. In 20 percent of the cases, the stalker uses a weapon to harm or threaten harm. Many victims are fearful of what will happen next, losing time from work, and other personal disturbances. By the early 1990s, every state criminalized stalking, but in half of the states it becomes a felony only after the second time, or if it is aggravated in some way. A more recent concern is cyber stalking. Email, chat rooms, websites, GPS, cell phones, video and digital cameras all allow easy access to personal information about victims. In some cases, personal contact information is posted online and others are encouraged to harass the victim. About one-third of the states address electronic stalking in their laws; others include electronic stalking under general harassment laws. A few states have separate cyber stalking laws (NCVC 2008b).

### Education and Modeling:
### A Solution Proposed by Men Can Stop Rape

This group was founded in 1997 to address the perpetrators of rape.[9] Rather than seeing men as the criminal offenders, it embraces them as allies "with the will and character to make healthy choices and foster safe, equitable relationships." It works to prevent rape by inspiring men to feel motivated and capable

---

9. www.mencanstoprape.org.

to end men's violence against women. It does youth development programming, public education messaging, and leadership training.

MOST Clubs (Men of Strength) are organized in high schools and MCC groups (Men Creating Change) in colleges and universities. Both groups use mentorship to mobilize male youth to create their own positive definitions of manhood, strength, healthy relationships, responsibility, and safe communities. The principles of healthy masculinity include recognizing unhealthy masculinity, empathy, gender equity, respect rather than risky and violent behaviors, and developing skills. The Strength Campaign is their method of starting with individuals and small groups, and growing to affect the whole school and then the community.

Men Can Stop Rape uses advertising to increase public awareness and to model healthy choices and behaviors associated with integrity and strength of character. The group regards this as "the most effective social marketing tool for young men." It addresses consent, drugs, alcohol, bystander intervention, reporting of violence, positive masculinity, and men's roles in preventing sexual assault in these campaigns.

Men Can Stop Rape training assists youth service professionals. It also provides technical assistance to agencies and organizations, including the military, rape crisis centers, and government agencies. The goal is to inspire a new generation of leaders for change who understand the harms associated with traditional masculinity and realize that broader definitions of social roles benefit everyone. Four theories inform this work: (1) Bystander intervention. Rather than just feeling uncomfortable when women are mistreated, men should realize that others feel the same, and express themselves. (2) Social-ecological model. Individuals exist in complex relationships, communities, and societies. New behavior has to be built on all levels. (3) Social and emotional learning. Includes self-awareness, social awareness, self-management, relationship skills, and responsible decision making. (4) Dominant stories. The group seeks to create new narratives of values and messages to counteract the old stories of winning and aggression that obscure alternatives.

The group has programs in one hundred locations in ten states, and has received some recognition, including being called "innovative" by Secretary of State Hillary Clinton and being featured in the national PTA magazine. Its recent conference included participants from military, law enforcement, and state, local, and federal government agencies.

## ■ QUESTIONS FOR REVIEW

1. What are the different types of rape?
2. How many rapes are there each year?
3. Why is it so important to prevent stalking?

## ■ QUESTIONS FOR FURTHER THOUGHT

1. How could the definition of rape be rephrased to include men?
2. Why do we hear so little about rape of men?
3. What is the main cause of rape on college campuses? How can it be avoided?
4. How would stalking laws need to be changed to include cyber stalking?
5. Why has the level of rape and sexual assault declined so much since 2000?

## ■ OTHER ADVOCATE GROUPS

American Civil Liberties Union (ACLU)
Arming Women Against Rape and Endangerment (AWARE)
Just Yell Fire
National Abortion Rights Action League (NARAL)
National Organization for Women
Planned Parenthood
Pro-Choice America
Rape, Abuse, and Incest National Network (RAINN)
Students Active for Ending Rape (SAFER)

## ▦ PROSTITUTION

Prostitution is often called one of the oldest professions, having been practiced in human societies throughout history. In the United States today, selling or advertising sex acts for money or other goods is illegal everywhere except in

┌─ ■■ ■■ ■■ BOX 9.1. ─────────────────────────────────────────

**HELP STOP SEXUAL VIOLENCE ON CAMPUS! AAUW (AN EMAIL)**

*This week, the AAUW Action Fund Capitol Hill Lobby Corps are visiting members of Congress to build support for a critical piece of legislation that would fight sexual violence on our nation's campuses. They hope to reinforce the message you can send today:* **Help stop sexual violence and assault by cosponsoring the Campus SaVE Act!**

A 2007 campus sexual-assault study by the U.S. Department of Justice found that around 28 percent of women are targets of attempted or completed sexual assault while they are college students. The Rape, Abuse, and Incest National Network (RAINN) reports that college-age women are four times more likely than any other age group to face sexual assault. There is an epidemic of sexual violence on campuses, and we must take steps to stop it.

The Campus Sexual Violence Elimination (SaVE) Act (H.R. 2016) would help to end sexual assault and violence on campus by requiring schools to spell out their policies, conduct prevention activities, and ensure necessary assistance for victims. It would constitute a step toward ending the sort of violence which prevents women from attaining their educational dreams.

**Ask your representative to cosponsor and support this important piece of legislation!**

To send a message, click on the "Take Action" link in the upper right hand corner of this email.

└──────────────────────────────────────────────────────────

some parts of Nevada, where it is regulated and controversial.[10] It is a victimless crime, or an illegal action where the victim is not obvious. Because it is illegal, it is hard to know the extent to which it occurs, although some estimate that a million U.S. women have worked as prostitutes (ProCon 2011). An early NORC poll found that approximately 15 percent of men in the United States have paid a prostitute at least once. There were more than 100,000 arrests related to prostitution in 2007—approximately 65 percent women and 35

---

10. The state requires prostitutes to register, to submit to fingerprinting, to pay a state business fee, and to provide up-to-date medical certification that they are free of STDs. The Nevada Coalition Against Sex Trafficking wants to make prostitution illegal in all of Nevada. www.nevadacoalition.org.

percent men. Men who were arrested were johns, pimps, and prostitutes. It is estimated that 10 percent of the total number of prostitutes are male, with mainly male customers. As to race, government data indicate that the number of African American women arrested declined dramatically from 1970, when they were 65 percent of those arrested, to 2006, when they were only 24.5 percent (Kendall 2010).

There are many different types of prostitutes or sex workers. Call girls or escorts are the best educated and make the most money. They are generally covert, contacted by phone, and meet at the client's home or a hotel. Where prostitution is legal, the next level consists of those who work in brothels, or premises explicitly dedicated to sex. In the United States, the equivalent would be massage parlors or other businesses that function as a cover. Prostitutes who work in these establishments share up to half of their earnings with the owner or manager (Harcourt and Donovan 2005).

Many prostitutes who are arrested are street workers, who solicit for business on the street or in a public place. They usually work with a pimp, who "protects" them and takes large portions of their earnings. Pimps exploit the women who work for them. Street workers are most at risk for violence and disease, and usually cannot refuse a potential customer. Some sex workers are considered indirect, in that sex is not the first or only job performed. Lap dancing, table dancers, strippers, and hustlers work in nightclubs and bars, as servers or at other jobs that allow them to encourage customers to buy drinks. Sex is sometimes, but not always, part of the job. Men who work as prostitutes in the United States are found in all the different levels. Some categories of sex workers are not common in the United States (Harcourt and Donovan 2005).

Most women and men who become prostitutes do it for the money. For escorts and nightclub dancers it is often a temporary job while they further their education or find a more stable occupation. Street workers are likely to be runaways who suffered abuse, often sexual abuse, as children. They are likely to be in their late teens or early twenties, some thrown out of the family home, and this is the best job they can get. Some have alcohol or drug problems. The most severely addicted are likely to exchange sex for drugs. But not all prostitutes have been abused or use drugs. A study in the Polytechnic Heights area of Fort Worth, Texas, found that 27 percent of those interviewed had not been abused and enjoyed their work; 20 percent had not used drugs, and 60 percent had not been arrested (Weddel 2002).

Prostitution is legal in many countries of the world; it was decriminalized in New Zealand in 2003. Even where it is illegal, it is often not prosecuted. A sex industry often develops in areas with a major U.S. military presence. In the Philippines bar girls are issued government badges and are required to have weekly STD checks and quarterly HIV tests. Thailand has the largest sex industry in the world. A recreation place during the Vietnam War, it is now a several billion dollar tourist industry involving an estimated 10 percent of the country's female population. Entertainment places are exempted from the otherwise illegal activity, and every kind of sex preference can be readily found, including the polished transvestite Tiffany's Show.

Some people want to legalize prostitution in the United States, arguing that to do so would make it safer for everyone, and bring more tax revenue to the government. Requiring health checks would make prostitution safer for customers, and making it legal would strengthen prostitutes' ability to protect themselves against abuse. A San Francisco prostitution task force (1996) that met with health officials, defense attorneys, scholars, police, clients, former prostitutes, neighborhood activists, and others, concluded that criminalizing prostitution marginalizes and victimizes prostitutes and makes it more difficult to leave the business if they want to. Further, it noted that most of the complaints that people have about prostitution are aimed at 10–20 percent of the industry in that city.

Many researchers seem to favor legalization. "Almost everywhere there are laws designed to limit and control prostitution but they rarely achieve their desired effect" (Harcourt and Donovan 2005, 205). Criminalizing prostitution limits the workers' power to protect themselves and leaves them vulnerable to corrupt officials.

Those who oppose legalization say it leads to increased crime (drugs, abuse, rape, murder) and to more sexually transmitted diseases; women in the industry have low self-esteem and don't know how to get out of the industry. And it leads to increased human trafficking, which has become more visible in recent years. Women and girls (and some males) from low income countries are either lured or coerced to come to the United States and other prosperous

278 ■ SOCIAL PROBLEMS

countries to become sex workers. They are often promised a good job or marriage, but upon arrival are restrained or confined through threats or actual
physical abuse. They are led to believe they must give away their services to
repay a debt they owe for their transport or other things. They are at risk for
disease, drug addiction, physical injuries, and psychological harm (DHHS
n.d.). In 2009 there were an estimated 12.3 million adults and children in
forced labor or prostitution around the world, with only 4,166 successful pros-
ecutions. Sex trafficking is a smaller but significant part of human trafficking,
with child sex trafficking approximately 16 percent (U.S. Dept. of State 2010;
KFF 2010).

Public opinion in the United States on the issue varies widely according to
how the question is asked. But in general, 22–29 percent approve of legalizing
prostitution with no conditions, while 38–49 percent consider it a major problem and 42–47 percent say the laws should be strictly enforced. On the other
hand, when people are asked about its seriousness compared to other things,
they consider it about as serious as minor shoplifting (Smith 1998).

### Educate: A Solution Proposed by
### Prostitution Research and Education

This group was founded by a clinical psychologist. Its goal is to eliminate prostitution, develop emotional alternatives, and provide health care for women
in prostitution.[11] It supplies research data to agencies that help women escape
prostitution.

Most of the effort of this group goes to collecting information about prostitution. It features writings on the subject from many different sources, including
personal accounts by women themselves. It keeps tabs on the legal situations
around the country and in some other countries as well. It looks at the way in
which prostitution and the attitudes that feed prostitution are prevalent in our
culture.

It also publishes resources for women who are interested in leaving prostitution, for several different states and four different countries. It is not particularly

---

11. www.prostitutionresearch.com.

active in lobbying for legal action but rather focuses on informing people—informing prostitutes of their choices and informing others about the ramifications of this industry.

■ **QUESTIONS FOR REVIEW**

1. What are the problems associated with prostitution?

2. Where is prostitution legal in the United States? What is the situation elsewhere in the world?

3. How many prostitutes are there? How many are male?

■ **QUESTIONS FOR FURTHER THOUGHT**

1. How would the situation regarding prostitution be different if it were legal in the United States?

2. Who is most harmed by prostitution? Why?

3. Is it possible to eliminate prostitution? If so, how?

4. Would legalizing prostitution be helpful in prosecuting human traffickers?

5. What kind of services/assistance is needed by those exiting the prostitution industry?

■ **OTHER ADVOCATE GROUPS**

Bay Area Sex Worker Advocacy Network (BAYSWAN)
Beyond the Streets
Call Off Your Old Tired Ethics (COYOTE)
Coalition Against Trafficking Against Women (CATW)
Family Partnership
Network of Sex Workers Projects (NSWP)
Nevada Coalition Against Sex Trafficking (NCAST)
Prostitution Research and Education (PRE)

---

**■■ ■■ ■■ BOX 9.2.**

### MONTANA METH PROJECT'S NOT EVEN ONCE CAMPAIGN

In 2005, a wealthy Montana resident, Thomas Siebel, invested about $15 million into an anti-drug campaign. The organization founded to run the campaign called Not Even Once is the Montana Meth Project. Ads were run in all the media. By 2007 there had been 45,000 TV ads, 35,000 radio ads, 10,000 print ads and 1000 billboard ads. "The ads pulled no punches, starkly portraying rape, prostitution, robbery and beatings, all as a result of getting hooked on meth. Other ads showed meth users with rotting teeth, gaunt, scarred bodies and hollow eyes" (Kemmick 2009: 10A).

Studies indicate that the campaign has been successful. In 2005, 8.3% of the teens in Montana used meth; in 2009 it was 3.1%, according to CDC studies. However, others say that not all of the drop in the number of teen users can be attributed to the ad campaign, as meth use was already on the decline, in Montana and around the country. For some reason, there are higher percentages of meth users in western states than most other states.

Nevertheless, the campaign has earned recognition. It was runner up for the Grand Effie marketing prize in 2007, and it has recognition of success by the White House. It has also expanded into six other states.

---

*Source:* http://www.montanameth.org.

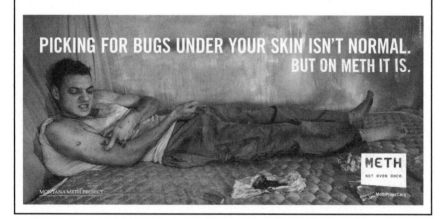

# :: SOCIAL PROBLEM
   ANALYSIS WORKSHEET

Your instructor may use this, or part of it, in assignments. But don't limit its use to class. It is a tool to be used anytime.

**I.  Social Problem** _____  **Name** _____

**A. Identifying the ingredients of the social problem**

Victim/target group _____

Social situation _____

Advocate group _____

Ameliorating action _____

Action group _____

Will to act _____

**B. Why did the social problem develop?** (development, aftermath of a natural event, inequality, self-interest, racism or discrimination, competing interests, history of enmity and conflict, ignorance, other)

_____

**C. Level of the social problem** (local, state, national, international)

_____


**II. About the Group**

**A. Type of advocate group** (political party, think tank, special interest group, social movement, crowd or riot) (Look at legal standing, type of action [in or out of system], size, resources, member identification)

_____

**B. What kind of support do members/supporters give?** (public activism, willingness to sacrifice, change personal behavior)

_____

**C. Why did the advocate group form?** (Desire for structural reform, reformation capacity, social reformer motivation)

_____

**D. What is the advocate group's view of human nature?** (rational human being, greater good human being, compassionate sacrificing human being)

---

**E. Dynamics within the advocate group** (structure, leaders, leadership style, productivity, impact on participants, rewards and equity, groupthink and other group decision processes)

---

**F. What stage of development best characterizes the advocate group?** (emergence, coalescence, action bureaucratization, decline, or change)

---

## III. Other Factors
**A. Claims making** (author bias, data bias, argument bias)

---

**B. What is the public reaction to the problem? To the proposed solution?** (fatalistic resignation, blame the victim, cynicism, romanticization, other)

---

**C. Is there an opposition group?** (If so, name it and explain why it formed—ideology, well-being threatened, afraid of change, other)

---

**D. What type of reform is sought?** (alternative, reformative, redemptive, transformative)

---

**E1. What type of solution does the advocate group seek?** (legal reform, government program, change addressed by professional agencies or nonprofit groups, education or public awareness, interpersonal interaction or reparation or apology, individual action, other)

---

**E2. If the group seeks legal reform, which social issue is it addressing?** (social discrimination, unequal distribution of resources, profiteering, different values, threats to physical or social well-being)

---

**F. What change model best fits?** (Marx's revolution, Gandhi's satyagraha, restructuring or critical mass, synthesis, emergence, redesign, manure)

---

**G. Looking at society as a whole, is change likely to be linear** (progress or development)**, cyclical** (growth and decay)**, or dialectic** (thesis, antithesis, synthesis)? **Why?**

---

**H. Are there likely to be unintended consequences?**

---

**I. Assess the overall benefit.** (Good or bad, for whom?)

---

# ■■ ADVOCATE GROUPS

Many groups have developed and proposed solutions to our social problems. Because some advocate for multiple issues, they are listed together here to avoid repetition. Each entry includes a brief description and an Internet address. (All addresses were current when included here, but some may have changed.) The reader can do research to get a more complete understanding of the merits of their positions. Some of the descriptions use language that comes from the organizations. Some advocate groups use acronyms to shorten their names for easy reference, others do not.

**AIDS Drugs Assistance Program Advocacy Association (AAA+).** One of the only grassroots groups to work exclusively on drug and AIDS assistance. It works to improve access to care for persons living with HIV/AIDS, pursues prevention, and strives to eliminate waiting lists for services. *www.adapadvocacyassociation.org.*

**AIDS Health Care Foundation (AHF).** A global organization providing medicine and advocacy in twenty-two countries. AHF pharmacies, thrift stores, health care contracts, and other strategic partnerships provide the operating capital. It brings lifesaving antiretroviral therapy to developing countries in Africa, Central America, and Asia. It has mobile HIV/AIDS testing and counseling clinics in California, Washington, D.C., and Florida. *www.aidshealth.org.*

**The AIDS Institute (TAI).** A nonprofit that promotes social change through public policy research, advocacy, and education. Research includes analysis and interpretation of AIDS information, related health care issues, and the social impact of disease on society. It coordinates studies and opportunities for students. *www.theAIDSInstitute.org.*

**AIDS Vaccine Advocacy Coalition (AVAC).** A nonprofit educational, policy analysis, and advocacy group working to improve global delivery of AIDS vaccines, male circumcision, microbicides, PrEP, and other emerging HIV prevention options. It works with other organizations to monitor, evaluate, and develop or expand advocacy around new and emerging HIV prevention strategies. *www.avac.org.*

**Al-Anon, Alateen.** Support groups for the friends and families of problem drinkers. *www.al-anon.alateen.org.*

**Alcoholics Anonymous (AA).** A fellowship of men and women who share their experiences, strengths, and hopes with each other, that they may solve their common problem and help others recover from alcoholism. Though AA is not allied with any sect or denomination, its 12 Step program features a God-based plan. *www.aa.org.*

**Alliance for Health Reform.** A nonpartisan, nonprofit educational group that organizes forums on health reform. It also serves as a resource for reporters, editorial writers, and newsrooms. Founded in 1991 and cochaired by a Democrat and a Republican, it aims to provide information to legislators, reporters, editors, and newsrooms. It holds forums on health and publishes health guides with the intention of providing access to detailed information. *www.allhealth.org.*

**Alliance for Retired Americans (ARA).** Formed in 2001, this group draws its membership from community organizations and the AFL-CIO union. It is concerned that, because of the National Commission on Fiscal Responsibility and Reform, programs like Social Security and Medicare and Medicaid are in serious jeopardy and facing significant reductions. Many of those who left AARP in 2003 defected to the Alliance for Retired Americans, or ARA. *www.retiredamericans.org.*

**American Academy of Pediatrics.** Official site used by 60,000 pediatricians committed to the physical, mental, and social well-being of children. *www.aap.org/advocacy/child healthmonth/prevteensuicide.htm.*

**American-Arab Anti-Discrimination Committee.** Founded in 1980, this civil rights organization defends the rights of people of Arab descent and promotes their rich cultural heritage. Combats stereotyping in the media and elsewhere, promotes a more balanced U.S. Middle East policy, sponsors cultural events, and participates in community activities. It offers legal services for victims of discrimination and has an active media and publications department. *www.adc.org.*

**American Association for Affirmative Action (AAAA).** A nonprofit association of professionals that promotes affirmative action. Founded in 1974, it does research, sponsors educational programs, and is a liaison with government agencies. *www.affirmative action.org.*

**American Association of Retired Persons (AARP).** A nonprofit organization founded in 1961 that advocates for the security, protection, and empowerment of people over fifty. It has more than 40 million members in all fifty states, and works as a service organization to provide information and some services to its members, as well as a lobby group (it is based in Washington, D.C.). On October 19, 2009, AARP released a joint statement with the American Medical Association (AMA) in support of health care reform. It sees privatization of Social Security as risky, and no guarantee against inflation, market down-turns, or loss of employment. Many AARP members left because of its support of the Medicare Modernization Act. *www.aarp.org; www.aarp.org/health/health-care-reform.*

**American Association of Suicidology.** Founded in 1968 by a psychologist, it is dedi-cated to researching and informing people about suicide. *www.suicidology.org.*

**American Association of University Women (AAUW).** This group's motto is "Advancing equity for women and girls through advocacy, education, philanthropy, and research." It argues that privatizing Social Security would cut disability and survivor benefits, which are particularly important for women. Also women would have smaller Social Security benefits because they earn less and spend less time in the workforce. It tentatively supports TANF because of its training program. It favors the Affordable Care Act because it restrains gender rating and practices detrimental to women. *www.aauw.org.*

**American Civil Liberties Union (ACLU).** Founded after World War I, it provided assistance to conscientious objectors. It was also involved in the Scopes trial in 1925. It works to defend individual freedoms, including speech and religion, a woman's right to choose, the right to due process, citizens' rights to privacy, and more. It works in court and in the legislature to serve minority interests. Lawsuits brought by the ACLU have been influential in the evolution of constitutional law. Issues of interest include capital punishment, criminal law reform, free speech, HIV/AIDS, human rights, immigrant rights, LGBT rights, national security, prisoner rights, racial justice, religion, reproductive freedom, voting rights, and women's rights. *www.aclu.org.*

**American Coalition for Clean Coal Electricity (ACCCE).** A partnership of industries involved in producing electricity from coal. It supports policies that promote the use of coal and make it cleaner, to include the capture and safe storage of $CO_2$ emissions. It looks to technology to ensure that coal is a fuel for America's future energy and environmental needs. *www.cleancoalusa.org.*

**American Family Association.** A well organized and efficient organization that promotes conservative Christian values and works to strengthen the moral foundation of American culture. Its activism makes use of Internet, radio, TV, email, publications, and lobbying. Its website includes broadcast files and mail/email information for supporters to write letters of protest on particular issues. It opposes abortion, same-sex marriage, and pornography. Founded in 1977, it is a large organization with many supporters. *www.afa.net.*

**American Federation of Labor (AFL-CIO).** Formed in 1886 in Columbus, Ohio, the AFL unionized workers to support legislation to reduce work hours and improve working conditions. In 1935 it had more than a million members. The Committee for Industrial Organization (CIO) formed within its ranks to organize workers by industry and admit African Americans. In 1945 they had a combined membership of 14 million. Today's membership is 13 million. It opposes privatizing Social Security, a move that would endanger a system that has kept retired and disabled persons out of dire poverty. The increased cost would benefit banks and investment companies, not workers. Also, raising the retirement age to seventy would mean that African American men, whose average age is sixty-six, would never receive benefits. It favors a single-payer health care system and TANF reform. *www.aflcio.org.*

**American Immigration Control Foundation.** A small, conservative group founded in 1983 to educate others about the disastrous effects of uncontrolled immigration. Activity is mainly publications. Unclear how big it is, maybe just a few people. *www.aic foundation.com*

**American Indian Movement (AIM).** Organization of Native Americans formed in the mid-twentieth century to advocate for their rights, restore their indigenous culture, and support each other. It also advocates for abolition of the Bureau of Indian Affairs and other issues. *www.aimovement.org.*

**Americans for Legal Immigration.** This group would like to see more immigrant controls and opposes amnesty for current illegal aliens. It supports candidates who make illegal immigration a top priority. Size of membership is unclear; may be just a few people. *www.alipac.us.*

**American Life League.** Catholic grassroots, pro-life education organization, committed to prevent abortion. *www.all.org.*

**American Lung Association.** The leading organization working to improve lung health and prevent lung disease through education, advocacy, and research. It sees air pollution as a serious threat to our nation's health. Medical experts, volunteers, and staff have testified in support of the Environmental Protection Agency's (EPA) proposed cleanup of the 386,000 tons of toxic pollutants pumped into the air annually. *www.lungusa.org www.info@lungusa.org.*

**American Medical Association.** Nationwide organization of doctors, founded in 1847. All policies are decided by democratic vote by the members. "It is understandable, though tragic, that some patients may come to decide that death is preferable to life. However, allowing physicians to participate in assisted suicide would cause more harm than good. Instead of participating in assisted suicide, physicians must aggressively respond to the needs of patients at the end of life." *www.ama-assn.org/ama/pub/physician-resources/medical-ethics/code-medical-ethics/opinion221.page.*

**American Psychiatric Association.** Members specialize in diagnosing and treating mental disorders. This URL is the group's online resource for mental health information. *www.healthyminds.org.*

**American Rivers.** A conservation organization that protects and restores rivers and clean water. It works in five areas: rivers and global warming, river restoration, river protection, clean water, promotion of change. Chicago disinfected sewage wastewater dumped daily into the Chicago River upon the recommendation of American Rivers. *www.amrivers.org.*

**Amnesty International.** A well-known international organization that seeks to ensure basic human rights for everyone in every country of the world. It works through research, campaigns (in the media and elsewhere), grassroots efforts, and in the courts to shape and promote legislation and policies to advance human rights, protect individuals, and free prisoners of conscience. Formed in 1961 by a British lawyer. *www.amnestyusa.org.*

**Anti-Defamation League (ADL).** A Jewish lobbying group founded in 1913 to stop defamation of Jewish people and secure justice and fair treatment for all. It fights anti-

Semitism and bigotry, defends democratic ideals, and protects civil rights through information, education, legislation, and advocacy. *www.adl.org.*

**Arise.** Nonprofit created in 1986 to provide alternatives for troubled youth and adolescents. Emphasizes families. *http://at-riskyouth.org/gangs.*

**Arming Women Against Rape and Endangerment (AWARE).** A nonprofit, all-volunteer organization to educate, support, train, and encourage spirit, knowledge, and determination. It teaches self-protection and emphasizes that the brain is anybody's best defense. In partnership with Verizon Wireless, AWARE provides emergency cell phones for stalking victims. *www.aware.org.*

**Bay Area Sex Worker Advocacy Network (BAYSWAN).** A nonprofit group that works to support prostitute and sex worker rights by improving working conditions, increasing benefits, and eliminating discrimination. It advises social services, policy reformers, media outlets and politicians, and has an educational website. *www.bayswan.org.*

**Beyond Coal.** A campaign of the Sierra Club, supported by Bloomberg (the current mayor of New York City) Philanthropies. It promotes a move from dirty coal to solar and wind power by (among other things) publicizing that the wind industry will employ more people. Campuses Beyond Coal is a related effort of young people seeking to get universities to stop using coal. *www.beyondcoal.org; www.sierraclub.org/coal; www.sierra club.org/coal/campus.*

**Beyond Pesticides.** Provides information on pesticides and alternatives. It identifies the risks of conventional pest management practices and promotes nonchemical and least toxic management alternatives. It has a newsletter and does research. It seeks safe air, water, land, and food for today and for future generations. *www.beyondpesticides.org.*

**Beyond the Streets.** Formerly National Christian Alliance on Prostitution or NCAP. The name change conveys a belief in the possibility of life beyond prostitution. A British group, it encourages discussion with local politicians and is committed to helping women who have left prostitution. It works with Freeset, a company that imports goods from India, to help Indian women escape prostitution. *www.beyondthestreets.org.uk; www.ncapuk.org.*

**Black Leadership Forum.** An alliance of African American organizations that lobbies for legislative and policy interests of African Americans and progressive public policy. It serves as a clearinghouse of black organizations. *www.blackleadershipforum.org.*

**Boys and Girls Clubs: Targeted Outreach.** Federally subsidized programs for gang prevention and gang intervention. *www.bgcnj.org/main_sublinks.asp?id=6&sid=97.*

**Brookings Institution.** A nonprofit public policy organization that conducts advanced research and develops practical recommendations. It aims to strengthen democracy, promote economic and social welfare among Americans, and help develop a cooperative international system. It is cautiously positive about the health care reform so far, but contends there is still a long way to go. Its view is that Medicare and Medicaid also need attention. *www.brookings.edu.*

**Caddo Lake Institute (CLI).** A nonprofit scientific and educational organization to protect the ecological, cultural, and economic integrity of Caddo Lake (shared between Texas and Louisiana), as well as its wetlands, plants, and wildlife habitats. Caddo Lake became the thirteenth of the Ramsar sites, which are wetlands of international importance. *www.caddolakeinstitute.us.*

**Call Off Your Old Tired Ethics (COYOTE).** A group working to decriminalize soliciting or engaging in consensual prostitution. It believes prostitution should be regulated like any other business. Founded in 1973, it has become rather inactive. *www.coyotela.org.*

**Catholics for Choice (CFC).** Supports Catholic women's right to follow their conscience regarding reproductive issues. Using discourse, education, research, and advocacy, this Washington-based group aims to be a counterpoint to the "powerful Roman Catholic hierarchy." It advocates for responsible choices in the best interests of all concerned. With a budget of $3 million, it works with sister organizations in Latin America and has a presence in Europe. *www.catholicsforchoice.org.*

**Cato Institute.** A nonprofit public policy research foundation dedicated to individual liberty, limited government, free markets, and peace. Founded in 1977 and located in Washington, D.C., it has ninety full-time employees and numerous others who contribute in a variety of ways. The group believes that Social Security must be reformed to remain viable, which includes private investment of Social Security taxes. On the other hand, it believes that Medicare should be reformed to look more like Social Security. *www.cato.org; www.cato.org/social-security.*

**Center for Biological Diversity.** Works to prevent extinction of animal species through science, law, and creative media. Uses biological data, legal expertise, and citizen petitions to establish new protections for animals, plants, and habitats: lands, water, and climates that they need to survive. *www.biologicaldiversity.org.*

**Center for Human Rights and Constitutional Law.** A nonprofit legal foundation dedicated to furthering and protecting the civil, constitutional, and human rights of immigrants, refugees, children, and the poor. Supported by the California Legal Services Trust Fund, private donations, and the receipt of attorneys' fees in major cases. *www.centerforhumanrights.org.*

**Center for Immigration Studies.** Founded in 1985 to provide immigration policy makers, new media, and others reliable information about the social, economic, environmental, security, and fiscal consequences of legal and illegal immigration. Researchers come from academia and politics. They try not to be predominantly "liberal" or "conservative." In general the group favors low immigration in order to maintain high standards in education, environment, security, and social fabric. *www.cis.org.*

**Center for Individual Rights.** Founded in 1989 by conservative lawyers. They work on various causes, including immigration. *www.cir-usa.org/index.html.*

**Center for Studying Health System Change.** A nonprofit, nonpartisan research organization that conducts studies and makes information available to others, especially lawmakers. *www.hschange.org.*

**Center on Addiction and Substance Abuse (CASA).** Professionals from all disciplines study and combat substance abuse. Founded by Joseph Califano in 1992, it aims to inform Americans of the economic and social costs of substance abuse, as well as remove the stigma and replace shame and despair with hope. *www.casacolumbia.org.*

**Century Foundation.** A nonpartisan, progressive organization founded in 1919. It advocates a mix of "effective government, open democracy, and competitive markets" as the solution to many of our social issues. It features research papers on many topics, including some authored by well-known persons. Opposed to privatization of Social Security, it favors universal health coverage and notes other problems in reform. *www.tcf.org.*

**Children's Assessment Center (CAC).** Provides services for sexually abused children, their siblings, and nonoffending caregivers. Includes medical professionals, police, therapists, and social workers; uses a holistic approach to restore the child's sense of self, comfort, and safety. *www.nationalcac.org.*

**Coalition Against Hate Crimes.** A group of Jewish and other professionals lobbying against hate crimes in Oregon. Founded 1997. *www.againsthate.pdx.edu.*

**Coalition Against Trafficking Women (CATW).** The first international nongovernmental organization (NGO) to focus on human trafficking, especially sex trafficking of women and girls. It works to reform prostitution laws, curb male demand for prostitution, and promote human rights. It addresses sexual exploitation, prostitution, pornography, sex tourism, and mail-order brides. *www.catwinternational.org.*

**Coalition to Defend Affirmative Action, Immigration, and Immigrant Rights and Fight for Equality by Any Means Necessary (BAMN).** Founded in 1995, it is a student and youth-based organization committed to making the promises of democracy and equality real. It campaigned to reverse the ban on affirmative action in the University of California system in 2001, and has pursued similar actions elsewhere. *www.bamn.com.*

**Committee on Women in Science and Engineering.** Formed in 1990 as a part of the National Research Council, it coordinates, monitors, and advocates to increase the number of women in science, engineering, and medicine. *http://sites.nationalacademies.org/PGA/cwsem/index.htm.*

**Commonwealth Fund.** A privately established think tank dedicated to the establishment of a high-quality health care system, particularly for society's most vulnerable, including low-income people, the uninsured, minority Americans, young children, and elderly adults. It contends that with innovation, the Affordable Care Act (2010) may be able to reduce health care costs and preserve or enhance care quality. *www.commonwealthfund.org.*

**Compassion and Choices.** Formed to assist persons with euthanasia decisions. *www.compassionandchoices.org.*

**Concerned Women for America.** Founded in 1979, it claims to be the largest public policy women's organization. It aims to bring Christian values into American culture. Focuses on policy research and activism. Pursues six core issues: family, sanctity of human life, religious liberty, education, pornography, and national sovereignty. Based in Washington, D.C. *www.cwfa.org/main.asp.*

**Council on Hemispheric Affairs.** A Washington-based think tank founded in 1975 to promote the common interests of the Americas and raise the visibility of regional affairs politically, economically, and diplomatically. It encourages rational and constructive U.S. policies toward Latin America. Researchers are professionals, civic and academic leaders, religious groups, and trade unions. *www.coha.org.*

**Court-Appointed Special Advocate Association.** Recruits, trains, and supports volunteers to represent abused and neglected children in the courtroom and elsewhere. They are appointed by the court to advocate for the most difficult foster children each year. These volunteers may be the only consistent adults in a child's life. *www.casa forchildren.org/site/c.mtJSJ7MPIsE/b.5301295/k.BE9A/Home.htm.*

**Cradle to Cradle Products Innovation Institute.** A nonprofit group based on the ideas of McDonnough and Braungart, it aims to transform the world of manufacturing and production. It promotes "innovation oriented models for eliminating toxic chemicals and other negative environmental impacts." *www.c2ccertified.org.*

**Death with Dignity.** Organized to work for legalizing euthanasia in Oregon, it mobilizes legal defense and maintains educational and outreach programs. *www.death withdignity.org.*

**Domestic Violence Resource Center.** A national center that provides a variety of services and information on domestic violence. Started in 1975 in Oregon. *www.dvrc-or.org.*

**Downwinders at Risk.** An activist nonprofit group founded in 1993 as a reaction to burning of hazardous waste in Midlothian, Texas, cement plants, upwind from the DFW metroplex. It is a full-time citizen group focusing on air quality. *www.downwindersatrisk.org.*

**Drug Abuse Resistance Education (DARE).** A police officer–led program founded in Los Angeles in 1983. Officers teach children from kindergarten through twelfth grade how to resist peer pressure and drugs. It is implemented in 75 percent of U.S. school districts and in forty-three countries. One student per state becomes a part of the Youth Advisory Board and is eligible for a $20,000 college scholarship. *www.dare.com.*

**Drug Free America Foundation (DFAF).** A nonprofit organization to develop and promote global strategies, policies, and laws to reduce illegal drug use and addiction. It is a consultant to the Economic and Social Council of the UN. It advocates abstinence-based drug education in schools. Students Taking Action Not Drugs (STAND), an affiliate, educates students about drugs. *www.dfaf.org.*

**Drug Policy Alliance.** A 2000 merger of Lindesmith Center and Drug Policy Foundation, both of which played an important role in advocating a more liberal drug policy in the twentieth century. The alliance advocates a policy that is grounded in science, compassion, health, and human rights. It wants reform of drug sentences for nonviolent offenders and medical marijuana. Lindesmith library remains as a resource. *www.drug policy.org.*

**Drug Strategies.** A research institute to identify and promote more effective approaches to substance abuse and to increase public understanding of current research on what works and what does not. It assesses education, prevention, and treatment initiatives and reviews drug policies and programs. It maintains a website to provide young people with information and assistance. *www.drugstrategies.com* [Research]; *www.drugstrategies .org* [Treatment].

**Eagle Forum.** Founded in 1972 by Phyllis Schlafly, it supports American sovereignty, American identity, the Constitution, exposes radical feminists, supports traditional education. Protecting the institution of marriage is important. It opposes feminists because they stereotype men as a danger to women but push the role of combat for military women. It opposes the ERA because of its hidden agenda of abortion and same-sex marriage. *www.eagleforum.org.*

**Earth First!** An unconventional, international environmental group that uses grassroots organizing, legal processes, civil disobedience, and "monkey wrenching." It is loosely organized and functions as a coordinating body for various local efforts. It is more of an activist group; one activity is "tree sits." *www.earthfirst.org.*

**Earth Justice.** A nonprofit public interest law firm, founded in 1971 as the Sierra Club Legal Defense Fund. It is dedicated to protecting natural resources and wildlife, and to defending the right to a healthy environment. It works through the courts and on Capitol Hill to ensure that government agencies and private interests follow the law and to strengthen federal environmental laws. Its 1997 name change reflects a change to include other clients. *www.earthjustice.org.*

**Emerge: Counseling and Education to Stop Domestic Violence.** The first abuser education program, founded in 1977. It teaches that violence is a learned behavior, not a disease or illness. Forty percent are self/partner referred, and 60 percent are referred by social services or through probation. *www.emergedv.com.*

**Environment Texas.** A citizen-based environmental group to protect the air, water, and open space in Texas. It uses research, practical ideas, and tough-minded advocacy to protect against toxic pollution, reduce material consumption, build sustainable transport, and shift to 100 percent clean energy. *www.environmenttexas.org.*

**Environmental Defense Fund (EDF).** A nonprofit organization founded in 1967 and composed of scientists and economists. It works with corporations to demonstrate the benefits of environmental innovation and to spur environmental gains throughout society. *www.edf.org.*

**Ethnic Majority.** Founded in 2002 to educate, assist, and empower African, Hispanic, and Asian Americans to achieve advancement in politics, business, at work, and in society. *www.ethnicmajority.com/racial_profiling.htm.*

**Euthanasia Prevention Coalition.** Canadian Catholics who oppose mercy killings and want to increase awareness of hospices and palliative care. *www.euthanasiaprevention.on.ca.*

**Families United Against Hate.** Support group for hate crime survivors. *www.cyber squattersagainsthate.com.*

**Families USA.** A nonpartisan organization that functions to keep a network of organizations and individuals informed on health issues. It acts as a watchdog over various government actions, alerting members to potential changes. It is critical of some aspects of the new health care bill and worries that premiums, deductibles, and copays will increase too much. *www.familiesusa.org.*

**Family Partnership.** An accredited human service nonprofit organization in Minneapolis that promotes strong families, vital communities, and capable children. PRIDE (from Prostitution to Independence, Dignity, and Equality) is a nationally recognized program it developed to help women get out and stay out of prostitution, based on self-help, advocacy, and support, plus assistance for children. *www.everyfamilymatters.org.*

**Family Research Institute.** Founded in 1982 to research controversial family issues from a conservative viewpoint: homosexuality, AIDS, sexual social policy, and drug abuse. It claims scientific objectivity but has come under criticism for its nonscientific views. *www.frc.org.*

**Fathers4Justice.** Formed in 2001 by a man from Britain who was denied access to his two sons. Campaigns for social justice in family law and is imitated by other groups in other countries. *www.Fathers-4-justice.org.*

**Feminist Majority.** The lobbying group associated with Feminist Majority Foundation. *http://feministmajority.org.*

**Feminist Majority Foundation.** Founded in 1987 to advocate for women's equality, health, and nonviolence, and empower women economically, socially, and politically. It does research, education, grassroots organizing, training. Cooperates with Feminist Majority in lobbying and political action. *http://feminist.org.*

**Final Exit Network.** A volunteer organization that assists persons with euthanasia decisions. It also aims to educate the American public and fights in court when necessary. *www.finalexitnetwork.org.*

**Focus on the Family.** A global organization that promotes God-centered marriages and families. It sees children as a gift, and all life as sacred, including fetuses. Founded in 1977, it advocates for responsible social policies that support the family. It offers counseling, forums, daily broadcasts, and a plethora of resources. It supports abstinence. *www.focusonthefamily.com.*

**Freedom to Marry.** Formed in 2003 as a campaign to win the right for same-sex marriage nationwide. It is working to overturn DOMA and win same-sex marriage in more states, as well as educate the public why it matters. *www.freedomtomarry.org.*

**Galveston Bay Foundation.** Founded to preserve, protect, and enhance the natural resources of Galveston Bay estuarine system and its tributaries. *www.galvbay.org.*

**GangFree.** A school-based program for younger children (second and fourth grades), as well as at-risk teens. *www.gangfree.org.*

**Gay Men's Domestic Violence Project (GMDVP).** This grassroots group provides crisis intervention for same-sex male domestic abuse—physical, emotional, financial, and sexual. It provides support and resources to victims and maintains a Facebook page. *www.gmdvp.org.*

**Glendon Association.** A private, California-based organization dedicated to enhancing mental health through research, education, and training. It particularly addresses suicide, child abuse, violence, and troubled interpersonal relationships. *http://glendon.org.index.*

**The Good Men Project.** Formed in 2009 as a film project to tell positive, life-changing stories about men. It did a survey of top 10 issues for men. Number one was father's rights. Number two was how feminism has harmed men. *http://goodmenproject.com.*

**grassroots.org.** Unconventional group that provides Internet business services to charities. Its mission is to be a catalyst for positive social change by providing nonprofits with free technologies and resources. *www.grassroots.org.*

**Gray Panthers.** Founded in 1970 by retired social workers. The public policy office in D.C. opened in 1985 to change health care, increase job opportunities and housing for elderly and others, and other issues. It aims to create a society where people's needs are more important than profit, and power is responsibly dealt with. Its neighborhood networks address problems on a local level. It opposes privatization of Social Security. *www.graypanthers.org.*

**Greenpeace.** One of the first environmental organizations. It started in Vancouver, Canada, in 1971. It is an activist group. *www.greenpeace.org.*

**Health Care for America Now (HCAN).** An organization of 1,000 organizations (doctors, nurses, community organizations, labor unions, small business owners, faith-based groups, people of color, seniors, and children's and women's rights groups) in forty-six states (30 million people) supporting comprehensive health care reform of private and public insurance that is affordable and comprehensive, and offers choice and quality. *http://healthcareforamericanow.org.*

**Health Care for the Homeless.** Formed in 1985 in Baltimore, it has become a nationally recognized model for delivery of health care to underserved populations. It delivers pediatric, adult, and geriatric medical care, mental health care, social services, addiction treatment, dental care, HIV services, outreach, prison reentry, supportive housing, access to education. Funded by Robert Wood Johnson Foundation, Pew Charitable Trust, and the U.S. Conference of Mayors. *www.hchmd.org.*

**Health Care Now.** A group of professionals and others that endorses a guaranteed national health insurance system—quality health care for everyone. It supports the HR 676 national legislation introduced by John Conyers—a single payer nonprofit health care system. *www.health care-now.org.*

**Heritage Foundation.** A research and educational institution founded in 1973. Promotes conservative public policies, free enterprise, limited government, individual freedom, strong national defense. It argues that Medicare reform has been accepted by doctors, provides patient choice, and is cost-effective. It wants to see less government regulation in the health care industry, additional Social Security reforms, adjustments in TANF, and limited immigration. *www.heritage.org.*

**Home for the Homeless.** New York–based provider of residential, educational, and employment training centers. Founded in 1986 as a public-private partnership between city government, private business, and the Cathedral of St. John the Divine. It aims to provide homeless families with the opportunities and support necessary to move out of shelter and live independently. It takes a family-based, child-centered, education-focused approach to all its programs and services. *www.homesforthehomeless.com.*

**Human Rights Campaign.** Founded in 1980, it is one of the largest civil rights organizations working for gay and lesbian rights. It works through advocacy, education, and outreach. *www.hrc.org.*

**Human Rights Watch.** An international group that monitors human rights violations worldwide. *www.hrw.org/campaigns/september11/hatewatch.htm.*

**Institute for American Values.** Founded in 1987 as a private, nonpartisan organization to research, educate, and publish on issues of family well-being and civil society. *www.americanvalues.org.*

**Institute for Marriage and Public Policy.** Founded in 2003, IMAPP is a private, nonpartisan organization with apparent connections to legislators in Washington. Its professed mission is high-quality research and public education on ways that law and public policy can strengthen marriage as a social institution. *www.marriagedebate.com.*

**Institute for Women's Policy.** Founded in 1987, it addresses women's needs in employment, education, religion, welfare issues, family and health issues. A Washington-based think tank intended to influence public policy. *www.iwpr.org.*

**Institute on Race and Justice.** An interdisciplinary research institute at Northeastern University (MA) established with a grant from the Bureau of Justice Assistance to research racial profiling. *www.racialprofilinganalysis.neu.edu.*

**Interagency Council on the Homeless.** Formed in 1987 to coordinate federal response to homelessness. Composed of nineteen cabinet secretaries and agency heads. *www.usich.gov.*

**Inter-American Dialogue.** A Washington-based think tank that promotes communication on issues related to the Western Hemisphere. It aims to help shape the agenda of democratic governance, social equity, and economic growth among public and private leaders. Members and board are drawn from throughout the region, including prominent politicians from other countries. Founded in 1982. *www.thedialogue.org.*

**International AIDS Society (IAS).** The world's leading independent association of HIV professionals in 191 countries. It hosts conferences, promotes dialogue, education, and networking, and advocates for an evidence-based response to HIV. Scientists, clinicians, public health, and community practitioners. Headquartered in Geneva. *www.iasociety.org.*

**International AIDS Vaccine Initiative (IAVI).** Works in partnership with more than forty nongovernmental research organizations and academic, biotechnology, pharmaceutical, and government institutions, to design and develop AIDS vaccine candidates, run clinical trials, and conduct clinical research on HIV epidemiology and disease. Operates in the United States, the United Kingdom, Africa, and India. Works with other international organizations. *www.iavi.org.*

**International Gay and Lesbian Human Rights Commission.** Started in 1990 in the United States, it has worked internationally to improve the rights of gays and lesbians around the world. *www.iglhrc.org.*

**International HIV/AIDS Alliance (The Alliance).** A global partnership of nationally based linking organizations, including an international secretariat, working to support community action on AIDS in developing countries, toward the goal of reversing the spread of AIDS by the year 2015. Based in the United Kingdom. *www.aidsalliance.org.*

**International Rivers.** A nonprofit group to protect rivers and the rights of communities that depend on them. It opposes destructive dams. *www.internationalrivers.org.*

**International Union of Gospel Missions.** Founded in 1913 as a Christian mission to help the homeless. It has 275 missions, serves 42 million meals a year, provides 15 million nights of lodging, and graduates 18,000+ from addiction recovery programs. *www.agrm.org/agrm/default.asp.*

**Joint Center for Political and Economic Studies.** An African American think tank formed in 1970 to help black politicians. It focuses on civil engagement and governance, health policies, media and technology, and environment. *www.jointcenter.org.*

**Just Yell Fire.** A nonprofit organization to teach teen girls safety from predators and sexual assault. Founded by fourteen-year-old Dallas Jessup (who has a black belt in Tae Kwon Do and has been an instructor in Filipino street fighting) in 2006, with a video showing girls a "no rules self-defense" that they can use to get away from frightening situations. It seeks to make self-defense and personal rights awareness mandatory in health classes and PE. Has one million members in fifty-two countries worldwide. *www.justyellfire.com.*

**Kaiser Family Foundation.** A respected nonprofit, nonpartisan, privately run think tank focusing on health care issues. It does research and makes it available to policy makers, media, the health care community, and the public. It is not associated with Kaiser Permanente or Kaiser Industries. Regarding Medicare and Medicaid, it is concerned that lower-income persons who need assistance are the dominant receivers and focus of policy discussions. *www.kff.org.*

**KidsHealth.** An educational organization dedicated to providing accurate, up-to-date medical information in a language easily understood by nonmedical persons. It is part of the Nemours Foundation's Center for Children's Health Media. It also provides programs and games to educate children. *http://kidshealth.org.*

**Lamberth Consulting.** A consulting group formed to assess racial profiling and provide training. Formed in 2000 to provide racial profiling assessment, training, and communication services to universities, governments, civil rights groups, and others. *www.lamberth consulting.com.*

**Law Enforcement Against Prohibition (LEAP).** An educational organization of law enforcement associated persons who want to eliminate prohibition of all drugs for adults and establish appropriate regulations and standards for distribution and use. Its view is that the drug war has wreaked havoc, funded terrorism, and caused corruption. Its speakers bureau is composed of former professionals. *www.leap.cc.*

**Leadership Conference on Civil and Human Rights.** A coalition of more than two hundred national organizations working together for a more just and open society. Started in 1950 by A. Philip Randolph, head of the Brotherhood of Sleeping Car Porters, Roy Wilkins of the NAACP, and Arnold Aronson, from the National Jewish Community Relations Advisory Council. Primarily a lobbying and educational group. It has lobbied for all major civil rights legislation, including the Civil Rights Act of 1964, the Voting Rights Act of 1965, and the Fair Housing Act of 1968. Its Education Fund keeps the public informed. http://civilrights.org.

**League of United Latin American Citizens (LULAC).** One of the main organizations to promote Latino rights. Founded in 1929 to fight prejudice and discrimination (including segregation) in Texas and elsewhere. It works in civil rights, economics, education, health, housing, immigration, public services, and technology. *www.lulac.org.*

**Legal Momentum.** Dedicated to the legal defense of the rights of women and girls. Started in 1970 as NOW (National Organization for Women), its New York and Washington, D.C., staff is mainly women. It pursues five areas of public policy relating to women: equal employment opportunities, workplace rights, strengthening the safety net for women, protection for victims of violence, promotion of gender equality. See Chapter 5 for a fuller description. *www.legalmomentum.org.*

**Live Action.** A young people's group founded in 2004 to opposed Planned Parenthood abortion clinics in a strictly nonviolent manner. Members tape and release videos of medical staff in abortion clinics and publish a campus magazine, *Advocate. http://liveaction.org.*

**Marriage Law Project (Marriage Watch).** Founded in 1996, the Marriage Law Project seeks to reaffirm marriage as the union of one man and one woman through (1) participating in key court cases, (2) sponsoring research, conferences, and publications, and (3) offering hands-on, pro bono legal assistance to interested policymakers and organizations. It is part of the Interdisciplinary Program in Law and Religion of the Catholic University of America. *www.marriagelaw.cua.edu* or *www.marriagewatch.org*.

**Men Can Stop Rape (MCSR).** An international organization mobilizing to create cultures free from violence, particularly male violence against women. MCSR schedules and conducts training programs with interactive group exercises, role-playing, and multimedia presentations for government employees, state and local coalition members, armed forces, law enforcement agencies, and universities. *www.mencanstoprape.org*.

**Men's Activism.** A site that primarily shares stories and information worldwide. Started in 2000, its goal is to provide information to help establish equal rights for men and improve men's lives. It believes that women can be violent and that many rape and abuse accusations are not true—but some are. *www.mensactivism.org/node/5631*.

**The Men's Center.** Formed to help men find positive resources, information, and support. It seeks to empower men to lead healthy, productive, and fulfilling lives. *www.the menscenter.com*.

**Mexican American Legal Defense and Education Fund.** Latino civil rights organization, founded in 1968 to address legal issues. It promotes social change through advocacy, communications, community education, and litigation in the areas of education, employment, immigrant rights, and political access. *www.maldef.org*.

**Montana Meth Project.** A privately formed media project to counter the use of methamphetamines. Started in 2005, several million dollars were invested in ads that portrayed the devastation of the drug. Studies indicate some success, but some claim the figures are exaggerated. *www.montanameth.org*.

**My Army One Source (Family Advocacy Program—FAP).** A program to prevent, educate, report, investigate, and intervene in spouse and child abuse. Includes information about the Transitional Compensation program (TC) for spouses, former spouses, or children who are victims of abuse. *www.myarmyonesource.com/familyprogramsand services/familyprograms/familyadvocacyprogram*.

**National Abortion Federation (NAF).** Professional association of abortion providers in North America. It believes that women should be trusted to make private medical decisions in consultation with their health care providers. NAF offers training and services to abortion providers, as well as information and services to women. *www.prochoice.org*.

**National Abortion Rights Action League (NARAL).** An activist group which believes women have a right to safe, legal abortion. It supports birth control and sex education to reduce the need for abortion. Members are pro-choice, reflecting the belief that a woman has control of her own body. It supports election of pro-choice leaders, works to prevent restrictions at the state level, protects pro-choice rights in court, and is active in other areas. *www.naral.org, www.prochoiceamerica.org*.

**National Alliance of HUD Tenants.** A tenant-controlled alliance of HUD assisted housing that works to preserve affordable housing, protect tenants' rights, and promote tenant ownership and control. Founded in 1991, it connects most HUD tenant groups in the country, and many coalitions. *www.saveourhomes.org.*

**National Alliance on Mental Illness (NAMI).** Formed in 1979 as a grassroots mental health advocacy organization. Its goals include helping communities be aware of mental illness and the resources needed, peer education and training for persons who deal with mental illness, and advocating for policy and services to serve those in need. *www.nami.org.*

**National Alliance to End Homelessness.** An alliance of providers and partners who aim to end homelessness in the United States. Formed in 1987, it analyzes policy and develops pragmatic solutions, working with public, private, and nonprofit sectors. Part of its mission is to provide data to inform and educate policy makers. *www.endhomelessness.org.*

**National Association for the Advancement of Colored Persons (NAACP).** One of the oldest and largest civil rights organizations, it was founded in 1909. Its mission is political, educational, social, and economic equality for all, and the elimination of racial discrimination. It seeks enactment and enforcement of civil rights laws and is committed to the democratic process. It also seeks to inform minorities of their constitutional rights and educate the public about the effects of discrimination. It maintains a presence in Washington and lobbies actively. *www.naacp.org.*

**National Association for Bilingual Education.** Teachers, administrators, college instructors, students, researchers, parents, and policy makers working to cultivate a multicultural society by supporting and promoting policy, programs, pedagogy, research, and professional development that yield academic success, value native language, lead to English proficiency, and respect cultural and linguistic diversity. *www.nabe.org.*

**National Association of Drug Court Professionals (NADCP).** A national corporation founded in 1994 by pioneers from the first twelve drug courts in the nation. Judges, prosecutors, defense attorneys, and clinical professionals who want justice system reforms, including judicial monitoring and effective treatment for offenders. The goal is to reduce crime, unburden our prison system, ease our health care load, and strengthen our society. *www.nadcp.org.*

**National Center for Homeless Education.** A North Carolina organization, funded by the U.S. Department of Education, to remove educational barriers and improve opportunities for children and youth experiencing homelessness. *http://center.serve.org/nche.*

**National Center for Policy Analysis.** A nonprofit, nonpartisan public policy research organization, established in 1983 with a goal to promote private, free market alternatives to government regulation and control. Most of the researchers are university professors. *www.ncpa.org; www.ncpa.org/sub/dpd/index.php?Article_Category=44.*

**National Coalition Against Domestic Violence.** Believes that violence against women and children is one of the top 10 political and legislative issues in the United States. It provides safe houses and other services for victims, as well as information for the public. *www.ncadv.org.*

**National Coalition for the Homeless.** A Washington, D.C.–based group engaging in public education, policy advocacy, and grassroots organizing. *www.nationalhomeless.org.*

**National Coalition for Homeless Veterans.** A nonprofit organization to help veterans negotiate the services available and find the assistance they need. *www.nchv.org.*

**National Coalition for Men.** Founded in 1977 to end sex discrimination. It fights for men's rights through information and civil rights actions, legislative reforms, protest and education. It finds antimale bias in the media, in sentencing, domestic violence policies, education, and false rape charges. Data regarding men and housework is biased. *www.ncfm.org.*

**National Committee to Preserve Social Security and Medicare (NCPSSM).** Formed in 1982 by the grandson of Theodore Roosevelt, it maintains an active lobby presence in Washington and actively involves any and all who want to participate in its educational and lobbying efforts. Its view is that the Social Security Administration has met its obligations for seventy-five years, at a cost of less than 2 percent. It is not in crisis, the group argues. For more discussion, see Chapter 5. *www.ncpssm.org.*

**National Council of La Raza.** Founded in 1968, it is one of the largest Hispanic civil rights advocacy organizations working to improve opportunities for Hispanic Americans. It works with a network of three hundred affiliated community-based organizations. It does research, policy analysis, and advocacy in five areas: investments, civil rights/immigration, education, employment, health. *www.nclr.org.*

**National Fatherhood Initiative.** Founded in 1994 to confront the widespread absence of fathers from children's lives. It aims to improve the situation by education and organizing—in the community and elsewhere—and developing programs and initiatives. *www.fatherhood.org.*

**National Gang Center.** A government site for the latest research about gangs. It publishes the results of the National Youth Gang Survey and other pertinent information and contacts. *www.nationalgangcenter.gov.*

**National Gay and Lesbian Task Force.** Founded in 1973, it works to build grassroots political muscle by training, strengthening infrastructure, and organizing campaigns. It has a policy think tank, organizes conferences, and lobbies government. *www.thetask force.org.*

**National Immigration Forum.** A Washington-based group established in 1982 to advocate for immigrants and immigration. It aims to help create a vision, consensus, and strategy to create a U.S. immigration policy that lives up to the country's ideals, protects human dignity, reflects our economic demands, celebrates family life, and provides opportunities for progress. It strives to be a trusted source for information, analysis, and advocacy, and examine a wider set of pro-immigration voices. *www.immigrationforum.org.*

**National Law Center on Homelessness and Poverty.** Founded in 1987 by a lawyer, Maria Foscarinis, who was instrumental in passing the McKinney-Vento Homeless Assistance Act two years earlier. It does policy advocacy, public education, impact litigation, and generally is the legal arm to end homelessness. *www.nlchp.org.*

**National Organization for Marriage.** Founded in 2007 to oppose same-sex marriage in state legislatures. *www.nationformarriage.org.*

**The National Organization for the Reform of Marijuana Laws (NORML).** A nonprofit, educational, and lobbying group to support the adult right to use marijuana responsibly and eliminate all penalties for its use, civil and criminal. It also supports legalizing hemp for industrial use. Notable board members: Willie Nelson, Bill Maher, Rick Steves (travel writer), Kary Mullis (1993 Nobel Laureate in chemistry), and Mark Stepnoski (former NFL). NORML has a database of attorneys across the United States. *www.norml.org.*

**National Organization for Women (NOW).** The largest organization of feminist activists, founded in 1966. It has 550 chapters in all 50 states. Supports women's equality in the workplace, schools, and justice system, and opposes violence against women. *www.now.org.*

**National Right to Life Committee.** Started in 1973, it is the largest pro-life advocate group, with more than 3,000 local chapters and a fully staffed office in Washington. It is recognized as an effective lobby group. Its three basic functions are education, legislation, and political action. General counsel defends pro-life legislation in court and takes legal action. Opposes euthanasia. *www.nrlc.org.*

**National Student Campaign Against Hunger and Homelessness.** Started in the 1980s, it now works as a clearinghouse for information and liaisons with student organizations. *www.studentsagainsthunger.org.*

**National Urban League.** Grassroots African American organization formed in 1910 to "elevate the standard of living in historically underserved urban communities." Its activities include urban programs, policy research, and advocacy. It focuses on education (early childhood literacy and college scholarships), economics (job training, homeownership), health, civic engagement, racial justice empowerment (proactive policies and programs). *www.nul.org.*

**National Wildlife Federation.** A conservation organization that works with communities to protect and restore wildlife habitat, confront global warming, and connect with nature. *www.nwf.org.*

**Natural Resources Defense Council (NRDC).** One of the largest environmental action groups working to protect right of all people to have a voice in what happens to their environment. It does grassroots activism as well as legal battles in the courtroom. Some 350 lawyers, scientists, and other professionals are associated. Founded in 1970 by a group of lawyers. *www.nrdc.org.*

**The Nature Conservancy.** Formed in 1951 to preserve the plants, animals, and natural communities that represent the diversity of life on earth. It works to protect lands and waters. Staff includes 550 scientists, located in all 50 states and 33 countries. It partners with individuals, governments, other nonprofits, and corporations. *www.nature.org.*

**Network of Sex Workers Projects (NSWP).** An international membership organization led by sex workers. Members must recognize sex work as work, oppose the criminalization of sex work. and support the self-organizing and self-determination of sex workers. It includes SWOPS (sex workers outreach projects), PONY (Prostitutes of New York), and BAYSWAN. *www.nswp.org.*

**Nevada Coalition Against Sex Trafficking (NCAST).** A group working to outlaw prostitution in Nevada. It runs educational campaigns, helps women escaping prostitution, and lobbies for more effective legal regulations. *www.nevadacoalition.org.*

**OCA National.** Founded in 1973 as Organization of Chinese Americans, it has redefined itself as an advocate group for Asian Pacific Americans. It has over eighty chapters and affiliates, and advocates for social justice and equal opportunity, promotes civic participation, and fosters cultural heritage. *www.ocanational.org.*

**Oceana.** A nonprofit working to protect the world's oceans. It uses science-based campaigns and claims to have protected over 1.2 million square miles of ocean and innumerable sea turtles, sharks, dolphins, and other sea creatures. It has offices in North, South, and Central America and Europe. *www.oceana.org.*

**Operation Rescue.** One of the most visible pro-life activist groups. It bought and closed an abortion clinic in Kansas in 2009. It advocates direct action to restore legal personhood to preborn babies and stop abortion. Its senior policy adviser advocates only peaceful activism after spending two years in prison for conspiring to damage an abortion clinic. *www.operationrescue.org.*

**Panzou Project.** Federally funded program to combat gang-related problems in Miami. An intense intervention program, it targets youth in their late teens or early twenties, especially those whose families need services. *www.panzouproject.org/home/services.*

**Partnership at Drug Free.** Helps parents relate to their teens and to understand addiction and treatment. Offers scientific insight into the problem and trains professionals to work with local leaders and others to prevent drug and alcohol abuse. Started by media people and uses advertising to reduce drug use. Has broadened into alcohol, as well. *www.drugfree.org.*

**Patients Rights Council.** An Ohio-based nonprofit organization established to lobby and inform about euthanasia. *www.patientsrightscouncil.org.*

**Pharmaceutical Research and Manufacturers of America (PHRMA).** Represents research and biotechnology companies that, in 2009, spent $45.8 billion on research and development of medicines "that allow patients to live longer, healthier, and more productive lives." It claims that medicine prices have not risen more than other health care services. *www.phrma.org.*

**Physicians for a National Health Program (PNHP).** Organized in 1987, it has more than 17,000 members and chapters. It advocates single payer national health insurance, in which the public or a quasi-public agency organizes health financing, but delivery of care remains largely private. For more discussion, see Chapter 5. *www.pnhp.org.*

**Planned Parenthood.** Maintains centers providing for women's sexual and reproductive health care and is one of the largest abortion providers in the United States. It also has an active education program and advocates on campuses, online, through legislation, and in communities. It is a national organization that works with many local centers and groups. *www.plannedparenthood.org.*

**Presbyterian Network to End Homelessness.** Newly organized to help end homelessness around the country. The Presbyterian Night Shelter, in existence for twenty-five years, is the largest provider of services for the homeless in Fort Worth. *www.pnteh.org; http://pns-tc.org.*

**Prevent Child Abuse America.** Formed in 1972, it builds awareness and educates people about child abuse. Local chapters work to prevent child abuse. It also works on the national level. *www.preventchildabuse.org/index.shtml.*

**Prostitution Research and Education (PRE).** A nonprofit that researches prostitution, pornography, and sex trafficking and consults with researchers, survivors, the public, and policy makers since 1995. Its information has been used around the world by groups that offer services to women escaping prostitution. *www.prostitutionresearch.com.*

**Public Citizen.** A nonpartisan public policy advocate group formed in 1971 to lobby concerns of private citizens on issues where their interests differ from large corporations. It has offices in Washington, D.C., and Austin, Texas. It favors a single payer health system, which would streamline administration and save money in the long run. *www.citizen.org.*

**Rainbow/PUSH Coalition.** Developed out of SCLC Operation Breadbasket in 1968 by Jesse Jackson. It combines theology and social justice with progressive economic, educational, and social policy. It has worked to protect black homeowners, workers, and businesses and to help youth develop in healthy ways, especially in the inner city. *www.rainbowpush.org.*

**Rape, Abuse, and Incest National Network (RAINN).** One of the largest anti–sexual assault organizations, it educates about sexual violence and works to improve victim services and ensure that rapists are brought to justice. Its National Sexual Assault Online hotline provides live and completely confidential help to victims. Especially concerned about college-age women, who are at greatest risk of being victims. *www.rainn.org.*

**Real Women of Canada.** Describes itself as an "alternative women's movement." Formed in 1983, it advocates for equality for women and takes into consideration the effects on the family. Its view is that career choices for women should include remaining at home. It advocates policies that would make that choice easier and calls for tolerance for all views. *www.realwomenca.com.*

**Ryan White HIV/AIDS Program.** A federal program for people with HIV/AIDS and their families, who have insufficient health care coverage or financial resources to cope with the disease. It provides services to more than half a million people each year. It provides grants, has resource lists, and publishes a newsletter. *http://hab.hrsa.gov.*

**Sachem Quality of Life Organization.** Citizens of Farmington, New York, who want to address the problem of day laborers, most of whom are illegal aliens, congregating on the streets of the community. This group apparently still exists but does not have a web presence. *www.cir-usa.org/articles/perez_SQL_mission_stmt.htm www.cir-usa.org/cases /perez_v_posse.html.*

**Safe Neighborhood Project.** Started in 2001, it is a nationwide program to link community programs that focus on gun crimes. Its goal is to reduce gun and gang crime through networking. *www.psn.gov.*

**The Salvation Army.** Has group homes, emergency shelters, and temporary living centers around the country. Founded in 1865 in England. *www.salvationarmyusa.org /usn/www_usn_2.nsf.*

**The Seniors Coalition.** Formed in 1989 to repeal the Medicare Catastrophic Coverage Act, this free market group has grown and expanded its work to include protecting the Social Security trust fund, saving Medicare from bankruptcy, and ensuring availability of low-cost generic drugs. Originally based in California, it has a membership of more than four million. *www.senior.org.*

**Sierra Club.** Founded in 1892 by naturalist John Muir to preserve communities, wild places, and the planet itself through work at a grassroots level. A large and well organized group, it works with local chapters to improve the natural environment around the country. It lobbies for federal protections for the environment. It also organizes hikes and outings, and publishes artistic photo books on nature. *www.sierraclub.org.*

**Simon Wiesenthal Center.** International Jewish human rights organization dedicated to preserving the collective memory of the Holocaust and fostering tolerance among various communities. *www.wiesenthal.com.*

**Sisters of Charity Foundation of South Carolina.** A faith-based (Catholic) organization dedicated to reducing poverty. It strives to understand the causes of poverty, advocate for the poor, promote education, strengthen families, and develop commu-nities. It forms alliances with individuals and organizations to mobilize resources and act as a change agent. *www.sistersofcharitysc.com; http://sistersofcharitysc.blogspot.com /2010/05/congress-needs-to-reauthorize-tanf-and.html.*

**Southern Christian Leadership Conference (SCLC).** Civil rights organization formed in 1957 by Martin Luther King and others. Known for its advocacy efforts. *http://sclc national.org.*

**Southern Poverty Law Center.** Formed by lawyers after the Civil Rights era to ensure legal enforcement of the nation's discrimination laws. It currently functions as a think tank on hate groups as well. *www.splcenter.org.*

**Standing Up to Texas' Biggest Polluters.** This group's Clean Air project won a land-mark settlement against Shell Oil in 2009, after the company agreed to reduce emissions at its Deer Park chemical plant by 80 percent—and pay a record penalty of almost $6 million. In 2010, using the same legal strategy, it settled a case with Chevron Phillips, which agreed to slash pollution by 85 percent at its Baytown chemical plant and pay a fine of $2 million.

**Street Gangs.** Originally run on a University of California server in 1995, this site has information about the history of gang formation in southern California. It stresses that not all gangs are criminal, and that police often use gang suppression as a means of appealing to the public. *www.streetgangs.com.*

**Students Active for Ending Rape (SAFER).** An all-volunteer group started by students at Columbia in 1999 to reform university sexual assault policy by covering backpacks with red tape symbolizing bureaucratic red tape. Conducts teach-ins, one day training for students, and mentoring programs around the country. Endorses the 2011 Campus Sexual Violence Elimination (SaVE) Act requiring better campus response to sexual violence. *www.safercampus.org.*

**Teen Suicide.** A site that has suicide statistics. Not clear who sponsors the site. *www.teensuicide.us.*

**Trust for Public Land (TPL).** Works to conserve land in and around cities for people to enjoy as parks, gardens, and other natural places. Founded in 1972 to bring a business approach to conservation, it fosters local land trusts. *www.tpl.org.*

**Union of Concerned Scientists (UCS).** This leading science-based nonprofit works for a healthy environment and safe world through scientific research and citizen action. It began as a collaboration between students and faculty members at the Massachusetts Institute of Technology in 1969. It now includes more than 250,000 citizens and scientists from all walks of life. Cleaner air and global warming are two of its big concerns. *www.ucsusa.org.*

**Urban Institute.** Founded in 1968 in response to then President Johnson's desire for an independent nonpartisan analysis of the problems in America's cities. It analyzes policies, evaluates programs and informs community development with the aim of im-proving social, civic, and economic well-being. Research findings are shared with policy makers, program administrators, businesses, academics, and public. Concerned about immigration, poverty, Medicaid and Medicare; wants to see universal health care. *www .urban.org.*

**Waterkeeper Alliance.** Founded in 1999 by Robert F. Kennedy Jr. and other water advocates who aim to patrol and protect over 100,000 miles of rivers, streams, and coastlines. There are nearly two hundred Waterkeeper Organizations on six continents defending their communities against anyone who threatens their right to clean water. *www.waterkeeper.org.*

**World Wildlife Fund (WWF).** A leading conservation organization that works in one hundred countries on extensive projects to preserve freshwater systems, the varied and endangered coral reefs, and some of the most productive fishing grounds. *www.world wildlife.org.*

**40 Days for Life.** A nonprofit, community-based activist group opposed to abortion. Biblically based, its activities are primarily demonstrations and public activism, such as door-to-door petitions, media contact, and campus outreach. It encourages activism in three areas: prayer and fasting, constant vigil, and community outreach. Active across the country, its visible, public centerpiece is a forty-day, round-the-clock prayer vigil outside a Planned Parenthood center or other abortion facility. *www.40daysforlife.com.*

**350.org.** A global grassroots movement founded by U.S. author Bill McKibben, who wrote on global warming, and his university friends. It organizes online campaigns, grassroots activities, and mass public actions such as the 10/10/10 day of climate solutions with over 7,000 events in more than 188 countries—from solar panel installations to community garden plantings. Its name, 350, is the safe upper limit for $CO_2$ parts per million in our atmosphere, according to climate experts. *www.350.org.*

# ▪▪ NOTES ON SIMILARITIES AND CONTRASTS OF SOCIAL PROBLEMS TEXTBOOKS

This appendix explains how words and concepts are used in various social problems texts.

## THE DEFINITION OF A SOCIAL PROBLEM

A social problem is defined here as a situation judged by an advocate group to be adversely affecting the personal or social well-being of a target group (or collectivity) to the extent that it needs to be redressed by means of an ameliorating action to be taken by an action group/organization or institution. An action group takes such action once there is sufficient will to act.

The six ingredients of a social problem are intended to be a clear and simple way to establish something as a social problem and bring all the aspects into the discussion. While other texts don't have all six ingredients, most have two or more in their definition.

- Henslin and Fowler: some aspect of society that people are concerned about and would like changed.
- Mooney, Knox, and Schacht: a social condition that a segment of society views as harmful to members of a society and in need of remedy.
- Macionis: a condition that undermines the well-being of some or all members of a society and is usually a matter of public controversy.
- Kendall: a social condition or pattern of behavior that harms some individuals or all people in a society; a sufficient number of people believe it warrants public concern and collective action to bring about change.

The term *target group* used here is similar to Best's "target population." Other texts are less specific. Henslin and Fowler: some aspect of society; Charron and Vigilant: a large number of people; Kendall: some individuals or all people in a society; Mooney, Knox, and Schacht: members of society.

The term *adverse social situation* (or adversely affecting personal or social well-being) is similar to other terms. Best: a troubling condition; Macionis: a condition; Kendall: a social condition or pattern of behavior.

307

The term *will to act* is intangible but important. Without the will to act, there would be no advocate group, and ultimately no social problem. Best's concept of "warrants" is similar, defined as the justification for doing something. However, w*ill to act* includes emotional motivation and is not always overtly specified.

The term *action group* can be confusing because it can refer to different parties. It is the group that will take action to solve the problem. For instance, to get drunks off the road, MADD persuaded the government to pass laws that could be enforced, with punishment as a deterrent. In this case, the action group is, first, the government that agrees to pass a law. Second, it is law enforcement that ensures the laws are obeyed.

## SOCIAL CONSTRUCTION OF SOCIAL PROBLEMS

Social construction is a common approach to the study of social problems. As a social constructionist, Best sees social problems as the process by which particular conditions come to be topics of interest and concern and action. Macionis identifies the social constructionist approach as one of the basic components. Kendall and Mooney et al. identify it as one of many approaches—a part of symbolic interactionism. Hensin and Fowler also look at social construction within the context of symbolic interactionism, but then under characteristics they state that social problems are relative, and there are competing views of reality—essentially a social constructionist viewpoint.

## CAUSES OF SOCIAL PROBLEMS

Causes are not always included in social problems texts. An exception is Charron and Vigilant, who think that causes of social problems are critical, controversial, and generally social. Best uses *causal stories* as subjective indicators of blame, as in accidents, inadvertent causes, and intentional actions. Levin and colleagues identify three levels of causation: individual, cultural, and structural. Discussion of cause here is intended to provide a philosophical and sociological underpinning to clarify the issues.

## NOTES ON SOCIAL MOVEMENTS

A common definition of social movement is given by Snow and colleagues (2004, 11) as "collectivities acting with some degree of organization and continuity outside institutional or organizational channels for the purpose of challenging or defending extant authority or world order of which they are a part."

The stages identified in advocate group development are taken from social movement theories and adapted slightly. The stages of Smelser's structural strain theory are the best known. The four stages identified by Tilly and others are (1) emergence, (2) coalescence, (3) formalization, and (4) decline. Best identifies six stages in what he calls the "natural history model of the social problems process": (1) claims making, (2) media coverage, (3) public reaction, (4) policy making, (5) social problems work, and (6) policy outcomes.

A good discussion of the typology of social movements is found in McAdam and Snow (1997). There are some differences in how the categories are applied to advocate groups here. Another discussion is found in Harper (1993).

## NOTE ON THREE SOCIOLOGICAL PERSPECTIVES

There has been no attempt to cover the three or four basic general sociological theories (conflict, interactionism, functionalism, interpretive approaches). Nor are sociological methods covered. Both topics can be covered in other classes. The intent is to make the study of social problems different from introduction to sociology. To that end, I emphasize the ability to evaluate claims makers as a crucial sociological analytical skill because the ability to evaluate the data of claims makers is crucial for analyzing social problems.

# :: GLOSSARY

**Acid rain**. Any atmospheric moisture that contains high levels of nitric and sulfuric acids which then combine with water, oxygen, and other chemicals to form an acidic compound.

**Acquaintance rape**. A forcible sexual encounter between two people who first meet in a social setting; excludes family members and incest.

**Action group**. The group that puts the change into effect.

**Active euthanasia**. Death that results from an intentional action, such as a lethal injection or breathing carbon monoxide.

**Active opposition group**. An advocate group that forms out of opposition to an action or proposed action by another advocate group. The action either changes some tradition within society, or is an extension of the authority of those in power. Former opposition groups tend to be more extreme as a means of bringing change to the establishment. If the opposition group acquires sufficient power, it will force compromises to the original resolution. Personal animosity may exist between members of the opposition group and the original advocate group.

**Adverse social situation**. Something that can be changed by human effort and probably has a human or social cause.

**Advocate group**. A collection of individuals motivated by self-interest, altruism, idealism, or other reasons who bring an issue into the public arena for discussion and action.

**Affirmative action**. The practice of giving minorities preferential treatment to compensate for the historical disadvantages they experienced, in order to put them on an equal footing in competing for jobs and admittance to institutions of higher education.

**Agents of change**. People, or in some cases forces of nature, who work to bring about change.

**Aid to Dependent Children (ADC)**. A modest welfare program set up by Franklin D. Roosevelt in 1935. It later became Aid to Families with Dependent Children (AFDC) and in 1996 was replaced by TANF (Temporary Assistance for Needy Families).

**Alternative change**. Limited change on an individual level, for example, Promise Keepers and anti-abortion groups.

**AMA (American Medical Association)**. Professional organization of doctors, founded in 1847, that regulates the practice of medicine in the United States. It works with the state to license practicing physicians and other medical practices.

311

**Ameliorating action**. Proposed change for a social problem.

**Argument bias**. Attempt to convince others by means other than careful weighing of the data.

**Author bias**. A distorted or misleading interpretation of information, of which the author may or may not be aware.

**Authoritarian personality**. Theory developed by Adorno and colleagues that people who are prejudiced are often intolerant and rigid, highly conforming to conventional norms, and projecting their own faults onto an "inferior" minority group.

**Autopoietic system**. A system that creates and recreates itself through inner reflexive and recursive processes.

**Battered child syndrome**. A condition of serious, chronic abuse that can cause permanent injury or death.

**Binge drinking**. Five or more drinks in a row for men; four for women.

**Blaming the victim.** A belief that the victim group is responsible for creating the problem it faces.

**Bracero program**. Guest worker program from 1949 to 1964 that permitted Mexicans to stay and work in the United States for nine months of the year.

**Bracketing**. Setting aside one's own worldview to understand the worldview of another.

**Bureaucratization**. The fourth stage in advocate group formation; a paid, skilled staff runs the group.

**Call girl or escort**. Least noticeable prostitute who contacts customers covertly by phone; the most educated prostitutes that make the most money.

**Capacity.** The human, social, and organizational resources that can be leveraged to solve social problems.

**Charter schools**. An alternative to regular public schools. They are set up by contract or charter through a state agency, are funded by the government, but do not have to follow the guidelines of the traditional public schools. There are some 3,000 charter schools in 40 states.

**Child abuse**. Physical or mental injury, sexual abuse, exploitation, neglect, or maltreatment of a child under eighteen, or specified by the state in terms of sexual abuse.

**Civil unions**. Legally recognized domestic partnerships given some rights, in some cases all the rights of married couples.

**Claims making**. The process by which a person tries to convince others of the truth and importance of something.

**Class consciousness**. According to Marx, workers' awareness that they are being taken advantage of.

**Coalescence**. The second stage in the formation of an advocate group; the problem is framed and defined, resources are gathered, leaders emerge, organizational structure emerges, and a plan of action is developed.

**Compassionate sacrificing human being**. People are at heart basically good, sympathetic, and generous.

**Complementary or alternative medicine**. Alternative approaches to health, including meditation, yoga, homeopathy, hypnosis therapy, herbal supplements (fish oil, glucosamine, Echinacea, etc.), and alternative practitioners such as acupuncturists, chiropractors, and massage therapists.

**Complex adaptive system**. A system with feedback loops that is open to external influences; it is self-regulating and morphogenic (can change its structure). Examples are psychological and sociocultural systems.

**Conflict theory of prejudice**. Prejudice comes from stratification: people who are powerful and privileged use disadvantaged minorities for their own benefit and tend not to see their own role in their situation.

**Conjunctive task**. One in which group productivity rests on the weakest member.

**Core and periphery nations**. Immanuel Wallerstein's term for wealthy and powerful versus poor and not powerful countries, respectively, in the world economic system.

**Coyotes**. Guides who transport illegal immigrants from Mexico to the United States for a fee.

**Cradle to cradle philosophy**. Production methods whereby products are designed so that the materials can be reclaimed and used again.

**Cradle to grave philosophy**. Production methods developed during the Industrial Revolution; resources are used for production, products are discarded when broken or no longer needed. It creates pollution, waste, and other problems.

**Critical mass**. The idea that change will come when a sufficient number of people who want it and are willing to work for it tip the scale toward change. See also Restructuring Model.

**Crowd**. A temporary gathering of persons with a similar focus.

**Cultural creatives**. David Korten's term for people who are willing to change the world in a positive way.

**Cyclical change**. The idea that history repeats itself, civilizations rise and fall, and there is no ultimate end goal. Change is a cycle of growth and decline.

**Cynicism**. The belief that nothing can be done to change something.

**Data bias**. Inaccuracy in the collection, analysis, or presentation of data; the conclusion is not supported as claimed.

**Deep poverty**. Income below 50 percent of federal poverty level.

**Development**. On a global scale, economic and social achievement of a society through transformation (in a pragmatic, scientific, or Western way) of conditions of poverty and low productivity.

**Dialectic change**. The idea that change is an interactive process whereby the stages and end result are undetermined. It has direction, but recurring patterns exist on different levels, similar to a spiral. Hegel incorporated the idea of thesis, antithesis, and synthesis—the original idea, division of the idea into two opposing aspects, and a final joining of the two opposing camps into one at a higher level.

**Diffuse impact**. Something that affects all aspects of someone's life.

**Diffusion**. Adoption of new ideas by others throughout the society.

**Discrimination**. Differential treatment of categories of people.

**Disjunctive task**. Task in which the group relies on the strongest or best member for a good outcome.

**Domestic partnerships.** Living arrangement of two persons sometimes granted rights of married couples.

**Dream Act.** Proposed legislation to allow those who came to this country illegally with their parents as children to be citizens.

**Drug maintenance.** A method of treating a drug addict by stabilizing the addict on the lowest possible amount of the drug, so he or she can function in society.

**Ecosystem.** The system of interacting, living organisms and their natural environment.

**Emergence.** First stage in the formation of an advocate group; a problem is noticed and discussed.

**Emergence model.** The idea that change comes from the bottom up (rather than top down), when people follow simple organizing principles: a new order emerges out of chaos.

**Environmental injustice.** Minorities and the poor who live in low-income communities and countries are more likely to be exposed to pollution and other harmful environmental factors, or be exploited for the benefit of others.

**Euthanasia.** Ending the life of someone who is terminally ill so death is more peaceful and less painful.

**Evolution.** An irreversible biological transformation of plant and animal populations.

**False consciousness.** According to Marx, a false sense of reality on the part of the workers, who don't recognize their unfair treatment by factory owners.

**Fatalistic resignation.** Resigned to a situation and not doing anything to change it.

**Feminism.** Working for equal women's rights in society and to end discrimination against women in all areas.

**Forced assimilation.** Pressure on people to acculturate to the mainstream society. For example, Native American children were sent to boarding schools where they were dressed in Western-style clothing and had to speak English.

**Free market competition health care system.** A consumer-driven, direct fee for service system, in the United States for example, where the patient selects the services he or she wants and is responsible for payment.

**Free rider.** Someone who makes use of collective resources without contributing.

**Glass ceiling.** Refers to barring women from the highest management positions in a company.

**Global warming.** The rise in worldwide temperatures presumably because of increased greenhouse gases.

**Government owned and managed health care system.** A health care system in which all medical practitioners are government employees. Found originally in socialist societies, such as China, Cuba, and the former Soviet Union.

**Greater good human being view of human nature.** In this view, people are essentially social and consequently will give up their individual rights to create a greater social whole.

**Group norms.** Unwritten behavioral rules within the group.

**Groupthink.** A group of ordinarily reasonable persons influence each other to make an irrational, flawed decision.

**Guest worker.** Immigration policy allowing people to temporarily reside in the United States in order to work, but not to stay permanently.

**Hate crimes**. Crimes motivated by biases of race, religion, sexual orientation, ethnicity/ national origin, and disability. *Crimes against persons* are murder and nonnegligent manslaughter, forcible rape, aggravated assault, simple assault, and intimidation. *Crimes against property* are robbery, burglary, larceny-theft, motor vehicle theft, arson, and destruction/damage/vandalism.

**Hate group**. A group of people who collectively have an extreme, even violent prejudice against another group, to the extent that they feel hate crimes are justified.

**Gentrification**. Investors bought up large segments of redlined neighborhoods that had fallen into disrepair to build upscale housing units that the original residents can't afford.

**Health**. A state of complete physical, mental, and social well-being and not merely the absence of disease or infirmity (WHO).

**Hippocratic Oath.** A vow taken by most medical professionals to preserve life and not cause harm.

**Homophobia.** People with an aversion to homosexuals.

**Hyperreality.** An experience of images that have no authenticity, for example, Disney-world.

**Ideal types**. An analytical, classifying construct against which real life is compared.

**Idealism**. Theory that looks to ideas or beliefs as the major factor of social change.

**Inequality**. Unequal distribution of social or material resources in a society.

**Infant mortality rate**. The number of deaths per 1,000 live births.

**Innovation**. The discovery or invention of something new; one kind of social change.

**Interest groups**. Political parties, think tanks, or special interest groups.

**International level social problem.** A problem resolved through cooperative efforts of multiple governments.

**Interpersonal interaction**. Members of two or more conflicting groups have the opportunity to interact on a personal basis over time.

**Juggernaut.** Anthony Giddens's view of the force of modernization that has come to be a "runaway engine of enormous power" threatening to control society instead of being controlled by people.

**Legal reform**. Efforts to effect change by passing laws. It is important when people resist change, when additional resources are needed, when two groups compete for resources or territory and other situations.

**Linear change**. Directional change, as in "things are getting better." It includes agents of change (people) and often proceeds in stages or steps toward some desired end state.

**Local level social problem**. A problem involving the local government as an action group, or some other way.

**Magnet schools**. Specialize in some subject, such as science or art. They are often in minority areas, so nonminority students are bused to the school.

**Managed competition health care system**. Health care is private but regulated by the government. Individuals choose their own insurance providers. Examples of this are found in France and Japan.

**Manure model**. A situation in which problems are solved by unforeseen new technology almost before proposed solutions can be implemented.

**Marielitos.** Persons imprisoned or suffering because they opposed Castro who came to United States in 1980.

**Marital rape.** A forcible sexual encounter between spouses.

**Marxian model.** Change based on Karl Marx's idea of revolution; the suffering group uses the power of its numbers to force the establishment to change—in short, a revolution.

**Materialism.** Theory that looks to the physical world for the factors that lead to change.

**Matriarchy.** A society in which women have dominant and powerful roles.

**Medical tourism.** People traveling from the United States to lower-income countries to get medical treatment.

**Western medical model.** Practice of medicine based on the scientific model; someone is a patient only when he or she is sick, unlike other approaches that focus on keeping people well.

**Medicaid.** Government health care program for the poor.

**Medicare.** Government health care program for the elderly and handicapped.

**Minority.** A category of people who have physically distinguishing characteristics and a subordinate status in society.

**Modernity.** The latest in industrial and scientific developments of Western society. Modern thinking is rational and utilitarian.

**Mommy track.** Refers to women who drop out of the workforce to raise their children.

**Narcotics.** Opium and its derivatives (heroine, morphine, codeine, etc); the coca leaf and its active ingredient cocaine, and derivative crack; and the cannabis plant, the source of marijuana and the powerful resin hashish.

**National level social problem.** A problem involving the federal government as an action group or in some other way.

**Opposition group.** A group that forms to counter the proposed ameliorating action of an advocate group.

**Passive euthanasia.** Death that results when medical treatment (feeding tubes or respirator) is withdrawn.

**Patriarchy.** A society in which men have the dominant and powerful roles.

**Physician-assisted suicide.** Death that results when a doctor prescribes a lethal dose of medicine but does not administer it.

**Pink collar.** Refers to lower paid occupations predominated by women: "women's jobs."

**Preference system.** Immigration policy where people are approved based on individual, not national, qualifications.

**Prejudice.** An irrational judgment about individuals based on one or more stereotypes about a category of people. It is irrational because there is little or no empirical evidence to support the judgment of the individual, or to support the stereotype.

**Privatization.** Putting all or some of Social Security taxes into individual savings/investment accounts.

**Pro-choice advocate groups.** they argue that a woman's body and health is her own business, and she has exclusive rights as to what happens to it. Some, but not all, pro choice advocates believe that life begins when a child is born and/or that the fetus has no rights. Legal abortions prevent unsafe practices and are therefore better for both baby and mother.

**Pro-life advocate groups**. Argue that life begins at conception, so abortion at any stage is killing of a human. This argument usually comes from their belief system (religion) and many pro-life advocates—but not all—subscribe to traditional religious and gender roles.

**Professional ethics.** Standards set by practicing professionals in a particular field.

**Profiteering.** An individual, group, company, or institution that profits at human expense or misfortune.

**Progress.** Linear change, moving toward a desired end goal.

**Prostitution.** Selling or advertising sex acts for money or other goods.

**Quota system**. Immigration policy as a result of the Immigration Act in 1924, whereby immigrants from a particular country or ethnic origin were limited to 2 percent of their presence in the 1890 census.

**Racism**. The belief that people with different biological traits (skin color) have different social value.

**Racial profiling**. Targeting members of a minority as criminal suspects.

**Racial steering.** Not being given full realtor information and/or steered toward minority neighborhoods when looking for housing.

**Rape**. Defined by the FBI as "carnal knowledge of a female forcibly and against her will." It includes attempts or assaults to commit rape by force or threat of force, but excludes statutory rape.

**Redlining**. Mortgage discrimination. Lenders identify a neighborhood as a high-risk area and refuse loans to residents or charge higher interest rates, or demand higher down payments.

**Reparation.** Some kind of repayment for an offense that recognizes the offense and to some measure, restores what was lost.

**Rational human being**. Humans are basically selfish and competitive, acting to benefit others only when it serves their own interests.

**Rationalization.** A change in thinking and values from tradition to practicality and efficiency.

**Redemptive change.** Radical change on an individual level, for example, Alcoholics Anonymous.

**Redesign model.** Rethinking methods of production—throwing out the old way and starting fresh to radically reduce waste and preserve and reuse natural resources.

**Reformative change.** Limited change on a structural level, for example, civil rights, gay rights, women's groups.

**Reframing.** Looking at a problem in a larger context.

**Resolution of a social problem.** When the advocate group or the public no longer advocate for the target group, the problem ceases to be a social problem.

**Restructuring model.** The idea that change will come when enough people want it and are willing to work for it. *See also* Critical Mass.

**Reverse discrimination.** Nonminorities are discriminated against because they were *not* minority.

**Revolution**. Marx's transformation of the social order, whereby the workers overthrow the owners of production.

**Riot**. An expressive and active crowd.

**Robin Hood funding**. Method of "recapturing" revenue from high-wealth districts to give it to lower-wealth districts in an effort to equalize school funding.

**Romanticization.** Seeing a situation as idyllic and believing that change would spoil things.

**Satyagraha model**. Change based on Mahatma Gandhi's idea of nonviolence; use of peaceful means, including self-sacrifice, to convince others to change.

**Scapegoat theory**. People who are disadvantaged blame minorities for their problems.

**SCHIP** (State Children's Health Insurance Program). A government health care program for children of low-income families, run by individual states.

**Second wave feminism.** The fight against discrimination against women that started in the 1960s. It focused on economics, education, abuse and domestic violence, abortion, and other issues.

**Segmented impact**. Something that affects only particular aspects of someone's life.

**Sexism.** The common prejudice that men are better than women (or entitled to certain social resources).

**Shaken infant syndrome**. Damage to a baby, toddler, or young child's brain because of shaking.

**Simulacrum.** Jean Baudrillard's observation that modern images that seem very real actually don't have any "real" references. *Pirates of the Caribbean,* for example, is an idealized version of a fantasy of pirates.

**Single payer health care system**. A kind of government insurance. Doctor bills and health care needs are paid with revenue from taxes and fees collected from the patient. The government also sets prices for services. Some single payer systems have a way for individuals to "opt out." Examples are found in the United Kingdom and Canada.

**Slippery slope argument.** The fear that legalizing euthanasia may lead to deaths for economic reasons.

**Social construction.** The process of arranging the various factors of one's experience into a coherent whole.

**Social control**. The means by which actions of individuals are controlled.

**Social Distance Scale.** A Thurstone scale that measures the level of understanding and intimacy between (social distance) groups, with values ranging from 1 (accept into your family by marriage) to 7 (reject the group as visitor to the country).

**Social dynamics**. An examination of the processes of movement, interaction, and change.

**Social facilitation**. The impact of a group on individual behavior.

**Social inequality.** Unequal distribution of social resources, including status, power, and prestige.

**Social movement**. A somewhat organized collectivity working outside institutional channels to bring social change.

**Social norms**. The unwritten rules of behavior of a group or society.

**Social problem**. A situation judged by an advocate group to be adversely affecting personal or social well-being.

**Social Security**. The government stipend paid to 58.7 million people—retired people, surviving spouses and minor children, and disabled.

**Social statics**. An examination of the parts of society, the influences they have on each other, and the way they are arranged in space at a particular point in time.

**Special interest group**. Smaller, more localized advocate group focused on a single issue.

**Stalking.** Persistent efforts to establish or reestablish a relationship against the will of the victim.

**State level social problem**. A problem involving the state government as an action group, or some other way.

**Status**. Social position.

**Satutory rape**. Nonforcible sexual intercourse with someone who is younger than the statutory age of consent.

**Stereotype.** A broad generalization about a category of people, usually exaggerated, often derogatory, although there can be positive stereotypes too.

**Stratification.** Organization of people according to differential access to resources and the consequent social positions in society.

**Structure**. Consistently arranged organization of members of a group or society.

**Synthesis**. Bringing two sides together to create something bigger than either one by itself.

**Synthesis model.** The idea of problem solving as taking the best from both sides to create something bigger and better than what existed before.

**Systems thinking**. Looking at the situation in terms of relationships rather than as linear cause and effect.

**TANF (Temporary Assistance for Needy Families)**. Replaced the earlier AFDC program when the Personal Responsibility and Work Opportunity Reconciliation Act was passed in 1996. A federally funded assistance program administered at the state level. Assistance is limited to a total of five years over a lifetime. Recipients are given child care and assisted to find jobs.

**Target group**. A collection of individuals whose personal well-being (life chances, life satisfaction, or emotional happiness) or their social well-being (equality, representation, and other social situations) is threatened.

**Think tank.** A research organization, usually with political affiliations, that collects and disseminates information.

**Thomas theorem**. If you think something is real, it will be real in its consequences.

**Trail of tears**. In 1839 the Cherokee nation was forcibly removed from the southeastern United States and traveled on foot to what is now Oklahoma.

**Transformative change**. Radical change on a structural level, for example, the Bolshevik revolution.

**Transnational communities**. Communities of people from one country living in another country and continuing to travel back and forth as if the border didn't exist.

***Verstehen.*** Interpretive understanding of social phenomena.

**Veterans programs**. Government health care program for former military personnel.

**Victimless crime**. Violation of law where the victim is not obvious.

**Wealth**. What you own minus what you owe.

**Wet foot, dry foot**. Cuban nickname for America's immigration policy: those who arrive safely can stay, but those caught in the water (between Cuba and the United States) are sent back.

**Wetlands**. Areas with surface or groundwater and vegetation that grows in saturated soils such as swamps, marshes, and bogs.

**White flight**. Large-scale migration of whites from racially mixed inner-city areas to racially homogeneous suburban areas.

**Will to act**. Willingness of the public, or of authorities, to pay the cost to bring change.

**Win/win**. Looking for solutions that give something to everyone, rather than zero-sum that creates polarization and makes people choose sides.

**Zero-sum.** When there is a fixed number of things; if one person has more, another automatically has less.

# :: SOURCES

Aasen, Eric. 2010. "Protestant, Catholic Teens from Northern Ireland Find Common Ground During Visit to Arlington." *Dallas Morning News*, July 11.

Abelson, Reed. 2008. "Health Care Costs Increase Strain, Studies Find." *New York Times*, September 24. www.nytimes.com/2008/09/25/business/25health.html. Accessed October 11, 2009.

Aberle, David. 1966. *The Peyote Religion Among the Navaho*. Chicago: Aldine.

ACF (Administration for Children and Families). 2009. "Child Maltreatment 2009." www.acf.hhs.gov/programs/cb/pubs/cn09. Accessed September 8, 2011.

ACLU (American Civil Liberties Union). 2009. "The Persistence of Racial and Ethnic Profiling in the United States," June 29. www.aclu.org/human-rights_racial-justice /persistence-racial-and-ethnic-profiling-united-states. Accessed July 24, 2011.

ACMA (Australian Communications and Media Authority). 2009. "Regulating Online Content," July 1. www.acma.gov.au/WEB/STANDARD/665330/pc=INT_IND _CONTENT_ABOUT. Accessed September 26, 2009.

Adams, Bert N., and R. A. Sydie. 2001. *Sociological Theory*. Thousand Oaks, CA: Pine Forge.

Adams, Mike. 2011. "America's Breadbasket Aquifer Running Dry: Massive Agriculture Collapse Inevitable." *Natural News,* March 10. www.naturalnews.com/031658 _aquifer_depletion_Ogallala.html. Accessed August 11, 2011.

Adorno, Theodor W., et al. 1950. *The Authoritarian Personality*. New York: Harper & Brothers.

Ahern, Louise Knott. 2009. "'The Burning Bed': A Turning Point in the Fight Against Domestic Violence." *Lansing State Journal*, October 20. www.lansingstatejournal .com/article/99999999/NEWS01/909270304/-Burning-Bed-turning-point-fight -against-domestic-violence. Accessed September 7, 2011.

Ahlborn, Richard, et al. "Mexican Americans: A Historical Perspective." Americans All: A National Education Program. www.americansall.com/PDFs/02-americans-all /8.9.pdf. Accessed July 27, 2011.

AllAbout. 2011. "History of the Pro-Choice Movement." www.allaboutpopularissues .org/history-of-the-pro-choice-movement-faq.htm. Accessed June 16, 2011.

Allan, Kenneth. 2006. *Contemporary Social and Sociological Theory: Visualizing Social Worlds*. Thousand Oaks, CA: Pine Forge.

Allen, Barbara L. 2007. "Environmental Justice, Local Knowledge, and After-Disaster Planning in New Orleans." *Technology in Society*. Vol 29 no 2, pp 153–159.

Allport, Gordon. 1979 (1954). *The Nature of Prejudice*. Reading, MA: Addison-Wesley.

Alonzo, Armando C. 2011. "Mexican-American Land Grant Adjudication." *Handbook of Texas Online*. www.tshaonline.org/handbook/online/articles/pqmck. Accessed July 20, 2011.

Alonzo-Zaldivar, Ricardo. 2009. "Studies Show Little Competition Among Insurers." *Fort Worth Star-Telegram*, August 23, p 8A.

Altenergy. N.d. "Alternative Energy." www.altenergy.org. Accessed August 11, 2011.

Amar, Akhil Reed. 2007. "How Women Won the Vote." In *Solutions to Social Problems: From the Bottom Up: Successful Social Movements*. Edited by D. Stanley Eitzen and Kenneth Stewart. Boston: Pearson Education.

American Signal Corp. www.americansignal.com/news/Richardson%20Texas.php. Accessed Sept 25, 2009.

Anrig, Greg. 2010. "The Next Priority for Health Care: Federalize Medicaid." http://tcf.org/publications/2010/9/the-next-priority-for-health-care-federalize-medicaid/pdf.

Ap, John. 2003. "Encountering SARS: Perspective from an Infected Area." eReview of Tourism Research. Vol 1 no 1.

APA (American Psychiatric Association). 2005. "Let's Talk Facts About Teen Suicide: Healthy Minds, Healthy Lives." www.healthyminds.org. Accessed September 8. 2011.

Arbreton, Amy J. A., and Wendy S. McClanahan. 2010. "Targeted Outreach: Boys & Girls Clubs of America's Approach to Gang Prevention and Intervention." Public/Private Ventures.

Arehart-Treichel, Joan. 2008. "Deep Sedation Gains Favor As Assisted Suicide Declines." *Psychiatry News,* May 2, 2008, p 30.

Armario, Christine, and Dorie Turner. 2010. "Shocking: Nearly 1 in 4 High School Graduates Can't Pass Military Entrance Exam." Huffpost Education, December 21. www.huffingtonpost.com/2010/12/21/high-school-grads-fail-military-exam_n _799767.html. Accessed June 16, 2011.

Armor, David. 1995. *Forced Justice: School Desegregation and the Law*. New York: Oxford University Press.

Armstrong, Karen. 2006. *The Great Transformation: The Beginning of our Religious Traditions*. New York: Knopf.

Associated Press. 2011. "Poverty in Mexico Rises to 46%, Study Says." *Fort Worth Star-Telegram,* July 30, p 2A.

Associated Press. 2011a. "10 Countries Now Allow Same-Sex Marriage." *Washington Post,* March 14. www.washingtonpost.com/wp-dyn/content/article/2011/03/14 /AR2011031402821.html. Accessed August 7, 2011.

Associated Press. 2011b. "Occupy Wall Street Has Money, Donated Supplies." October 17. *Fort Worth Star-Telegram,* p 10A.

Austin, W., and E. Walster. 1974. "Participants' Reactions to 'Equity with the World.'" *Journal of Experimental Social Psychology*. Vol 10, pp 528–548.

Avert. 2010. "Worldwide HIV and AIDS Statistics Commentary." www.avert.org/worl statinfo.htm. Accessed August 16, 2011.

Balabanova, Dina, et al. 2004. "Health Service Utilization in the Former Soviet Union: Evidence from Eight Countries." http://findarticles.com/p/articles/mi_m4149 /is_6_39/ai_n8577383/?tag=content;col1. Accessed October 16, 2009.

Balmer, Randall. 2006. *Thy Kingdom Come: An Evangelist's Lament: How the Religious Right Distorts the Faith and Threatens America.* Philadelphia: Basic Books.

Balsdon, J. P. V. D. 1990. *Roman Women.* New York: Barnes & Noble Books.

Barnes, Sarah. 2011. http://www.campbellcompany.com/news/bid/56140/U-S-charitable -giving-shows-modest-uptick-in-2010-following-two-years-of-declines. Accessed December 14, 2011.

Barr, Andrew. 1998. *Drink: A Social History of America.* New York: Carroll & Graf.

Bass, B. M. 1990. *Bass and Stogdill's Handbook of Leadership: Theory, Research, and Managerial Applications.* 3rd edition. New York: Free Press.

Baudrillard, Jean. 1994. *Simulacra and Simulation.* Ann Arbor: University of Michigan Press.

BBC. 2008. "Rwanda: How the Genocide Happened," December 18. http://news.bbc .co.uk/2/hi/1288230.stm. Accessed September 29, 2009.

BBC. 2011. "Japan Nuclear Crisis Over in Nine Months," April 17. www.bbc.co.uk /news/world-asia-pacific-13107846. Accessed August 11, 2011.

Beaubien, Jason. 2011. "Brutal Cartels Make Crossing US Border Even Riskier." All Things Considered, July 8. www.npr.org/2011/07/08/137647286/brutal-cartels -make-crossing-u-s-border-even-riskier. Accessed July 29, 2011.

Beck, E. M., and Steward E. Tolnay. 1990. "The Killing Fields of the Deep South: The Market for Cotton and the Lynching of Blacks, 1882–1930." *American Sociological Review.* Vol 55 no 4, pp 526–539.

Becker, Gary. 1957. *The Economics of Discrimination.* Chicago: University of Chicago Press.

Bernstein, Henry. 1995. "Development and Underdevelopment." In *The Blackwell Dictionary of 20th Century Social Thought.* Edited by William Outhwaite and Tom Bottomore. Cambridge, MA: Blackwell, pp 151–154.

Best, Joel. 2008. *Social Problems.* New York: Norton.

Bhaskar, Roy. 1995. "Dialectic." In *The Blackwell Dictionary of 20th Century Social Thought.* Edited by William Outhwaite and Tom Bottomore. Cambridge, MA: Blackwell, pp 154–157.

Bihari, Michael. 2010. "Understanding the Medicare Part D Donut Hole." http://health insurance.about.com/od/medicare/a/understanding_part_d.htm. Accessed February 2, 2011.

BJS. 2010. "National Crime Victimization Survey: Criminal Victimization, 2009." October Bulletin. U.S. Department of Justice, Office of Justice Programs, Bureau of Justice Statistics.

Blue Cross Blue Shield Association. 2009. "History of Blue Cross Blue Shield." www.bcbs.com/about/history. Accessed October 12, 2009.

Bluestein, Greg, and Jay Reeves. 2011. "Appeals Court Blocks Part of Alabama Immigration Law." October 14. *Fort Worth Star-Telegram.*

Blumrosen, Alfred W., and Ruth G. Blumrosen. 1999. "The Reality of Intentional Job Discrimination in Metropolitan America, 1999." www.eeo-1.info/1999_NR/Title.pdf. Accessed July 23, 2011.

Bogardus, Emory S. 1933. "A Social Distance Scale." *Sociology and Social Research.* Vol 17, pp 265–271.

Bogardus, Emory S. 1958. "Racial Distance Changes in the US During the Past Thirty Years." *Sociology and Social Research.* Vol 43 no 2, pp 127–135.

Bond, Sharon. 2009. "US Charitable Giving Estimated to be $307.65 billion in 2008," June 10, 2009. www.philanthropy.iupui.edu/News/2009/docs/GivingReaches300 billion_06102009.pdf. Accessed August 10, 2010.

Bond, Sharon. 2011. "US Charitable Giving Shows Modest Uptick in 2010 Following Two Years of Declines," June 20. www.campbellcompany.com/news/bid/56140 /U-S-charitable-giving-shows-modest-uptick-in-2010-following-two-years-of -declines. Accessed July 30, 2011.

Boyko, Edward J., et al. 1994. "Attitudes Toward Assisted Suicide and Euthanasia Among Physicians in Washington State." *New England Journal of Medicine.* Vol 331 no 2, pp 89–94.

Brandenburg, Katie. 2010. "Virtual Fence on Border is Called Virtually Useless." *Fort Worth Star-Telegram,* March 19, p 6B.

Brodie, Mollyann, et al. 2006. "Experiences of Hurricane Katrina Evacuees in Houston Shelters: Implications for Future Planning." *American Journal of Public Health.* Vol 96 no 8, pp 1402–1408.

Brothers, Robert. 1993. "Operation Rescue Disavows Violence." *New York Times,* February 8. www.nytimes.com/1993/02/08/opinion/l-operation-rescue-disavows-violence-726 293.html. Accessed August 3, 2011.

Brown, Lester. 2006. *Plan B 2.0: Rescuing a Planet Under Stress and a Civilization in Trouble.* New York: Norton.

Brownstein, Ronald. 2009. "Healthy Competition: Creating a Public Option Has Not Been the Country's Usual Response to Uncompetitive Markets." *National Journal Magazine,* September 26. www.nationaljournal.com/njmagazine/nj_20090926 _6036.php. Accessed October 12, 2009.

Buckley, Walter, ed. 1968. *Modern Systems Research for the Behavioral Scientist.* Chicago: Aldine.

Burleson, Elizabeth. 2011. "Cancun Climate Negotiations." www.bepress.com/elizabeth _burleson/21. Accessed August 10, 2011.

Buscher, Sarah, and Bettina Ling. 1999. *Mairead Corrigan and Betty Williams: Making Peace in Northern Ireland.* New York: Feminist Press.

Buzawa, Eve S., and Carl G. Buzawa. 1993. "The Scientific Evidence Is Not Conclusive: Arrest Is No Panacea." In *Current Controversies on Family Violence.* Edited by Richard J. Gelles and Donileen R. Loseke. Newbury Park, CA: Sage, pp 337–356.

Caddell, David P., and Rae R. Newton. 1995. "Euthanasia: American Attitudes Toward the Physician's Role." *Social Science and Medicine.* Vol 40 no 12, pp 1671–1681.

Camarota, Steven A. 2010. "Immigration and Economic Stagnation: An Examination of Trends 2000 to 2010." November 10. www.cis.org/highest-decade Accessed October 8, 2011.

Carafano, James Jay, and Laura Keith. 2006. "The Solution for Immigration Enforcement at the State and Local Level." Heritage Foundation, Web Memo 1096, May 25.

Caruso, David B. 2011. "'Occupy' Protests Evolved from Magazine Appeal." October 13. *Fort Worth Star-Telegram,* p 2A.

Casey, Kay. 2011. "TANF Reauthorization." January 7, 2011. www.publicconsultinggroup .com/research/post/2011/01/07/TANF-Reauthorization.aspx#. Accessed January 26, 2011.

Castillo, Richard Griswold del. 1990. *The Treaty of Guadalupe Hidalgo: A Legacy of Conflict.* Norman: University of Oklahoma Press.

Catalyst. 2011. "Women CEOs and Heads of the Financial Post 500," March. www .catalyst.org/publication/271/women-ceos-of-the-fortune-1000. Accessed August 5, 2011.

CBP (Customs and Border Protection). 2010. "Border Patrol History." www.cbp.gov/xp /cgov/border_security/border_patrol/border_patrol_ohs/history.xml. Accessed July 27, 2011.

CDC (Centers for Disease Control). 2010 "Trends in Sexually Transmitted Diseases in the United States: 2009 National Data for Gonorrhea, Chlamydia, and Syphilis." www.cdc.gov/std/stats09/trends.htm. Accessed August 16, 2011.

CDC (Centers for Disease Control). 2011. "Sexually Transmitted Diseases." www.cdc .gov/stf. Accessed August 16, 2011.

CDC. (Centers for Disease Control). 2011a. "New Multi-Year Data Show Annual HIV Infections in US Relatively Stable." NCHHSTP Newsroom, August 3. www.cdc .gov/nchhstp/newsroom/HIVIncidencePressRelease.html. Accessed August 16, 2011.

CDC (Center for Disease Control). 2011b. "Illegal Drug Use." www.cdc.gov/nchs /fastats/druguse.htm. Accessed August 29, 2011.

Center for Responsive Politics. 2009. "Influence and Lobbying–Health." www.open secrets.org/lobby/indus.php?lname=H&year=a. Accessed October 16, 2009.

Centers for Medicare and Medicaid. www.cms.hhs.gov.

Chardin, Pierre Teilhard de. 1964. *The Future of Man.* New York: HarperCollins.

Charon, Joel M., and Lee Garth Vigilant. 2006. *Social Problems: Readings with Four Questions.* Belmont, CA: Thomson Wadsworth.

Chaskin, Robert J., et al. 2001. *Building Community Capacity.* New York: Aldine De Gruyter.

Chatterjee, N. 1999. "They Have Not Heard of AIDS: HIV/AIDS Awareness Among Married Women in Bombay." *Public Health.* Vol 113 no 3, pp 137–140.

Chu, Jeff. 2011. "Michelle Rhee Wants to Spend $1 Billion Fixing Education." *Fast Company.* www.fastcompany.com/magazine/152/forget-100-million-michelle-rhee -wants-to-spend-a-billion.html. Accessed July 21, 2011.

Chudacoff, Howard, and Judith Smith. 2000. *The Evolution of American Urban Society.* Upper Saddle River, NJ: Prentice Hall.

CIA (Central Intelligence Agency). 2009a. *World Factbook.* https://www.cia.gov/library/publications/the-world-factbook/rankorder/2102rank.html. Accessed October 10, 2009.

CIA (Central Intelligence Agency). 2009b. *World Factbook.* https://www.cia.gov/library/publications/the-world-factbook/rankorder/2091rank.html. Accessed October 10, 2009.

Cirtautas, Arista Maria. 1997. *The Polish Solidarity Movement: Revolution, Democracy, and Natural Rights.* London: Routledge.

CIS (Center for Immigration Studies). 2011. www.cis.org/CurrentNumbers. Accessed July 27, 2011.

CIS (Center for Immigration Studies). 2011a. www.cis.org/highest-decade. Accessed July 27, 2011.

Clarridge, Brian R., et al. 1996. "Euthanasia and Physician-Assisted Suicide: Attitudes and Experiences of Oncology Patients, Oncologists, and the Public." *Lancet.* Vol 347 no 9018, pp 1805–1810.

CNN. 2010. "Nebraska Immigration Law Passes." http://articles.cnn.com/2010–06–22/us/nebraska.immigration_1_immigration-policy-farmers-branch-ordinance?_s=PM:US. Accessed July 28, 2011.

CNN. 2011. "Arizona Takes Controversial Immigration Law to Supreme Court," May 9. www.cnn.com/2011/US/05/09/arizona.immigration. Accessed June 6, 2011.

"Coalition to Invest in Texas Schools." 2004. *School Funding 101: A Brief History of School Funding in Texas.* www.investintexasschools.org/schoolfunding/history.php. Accessed June 15, 2011.

Cohn, Raymond L. 2010. "Immigration to the United States." http://eh.net/encyclopedia/article/cohn.immigration.us. Accessed July 27, 2011.

Colley, David P. 2003. *Blood for Dignity: The Story of the First Integrated Combat Units in the US.* New York: St. Martin's.

Collins, Dave. 2008. "Connecticut Becomes Third State in U.S. to Allow Same-Sex Marriage." *Fort Worth Star-Telegram,* October 11, p 7A.

Committee for Skeptical Inquiry. www.csicop.org. Accessed October 4, 2009.

Comte, August. 1973. (B. Franklin, ed.) *System of Positive Polity or Treatise on Sociology.* University of Michigan.

Conger, J. A., R. N. Kanungo, and S. T. Mennon. 2000. "Charismatic Leadership and Follower Outcome Effects." *Journal of Organizational Behavior.* Vol 21, pp 747–767.

Conley, Mark W., and Kathleen A. Hinchman. 2004. "No Child Left Behind: What It Means for US Adolescents and What We Can Do About It." *Journal of Adolescent & Adult Literacy.* Vol 48 no 1, pp 42–50.

Conover, Ted. 1987. *Coyotes: A Journey Through the Secret World of America's Illegal Aliens.* New York: Vintage.

Coontz, Stephanie. 2005. *Marriage: A History.* New York: Viking.

Cooper, Robert Alan. 1981. "Jeremy Bentham, Elizabeth Fry, and English Prison Reform." *Journal of the History of Ideas.* Vol 42 no 4, pp 675–690.

Coser, Lewis A. 1977. *Masters of Sociological Thought: Ideas in Historical and Social Context.* New York: Harcourt Brace Jovanovich.

Coulson, Andrew J. 1999. *Market Education: The Unknown History.* New Brunswick, NJ: Transaction.

Council for Secular Humanism. 1980. "A Secular Humanists Declaration." www.secular humanism.org/index.php?page=declaration&section=main. Accessed October 4, 2009.

Cowell, Alan. 1988. "War on Smog Is Rude Awakening for Athens." *New York Times,* February 14. www.nytimes.com/1988/02/14/world/war-on-smog-is-rude-awakening-for -athens.html. Accessed August 10, 2011.

Crile, George. 2003. *The Extraordinary Story of the Largest Covert Operation in History.* New York: Atlantic Monthly Press.

Cunningham, Peter J. 2008. "Trade-Offs Getting Tougher: Problems Paying Medical Bills Increase for US Families, 2003–2007." Tracking Report 21. Center for Health Systems Change. www.hschange.org/CONTENT/1017/?topic=topic05. Accessed October 11, 2009.

Dafny, Leemore. 2008. "Are Health Insurance Markets Competitive?" Working paper 14572, National Bureau of Economic Research. www.nber.org/papers/w14572. Accessed October 12, 2009.

Daniels, Roger. 2008. "The Immigration Act of 1965: Intended and Unintended Consequences for the 20th Century." www.america.gov/st/educ-english/2008/April /20080423214226eaifas0.9637982.html. Accessed July 27, 2011.

Darity, William Jr. 2008. "Forty Acres and a Mule in the 21st Century." *Social Science Quarterly.* Vol 89 no 3, pp 656–664.

Data Collection Resource Center. N.d. "Background and Current Data Collection Efforts: History of Racial Profiling Analysis." www.racialprofilinganalysis.neu.edu /background/history.php. Accessed July 24, 2011.

Davenport, Paul. 2011. "Arizona Launched Website to Raise Money for Border Fence." *Fort Worth Star-Telegram,* July 11, p 5A.

Davies, Paul. 1988. *The Cosmic Blueprint.* New York: Simon & Schuster.

DeLamater, John D., and Daniel J. Myers. 2007. *Social Psychology.* Belmont, CA: Thomson Wadsworth.

Demirjian, Karoun. 2011. "Harry Reid Reintroduces the Dream Act." *Las Vegas Sun,* May 11. www.lasvegassun.com/news/2011/may/11/harry-reid-reintroduces-dream-act. Accessed July 29, 2011.

Denby, David. 2010. "School Spirit: Waiting for 'Superman.'" *New Yorker,* October 11. www.newyorker.com/arts/critics/cinema/2010/10/11/101011crci_cinema_denby. Accessed July 11, 2011.

DeSipio, Louis. 2000. "Sending Money HomeFor Now Remittances and Immigrant Adaptations in the United States." www.thedialogue.org/publications/Desipio.pdf. Accessed January 25, 2009.

Deutsch, M. 1985. *Distributive Justice: A Social Psychological Perspective.* New Haven: Yale University Press.

Deyhle, Donna, and Karen Swisher. 1997. "Research in American Indian and Alaska Native Education: From Assimilation to Self-Determination." *Review of Research in Education.* Vol 22, pp 113–194.

DHHS (Department of Health and Human Services). N.d. "Sex Trafficking Fact Sheet." www.acf.hhs.gov/trafficking/about/fact_sex.pdg. Accessed August 13, 2011.

Dickson, Gordon. 2011. "Fort Worth Buses Crack Down on Saggy Pants." *Fort Worth Star-Telegram,* May 31. www.star-telegram.com/2011/05/31/3117485/fort-worth -buses-crack-down-on.html. Accessed June 16, 2011.

Diehl, Paul Francis. 1999. *A Road Map to War: Territorial Dimensions of International Conflict.* Nashville, TN: Vanderbilt University Press.

Dietz, Thomas, et al. 1999. "A Value-Belief-Norm Theory of Support for Social Movements: The Case for Environmentalism." *Human Ecology Review.* Vol 6 no 2, pp 81–97.

Docteur, Elizabeth, and Robert A. Berenson. 2009. "How Does the Quality of US Health Care Compare Internationally?" www.rwjf.org/qualityequality/product .jsp?id=47508. Accessed October 9, 2009.

DOJ (Department of Justice). 2003. "Fact Sheet: Racial Profiling." www.justice.gov /opa/pr/2003/June/racial_profiling_fact_sheet.pdf. Accessed July 24, 2011.

Dollard, John, et al. 1939. *Frustration and Aggression.* New Haven: Yale University Press.

Dosani, Rahima. 2009. "Lessons from the Cuban Health System: Comparative Mortality of Cuba, India, and the United States." *Global Pulse: AMSA's International Health Journal.* www.globalpulsejournal.com/about.html. Accessed October 16, 2009.

Douglas, T. 1995. *Scapegoats: Transferring Blame.* New York: Routledge.

Doyle, Arthur Conan. 1975 (1926). *The History of Spiritualism.* Vol 1. New York: Arno.

Dubay, Lisa, John Holahan, and Allison Cook. 2007. "The Uninsured and the Afford- ability of Health Insurance Coverage." *Health Affairs.* Vol 26 no 1, w22–w30.

Duhigg, Charles. 2009. "Cleaning the Air at the Expense of Waterways." *New York Times,* October 12. www.nytimes.com/2009/10/13/us/13water.html. Accessed Au- gust 10, 2011.

Dye, Scott. 2011. "Water Sentinels Program." www.sierraclub.org/watersentinels. Ac- cessed August 11, 2011.

Eastland, Terry. 1996. *Ending Affirmative Action: The Case for Colorblind Justice.* New York: Basic Books.

Edwards, Bob, and John D. McCarthy. 2004. "Resources and Social Movement Mobi- lization." In *The Blackwell Companion to Social Movements.* Edited by David A. Snow, Sarah A. Soule, and Hanspeter Kriesi. Malden, MA: Blackwell, pp 116–152.

Egeberg, Morten. 1995. "Bureaucrats as Public Policy-Makers and Their Self-Interests." *Journal of Theoretical Politics.* Vol 7 no 2, pp 157–167.

Egelko, Bob. 2011. "Feds' Response to Marriage Act in Flux." *San Francisco Chronicle,* July.

EIA (Energy Information Administration). 2011. "Annual Energy Outlook 2011." www .eia.gov/forcasts/aeo. Accessed August 11, 2011.

Eigenberg. Helen M. 2001. *Woman Battering in the United States: Till Death Do Us Part.* Prospect Heights, IL: Waveland, pp 1–30, 197–225.

Eigenberg, Helen M., and Victor E. Kappeler. 2011. "When the Batterer Wears Blue: A National Study of the Institutional Response to Domestic Violence Among Po- lice." In *Woman Battering in the United States: Till Death Do Us Part.* Edited by Helen M. Eigenberg. Prospect Heights, IL: Waveland, pp 248–268.

Eisenberg, Bonnie, and Mary Ruthsdotter. 1998. "Living the Legacy: The Women's Rights Movement, 1848–1998." www.legacy98.org/move-hist.html. Accessed August 4, 2011.

El-Nasser, Haya. 2010. "Census Data Show 'Surprising' Segregation." *USA Today,* December 20. www.usatoday.com/news/nation/census/2010–12–14-segregation_N.htm. Accessed July 22, 2011.

Elliott, James R., and Jeremy Pais. 2006. "Race, Class, and Hurricane Katrina: Social Differences in Human Responses to Disaster." *Social Science Research.* Vol 35 no 2, pp 295–321.

Ellsworth, Scott. 2007. "Tulsa Race Riot." Oklahoma Historical Society's Encyclopedia of Oklahoma History and Culture. http://digital.library.okstate.edu/encyclopedia /entries/T/TU013.html. Accessed July 23, 2011.

Elshtain, Jean Bethke. 1987. *Women and War.* New York: Basic Books.

Emory University Health Sciences Center. 2002. "Emory Brain Imaging Studies Reveal Biological Basis for Human Cooperation." ScienceDaily. www.sciencedaily.com /releases/2002/07/070218075131.htm.

Encyclopedia of the Nations. "Cyprus: Location, Size, and Extent." www.nations encyclopedia.com. Accessed September 29, 2009.

ENS (Environment News Services). 2011. "House Republicans Try to Undo EPA Air Pollution Rules." www.ens-newswire.com/ens/jan2011/2011–01–11–01.html.

EPA (Environmental Protection Agency). 2007. "What Is Acid Rain?" www.epa.gov /acidrain/what. Accessed August 10, 2011.

EPA (Environmental Protection Agency). 2011. "Laws, Regulations, Treaties." www.epa .gov/aboutow/owow/laws.cfm. Accessed August 10, 2011.

EPA (Environmental Protection Agency). 2011a. "Clean Air Act." www.epa.gov/air/cca. Accessed August 10, 2011.

EPA (Environmental Protection Agency). 2011b. "Summary of the EPA Municipal Solid Waste Program." www.epa.gov/reg3wcmd/solidwastesummary.htm. Accessed August 10, 2011.

Ertelt, Steven. 2011. "Senate Parental Notification Bill Would Stop Teen Abortions." www.lifenews.com/2011/05/18/senate-parental-notification-bill-would-stop-teen -abortions. Accessed August 2, 2011.

Ertelt, Steve. 2011a. "Assisted Suicide Support Drops to Lowest Level in 8 Years." www.lifenews.com/2011/05/31/assisted-suicide-support-drops-to-lowest-level-in -8-years. Accessed August 7, 2011.

Eskinazi, Daniel P. 1998. "Factors That Shape Alternative Medicine." *Journal of American Medical Association.* Vol 280 no 18, pp 1621–1623.

Espenshade, Thomas J., and Alexandria Walton Radford. 2009. *No Longer Separate, Not Yet Equal: Race and Class in Elite College Admission and Campus Life.* Princeton: Princeton University Press.

Etzioni, Amitai. 1988. *The Moral Dimension: Toward a New Economics.* New York: Free Press.

Eve, Raymond, Sara Horsfall, and Mary Lee. 1997. *Chaos, Complexity, and Sociology: Myths, Models, and Theories.* Thousand Oaks, CA: Sage.

FBI (Federal Bureau of Investigation). 2009. "Forcible Rape." Crime in the United States. http://www2.fbi.gov/ucr/cius2009/offenses/violent_crime/forcible_rape.html. Accessed August 15, 2011.

FBI (Federal Bureau of Investigation). 2010. "Hate Crime Statistics 2009." http://www2 .fbi.gov/ucr/hc2009/index.html. Accessed July 23, 2011

FindLaw. 2011. "Legal Rights of Nursing Home Residents." http://injury.findlaw.com /nursing-home-abuse/nursing-home-abuse-basics-rights.html. Accessed June 15, 2011.

Finkelstein, Joel B. 2003. "Medicaid Reform Is Waiting on Medicare Pact: The Bush Administration Still Wants Medicaid to Become More Economical," *AMA News,* November 10. www.ama-assn.org/amednews/2003/11/10/gvsc1110.htm.

Finkelstein, Sydney, Jo Whitehead, and Andres Campbell. 2008. *Think Again: Why Good Leaders Make Bad Decisions and How to Keep It From Happening to You.* Watertown, MA: Harvard Business Press.

Finney, Dee. "The Age of the Kali Yuga." www.greatdreams.com/sacred/age_kali.htm. Accessed July 23, 2010.

Fitzpatrick, Laura. 2009. "A Brief History of Affirmative Action." *Time.* July 13. www.time.com/time/magazine/article/0,9171,1908430,00.html#ixzz1T8rRKwcY. Accessed July 25, 2011.

Flemming, Walter L. 1906. "Forty Acres and a Mule." *North American Review,* May. Vol 182, p 594.

Fletcher, Michael A. 1998. "Affirmative Action Tops NAACP List." *Washington Post,* July 14. www.washingtonpost.com/wp-srv/politics/special/affirm/stories/naacp071 498.htm. Accessed July 25, 2011.

Foner, Eric. 1993. *Freedom's Lawmakers: A Directory of Black Officeholders During Reconstruction.* New York: Oxford University Press.

*Fort Worth Star-Telegram.* 2008. "Less Money Is Going to Mexico as US Economy Falters." October 2, p 2A.

*Fort Worth Star-Telegram.* 2010. "Few Texas 'Robin Hood' School Districts are Renegades," November 16. www.star-telegram.com/2010/11/16/2637250/few-texas -robin-hood-school-districts.html

Fourney, Matthew. 2003. "China's Failing Health System." *Time,* May 12. www.time .com/time/magazine/article/0,9171,451006,00.html. Accessed October 16, 2009.

Frey, William H. 2010. "Census Data: Blacks and Hispanics Take Different Segregation Paths." www.brookings.edu/opinions/2010/1216_census_frey.aspx. Accessed July 22, 2011.

Frickel, Scott, and Bess Vincent. 2007. "Hurricane Katrina, Contamination, and the Unintended Organization of Ignorance." *Technology in Society.* Vol 29 no 2, pp 181–188.

Friedman, Lisa. 2011. "US Negotiator Warns Kyoto Fight Could Derail Climate Talks." *New York Times,* April 22. www.nytimes.com/cwire/2011/04/22/22climatewire-us -negotiator-warns-kyoto-fight-could-derail-88722.html. Accessed August 10, 2011.

Frieze, Irene H. "Female Violence Against Intimate Partners: An Introduction." *Psychology of Women Quarterly.* Vol 29, p 2290237.

Frum, David. 2000. *How We Got Here: The '70s.* New York: Basic Books.

Fry, Elizabeth Gurney, and Edward Ryder. 1883. *Elizabeth Fry: Life and Labors of the Eminent Philanthropist, Preacher and Prison Reformer: Compiled from Her Journal and Other Sources.* New York: E. Walker's Son.

Gallup. 2011. "Doctor Assisted Suicide Is Moral Issue Dividing Americans Most." www.gallup.com/poll/147842/doctor-assisted-suicide-moral-issue-dividing-americans.aspx. Accessed August 7, 2011.

Gallup. 2011a. "Water Issues Worry Americans Most, Global Warming Least." www.gallup.com/poll.146810/water-issues-worry-americans-global-warming-least.aspx. Accessed August 10, 2011.

Gandhi, Mohandas. 1960. *All Men Are Brothers.* www.mkgandhi-sarvodaya.org/ama brothers/amabrothers.htm. Accessed July 23, 2010.

Gandhi, Mohandas K. 2004 (1927). *An Autobiography: Or My Story of My Experiments with Truth.* Ahmedabad, India: Navajivan Publishing House.

Garreau, Joel. 2004. *Radical Evolution: The Promise and Peril of Enhancing Our Minds, Our Bodies—and What It Means to Be Human.* New York: Doubleday.

Garrido, Jon. "How Cubans Come to America." 2010. Hispanic News. http://hispanic.cc/how_cubans_come_to_america.htm. Accessed July 27, 2011.

Gazzar, Brenda. 2005. "Mexican 'Coyote' Smuggles Immigrants into the US." www.banderasnews.com/0509/eded-coyote.htm. Accessed July 29, 2011.

Gelles, Richard J. 1993. "Alcohol and Other Drugs Are Associated with Violence: They Are Not Its Cause." In *Current Controversies on Family Violence.* Edited by Richard J. Gelles and Donileen R. Loseke. Newbury Park, CA: Sage, pp 182–196.

GEP. 2005. "World Energy Supply." www.theglobaleducationproject.org/earth/energy-supply.php. Accessed August 11, 2011.

Giddens. Anthony. 1990. *The Consequences of Modernity.* Stanford, CA: Stanford University Press.

Gilbert, T.F. 1978. *Human Competence.* New York: McGraw-Hill.

Giljum, Stefan, et al. 2009. "Overconsumption? Our Use of the World's Natural Resources." www.foeeurope.org/publications/2009/Overconsumption_Sep09.pdf. Accessed August 11, 2011.

Gilley, Brian Joseph. 2006. *Becoming Two-Spirit: Gay Identity and Social Acceptance in Indian Country.* Lincoln: University of Nebraska Press.

Giving USA Foundation. 2011. www.givingusareports.org.

Gleick, James. 1987. *Chaos: Making a New Science.* New York: Penguin.

Goble, Danney. 2000. "Final Report of the Oklahoma Commission to Study the Tulsa Race Riot of 1921." www.tulsareparations.org/FinalReport.htm. Accessed July 23, 2011.

Goleman, Daniel. 2006. *Social Intelligence: The New Science of Human Relationships.* New York: Bantam.

Goode, Jennifer L. 2004. "Some Considerations on the Disease Concept of Addiction." In *The American Drug Scene,* Edited by James A. Inciardi and Karen McElrath. Los Angeles: Roxbury, pp 27–40.

Goodman, John. 2011. "What Will President Obama Say About Medicine?" *Kaiser Health News,* January 25. www.kaiserhealthnews.org/columns/2011/january/0125 11goodman.aspx. Accessed February 2, 2011.

Goodsell, Willystine. 1915. *A History of the Family as Social and Educational Institution.* New York: Macmillan.

Gorman, Martha, and Carolyn S. Roberts. 1996. *Euthanasia.* Santa Barbara, CA: ABC-CLIO.

Gould, Stephen Jay. 1981. *The Mismeasure of Man.* New York: Norton.

Gould, William B. 1977. *Black Workers in White Unions: Job Discrimination in the United States.* Ithaca, NY: Cornell University Press.

Gray, Mike. 2000. *Drug Crazy: How We Got into This Mess and How We Can Get Out.* New York: Routledge.

Greenbook. 2008. "Background Material and Data on the Programs Within the Jurisdiction of the Committee on Ways and Means 2008." http://waysandmeans.house .gov/Documents.asp?section=2168.

Greenburg, Warren. 1982. "Insurance, Competition, and Cost Containment." *Social Science and Medicine.* Vol 16 no 7, pp 805–810.

*Guardian.* 2010. "Charitable Giving by Country: Who Is the Most Generous?" September 8. www.guardian.co.uk/news/datablog/2010/sep/08/charitable-giving-country. Accessed July 30, 2011.

Guggenheim, David. 2010. *Waiting for Superman.* www.waitingforsuperman.com. Accessed July 21, 2011.

Gusfield, Joseph R. 1994. "The Reflexivity of Social Movements: Collective Behavior and Mass Society Theory Revisited." In *New Social Movements: From Ideology to Identity.* Edited by Enrique Larana, Hank Johnston, and Joseph R. Gusfield. Philadelphia: Temple University Press, pp 58–78.

Guttmacher Institute. 2011. "States Enact Record Number of Abortion Restrictions in First Half of 2011," July 13. www.guttmacher.org/media/inthenews/2011/07/13 /index.html. Accessed August 1, 2011.

Guttmacher Institute. 2011a. "Facts on Induced Abortion in the United States," May. www.guttmacher.org/pubs/fb_induced_abortion.html. Accessed August 1, 2010.

Guttmacher Institute. 2011b. "Parental Involvement in Minors' Abortion," August 1. www.guttmacher.org/statecenter/spibs/spib_PIMA.pdf. Accessed August 2, 2011.

Halpern, Robert. 1995. *Rebuilding the Inner City: A History of Neighborhood Initiatives to Address Poverty in the United States.* New York: Columbia University Press.

Hannigan, Johyn A. 1985. "Alain Touraine, Manuel Castells, and Social Movement Theory: A Critical Appraisal." *Sociological Quarterly.* Vol 26, no 4, pp 435–454.

Harcourt, Christine, and B. Donovan. 2005. "Many Faces of Sex Work." *Sexually Transmitted Infections.* Vol 81 no 3, pp 201–206.

Hareyan, Armen. 2009. "Medical Tourism or Health-Seeking Travel." *ExMax Health,* February 15. www.emaxhealth.com/1/41/29260/medical-tourism-or-healthseeking -travel.html.

Harkins, S. G., and K. Szymanski. 1987. "Social Loafing and Social Facilitation." In *Group Processes and Intergroup Relations.* Edited by C. Hendrick. Newbury Park, CA: Sage, pp 167–188.

Harmstone, Teresa Rakowska. 1984. *Communism in Eastern Europe.* Indiana: Indiana University Press.

Harper, Charles L. 1993. *Exploring Social Change.* Englewood Cliffs, NJ: Prentice Hall.

Hasday, Judy L. 2007. *The Civil Rights Act of 1964: An End to Racial Segregation.* New York: Chelsea House.

Hatvalne, Prakash. 2010. "Seven Guilty in Toxic Gas Leak in 1984." *Arlington Star-Telegram,* June 8, sec A.

Havel, Vaclav. 1995. "The Need for Transcendence in the Postmodern World." *Futurist,* July-August. http://dieoff.org/page38.htm. Accessed August 10, 2010.

Healey, Thomas J. 2004. "Is It Really Social Insecurity? The Situation May Not Be As Black As It's Been Painted." *Fort Worth Star-Telegram,* July 18.

Hegel, G. W. F. 1977. *Phenomenology of Spirit.* Translated by A. V. Miller. Oxford: Clarendon.

Heininger, Mary Lynn Stevens. 1984. "Children, Childhood, and Change in America, 1820–1920." In *A Century of Childhood, 1820–1920.* Rochester, NY: Margaret Woodbury Strong Museum.

Henslin, James M., and Lori Ann Fowler. 2010. *Social Problems: A Down-to-Earth Approach.* Boston: Allyn & Bacon.

Henson, Robert. 2011. "What Is the Kyoto Protocol and Has It Made Any Difference?" *Guardian,* March 11. www.guardian.co.uk/environment/2011/mar/11/kyoto-protocol. Accessed August 10, 2011.

HHS (US Department of Health and Human Services). 2010. News Release, November 3. www.hhs.gov/news/press/2010pres/11/20101103a.html. Accessed January 31, 2011.

Himmelstein, D., et al. 2009. "Medical Bankruptcy in the United States, 2007: Results of a National Study." *American Journal of Medicine.* Vol 122 no 8, pp 741–746.

Hochschild, Jennifer L., and Nathan Scrovronick. 2003. *The American Dream and the Public Schools.* New York: Oxford University Press.

Hoffman, Abraham. 1974. *Unwanted Mexican Americans in the Great Depression: Repatriation Pressures, 1929–1939.* Tucson: University of Arizona Press.

Horsfall, Sara. 1982. Interview, World Health Organization, Athens, Greece.

Howell, James C. 2010. "Gang Prevention: An Overview of Research and Programs." Office of Juvenile Justice and Delinquency Prevention, December.

Howell, James C., et al. 2011. "US Gang Problem Trends and Seriousness, 1996–2009." National Gang Center Bulletin. No. 6.

Hsiao, W. C. 1995. "The Chinese Health Care System: Lessons for Other Nations." *Social Science Medicine.* October. Vol 41 no 8, pp 1047–1055.

Hsu, Spencer S. 2010. "Work to Cease on 'Virtual-Fence' Along US-Mexico Border." *Washington Post,* March 16. www.washingtonpost.com/wp-dyn/content/article/2010/03/16/AR2010031603573.html. Accessed July 27, 2011.

Hubbart, Jason A., and Michael Pidwirny. 2011. "Hydrologic Cycle." In *Encyclopedia of Earth,* February 23. www.eoearth.org/article/Hydrologic_cycle. Accessed August 11, 2011.

Huber, Ruth, Virginia Meade Cox, and William B. Edelen. 1992. "Right-to-die Responses from a Random Sample of 200." *Hospice Journal.* Vol 8 no 3, pp 1–19.

Human Rights Campaign. 2009. "Matthew Shepard and James Byrd, Jr. Hate Crimes Prevention Act: Public Law No. 111–84." www.hrc.org/issues/5660.htm. Accessed July 23, 2011.

Hunt, Diana. 2009. "Medical Bills Leading to a Rise in Bankruptcies." *Fort Worth Star-Telegram*, October 11, p D1.

Hutchinson, W. D., et al. 1999. "Pain-related Neurons in the Human Cingulate Cortex." *Nature Neuroscience.* Vol 2, pp 403–405.

Iacobani, M., et al. 1999. "Cortical Mechanisms." *Science*, December 24.

Ibn Khaldun, Mokaddimat. 2004 (1377). *The Maqaddimah: An Introduction to History.* Translated by Franz Rosenthal. Edited by N. J. Dawood. Princeton: Princeton University Press.

IDB (Inter-American Development Bank). 2010. "Remittances to Latin America Stabilizing After 15% Drop Last Year." www.iadb.org/en/news/news-releases/2010 –03–04/remittances-to-latin-america-stabilizing-after-15-drop-last-year-mif ,6671.html. Accessed July 28, 2011.

Issues 2000. www.issues2000.org.

Janis, I. L. 1982. *Groupthink.* 2nd edition. Boston: Houghton Mifflin.

Jarvis, Jan. 2010. "Big Insurance Hikes Stir Push for Action." *Fort Worth Star-Telegram*, November 3, pp C1, D5.

Jasanoff, Sheila. 1994. *Learning from Disaster: Risk Management After Bhopal.* Philadelphia: University of Pennsylvania Press.

Jonas, Wayne B. 1996. "Testimony on Access to Medical Treatment Act." Senate Committee on Labor and Human Resources, Department of Health and Human Services, July 30. www.hhs.gov/asl/testify/t960730b.html. Accessed on October 8, 2009.

Judge, T. A., and J. E. Bono. 2000. "Five-Factor Model of Personality and Transformational Leadership." *Journal of Applied Psychology.* Vol 60, pp 193–202.

Kadushin, Alfred, and Judith A Martin. 1980. *Child Abuse: An Interactional Event.* Irvington, NY: Columbia University Press.

Kaiser Family Foundation. 2005. "Medicare and Medicaid at 40," July 26. www.kff .org/medicaid/40years.cfm. Accessed January 31, 2011.

Kaiser Family Foundation. 2010. "US State Department Releases 2010 Report on Human Trafficking." *Kaiser Daily Global Health Policy Report.* http://globalhealth .kff.org/Daily-Reports/2010/June/15/GH-061510-Trafficking-Report.aspx. Accessed August 13, 2011.

Kaiser Family Foundation. 2009. "HIV/AIDS Policy: The Ryan White Program." www.kff.org/hivaids/upload/7582_05.pdf. Accessed August 16, 2011.

Kakutani, Michiko. 2006. "Al Gore Revisits Global Warming, with Passionate Warnings and Pictures." *New York Times,* May 23. www.nytimes.com/2006/05/23/books /23kaku.html. Accessed August 8, 2011.

Kallman, Matt. 2007. "Talking Trash: The World's Waste Management Problem." www.earthtrends.wri.org/updates/node/314. Accessed August 10, 2011.

Karau, S. J., and K. D. Williams. 2001. "Understanding Individual Motivation in Groups: The Collective Effort Model." In *Groups at Work: Advances in Theory and Research.* Edited by M. E. Turner. Mahwah, NJ: Erlbaum, pp 113–141.

Katz, Jennifer, Stephanie Washington Kuffel, and Amy Coblentz. 2002. "Are There Gender Differences in Sustaining Dating Violence? An Examination of Frequency, Severity, and Relationship Satisfaction." *Journal of Family Violence.* Vol 17 no 3, pp 247–271.

Kauffman, Albert H., and Roger Gonzalez. 1997. *Affirmative Action's Testament of Hope: Strategies for a New Era in Higher Education.* Edited by Mildred Garcia. Albany: State University of New York Press, pp 227–250.

Kaye, Lenard, and Jeffrey Applegate. 1990. "Men as Elder Caregivers: A Response to Changing Families." *American Journal of Orthopsychiatry.* Vol 60, pp 86–95.

Kemble, Fanny. 2000. *Fanny Kemble's Journals.* Cambridge: Harvard University Press.

Kemmick, Ed. 2009. "Montana Meth Project: Message Heard, Results Debated." *Billings Gazette,* July 5, p 1.

Kemp, Alan. 1998. *Abuse in the Family: An Introduction.* Pacific Grove, CA: Brooks/Cole.

Kendall, Diana. 2010. *Social Problems in a Diverse Society.* New York: Allyn & Bacon.

Kessler, Ronald C., and Hurricane Katrina Community Advisory Group et al. 2006. "Mental Illness and Suicidality After Hurricane Katrina." *Bull World Health Organ.* Vol 84 no 12, pp. 930–939.

King, Joyce. 2002. *Hate Crime: The Story of a Dragging in Jasper.* New York: Pantheon.

Kinsey, Alfred, Wardell Baxter Pomeroy, and Clyde Martin. 1948. *Sexual Behavior in the Human Male.* Philadelphia: Saunders.

Kirkpatrick, David. 2009. "Lobbyists Fight Last Big Plans to Cut Health Care Costs." *New York Times,* October 11.

Klandermans, Bert. 2004. "The Demand and Supply of Participation: Social-Psychological Correlates of Participation in Social Movements." In *The Blackwell Companion to Social Movements.* Edited by David A. Snow, Sarah A Soule, and Hanspeter Kriesi. Malden, MA: Blackwell, pp 360–379.

Klarman, Michael J. 2004. *From Jim Crow to Civil Rights: The Supreme Court and the Struggle for Racial Equality.* New York: Oxford University Press.

Kleg, Milton, and Kaoru Yamamoto. 1998. "As the World Turns: Ethno-Racial Distances After 70 Years." *Social Science Journal.* Vol 35 no 2, pp 183–191.

Kluger, Jeffrey. 2010. "Flushed Away." *Time,* April 1. www.time.com/time/specials/packages/article/0,28804,1976909,1976907,1976871,00.htm. Accessed August 10, 2011.

Kochhar, Rakesh, Richard Fry, and Paul Taylor. 2011. "Wealth Gaps Rise to Record Highs Between Whites, Blacks, and Hispanics," July 26. http://pewsocialtrends.org/2011/07/26/wealth-gaps-rise-to-record-highs-between-whites-blacks-hispanics. Accessed July 26, 2011.

Korf, Benedikt. 2007. "Antinomies of Generosity: Moral Geographies, and Post-Tsunami Aid in Southeast Asia." *Geoforum.* Vol 38 no 2, pp 366–378.

Kornhauser, William. 1959. *The Politics of Mass Society*. Glencoe: The Free Press.

Korten, David. 2006. *The Great Turning*. Bloomfield, CT: Kumarian.

Kozol, Jonathan. 2005. "Overcoming Apartheid." *The Nation,* December 19.

Kozol, Jonathan. 2006. "Segregation and Its Calamitous Effects: America's 'Apartheid' Schools." *VUE* (Voices in Urban Education). Vol 10. Providence, RI: Annenberg Institute for School Reform at Brown University.

Krauss, Cilfford. 2008. "Move Over, Oil, There's Money in Texas Wind." *New York Times,* February 23. www.nytimes.com/2008/02/23/business/23wind.html. Accessed August 11, 2011.

Kravitz, D. A., and B. Martin. 1986. "Ringelmann Rediscovered: The Original Article." *Journal of Personality and Social Psychology*. Vol 32, pp 1134–1146.

Kumar, Krishnan. 1995. "Modernity." In *The Blackwell Dictionary of 20th Century Social Thought*. Edited by William Outhwaite and Tom Bottomore. Cambridge, MA: Blackwell, pp 391–392.

La Corte, Rachel. 2008. "Washington Mulls Assisted Suicide." *Fort Worth Star-Telegram,* October 12, p 12A.

Larana, Enrique, Hank Johnston, and Joseph R. Gusfield, eds. 1994. *New Social Movements: From Ideology to Identity*. Philadelphia: Temple University Press.

Laumann, E. O., et al. 1994. *The Social Organization of Sexuality: Sexual Practices in the United States*. Chicago: University of Chicago Press.

LCCR (Leadership Conference on Civil and Human Rights/Leadership Conference Education Fund). 2011. "Hate Crimes Against Jews." www.civilrights.org /publications/hatecrimes/jews.html. Accessed July 23, 2011.

LCCR (Leadership Conference on Civil and Human Rights/Leadership Conference Education Fund). 2011a. "Hate Crimes Against Women." www.civilrights.org /publications/hatecrimes/women.html. Accessed July 23, 2011.

Leake, Jonathan. 2010. "UN Wrongly Linked Global Warming to Natural Disasters." *Sunday Times,* January 24. www.timesonline.co.uk/tol/news/environment/article 7000063.ece. Accessed August 9, 2011.

LeCuyer, Nick A., and Shubham Singhal. 2007. "Overhauling the US Health Care Payment System." *McKinsey Quarterly,* June, pp 1–11.

Lefkowitz, Mary R., and Maureen B. Fant. 1992. *Women's Life in Greece and Rome*. Baltimore: Johns Hopkins University Press.

Legal Momentum. www.legalmomentum.org. Accessed January 10, 2011.

LeMay, Michael. 2007. *Illegal Immigration: A Reference Handbook*. Contemporary World Issues. Santa Barbara, CA: ABC-CLIO/Greenwood.

LeMay, Michael. 2004. *US Immigration*. Contemporary World Issues. Santa Barbara, CA: ABC-CLIO/Greenwood.

Lenski, Gerhard. 1966. *Power and Privilege: A Theory of Social Stratification*. New York: McGraw-Hill.

Lenski, Gerhard. 1995. "Evolution." In *The Blackwell Dictionary of 20th Century Social Thought*. Edited by William Outhwaite and Tom Bottomore. Cambridge, MA: Blackwell, pp 212–213.

Lenski, Gerhard, Patrick Nolan, and Jean Lenski. 1995. *Human Societies: An Introduction to Macrosociology.* 7th ed. New York: McGraw-Hill.

LeoGrande, William M. 1998. "From Havana to Miami: US Cuba Policy as a Two-Level Game." *Journal of Interamerican Studies and World Affairs.* Vol 40 no 1, pp. 67–86.

Letchford, C. W., H. S. Norville, and J. Bilello, 2000. "Damage Survey and Assessment of Fort Worth Tornado, 28 March 2000." www.depts.ttu.edu/weweb/Pubs/pdfs/D3–28–00%20Tor%20FtWorth.pdf. Accessed September 25, 2009.

Levey, Naomi N. 2010. "Health Costs Still Rising at Record Pace." *Fort Worth Star-Telegram*, February 3, p 5A.

Lewin, Roger. 1992. *Complexity: Life at the Edge of Chaos.* New York: Macmillan.

Lewis, Jone Johnson. 2011. "A Brief History of the Abortion Controversy in the United States." http://womenshistory.about.com/od/abortionuslegal/a/abortion.htm. Accessed June 16, 2011

Liazos, Alexander. 1972. "The Poverty of the Sociology of Deviance: Nuts, Sluts, and Perverts." *Social Problems.* Vol 20, pp 403–420.

Lindesmith, Alfred R. 2004. "A Sociological Theory of Drug Addiction." In *The American Drug Scene.* Edited by James A Inciardi and Karen McElrath. Los Angeles: Roxbury, pp 14–26.

Lockette, Tim. 2010. "The New Racial Segregation at Public Schools." www.alternet.org/rights/145553/the_new_racial_segregation_at_public_schools?page=1. Accessed July 21, 2011.

Loh, L. C., et al. 2004. "Change in Infection Control Practices and Awareness of Hospital Medical Staff in the Aftermath of SARS." *Medical Journal of Malaysia.* Vol 59 no 5, pp 659–664.

Lower-Basch, Elizabeth. 2011. "Goals for TANF Reauthorization," January 24. www.clasp.org/admin/site/publications/files/TANF-Reauthorization-Goals.pdf. Accessed January 25, 2011.

Loye, David, and Riane Eisler. 1987. "Chaos and Transformation: Implication of Nonequilibrium Theory for Social Science and Society." *Behavioral Science.* Vol 32, pp 53–65.

Lynch, Sarah N. 2008. "An American Pastime: Smoking Pot." *Time Health.* July 11. www.time.com/time/healt h/article/0,8599,1821697,00.html#ixzz1WSpexbg2. Accessed August 29, 2011.

MacDonald, David Bruce. 2002. *Balkan Holocausts? Serbian and Croatian Victim-Centered Propaganda and the War in Yugoslavia.* Manchester, UK: Manchester University Press.

Macionis, John J. 2005. *Social Problems.* 2nd edition. Upper Saddle River, NJ: Pearson Education, Inc.

Macionis, John. 2011. *Sociology.* Upper Saddle River, NJ: Pearson Prentice Hall.

Malcolm, Andrew H. 1990. "What Medical Science Can't Seem to Learn: When to Call It Quits." *New York Times*, December 23.

Malkin, Michelle. 2010. "The Death of an Arizona Rancher; Updated: Cattle Growers' Association Offers Reward." http://michellemalkin.com/2010/03/29/the-death-of-an-arizona-rancher. Accessed July 28, 2011.

Mann, J. 1990. "AIDS: A Worldwide Pandemic." *Current Topics in AIDS*. Vol 2. Edited by D. J. Jeffries et al. Hoboken, NJ: John Wiley.

Mansbridge, Jane, and Aldon Morris, eds. 2001. *Oppositional Consciousness: The Subjective Roots of Social Protest*. Chicago: University of Chicago Press.

Marchione, Marilynn, and Mike Stobbe. 2009. "Billions Spent on Alternative Medicine." *Fort Worth Star-Telegram*. August 2, p 1D.

Marker, Rita L., and Kathi Hamlon. 2010. "Euthanasia and Assisted Suicide: Frequently Asked Questions." www.patientsrightscouncil.org/site/frequently-asked-questions. Accessed August 8, 2011.

Martin, Gary. 2009. "300 Miles of Border Fence Rejected." *Fort Worth Star-Telegram*, p 6a.

Martin, Richard. 2010. "What Peak Oil? Why an Oil Glut Is Ahead." CNNMoney, September 8. money.cnn.com/2010/09/07/news/economy/coming-oil-glut.fortune /index.htm. Accessed August 11, 2011.

Martinez, James Michael. 2007. *Carpetbaggers, Cavalry, and the Ku Klux Klan: Exposing the Invisible Empire*. Lanham, MD: Rowman & Littlefield.

Marx, Karl. 1967 (1867). *Capitalism: A Critical Analysis of Capitalist Production*. New York: International.

Marx, Karl, and Friedrich Engels. 1971 (1847). *The Communist Manifesto*. New York: International.

Maryland Budget and Tax Policy Institute. 2006. "TANF in Brief." www.maryland policy.org/TANFInformation.asp. Accessed June 15, 2011.

Mascaro, Lisa. 2011. "Patriot Act Provisions Extended Just in Time." *Los Angeles Times*. May 27. http://articles.latimes.com/2011/may/27/nation/la-na-patriot-act-2011 0527. Accessed July 24, 2011.

Massey, Douglas S., and Nancy A. Denton. 1998. *American Apartheid : Segregation and the Making of the Underclass*. Cambridge: Harvard University Press.

Matthew Shepard Foundation. 2010. "Our Story." www.matthewshepard.org/our-story. Accessed August 6, 2011.

Matz, William M. Jr. 2010. "Medicare's Drug Benefit Is a Remedy That Really Works: A Striking Success for Veterans' Families." *Senior Citizen Opinions & Analysis,* November 16. http://seniorjournal.com/NEWS/Opinion/2010/20101116-Medicares DrugBenefit.htm. Accessed February 2, 2011.

Mauss, Armand L. 1975. *Social Problems of Social Movements*. Philadelphia: Lippincott.

McAdam, Doug, and David A. Snow. 1997. Introduction to *Social Movements: Readings on Their Emergence, Mobilization, and Dynamics*. Edited by Doug McAdam and David A. Snow. Los Angeles: Roxbury.

McAdam, Doug, and Ronnelle Paulsen. 1997. "Specifying the Relationship Between Social Ties and Activism." In *Social Movements: Readings on Their Emergence, Mobilization, and Dynamics*. Edited by Doug McAdam and David A. Snow. Los Angeles: Roxbury, pp 145–157.

McBride, Timothy D. 2002. "Ending the Blame Game: Economic Forces Behind Our Health Care Problems." In *A Physician's Guide to Health Care Management*. Edited by Daniel M. Albert. Malden, MA: Blackwell Science, pp 81–100.

McCarthy, John D., and Mayer N. Zald. 1973. *The Trend of Social Movements in America: Professionalization and Resource Mobilization.* Morristown, NJ: General Learning Press.

McCarthy, John D., and Mayer N. Zald. 1977. "Resource Mobilization and Social Movements: A Partial Theory." *American Journal of Sociology.* Vol 82, pp 1212–1241.

McCarty, Teresa L. 1998. "Schooling, Resistance, and American Indian Languages." *Journal of the Sociology of Language.* Vol 132 no 1, pp 27–42.

McDonough, William, and Michael Braungart. 2002. *Cradle to Cradle: Remaking the Way We Make Things.* New York: North Point.

McGuire, Meredith. 1997. *Religion: The Social Context.* Belmont, CA: Wadsworth.

McLaughlin, Corinne, and Gordon Davidson. 1994. *Spiritual Politics: Changing the World from the Inside Out.* New York: Ballantine.

McMillen, Neil R. 1990. *Dark Journey: Black Mississippians in the Age of Jim Crow.* Chicago: University of Illinois Press.

Medhoff, Peter, and Holly Sklar. 1994. *Streets of Hope: The Fall and Rise of an Urban Neighborhood.* Boston: South End.

Medicare. www.medicare.gov.

MedicineNet. 2011. "Date Rape Drugs." www.medicinenet.com/date_rape_drugs /article.htm. Accessed August 15, 2011.

Mendoza, Marlene. 2011. "Giant Salvinia Problem Growing in Ark-La-Tex Lakes." June 28. *www.kmsstv.com/local/giant-salvinia-rapidly-growing-in-tx-la-lakes.* Accessed August 15, 2011.

Merton, Robert. 1968. *Social Theory and Social Structure.* New York: Free Press.

Metrocode. 2009. "Architecture in Fort Worth: The Tower." www.fortwortharchitecture .com/bankone.htm. Accessed October 2, 2009.

Metzger, John T. 2000. "Planned Abandonment: The Neighborhood Life-Cycle Theory and National Urban Policy." *Housing Policy Debate.* Vol 11 no 1, pp 7–40.

Michaels, Daniel W. 2002. "The Gulag: Communism's Penal Colonies Revisited." *Journal for Historical Review.* Vol 21 no 1. p 39. www.ihr.org. Accessed June 21, 2011.

Migration Policy Institute. 2011. "US Historical Immigration Trends." www.migration information.org/datahub/historicaltrends.cfm#history. Accessed July 27, 2011.

Miller, C. E., and S. S. Komorita. 1995. "Reward Allocation in Task-Performing Groups." *Journal of Personality and Social Psychology.* Vol 69, pp 80–90.

Mingione, Enzo. 1995. "Urbanism." In *The Blackwell Dictionary of 20th Century Social Thought.* Edited by William Outhwaite and Tom Bottomore. Cambridge, MA: Blackwell, pp 386–389.

Monckton, Christopher. 2009. "Climategate: Caught Green-Handed! Cold Facts About the Hot Topic of Global Temperature Change After the Climategate Scandal." http://scienceandpublicpolicy.orgoriginals/climategate.html.

Mooney, Linda A., David Knox, and Caroline Schacht. 2005. *Understanding Social Problems.* Belmont, CA: Thomson Wadsworth.

Morris, Aldon. 2000. "Reflections on Social Movement Theory: Criticisms and Proposals." *Contemporary Sociology.* Vol 29 no 3, pp 445–454.

Morris, Aldon, and Naomi Braine. 2001. "Social Movements and Oppositional Consciousness" in Jane Mansbridge and Aldon Morris, eds., *Oppositional Consciousness: The Subjective Roots of Social Protest.* Chicago: University of Chicago Press, pp. 20–37.

Morris, Aldon D., and Suzanne Staggenborg. 2004. "Leadership in Social Movements." In *The Blackwell Companion to Social Movements.* Edited by David A Snow, Sarah Ann Soule, and Hanspeter Kriesi. Malden, MA: Blackwell, pp 171–196.

Morris, Benny. 2001. *Righteous Victims: A History of the Zionist-Arab Conflict, 1881–1999.* New York: Vintage.

Moynihan, Daniel P., and Bob Kerrey. 2000. "The Lessons of History: Elections Are at Stake: The Proposed Fixes Fall Painfully Short." *Newsweek,* July 3.

Mueller, Milton. 2009. "Internet Content Regulation and the Limits of Sovereignty." *World Politics Review,* September 1.

Munson, Ziad W. 2002. *The Making of Pro-Life Activists: How Social Movement Mobilization Works.* Chicago: University of Chicago Press.

Murdoch, Stephen. 2007. *IQ: A Smart History of a Failed Idea.* Hoboken, NJ: John Wiley.

Murphy, Jarrett. 2009. "Remembering the Killing Fields." CBS News, February 11. www.cbsnews.com/stories/2000/04/15/world/main184477.shtml. Accessed June 21, 2011.

Musto, David F. 1999. *The American Disease: Origins of Narcotic Control.* New York: Oxford University Press.

Myers, Daniel J. 1997. "Racial Rioting in the 1960s: An Event History Analysis of Local Conditions." *American Sociological Review.* Vol 62, pp 94–112.

Myers-Lipton, Scott J. 2006. *Social Solutions to Poverty: America's Struggle to Build a Just Society.* Boulder: Paradigm.

NAACP (National Association for the Advancement of Colored People). 2009–2011. "Responsible Mortgage Lending Principles." www.naacp.org/pages/responsible -lending-principles. Accessed July 25, 2011.

NAACP (National Association for the Advancement of Colored People). 2009–2011a. "A Brief Review of Public Opinion on Affirmative Action." *Research.* http://leadership500 .naacp.org/advocacy/research/affaction/index.html. Accessed July 25, 2011.

NAEH (National Alliance to End Homelessness). 2011. Frequently Asked Questions. www.endhomelessness.org/section/about_homelessness/faqs. Accessed September 1, 2011.

NAEH (National Alliance to End Homelessness). 2011b. "Snapshot of Homelessness." www.endhomelessness.org/section/about_homelessness/snapshot_of_homelessness. Accessed September 1, 2011.

NAEH (National Alliance to End Homelessness). 2011c. "Cost of Homelessness." www .endhomelessness.org/section/about_homelessness/cost_of_homlessness. Accessed September 1, 2011.

NAF (National Abortion Federation). 2010. "History of Abortion." www.prochoice.org /about_abortion/history_abortion.html. Accessed August 1, 2011.

NAMI (National Alliance on Mental Illness). 2011. "Suicide in Youth." www.nami.org /Content/ContentGroups/Illness/Suicide_Teens.htm. Accessed September 8, 2011.

NASA (National Aeronautics and Space Administration). N.d. "A Blanket Around the Earth." http://climate.nasa.gov/causes. Accessed August 9, 2011.

National Conference on State Legislators. 2011 "Same Sex Marriage, Civil Unions, and Domestic Partnerships," July 14. www.ncsl.org/default.aspx?tabid-16430. Accessed August 6, 2011.

National Geographic. 2011. "Causes of Global Warming." http://environment.national geographic.com/environment/global-warming/gw-causes. Accessed August 9, 2011.

National Research Council. 1997. *The New Americans: Economic, Demographic, and Fiscal Effects of Immigration.* Washington, D.C.: National Academy Press.

Nature Conservancy. 2011. "Rainforests: Facts about Rainforests." July 29. www.nature.org /ouriniatives/urgentissues/rainforests/rainforsts-facts.xml. Accessed August 11, 2011.

NBC4i. 2009. "Third Person Dies After Ohio Buggy Accident," September 6. http:// www2.nbc4i.com/cmh/news/local/article/third_person_dies_after_ohio_buggy_ accident/22728. Accessed September 30, 2009.

NCCAM (National Center for Complementary and Alternative Medicine). 2009. "Americans Spend $33.9 billion Out-of-Pocket on Complementary and Alternative Medicines," August 30. http://nccam.nih.gov/news/2009/073009.htm. Accessed October 13, 2009.

NCH (National Coalition for the Homeless). 2009. "Who Is Homeless?" www.hnational homeless.org/factsheets/who.html. Accessed September 1, 2011.

NCH (National Coalition for the Homeless). 2009b. "Why Are People Homeless?" www.hnationalhomeless.org/factsheets/why.html. Accessed September 1, 2011.

NCVC (National Center for Victims of Crime). 2008. "Male Rape." www.ncvc.org /ncvc/main.aspx?dbName_DocumentViewer&DocumentID=32361. Accessed August 15, 2011.

NCVC (National Center for Victims of Crime). 2008a. "Acquaintance Rape." www.ncvc .org/ncvc/main.aspx?dbName_DocumentViewer&DocumentID=32306. Accessed August 15, 2011.

NCVC (National Center for Victims of Crime). 2008b. "Stalking in Society." www.ncvc .org/src/main.aspx?dbID=DB_stalkinginsociety113. Accessed August 15, 2011.

NCVC (National Center for Victims of Crime). 2009. "Rape-Related Posttraumatic Stress Disorder." www.ncvc.org/ncvc/main.aspx?dbName_DocumentViewer& DocumentID=32366. Accessed August 15, 2011.

Nelson, Marla. 2009. "Are Hospitals an Export Industry? Empirical Evidence from Five Lagging Regions." *Economic Development Quarterly.* Vol 23 no 3, pp 242–253.

Newport, Frank. 2011. "For First Time, Majority of Americans Favor Legal Gay Marriage." www.gallup.com/poll.147662/firt-time-majority-americans-favor-legal-gay -marriage.aspx. Accessed August 6, 2011.

*New York Times.* 2004. "Study Says White Families' Wealth Advantage Has Grown," October 18. http://query.nytimes.com/gst/fullpage.html?res=9B02EFD7153AF 93BA25753C1A9629C8B63. Accessed July 20, 2011.

*New York Times.* 2009. "Stonewall Rebellion." http://topics.nytimes.com/topics/reference /timestopics/subjects/s/stonewall_rebellion/index.html. Accessed August 6, 2011.

*New York Times.* 2011. "Global Warming," January 13. http://topics.nytimes.com/top /news/science/topics/globalwarming/index.html. Accessed August 10, 2011.

*New York Times.* 2011a. "Editorial: A Decision for Clean Air," July 26. www.nytimes .com/2011/07/27/opinion/27wed3.html. Accessed August 10, 2011.

NGC (National Gang Center). 2009. "National Youth Gang Survey Analysis." www .nationalgangcenter.gov/Survey-Analysis. Accessed September 8, 2011.

NGC (National Gang Center). 2009a. "Evaluation and Evolution of the Gang Resistance Education and Training (G.R.E.A.T.) Program." www.nationalgangcenter.gov /Publications/GREAT-Evaluation. Accessed September 8, 2011.

Nicholson, Linda J. 1986. *Gender and History: The Limits of Social Theory in the Age of the Family.* New York: Columbia University Press.

NIH (National Institutes of Health). 2011. "Sexually Transmitted Diseases." Medline Plus. http://www/nlm.nih.gov/medlineplus/sexuallytransmitteddiseases.html.

NLCHP (National Law Center on Homelessness and Poverty). 2010. "Homelessness and Poverty in America." http://nlchp.org/hapia.chm. Accessed September 1, 2011.

NPS (National Park Service). 2010. "Theodore Roosevelt and Conservation." www.nps .gov/thro/historyculture/theodore-roosevelt-and-conservation.htm. Accessed August 11, 2011.

NPS (National Park Service). 2011. "John Muir." www.nps.gov/jomu/index.htm. Accessed August 11, 2011.

Obama-Biden. 2009. "Barack Obama and Joe Biden's Plan to Lower Health Care Costs and Ensure Affordable, Accessible Health Coverage for All." Organizing for America. www.barackobama.com/pdf/issues/Health careFullPlan.pdf. Accessed October 16, 2009.

Ogburn, William F. 1938. *Social Change.* New York: Viking.

O'Grady, Candice. 2008. "Sarah Palin: Maverick Feminist?" Fairness and Accuracy in Reporting. www.fair.org/index.php?page=3677. Accessed August 6, 2011.

O'Leary, Kevin. 2010. "The Feds' Homelessness-Prevention Program." *Time,* January 25. www.time.com/time/nation/article/0,8599,1956213,00.html. Accessed September 3, 2011.

OSU (Ohio State University) Medical Center. 2011. "Teen Suicide." http://medical-center.osu.edu/patientcare/health care_services/mental_health/mental_health_a. Accessed September 8, 2011.

Pachauri, Rajendra. 2010. Opening Statement by Dr. Rajendra Pachauri, Chairman of the Intergovernmental Panel on Climate Change, at a Press Conference at the United Nations in New York. www.ipcc.ch/news_and_events/press_information .shtml. Accessed August 9, 2011.

Palfreman, Jon. 1979. "Between Skepticism and Credulity: A Study of Victorian Attitudes to Modern Spiritualism." In *On the Margins of Science: The Social Construction of Rejected Knowledge.* Edited by Roy Wallis. Keele, Canada: University of Keele, pp 201–236.

Pareto, Vilfredo. 1966. *Sociological Writings.* New York: Praeger.

Park, Robert, and Ernest Burgess. 1967. "Collective Behavior." In *Robert Park on Social Control and Collective Behavior*. Edited by Ralph Turner. Chicago: University of Chicago Press.

Park, Robert E. 1924. "The Concept of Social Distance: As Applied to the Study of Racial Relations." *Journal of Applied Sociology*. Vol 8, pp 329–334.

Park, W. 1990. "A Review of Research on Groupthink." *Journal of Behavioral Decision Making*. Vol 3, pp 229–245.

Parsons, Talcott. 1964. *The Social System*. New York. Free Press Paperback.

Parsons, Talcott. 1966. *Societies: Evolutionary and Comparative Perspectives*. Upper Saddle River, NJ: Prentice Hall.

Passell, Jeffrey S., and D'Vera Cohn. 2011. "Unauthorized Immigrant Population: National and State Trends, 2010." http://pewresearch.org/pubs/1876/unauthorized -immigrant-population-united-states-national-state-trends-2010 Accessed October 7, 2011.

Pate, Tempe. 2002. "Outcasts on Presidio: Homeless in Polytechnic Heights." In *A Neighborhood Portrait: Polytechnic Heights of Inner City Fort Worth*. Edited by Sara Horsfall. Austin, TX: Eakin, pp 89–100.

Paulus, P.B. 1998. "Developing Consensus About Group-think After All These Years." *Organizational Behavior and Human Decision Processes*. Vol 73, pp 362–374.

PBS. 2011. "Forty Acres and a Mule: Primary Sources." *Reconstruction: The Second Civil War*. www.pbs.org/wgbh/amex/reconstruction/40acres/ps_so15.html. Accessed June 15, 2011.

PBS. 2011a. "Obama Makes Immigration Reform Pitch in El Paso." PBS NewsHour. www.pbs.org/newshour/rundown/2011/05/president-obama-launches-immigration -reform-pitch.html. Accessed July 29, 2011.

Perdue, Theda. 1989. "Cherokee Women and the Trail of Tears." *Journal of Women's History*. Vol 1 no 1, pp 14–30.

Perrow, Charles. 1984. *Normal Accidents*. New York: Basic Books.

Pew Forum on Religious and Public Life. 2010. "Religious Groups' Official Positions on Abortion." http://pewforum.org/Abortion/Religious-Groups-Official-Positions -on-Abortion.aspx. Accessed August 2, 2011.

Pew Hispanic Center. 2004. "Wealth Gap Widens Between Whites and Hispanics." http://pewhispanic.org/newsroom/releases/release.php?ReleaseID=15. Accessed July 20, 2011.

Pew Hispanic Center. 2011. "Illegal Immigration in the US." http://pewhispanic.org /unauthorized-immigration. Accessed July 28, 2011.

Pew Research Center. 2000. "Self-Censorship: How Often and Why: Journalists Avoiding the News." http://people-press.org/2000/04/30/self-censorship-how-often-and -why. Accessed June 15, 2011.

Pfohl, Stephen J. 1977. "The Discovery of Child Abuse." *Social Problems*. Vol 24, pp 310–323.

Pierlot, Paul A. 2000. "Canada Self-Regulation of Internet Content: A Canadian Perspective." www.isoc.org/inet2000/cdproceedings/8k/8k_2.htm. Accessed Sept 26, 2009.

Pipes, Sally C. 2008. "Earth Day Doomsayers Need to Get Their Facts Right." www .pacificresearch.org/docLib/20080423_Voice_SM041008.pdf. Accessed August 10, 2011.

Popenoe, David. 1994. "Scandinavian Welfare." *Society*. Vol 30 no 6, pp 78–81.

Preble, Edward, and John J. Casey. 2004. "Taking Care of Business: The Heroin Addict's Life on the Street." In *The American Drug Scene*. Edited by James A Inciardi and Karen McElrath. Los Angeles: Roxbury, pp. 174–187.

Presgraves, Daryl. 2010. "2009 National School Climate Survey: Nearly 9 out of 10 LGBT Students Experience Harassment in School." www.glsen.org/cgi-bin/iowa/all/library /record/2624.html?state=research&type=research. Accessed August 6, 2011.

Preston, Jennifer. 2011. "Social Media Pick up Populist Message." October 9. *Fort Worth Star-Telegram,* p 10A.

Preston, Julia. 2010. "Number of Illegal Immigrants in US Fell, Study Says." *New York Times,* September 1. www.nytimes.com/2020/09/02/us/02immig.html. Accessed July 27, 2011.

Price, Barbara Raffel. 1996. "Female Police Officers in the United States." In *Policing in Central and Eastern Europe: Comparing Firsthand Knowledge with Experience from the West.* https://www.ncjrs.gov/policing/fem635.htm. Accessed July 19, 2011.

Pritchard, R. D., et al. 1988. "Effects of Group Feedback, Goal Setting, and Incentives on Organizational Productivity." *Journal of Applied Psychology*. Vol 73, pp 337–358.

Pritchard, R. D., and M. D. Watson. 1992. "Understanding and Measuring Group Productivity." In *Group Process and Productivity*, Edited by S. Worchel, W. Wood, and J. A. Simpson. Newbury Park, CA: Sage, pp 251–275.

ProCon.org. 2011. "Prostitution." www.prostitution.procon.org. Accessed August 13, 2011.

Quinn, Jane Bryant. 2000. "Social Security Isn't Doomed." *Newsweek,* March 29.

Ralston, David A., et al. 1995. "Pre-Post Tiananmen Square: Changing Values of Chinese Managers." *Asia Pacific Journal of Management*. Vol 12 no 1, pp 1–20.

Ramirez, Deborah, Jack McDevitt, and Amy Farrell. 2000. *A Resource Guide on Racial Profiling Data Collection Systems: Promising Practices and Lessons Learned.* https:// www.ncjrs.gov/pdffiles1/bja/184768.pdf. Accessed July 24, 2011.

Rasmussen Reports. 2009. "Americans Support Universal Health Coverage, But Not If It Covers Illegal Immigrants," June 12. www.rasmussenreports.com/public_ content/politics/current_events/health care/june_2009/americans_support_universal _health_coverage_but_not_if_it_covers_illegal_immigrants. Accessed October 16, 2009.

Ravilious, Kate. 2007. "Mars Melt Hints at Solar, Not Human Cause for Warming, Scientist Says." National Geographic News. http://news.nationalgeographic.com/news /2007/02/070229-mars-warming.html. Accessed August 9, 2011.

Reagan, Leslie. 1998. *When Abortion Was a Crime: Women, Medicine, and Law in the United States, 1897–1973.* Berkeley: University of California Press.

Reid, T. R. 2009. *The Healing of America: A Global Quest for Better, Cheaper, and Fairer Health Care.* New York: Penguin.

Religious Tolerance. www.religioustolerance.org.

Renewable Energy World. 2010. "US Energy Use Declines, Renewables Increase," August 6. www.renewableenergyworld.com/real/news/article/2010/08/u-s-energy-use-declines-while-renewables-increase. Accessed August 11, 2011.

Renzetti, Claire M. 2011. "Toward a Better Understanding of Lesbian Battering." In *Shifting the Center: Understanding Contemporary Families*. Edited by Susan Ferguson. New York: McGraw-Hill, pp 595–607.

Richardson, Terri. 2010. "Salvinia Munchers on the Way," October 23. www.marshall newsmessenger.com/news/article_725d721a-de75–11df-87ae-001cc4c03286.html. Accessed August 15, 2011.

Robbin, Alice. 1999. "The Problematic Status of US Statistics on Race and Ethnicity: An Imperfect Representation of Reality." *Journal of Government Information*. Vol 26 no 5, pp 467–483.

Rodriguez, Nestor. 1999. "The Battle for the Border: Notes on Autonomous Migration, Transnational Communities, and the State." In *Immigration: A Civil Rights Issue for the Americas*. Edited by Susanne Jonas and Suzie Dodd Thomas. Wilmington, DE: Social Justice, pp 27–44.

Rogers, Everett M. 1962. *Diffusion of Innovations*. New York: Free Press.

Rose, Jerry D. 1982. *Outbreaks*. New York: Free Press.

Rosen, Mike. 2011. "Cities Sovereign?" *California Lawyer,* January. www.callawyer.com /story.cfm?eid=913374&evid=1. Accessed July 28, 2011.

Rosenfeld, Boris A. 1995. "The Crisis of Russian Health Care and Attempts at Reform." In *Russia's Demographic "Crisis,"* Edited by Julie DaVanzo and Gwen Farnsworth. Arlington, VA: Rand. www.rand.org/pubs/conf_proceedings/CF124/CF124.chap5.html. Accessed October 16, 2009.

Rothenberg, Paula. 2008. *White Privilege*. New York: Worth.

Ruane, Joseph, and Jennifer Todd. 2000. *The Dynamics of Conflict in Northern Ireland: Power, Conflict, and Emancipation*. Cambridge, UK: Cambridge University Press.

Rubin, Joel. 2010. "Justice Department Warns LAPD to Take a Stronger Stance Against Racial Profiling." *Los Angeles Times,* November 14. http://articles.latimes.com /2010/nov/14/local/la-me-lapd-bias-20101114 Accessed July 24, 2011.

Saito, Y. 1988. "Situational Characteristics as the Determinants of Adopting Distributive Justice Principles: II." *Japanese Journal of Experimental Social Psychology*. Vol 27, pp 131–138.

San Francisco Prostitution Task Force. 1996. www.bayswan.org/SFTFP.html. Accessed August 13, 2011.

Sanchez, Rene. 2004. "Immigrant Smuggling Thrives Near Border: 100 People Are Found Trapped in L.A. 'Drop House.'" *Washington Post,* April 23, p A03.

Sanford, Wendy C. 1998. *Our Bodies, Ourselves: For the New Century*. New York: Simon & Schuster.

Sapien, Joaquin. 2009. "With Natural Gas Drilling Boom, Pennsylvania Faces Flood of Wastewater." *Scientific American*. www.scientificamerican.com/article.cfm?id =wastewater-sediment-natural-gas-mckeesport-sewage. Accessed August 10, 2011.

Scheer, Robert. 2006. "An Old Story: Scapegoat Immigrants." *San Francisco Chronicle,* March 29. www.commondreams.org/views06/0329–26.htm. Accessed July 19, 2011.

Schlafly, Phyllis. 2011. "Equal Rights Amendment." www.eagleforum.org/era. Accessed August 5, 2011.

Schmidt, G. 1997. "The Social Organization of Sexuality: Sexual Practices in the United States." *Archives of Sexual Behavior*. Vol 26, pp 327–333.

Schneider, Keith. 2011. "Dr. Jack Kervorkian Dies at 83; A Doctor Who Helped End Lives." *New York Times,* June 3. www.nytimes.com/2011/06/04/us/04kervorkian.html?oagewanted=all. Accessed August 7, 2011.

Schwartz, Brian. 2011. "Colorado Medicaid Reform: Federal Matching Funds Promote Waste." *Patient Power,* January 18. www.patientpowernow.org/2011/01/colorado-medicaid-reform-block-grant-matching-funds/#. Accessed January 31, 2011.

Scott, George P. 1991. *Time, Rhythm, and Chaos in the New Dialogue with Nature.* Ames: Iowa State University Press.

Sedeno, David. 2004. "The Cost of Freedom." *Fort Worth Star-Telegram,* July 4.

Sen, Amartya K. 1977. "Rational Fools: A Critique of the Behavioral Foundations of Economic Theory." *Philosophy and Public Affairs*. Vol 6 no 4, pp 317–344.

Seper, Jerry. 2009. "16 Illegals Sue Arizona Rancher." *Washington Times,* February 9. www.washingtontimes.com/news/2009/feb/09/16-illegals-sue-arizona-rancher/#. Accessed July 27, 2011.

Shook, Nancy, et al. "Courtship Violence Among College Students: A Comparison of Verbally and Physically Abusive Couples." *Journal of Family Violence*. Vol 15 no 1, pp 1–23.

Siegal, Harvey A., and James A. Inciardi. 2004. "A Brief History of Alcohol." In *The American Drug Scene*. Edited by James A Inciardi and Karen McElrath. Los Angeles: Roxbury, pp 74–79.

Siskind, Gregory. N.d. "Summary of the Secure America and Orderly Immigration Act." www.visalaw.com/05may4/3may405.html. Accessed July 29, 2011.

Sisters of Charity Foundation of South Carolina. 2010. "Congress Needs to Reauthorize TANF and Change the Distribution Formula; But Right Now Replenish the Contingency Fund," May 26. http://sistersofcharitysc.blogspot.com/2010/05/congress-needs-to-reauthorize-tanf-and.html. Accessed January 25, 2011.

Sloan, Allan. 2000. "The Social Security Crackup." *Newsweek,* July 3.

Smelser Neil. 1962. *Theory of Collective Behavior.* London: Routledge & Kegan Paul.

Smith, Anne Kates. 2009. "A Makeover for Health Care: Congress Promises to Deliver a Package by Year-end. But There's Still a Lot of Iron Out." *Kiplinger's Personal Finance*, October, pp 13–14.

Smith, Tim W. 1998. "Public Opinion on Prostitution: Trends, Comparisons, and Models." *GSS Topical Report*. No 31. NORC National Opinion Research Center, University of Chicago.

Snodgrass, Sara E. 1985. "Women's Intuition: The Effect of Subordinate Role on Interpersonal Sensitivity." *Journal of Personality and Social Psychology*. Vol 49, pp 146–155.

Snow, David A., Sarah A. Soule, and Hanspeter Kriesi. 2004. "Mapping the Terrain." In *The Blackwell Companion to Social Movements*. Edited by David A. Snow, Sarah A. Soule, and Hanspeter Kriesi. Malden, MA: Blackwell, pp 3–16.

Social Security Administration. 2011. "Historical Background and Development of Social Security." www.ssa.gov/history/briefhistory3.html. Accessed January 8, 2011.

Solis, Dianne. 2010. "Farmers Branch Rental Ordinance Again Struck Down." *Fort Worth Star-Telegram,* March 25, p 1B.

Solomon, Robert. 1983. *In the Spirit of Hegel.* New York: Oxford University Press.

Sorensen, Aja. 2004. "Rosie the Riveter: Women Working During World War II." *www.nps.gov/pwro/collection/website/rosie.htm.* Accessed August 5, 2011.

Sorokin, Pitirim. 1937. *Social and Cultural Dynamics.* Vols 1–4. New York: American Book Company.

SOSU (Southeastern Oklahoma State University). 2011. "Affirmative Action." http://homepages.se.edu/affirmative-action/4. Accessed July 25, 2011.

Sowell, Thomas. 1981. *Ethnic America.* New York: Basic Books.

Spangler, Anthony. 2009. "Texas Leads US in Percentage of Uninsured." *Fort Worth Star-Telegram*, September 11, p B1.

Spengler, Oswald. 1939 (1918). *The Decline of the West.* New York: Knopf.

SPLC (Southern Poverty Law Center). 2011. "US Hate Groups Top 1,000." www.splcenter.org/get-informed/news/us-hate-groups-top-1000. Accessed July 23, 2011.

SPLC (Southern Poverty Law Center). 2011a. "Ideology." www.splcenter.org/get-informed/intelligence-files/ideology. Accessed July 24, 2011.

Steinfels, Peter. 2009. "Despite a Decade of Controversy, the 'Faith-Based Initiative' Endures." *New York Times,* July 31. www.nytimes.com/2009/08/01/us/01beliefs.html?ref=faithbasedinitiatives. Accessed September 5, 2011.

Stent, Gunther. 1978. *Paradoxes of Progress.* San Francisco: W. H. Freeman.

Strassmann, Mark. 2010. "America's Dwindling Water Supply." CBS Evening News, January 9. www.cbsnews.com.stories/2010/01/08/eveningnews/main6073416.shtml. Accessed August 11, 2011.

Strong, Bryan, Christine DeVault, and Theodore F. Cohen. 2008. "Intimate Violence and Sexual Abuse." In *The Marriage and Family Experience.* Edited by Bryan Strong et al. Belmont, CA: Thompson Wadsworth, pp 455–486.

Sturm, Susan, and Lani Guinier. 1996. "The Future of Affirmative Action: Reclaiming the Innovative Ideal." *California Law Review.* Vol 84 no 4, pp 953–1036.

Swarns, Rachel L. 2006. "Failed Amnesty Legislation of 1986 Haunts the Current Immigration Bills in Congress." *New York Times,* May 23. www.nytimes.com/2006/05/23/washington/23amnesty.html. Accessed July 27, 2011.

Swartz, Spencer, and Shai Oster. 2010. "China Tops US in Energy Use." *Wall Street Journal,* July 18. www.wsj.com/article/SB10001424052748703720045753767 12353150310.html. Accessed August 11, 2011.

Sweeney, Paul D., Dean B. McFarlin, and Edward J. Inderrieden. 1990. "Using Relative Deprivation Theory to Explain Satisfaction with Income and Pay Level: A Multistudy Examination." *Academy of Management Journal.* Vol 33 no 2, pp 423–436.

Swindler, Ann. 2003. "Cultural Power and Social Movements." In *Social Movements and Culture.* Edited by Hank Jonston and Bert Klandermans. Abingdon, UK: Routledge, pp 25–40.

Swinton, Daniel C. 2005. "Criminal Liability, Failure to Report Child Abuse, and School Personnel: An Examination of History, Policy, and Caselaw." www.educationlaw-consortium.org/forum/2005/papers/swinton.pdf. Accessed September 7, 2011.

Symonds, John Addington. 1879. *Studies of the Greek Poets*. London: Smith, Elder & Co.

Sztompka, Piotr. 1993. *The Sociology of Social Change*. Oxford, UK. Blackwell.

Tam, Kim-Pong, Ivy Yee-Man Lau, and Chi-Yue Chiu. 2004. "Biases in the Perceived Prevalence and Motives of Severe Acute Respiratory Syndrome Prevention Behaviors Among Chinese High School Students in Hong Kong." *Asian Journal of Social Psychology*. Vol 7 no 1, pp 67–81.

Tang, Catherine So-kum. 2007. "Trajectory of Traumatic Stress Symptoms in the Aftermath of Extreme Natural Disaster: A Study of Adult Thai Survivors of the 2004 Southeast Asian Earthquake and Tsunami." *Journal of Nervous and Mental Disease*. Vol 195 no 1, pp 54–59.

Tanner, Michael D. 2008. "The Grass Is Not Always Greener: A Look at National Health Care Systems Around the World." www.cato.org/pub_display.php?pub_id=9272. Accessed October 13, 2009.

Tavris, Carol. 1992. *Mismeasure of Woman*. New York: Simon & Schuster.

Tavris, Carol, and Carol Wade. 2001. *Psychology in Perspective*. Upper Saddle River, NJ: Prentice Hall.

Teichert, Nancy Weaver. 2002. "US Seniors Finding Drug Relief in Canada." *Sacramento Bee,* September 14. www.seniors.org/doc.asp?id=1681.

Theocracywatch. 2011. "Faith-Based Initiative." www.theocracywatch.org/faith_base.htm. Accessed June 15, 2011.

Thomasson, Melissa A. 2002. "From Sickness to Health: The Twentieth Century Development of US Health Insurance." *Explorations in Economic History*. Vol 39 no 3, pp 233–253.

Thompson, J. Walter. N.d. "Women in War Jobs–Rosie the Riveter (1942–1945)." www.adcouncil.org/default.aspx?id+128. Accessed August 5, 2011.

Thornton, Mark. 1991. "Alcohol Prohibition was a Failure," July 17. www.cato.org/pub_display.php?pub_id=1017. Accessed June 16, 2011.

Tietze, C., and S. K. Henshaw. 1986. *Induced Abortion: A World Review*. New York: Guttmacher Institute.

Tilly, Charles. 1978. *From Mobilization to Revolution*. Reading, MA: Addison-Wesley.

Tinsley, Anna M. 2006. "Proposal Puts City in Spotlight." *Fort Worth Star-Telegram,* August 26, p 4A.

Touraine, Alain. 1981. *The Voice and the Eye. An Analysis of Social Movements*. New York: Cambridge University Press.

Touraine, Alain, G. Gesicka, and D. Denby. 1983. *Solidarity: The Analysis of a Social Movement: Poland 1980–1981*. New York: Cambridge University Press.

Triplett, N. 1898. "The Dynamogenic Factors in Pacemaking and Competition." *American Journal of Psychology*. Vol 9, pp 507–533.

Truth or Fiction. "The Slavery Tax Refund." www.truthorfiction.com/rumors/s/slaverytaxrefund.htm. Accessed June 15, 2011.

Tsonis, Anastasios. 1992. *Chaos and Fractal Forms: Irregularity in Nature*. Video. Winchester, MA: Blue Sky Associates.

Tu, Ha T., and Genna Cohen. 2009. "Financial and Health Burdens of Chronic Conditions Grow." www.hschange.org/CONTENT/1049/?topic=topic05. Accessed October 11, 2009.

Tulsa Reparations Committee. 2000. Center for Racial Justice. www.tulsareparations .org/index.html. Accessed July 23, 2011.

Turrell, David J. 2004. *Science vs. Religion: The 500 Year War Finding God in the Heat of the Battle*. Baltimore: Publish America.

Tuveson, Ernest. 1995. "Progress." In *The Blackwell Dictionary of 20th Century Social Thought*. Edited by William Outhwaite and Tom Bottomore. Cambridge, MA: Blackwell, pp 515–517.

Tyler, Jerry. 1997. *Readings in Contemporary Social Issues*. New York: McGraw-Hill.

Tyler, S. Lyman. 1973. *A History of Indian Policy*. Washington, D.C.: US Department of the Interior, Bureau of Indian Affairs.

Ungar, Sheldon. 2008. "Selling Environmental Problems." In *Social Problems Readings*. Edited by Ira Silver. New York: Norton, pp 243–259.

United Nations Peace Keeping Force in Cyprus. www.un.org/Depts/dpko/missions /unficyp. Accessed September 29, 2009.

Urban Institute. 2006. "A Decade of Welfare Reform: Facts and Figures: Assessing the New Federalism." www.urban.org/UploadedPDF/900980_welfarereform.pdf. Accessed January 10, 2011.

*USA Today*. 2007. "Americans Give Record $295B to Charity." www.usatoday.com /news/nation/2007–06–25-charitable_N.htm. Accessed June 15, 2011.

*USA Today*. 2010. "Giving and Volunteering." www.usatoday.com/yourlife/mind-soul /doing-good/2010–11–29-sharing-by-the-numbers-graphic_N.htm. Accessed June 15, 2011.

US Census Bureau. 2007. www.census.gov/did/www/saipe/publications/files/Tech-0607 .pdf. Accessed December 14, 2011.

US Census Bureau. 2009. "Health Insurance Coverage:2008." www.census.gov/hhes /www/hlthins/hlthin08.html. Accessed October 12, 2009.

US Census Bureau. 2010. "Income, Poverty and Health Insurance Coverage in the United States: 2009." www.census.gov/newsroom/releases/archives/income_wealth /cb10–144.html September 16. Accessed July 20, 2011.

US Census Bureau. 2010a. Table 225, Educational Attainment by Race and Hispanic Origin. www.census.gov/compendia/statab/2011/tables/11s0225.xls. Accessed July 20, 2011.

US Census Bureau. 2011. "Births, Deaths, Marriages, and Divorces: Family Planning, Abortions," January 20. www.census.gov/compendia/statab/cats/births_deaths _marriages_divorces/family_planning_abortions.html. Accessed August 2, 2011.

US Census Bureau. 2011a. "US and World Population." www.census.gov/main/www /popclock.html. Accessed July 26, 2011.

US Dept. of Commerce, Economics, and Statistics Administration and the Executive Office of the President, Office of Management and Budget. 2011. *Women in America: Indicators of Social and Economic Well-Being*, March.

US Dept. of State. 2009. "Northern Ireland Peace Process." www.state.gov/p/eur/ci/uk /c17916.htm. Accessed September 29, 2009.

US Dept. of State. 2010. *Trafficking in Persons Report 2010.*

US EEOC (Equal Employment Opportunity Commission). 2009. "Federal Laws Prohibiting Job Discrimination: Questions and Answers," November 21. www.eeoc .gov/facts/qanda.html. Accessed July 23, 2011.

*US News.* 2010. "Poll: No Consensus on Legalized Euthanasia," February 11. htttp:// www.upi.com/Top_News/US/2010/02/11/Poll-No-consensus-on-legalized -euthanasia/UPI-48731265922614. Accessed August 7, 2011.

Vicini, James. 2011. "UPDATE 3: Obama's Health Care Law Appealed to Supreme Court." Reuters. September 28. www.reuters.com/article/2011/09/28/usa-health care-court-idUSS1E78R0ZI20110928. Accessed October 16, 2011.

Vico, Giambattista. 1961 (1725). *The New Science of Giambattista Vico.* New York: Doubleday Anchor.

Vienonen, Mikko A., and Ilkka J. Vohlonen. 2001. "Integrated Health Care in Russia: To Be or Not to Be?" *International Journal of Integrated Care.* Vol 1 no 38. www .ncbi.nlm.nih.gov/pmc/articles/PMC1525341. Accessed October 16, 2009.

Waldman, D. A., et al. 2001. "Does Leadership Matter? CEO Leadership Attributes and Profitability Under Conditions of Perceived Environmental Uncertainty." *Academy of Management Journal.* Vol 44, pp 134–143.

Waldman, Simon. 2008. "Harmful Content on the Internet: Self-regulation Is The Best Way Forward," August 1. www.guardian.co.uk/media/organgrinder/2008/aug/01 /post88. Accessed September 26, 2009.

Walker, C. 2008. "Marxism 101: Are People Too Greedy for Socialism?" *Dynamic.* Vol 19. www.yclusa.org/article/articleprint/1864/-1/341. Accessed September 27, 2009.

Walker, Lenore. 1993. "The Battered Woman Syndrome Is a Psychological Consequence of Abuse." In *Current Controversies on Family Violence.* Edited by Richard J. Gelles and Donileen R. Loseke. Newbury Park, CA: Sage, pp 133–153.

Wall, Tim. 2011. "NASA's Glory Satellite Will Study Climate Change Causes," January 12. http://news.discovery.com/earth/nasas-glory-satellite-will-study-climate-change -causes.html. Accessed August 9, 2011.

Wallace, Ruth A., and Alison Wolf. 2005. *Contemporary Sociological Theory: Expanding the Classical Tradition.* Upper Saddle River, NJ: Pearson, Prentice Hall.

Walsh, Andrew. 1999. "Addressing the Rising Cost of Prescription Drugs." www.trin coll.edu/depts./tcn/Research_Reports/51.htm.

Wang, Tina. 2009. "China Takes a Stab at Universal Health Care." www.forbes.com /2009/01/22/china-health-care-markets-econ-cx_twdd_0122markets04.html. Accessed October 16, 2009.

Watts, Alan. 1972. *The Supreme Identity: An Essay on Oriental Metaphysic and the Christian Religion.* New York: Vintage.

Weber, Max. 1958 (1905). *The Protestant Ethic and the Spirit of Capitalism.* New York: Charles Scribner's Sons.

Wechsler, Henry, et al. 2004. "College Binge Drinking in the 1990s." In *The American Drug Scene*. Edited by James A Inciardi and Karen McElrath. Los Angeles: Roxbury, pp 86–100.

Weddel, Lea Ann. 2002. "A Study of Prostitution in Polytechnic Heights." In *A Neighborhood Portrait: Polytechnic Heights in Inner City Fort Worth.*" Edited by Sara Horsfall. Austin, TX: Eakin.

Weil, Elizabeth. 2004. "Senior Drug Smugglers." New York Times Service, July 5.

Wesley, Cynthia. 2001. "Birmingham Church Bomber Guilty, Gets Four Life Terms." CNN, May 1. http://articles.cnn.com/2001–05–01/justice/church.bombing.05_1 _cynthia-wesley-carole-robertson-whites-and-four-blacks?_s=PM:LAW. Accessed July 23, 2011.

White, Matthew. 2011. "Source List and Detailed Death Tolls for the Primary Megadeaths of the Twentieth Century," February. http://necrometrics.com/20c5m.htm. Accessed June 21, 2011.

Whiteley, Michael. 2002. "Owners, Fort Worth in Standoff with State Over 'Plank One' Tower." *Dallas Business Journal*, July 19.

WHO (World Health Organization). 1946. Preamble to the Constitution of the World Health Organization As Adopted by the International Health Conference, New York, 19 June–22 July, Signed by 61 States. *Official Records of the World Health Organization.* No. 2, p. 100.

WHO (World Health Organization). 2000. "World Health Organization Assesses the World's Health Systems," June 21. www.who.int/whr/2000/media_centre/press _release/en/index.html. Accessed October 10, 2009.

WHO (World Health Organization). 2008. *The World Health Report 2008: Primary Health Care (Now More Than Ever).* www.who.int/whr/2008/08_overview_en.pdf.

WHO (World Health Organization). 2009. "Countries." www.who.int/countries/en. Accessed October 12, 2009.

Whyte, David. 1994. *The Heart Aroused: Poetry and the Preservation of the Soul in Corporate America.* New York: Currency & Doubleday.

Wilcher, Shirley J. 2003. "The History of Affirmative Action Policies." *Inmotion,* August 7. www.inmotionmagazine.com/aahist.html. Accessed July 25, 2011.

Wildman, Stephanie M., Margalynne Armstrong, and Adrienne D. Davis. 1996. *Privilege Revealed: How Invisible Preference Undermines America.* New York: NYU Press.

Williams, Steven. 2010. "Which Countries Have Legalized Gay Marriage." www.care2.com /causes/which-countries-have-legalized-gay-marriages.html. Accessed August 7, 2011.

Winfrey, Oprah. 2010. "The Shocking State of our Schools." *Oprah Winfrey Show*, September 20. www.oprah.com/oprahshow/The-Shocking-State-of-Our-Schools/5. Accessed July 21, 2011.

Wirth, Louis. 1945. "The Problem of Minority Groups." In *The Science of Man in the World Crisis.* Edited by Ralph Linton. New York: Columbia University Press, pp 347–372.

Wit, A., and H. Wilke. 1988. "Subordinates' Endorsement of an Allocating Leader in a Commons Dilemma: An Equity Theoretical Approach." *Journal of Economic Psychology.* Vol 9, pp 151–168.

Wit, A. P., H. A. M. Wilke, and E. Van Dijk. 1989. "Attribution of Leadership in a Resource Management Situation." *European Journal of Social Psychology*. Vol 19, pp 327–338.

Withrow, Brian L. 2006. *Racial Profiling: From Rhetoric to Reason*. Upper Saddle River, NJ: Pearson/Prentice Hall.

Wolfe, Warren. 2010. "Senior Federation Shuts Down." *Minneapolis-St. Paul Star Tribune,* February 5. www.startribune.com/local/45368147.html?page=1&c=y. Accessed February 2, 2011.

Women's Health. N.d. "Facts About Sexually Transmitted Diseases." www.idph.state .il.us/about/womenshealth/factsjeets/std.htm. Accessed August 16, 2011.

Wood, Daniel B. 2011. "Why One City Is Spending More on Antigang Efforts Despite Budget Cuts." *Christian Science Monitor,* June 10. www.csmonitor.com/USA/2011 /0610/Why-one-city-is-spending-more-on-antigang-efforts-despite-budget-cuts. Accessed September 10, 2011.

WWTG (World Wide Travellers Guide). 2011. "The Lethal London Smog Event 5th-9th December 1952." www.world-weather-travellers-guide.com/london-smog.html. Accessed August 10, 2011.

Xu, Jiaquan, Kenneth D. Kochanek, and Betzaida Tejada-Vera. 2009. "Deaths: Preliminary Data for 2007." *National Vital Statistics Report*. Vol 58 no 1. www.cdc/gov /nchs/data/nvsr/nvsr58/nvsr58_01.pdf. Accessed October 10, 2009.

Yllo, Kersti A. 2011. "Gender, Diversity, and Violence: Extending the Feminist Framework." In *Shifting the Center: Understanding Contemporary Families*. Edited by Susan Ferguson. New York: McGraw-Hill, pp 572–583.

Zajonc, R. B. 1968. "The Attitudinal Effects of Mere Exposure." *Journal of Personality and Social Psychology*. Vol 9, pp 1–27.

Zimmerman, Carle C. 1968. *Sorokin: The World's Greatest Sociologist: His Life and Ideas on Social Time and Change*. Saskatoon: University of Saskatchewan Press.

# ▪▪ INDEX